The Emergence of Value

SUNY series in American Philosophy and Cultural Thought
―――――――
Randall E. Auxier and John R. Shook, editors

The Emergence of Value

Human Norms in a Natural World

LAWRENCE CAHOONE

Published by State University of New York Press, Albany

© 2023 State University of New York

All rights reserved

Printed in the United States of America

No part of this book may be used or reproduced in any manner without written permission. No part of this book may be stored in a retrieval system or transmitted in any form or by any means including electronic, electrostatic, magnetic tape, mechanical, photocopying, recording, or otherwise without the prior permission in writing of the publisher.

For information, contact State University of New York Press, Albany, NY
www.sunypress.edu

Library of Congress Cataloging-in-Publication Data

Name: Cahoone, Lawrence E., 1954– author.
Title: The emergence of value : human norms in a natural world / Lawrence Cahoone.
Description: Albany : State University of New York Press, [2023] | Series: SUNY series in american philosophy and cultural thought | Includes bibliographical references and index.
Identifiers: LCCN 2022055897 | ISBN 9781438494456 (hardcover : alk. paper) | ISBN 9781438494470 (ebook) | ISBN 9781438494463 (pbk. : alk. paper)
Subjects: LCSH: Ethics. | Truth. | Naturalism. | Truth.
Classification: LCC BJ21 .C2466 2023 | DDC 121/.8—dc23/eng/20230530
LC record available at https://lccn.loc.gov/2022055897

10 9 8 7 6 5 4 3 2 1

For EMB
one more time

I sit with Shakespeare, and he winces not . . . From out of the caves of evening that swing between the strong-limbed Earth and the tracery of stars, I summon Aristotle and Aurelius and what soul I will, and they come all graciously with no scorn nor condescension. So, wed with Truth, I dwell above the veil.

—W. E. B. Du Bois, *The Souls of Black Folk*

Contents

List of Illustrations	ix
Acknowledgments	xi
Introduction	1

I. Approaching the Fact-Value Problem

1	Facts, Values, and Other Dichotomies	13
2	An Objective Relativism	31
3	Emergence in Nature	49

II. Nature and Human Judgments

4	The Feud over Purpose	63
5	Animal Minds, Theirs and Ours	85
6	Dimensions of Human Agency	101
7	Beyond the Naturalistic Fallacy	121
8	Values in Judgments	137
9	What Modernity Did to Values	153

III. Emergent Norms

10	Objective Morality	173
11	Truth and Logical Validity	191
12	Ethics of the Truly Social Animal	209
13	Political Rights, Political Wrongs	229
14	Art Works	251
15	The Good	277
Notes		287
Works Cited		299
Index		319

Illustrations

Figure 2.1	A Complex	38
Figure 4.1	Values in Relation	81
Figure 6.1	Logic of Joint Intentionality	105
Figure 7.1	Sellars on Sensation and Belief	126
Figure 7.2	Sellars Revised	128
Figure 12.1	Contexts of the Act	220
Figure 14.1	Contexts of the Artwork	273

Acknowledgments

Few things are more boring than the details of a philosophy professor's life. A colleague who gave up a thriving legal practice to become a philosopher described her new job this way: "I *love* it. But you have to get used to a permanent adrenaline deficit." Nevertheless, I will hazard a personal note. Its moral is the glorious results of a misspent academic youth.

After not getting into my top choice of undergraduate colleges, doubtless for good reasons, I wound up at a small university hosting many Ivy League rejects. Oddly, it contained the remnants of a forgotten school of developmental psychology, the "Organismic Developmental Perspective" of the German émigré Heinz Werner and his student Bernard Kaplan. So, as a psychology major, in addition to reading learning theory and perceptual psychology, I was forced to read Ernst Cassirer, Sigmund Freud, Kurt Goldstein, Kurt Lewin, Jean Piaget, and Lev Vigotsky! I wrote a long paper on, what I only now realize, was emergence in psychology. But I was a philosophy major too. I hoped to get further degrees in both fields, but for starters I chose a graduate program strong in European or "continental" philosophy. There I discovered a pocket of refugees from a forgotten school called Columbia Naturalism, where the reading totally diverged from my courses in continental and analytic philosophy. Finally, in my first tenure-track job, at a formerly prominent department that had fallen on hard times, I became colleagues not only with continental and analytic philosophers but also a pocket of unrepentant process philosophers and a coven of anachronistic Carnapians who exposed me to the work of neglected, interdisciplinary scientist-philosophers, like Donald Campbell, Marjorie Grene, Herbert Simon, and William Wimsatt.

Doubtless, students are best off at the most highly reputed and competitive schools they can manage to attend. But because those schools must keep up with the trends of the moment, there are things you can't learn there. They cannot afford anachronism or eccentricity. That is the burden of their success. Hence my gratitude to non-elite schools: may they live long and not prosper too much! They may be the proper home for thinkers who can't understand why everyone else seems so sure.

More particular thanks are due to Elizabeth Baeten, for innumerable conversations on biology, anthropology, and philosophy; Alo Basu for instruction in neuroscience; Andrea Borghini for our discussions on logic; Karsten Stueber, for his reading of my ethics and moral psychology; and Paul Guyer, for his comments on my work in aesthetics. My thanks to Holly Hunt and Patricia Chuplis for the figures and index, and the Metaphysical Society for offering me a venue for my work. I am grateful to Diane Ganeles for her excellent production of the book. And lastly, I thank my students, who during this decade-long project let me learn by teaching them.

I appreciate Harvard University Press, and Robert Brandom, for use of a diagram in his Study Guide to Wilfred Sellars's *Empiricism and the Philosophy of Mind* (Harvard, 1997). Thanks as well to a number of venues where earlier versions of chapters, or parts of chapters, have appeared: "A Most Contradictory Family: Cohen, Nagel, and Buchler on Logical Realism," Michael Berman, editor, *Nature, Judgment, and Complexes: Justus Buchler in 21st Century Philosophy* (SUNY Press, 2023); "Toward an Ordinal Naturalism," *Review of Metaphysics* 75.1 (September 2021: 115–34); "Truth, Nature, and Sellars' Myth of the Given," *Journal of Speculative Philosophy* 34.4 (2020: 463–77); my review of Hilary Putnam and Ruth Anna Putnam, *Pragmatism as a Way of Life: The Lasting Legacy of William James and John Dewey*, edited by David Macarthur (Harvard University, 2017) in *Metaphilosophy* 51.2–3 (April 2020: 472–78); "Mead and the Emergence of the Joint Intentional Self," *European Journal of Pragmatism and American Philosophy*, XI-2, 2019 (https://journals.openedition.org/ejpap/1592); "Self-, Social-, or Neural-Determination," *Journal of Philosophical Investigations* (13.28.1398: 95–108, https://philosophy.tabrizu.ac.ir); "Physicalism, the Natural Sciences, and Naturalism," *Philo* 16.2 (2013: 130–44). The shades of fallen comrades continue to haunt me: Sandra Bartky, Bob Cohen, Burt Dreben, Ber Elevitch, Jean Elshtain, Val Geist, Erazim Kohák, Joe Margolis, Gary Overvold, Hilary Putnam, and Leroy Rouner. Pleasantly, but hauntings nonetheless.

Introduction

> If there is a coherent specialty lying in this interdisciplinary space . . . it may have to be done by marginal scholars who are willing to be incompetent in a number of fields at once. . . .
>
> —Donald Campbell, "Evolutionary Epistemology"[1]

A human being unable to recognize that something is a fact independent of how good or bad or beautiful or useful or just or satisfying it is would be in serious trouble. Dead, actually, unless cared for or directed by others. But a human being not capable of recognizing that some fact, or even a potential or possible fact, was or would be useful or good or bad or beautiful or just or satisfying would be in just as much trouble. Dead again.

Vines are not like that, nor are cameras. Vines grow if exposed to water, minerals, and sunlight. They don't perceive or recognize or represent their environments. They don't have to. They have needs, and when energy or chemicals hit their surfaces, they respond or develop to take advantage of these good things. That's what living things do. Vines need not bother with perceiving or knowing. Cameras do a different amazing thing: they represent states of affairs that reflect visible light. They produce images that can be relatively accurate depictions of some kinds of things, albeit on a two-dimensional plane. But while cameras need batteries, they cannot go out and buy them. They don't get hungry or wait impatiently for them to show up. They aren't alive.

Like many other animals, we have to do both. We recognize situations and evaluate some of them. Hence we can act, which cameras and vines cannot. Actions have to be based, on the one hand, on perceiving and cognizing the state of our environment, and on the other, on feeling the state of our bodies and being motivated to do something. As Aristotle said, we are animals, which means capable of desires, perceptions, and actions.

But special animals. We argue about which beliefs are true. We disagree, a lot, but we all want to believe that what we believe is true, not just that it feels good to believe it. We get ashamed and suffer for acting badly, are angry and depressed that others treat us poorly. We want our dancing at the ceremony to be right, our arrangement of plants in the window to be beautiful. We don't just want to bag the biggest boar so we can eat a lot; we want everyone to see it, and then give the extra away—whether out of kindness or to achieve status, it doesn't much matter. We don't just want to live or exist, but to live *well*, something else Aristotle said.

Just what is "living well"? That question is pursued by a family of subfields of philosophy called the *philosophy of value*. This usually includes ethics, which studies what is morally right or wrong action, aesthetics, concerning what is beautiful or aesthetically compelling, and political philosophy or political theory, which is about what kind of society and government we ought to have. What follows is a book in the philosophy of value, so it will eventually get around to questions of ethics, aesthetics, and political philosophy. But it will take a while to get there.

It has to. Part of the motivation of this book is a belief that the mainstream of modern Western intellectual culture has pursued a set of conceptual habits that blocks any plausible advance in our philosophical understanding of values. And because a layer or dimension of Western culture has spread all over the world, there is more than enough blockage to go around. I don't mean the modern West was all wrong, or the world is doomed, or that a different set of ideas could "save" either one. The current project merely desires to loosen up a traffic jam, a jam caused partly by smart people thinking there are only two roads to where they want to go. This means that where the two roads cross we find a massive and frozen collection of honking horns and exasperated drivers. The point of this book is that there are more roads to take.

Part of the reason modernity makes it very hard rationally to think about moral values, political values, aesthetic values, and even cognitive values like truth, is the famous *fact-value dichotomy*. Its source has to do with modern science and even modern society. But philosophy, which is the most general form of inquiry in human cultures, has absorbed and to some extent exacerbated the scientific and social problems. Some of the most important philosophical work of the last century, in very different and opposed schools of thought, denied that values can be anything but human "projections" and held that no rational decisions about values are possible. The most extreme of these—such as existentialism and logical positivism, prominent just before and after the Second World War—have been replaced in recent decades by more subtle analyses. Recent ethics, aesthetics, and political theory remain important, fecund areas of philosophical work. But they tend to deal with the problem of value by becoming highly specialized or merely critical: specialized by proposing which normative principles or rules in a particular field of values survive which counter-examples; and merely critical in showing that the more fundamental attempts to justify all moral or political or aesthetic judgments by the deepest or broadest principles, or "foundations," cannot work. Much more rare is the attempt to think about the nature of the major kinds of values or norms *together*.

One of the most promising developments of recent decades has been a new naturalism in the treatment of ethics, largely inspired by evolutionary psychology. Whereas it was common for a long time to think humans are naturally selfish, and therefore morality couldn't possibly be accounted for in evolutionary or naturalistic terms, there are today numerous scientists and philosophers who argue that humans are naturally *pro-social*, meaning that our ethical judgments and practices evolved under natural selection. That is part of what made us more capable of collaboration with non-kin than any other species on Earth.

But there are problems with this. For some of its philosophical critics, the attempt fails right off the bat. For them, showing that humans are often caused to behave a certain way has nothing to do with showing that this is the *right* way, that the forms of human socialization are the morally right way to act. Evolutionary psychology, like naturalism in general, leaves us a "descriptive" account of what humans tend to do, not a "normative" account of what they should do. After all, if ethics means doing whatever works, or following whatever rules or norms bring success in a given society and historical period, then whatever form of life dominates a given society or period dictates what is right. The notion that I should do whatever "works" could lead to a pretty lousy ethics.

But even the new naturalists themselves recognize another problem. If humans evolved to be highly social, to cooperate and collaborate with non-kin to hunt and gather, that also means they evolved to be *tribal*, to distrust outsiders, members of other societies, even to fight them. If normative ethics is going to live with naturalism, it must die with it too—that is, it must recognize when it is "natural" for us to do awful, nasty, immoral things to members of other tribes. After all, most modern value theorists want to believe in a universal, cosmopolitan morality of human rights and equality, with a concern for social justice, applying not just to "us" but to "them," the others. But that doesn't seem to be the kind of morality that evolutionary psychology would be able to generate.

Naturalistic, evolutionary psychology by itself may fail to give a philosophically adequate account of normativity, the difference between "is" and "ought," but it does make a beginning in showing us that cooperation-enabling morality is indeed very likely to be natural. The ethicists who question its philosophical adequacy are also partly right, but they fail to consider the causal relations that undergird the human ability and need to be ethical in the first place. At the same time, many thinkers, including scientists, tend to think the human mind is utterly different from everything else in nature. There is a tendency for each relevant discipline and each method within each discipline to regard its own research field as the key to everything while denying that a more generalized metaphysical or systematic approach makes any sense.

My claim will be that naturalism can pass these tests, but only if it is the right kind. Hence this book. I will suggest that a naturalism broadly enough conceived can provide the intellectual background for understanding the main areas of human valuing, and as well the resources for rational normative decision making. But to show this we must do several things at once. To get plausible accounts of the norms of ethics, politics, aesthetics, and their relation to truth, we are going to need a theory of human judgment that includes all of them; to do that we will need a naturalism that accepts that culture, mind, biological processes, and the physical world are all related and potentially causal; and to do that we need an approach to metaphysics that sees each thing as related to others, and no one kind of thing as ultimate or foundational. Finally, we need to see how modern thought altered our understanding of values, for good and ill. This means we have to do some *systematic* philosophy. This need not involve creating a "system" that claims to address or answer everything. But it does require doing several things at once.

Which is no longer a common approach in philosophy. Contemporary philosophy, at least since the Second World War, is quite different from earlier philosophy. In the 1930s, Western philosophy famously split into divergent cultures that eventually, in the postwar period, stopped talking to each other, not just "schools" with different answers to the same questions competing against each other like multiple baseball teams, but traditions who don't ask the same questions or speak the same language. More like a baseball team playing a hockey team playing a volleyball team. Not a lot of fun for spectators.

The dominant culture in the English-speaking world is "analytic" philosophy, rooted in modern logic and philosophy of language, plied by Bertrand Russell, G. E. Moore, and Wittgenstein, among others. Its smaller, loyal opposition is "continental" philosophy, rooted in German and French thinkers like Hegel, Nietzsche, Husserl, Heidegger, and Derrida. Both of these mostly reject traditional, systematic philosophy. The analysts, starting with Russell but doubling down with Wittgenstein and Carnap, rejected metaphysics and foundational approaches to philosophical questions, which they thought were unjustifiable and wrong-headed, a kind of remnant of religion. As time went on, they became extremely specialized into subfields, like much of science, pushing the entire philosophy profession into specializations where nobody wanted to do or even approve of systematic work. The continentals, starting with Nietzsche, then more so with Heidegger, also rejected foundational approaches to philosophical questions, but they developed a different form of specialization in historical literatures or key figures. Following Derrida, Foucault, Rorty, and Butler, some continental philosophers came to regard the aim of philosophy itself as aesthetic or political or both, rather than as inquiry into truth. Thus the two main schools of philosophy—analytic and continental—mostly stopped doing traditional systematic philosophy.

These two schools reflected something called "the two cultures." In a 1959 lecture, C. P. Snow, an English novelist trained in chemistry, argued that Western intellectual life was becoming badly separated into scientists and humanists who could no longer talk to teach other. The analytic-continental divide in philosophy very accurately mirrored this division. Analytic philosophers agree they are inquiring into truth, but mostly think of their work like science, as responses to recent candidate solutions to narrow problems in a subfield, highly suspicious of more speculative and older work. Most continental philosophers engaged in the interpretation of particular philosophical writers and historical periods, like other humanities professors. They read a lot of history but deny the traditional goal of describing and explaining reality in general. All are philosophers, but one modeled on the sciences, the other on the humanities.

Now, every form of human endeavor that seeks to progress in the modern age has a strong tendency to specialization. That is how the modern thing we call "progress" works. No inquirer can doubt that the best standard work, the state of the art of a research field, is usually established by specialists. The most complete and well-informed account of causality in science will probably be done by analysts; the most complete and well-informed account of Heidegger's philosophy will be continental. But the glories of specialization carry a couple of dangers that are mostly invisible to the specialist, and are particularly unbecoming for philosophy.

One downside is that a lot of work disappears from consideration. Inquiry in science progresses by dropping candidate solutions. But sometimes we drop more than we should. As philosopher Hilary Putnam wrote, each new generation of philosophers tends to throw everybody else's baby out with the bathwater. A concept that fails to solve today's problem may turn out to be helpful in addressing the problems of tomorrow or in a different area. The cost of specialization is often worth it in the sciences. But in the most general of all forms of inquiry, philosophy, that cost inflates.

Specialization also means each inquiry inhabits a narrow research community with shared presuppositions, a technical language, and its own little canon of stock problems and candidate solutions, represented in journals, which are community organs. In addressing the issue x, specialists create alternative analyses and candidate solutions x', x'', x''', et cetera. But the research community's conception of its own subject matter must rest on a distinction from other subject matters. The student exclusively concerned with x or even x' versus x'' must have some background conception of what makes x, x. That presumes a notion of not-x, hence some knowledge of a, p, q, or r—not knowledge of *all* other things, but of *some*. For what if the specialist's conception of *not-x*, on which x rests, is faulty? The specialist can never learn that. Since it is not their job, they cannot find out. We don't need to know much about snails to be an expert on dogs. But what if we ask, "What makes dogs, your specialty, different from all other animals?" To be right about this requires knowing something about a lot of other animals. What if such general questions happen to be key to the next advance in knowledge of animals, including dogs? It might turn out that advancing our understanding of x presumes answers to other issues like p or q.

The social realities of academia exacerbate this. The top philosophy programs, where they make new PhDs, are excellent. But they cannot afford to waste faculty lines on forms of thought not generally regarded as intellectually competitive right now. The most successful practitioners must be most concerned with the fashions of, if not the day, then at least the decade. If you are hot, you want to stay that way; if you want to become hot, you'd better get busy. This applies even to the study of the history of philosophy, where some current interpretations are hot, others not. Such programs cannot waste precious faculty lines on philosophers who study yawn-producing ideas of yesterday. Top graduate students do not want to yawn. Few faculty in such programs—at least, until late in their tenured careers—spend time reading what is outside their specializations. Indeed, the task of assiduously making yourself an expert virtually requires that you *un-learn* any other way of thinking or talking. Schools lower down the success ladder can and do represent the "non-hot," not by design but because they don't have the resources to do otherwise. Lacunae of forgotten theories persist in those shallows. Every now and then they might be right about something that matters.

The opposite of specialized philosophy is systematic philosophy. Whatever else it is, philosophy is the most general or comprehensive form of inquiry. I am not saying philosophy is only inquiry: some think it is also the search for wisdom, or the fulfillment of thinking, or conceptual clarification, or construction of novel modes of experience. But whatever else it is, philosophy contains within itself the most general, unrestricted mode of inquiry. Systematic philosophy is the attempt philosophically to coordinate inquiries into different subject matters. It is based in a gamble that some areas of philosophic inquiry can only be advanced if we relate their investigation to other areas, that getting a better account of mind or agency might require a better account of the physical, or a better understanding of politics might require a better understanding of aesthetics or evolutionary theory, et cetera. It may be that the undergrowth blocking several different lines of inquiry can only be removed all at once because it is entangled.

But this is not a competition. Systematizers must always stand on the shoulders of specialists. And systematic philosophy, contrary to its reputation, must be approached in a fallibilist spirit. The broader you go, the more fallibilist you had better be. As Donald Campbell quipped, we must be willing to be "incompetent in many fields at once." The systematizer, in considering her complex journey, must recognize that every province she traverses can be expanded into endless complexity, some of which may be dispositive for the journey as a whole. The investigators of those provinces have the right to, indeed ought to, complain about the systematizer's quick passage through their domain. The systematizer remains permanently responsible to all their objections. So she cannot fly over the traffic jam, nor speed around it. She must take the long walk through.

Few recent philosophers brave this muddle, where there is lots of stuff but little structure, where "foundations" are shallow and porous, and no formulation can be taken for granted.[2] Charles Peirce, the inventor of pragmatism, fired in 1884 at age forty-five from the only regular teaching position he would ever hold, was neglected for seventy years after his death in 1914. At one point he lamented, "Only once . . . in all my lifetime have I ever experienced the pleasure of praise. . . . and the praise . . . was meant for blame. It was that a critic said of me that I did seem to be *absolutely sure of my own conclusions*. Never, if I can help it, shall that critic's eye ever rest on what I am now writing; for I owe a great pleasure to him . . ."[3] Fallibilist, interdisciplinary systematizers are not engineering a sturdy building of knowledge, a set of floors anchored to a foundation. They are more like nomads traveling the steppe, in need of a tent, a structure that is stable but pliable and moveable, fixed to reality at a finite number of key points.

So what are we going to use to stake the corners of our tent? First, we will need the most pluralistic philosophical approach to reality we can find. There is such a view. Developed in American philosophy in the mid-twentieth century by philosophers associated with American pragmatism, it is called *objective relativism*. It was created around the time of the First World War, named a bit later, and endorsed by a school of philosophy at Columbia University called "Columbia Naturalism." Why this matters can only be seen later, but it will mean that a host of philosophical habits that obscure the inquiry into values can be jettisoned. We will be using the Columbians' ideas, but with some differences. For example, they thought objective relativism was a kind of naturalism. They were wrong. But that turns out to be an advantage.

Second, we need a naturalism that accepts the idea of *emergence*. The concept of emergence was invented at the start of the twentieth century, mostly by philosopher-ethologists, before psychology had totally separated from philosophy. It disappeared for fifty years but has received a lot of attention in recent decades. We are going to formulate a concept of emergence that can be used to understand nature in general. There is nothing mystical about it; it is simply the notion that natural systems can exhibit properties that cannot be reduced to the properties of their components, and that those exhibited properties can play a causal role, can *do* something. A system can have some properties that are fully reducible and other properties that are not. The result is, when applied broadly, a hierarchical view of nature, in which some kinds of natural phenomena are asymmetrically dependent on, but not reducible to, others, for example, culture on minded, linguistic animals, mind on neurology, life on chemical processes, and chemical materials on mass-energy distributed in time and space. This was the subject of an earlier book of mine (Cahoone 2013a). We are now using it to talk about values.

A third requirement is a *multifunctional theory of human judgment*. The point of this theory is to regard our assertions about what is true or false, our actions, and our artworks all as judgments. All are selective responses to the world, embody a perspective and take a position, and can be valid and rational, but in different ways. The point of this approach is to allow us to think about our so-called "cognitive" judgments or assertions or propositions, our considered actions and choices of what to do, and our arrangements of things that express some quality—in short, our sayings, actions, and makings—as falling under one category. This doesn't mean merging them but relocating what distinguishes them.

Fourth and last, we need to recognize that *modernity has changed the relations among human values*. My point is not just that the modern world is different, that we now have different values than more traditional peoples. Everybody agrees on that. It is that the relations among truth, beauty, moral goodness, and political rightness have changed. Sometimes philosophers discussing ethics or aesthetics or politics write on modern theories and modern situations as if their conclusions ought to hold universally for all humans at all times. Others write on older, medieval or ancient views of value as if those could apply directly to the modern world. But modern society is very different from all prior human societies. Not totally, but very. Our account of what is true, right, just, and beautiful has to apply to human societies in general and yet inform our judgments of our extremely novel, modern way of life. We can still judge modern equality and human rights and democracy superior, but we can't do it by simply defining all ethics and politics in modern terms.

Where can we find these particular tent stakes? They come from roughly the first half of the twentieth century, from 1900 to the 1950s. There is a reason for this. The period from 1900 to 1930 was a time when what would be called analytic and continental philosophy were not yet separate disciplines, and both regarded American pragmatism as an interlocutor. In that period we find philosophers who are just as "modern" as we are—who presume Darwinian evolution, modern logic, physical relativity and quantum theory, early abstract art, industrial mass society—yet before Western philosophy split into the two cultures of scientific or analytic philosophers and the humanistic or continental philosophers, which corresponded to the general abandonment of systematic philosophy. In the 1920s, philosophers as different as Russell, Wittgenstein, Carnap, Husserl, Heidegger, Dewey, C. I. Lewis, Whitehead, Bergson, and Husserl were all part of one conversation.

Second, during that time through the 1950s there occurred an intermixing of scientific fields, such as ethology, the study of animal behavior, with both analytic and continental philosophy, including figures like Lloyd Morgan, Conrad Waddington, Jacob von Uexküll, Heinz Werner, Kurt Goldstein, Konrad Lorenz, and Merleau-Ponty. Third and last, immediately after the Second World War, the successors to logical positivism, the "ordinary language" philosophers, G. E. Anscombe, R. M. Hare, Bernard Williams, and Alasdair MacIntyre, brought a new approach to ethics, rationality, and human agency that was intertwined with anthropology. In all these periods there was strong interaction between American pragmatism and analytic philosophy, before all three schools finally went to their opposite corners. And it so happens that a specific form of naturalism, at home at Columbia University from 1930 to 1955 combined pragmatism and analytic philosophy to make made major contributions to logic, the theory knowledge, metaphysics, and, oddly, the philosophy of art. We will see their unique view.

The three chapters of part I will sketch our approach to nature, setting the stage for the rest of the book: stating the fact-value problem (chapter 1), explaining objective relativism (chapter 2), and presenting our emergent naturalism (chapter 3). Part II will describe how biology (chapter 4), animal psychology (chapter 5), and human agency (chapter 6) display values; how this defeats the "naturalistic fallacy" (chapter 7); and how human value judgments (chapter 8) are altered by modernity (chapter 9). In part III, I will propose a way of understanding moral norms (chapters 10 and 12), truth as the norm of inquiry (chapter 11), the norms of political activity (chapter 13) and art (chapter 14), and finally "The Good" (chapter 15). In none of these chapters do I hope to offer the one right or final understanding of the True, the Good, the Just, or the Beautiful. But taken together these chapters do suggest a way of regarding these norms, and their rational consideration, within the naturalism of parts I and II.

If our supplies and bedroll are handy, let's grab our compass and begin.

I

Approaching the Fact-Value Problem

Chapter One

Facts, Values, and other Dichotomies

> Tolstoi has [written that] . . . science is meaningless because it gives no answer to . . . the only question important . . . 'What shall we do and how shall we live?' That science does not give an answer to this is indisputable. The only question that remains is the sense in which science gives 'no' answer, and whether or not science might yet be of some use to the one who puts the question correctly.
>
> —Max Weber, "Science as a Vocation"[1]

Steven Weinberg, the erudite Nobel Prize–winning physicist, famously closed his excellent 1977 book on the origin of our universe *The First Three Minutes*, writing, "The more the universe seems comprehensible, the more it also seems pointless."[2] His morose view was merely the latest, and by no means most depressing, of a tradition of gloom regarding nature stretching back to the nineteenth century. Forty years earlier, Jean-Paul Sartre, who was to become the most famous philosopher in the world for a decade after the Second World War, published his 1938 novel *La Nausée* at age thirty-three. His narrator Antoine Roquentin visits a city park, looking at the roots of the trees. He has a vision.

> I sank down on the bench, stupefied, stunned by the profusion of beings without origin: everywhere blooming, hatching out, my ears buzzed with existence, my very flesh throbbed and opened, abandoned itself to the universal burgeoning. It was repugnant . . . Those trees, those great clumsy bodies . . . *They did not want to exist*, only they could not help themselves. . . . I hated this ignoble mess . . . filling everything with its gelatinous

slither. . . . I was afraid of cities. But you mustn't leave them. If you go too far you come up against the vegetation belt. Vegetation has crawled for miles toward the cities . . . you must never penetrate alone this great mass of hair waiting at the gates . . .[3]

Six years later, Sartre would complete the play *No Exit* (*Huis Clos*), with the famous line "Hell is other people." But evidently social hell was still better than natural hell. Sartre was a continental philosopher, a practitioner of a twentieth-century philosophical tradition concerned with the experiencing human subject, its history and culture, building on German thinkers like G. W. F. Hegel, Edmund Husserl, and Martin Heidegger. One might imagine that members of the more scientifically minded English analytic tradition would be less florid than the Gallic Sartre. But in 1903 at the age of thirty-one, the same year that he invented analytic philosophy with his *Principles of Mathematics*, Bertrand Russell published his popular essay "A Free Man's Worship" in which he famously wrote,

> Even more purposeless, more void of meaning, is the world which science presents for our belief. . . . That man is the product of causes which had no prevision of the end they were achieving; that his origin, his growth, his fears, his loves and his beliefs, are but the outcome of accidental collocations of atoms . . . that all the labors of the ages, all the devotion, all the inspiration, all the noonday brightness of human genius, are destined to extinction in the vast death of the solar system, and the whole temper of Man's achievement must inevitably be buried beneath the debris of a universe in ruins—these things, if not quite beyond dispute, are yet so nearly certain that no philosophy which rejects them can hope to stand. Only within the scaffolding of these truths, only on the firm foundation of unyielding despair, can the soul's habitation henceforth be safely built.[4]

And this was written a decade before the Great War, which would make a lot more British writers begin to sound like existentialists.

We must not forget the Germans. While Heidegger's thought in the 1920s was the source of most twentieth-century existentialism, it was partly inspired by the work of Friedrich Nietzsche, the radical nineteenth-century critic of Judeo-Christian thought. Nietzsche had remarked in 1886, in perhaps the best compilation of his philosophy, *Beyond Good and Evil*, "So you want to *live* 'according to nature'? Oh you noble Stoics, what a fraud is in this phrase! Imagine something like nature, profligate without measure, indifferent without measure, without purpose and regard, without mercy and justice, fertile and barren and uncertain at the same time, think of indifference as a power—how *could* you live according to this indifference?"[5] But even Nietzsche seems mild compared to this passage from the most important British philosopher of the nineteenth century, the steady utilitarian John Stuart Mill, who wrote in his 1874 essay "Nature,"

> In sober truth, nearly all the things which men are hanged or imprisoned for doing to one another are nature's every-day performances.... Nature impales men, breaks them as if on the wheel ... burns them to death, crushes them with stones like the first Christian martyr.... Even when she does not intend to kill she inflicts the same tortures in apparent wantonness.... A single hurricane destroys the hopes of a season; a flight of locusts, or an inundation, desolates a district; a trifling chemical change in an edible root starves a million of people.... Anarchy and the Reign of Terror are overmatched in injustice, ruin, and death by a hurricane and a pestilence. But, it is said, all these things are for wise and good ends ... whether they are so or not is altogether beside the point. Supposing ... these horrors ... promote good ends, still, as no one believes that good ends would be promoted by our following the example, the course of Nature cannot be a proper model for us to imitate.[6]

In the Western tradition we are used to some Christians portraying nature as the source of temptation, as a cage from which the soul needs to escape. But the modern secular worldview has done one better. After all, some Christians had seen the natural world as an expression of God's grace, and at any rate as the pre-school for paradise. The modern secular thinkers are like Christian ascetics, but worse, since nature is no longer part of a moral test, and there is no Heaven after graduation. Humans are merely strangers in a strange land where their values and hopes, expressed by words like "good," "right," "beautiful," "ought," and "should" are strictly domestic projections, with no relation to reality. Nothing in nature is good. Then you die.

In such a philosophical milieu, where nature is either devoid of or hostile to human values, how could affirmations of value be rational, or valid? How could we know or justify claims about them and acts based on them? Philosophers have always had major questions about our knowledge of facts, but modern knowledge of values has seemed to some simply unavailable. Therein lies a tale.

The Fact-Value Dichotomy

In the early twentieth century, what was called the "fact-value" dichotomy became prominent in part because it was adopted by the most powerful movement of the new analytic philosophy, which, starting in the 1920s, spread from England to Austria and then across North Atlantic philosophy. This was logical positivism, also called logical empiricism. It was pioneered by the early Wittgenstein and the members of the Vienna Circle, especially Rudolf Carnap. They took the view that value claims could not be true or false, and therefore had no rational justification. Part of their reasoning involved the "verifiability criterion of meaning," that a statement does not have meaning if you cannot imagine it being confirmed or disconfirmed by evidence. This was in a sense ironic as the logical positivists were by and large men of strong moral and political opinions, mostly democratic socialists, with deep objections to the development of fascism in Germany and Austria, and had to escape central Europe in the 1930s. They did in fact believe that science, logic, and inquiry into truth in general are morally valuable and a bulwark of liberal society against irrational social thought. But their moral commitments were maintained, so to speak, off the books. Positivism's only ethical theory, "emotivism," claimed that moral statements are nothing but emotional expressions; for example, "murder is wrong" means "I hate murder" or even "Boo to murder."

But starting in the 1950s, analytic ethics was reborn with the new generation of linguistic or "ordinary language" philosophy housed above all at Oxford University. Philosophers like R. M. Hare rejected emotivism on the grounds of ordinary language use. After all, no everyday language speaker of "murder is wrong" would say its meaning matches "I don't like murder"! They focused their inquiry instead on the question of whether value statements could ever be "cognitive" or "descriptive," or known to be true like our true descriptions of facts, as opposed to being valid as commands or based in contractual agreements that are not "true." The latter might still be open to rational agreement. After all, the rules of chess do not describe natural facts, but it is perfectly rational, in fact accurate, to say to a chess player who is moving her rook diagonally, "No, that's wrong."

At the same time in the 1950s other young analytic philosophers were attacking the "analytic-synthetic" distinction that had been crucial to positivism. That distinction segregated statements known to be true just because of the meanings of their terms—like "all bachelors are unmarried," which is true by definition—from normal empirical statements that applied concepts to facts—like "Fred is a bachelor" or "There are bachelors in the world." This distinction went back to Hume; the positivists connected it to the distinction within a scientific theory between the "theoretical" statements that related abstract concepts to each other and the "observation" statements merely reporting sense data. But after the Second World War, younger positivists—like W. V. O. Quine and Morton White at Harvard—saw that the usual distinction between synthetic statements of observations and analytic statements was blurry. And if the fact/theory and fact/definition distinctions were blurry, then that *from which* values were supposed to be utterly distinct—empirical facts—might be blurry too. This led the analytic offspring of the logical positivists in a *pragmatic* direction, a belief that theoretical statements might be valid as guides to action, even if not proved valid by facts. And as they knew, pragmatism had earlier been the most famous doctrine in American philosophy for the first half of the twentieth century.

Pragmatism was arguably a long cultural impulse in American thought, imbibed from its Scottish heritage. But the official doctrine of pragmatism was invented in the late nineteenth century by Charles Sander Peirce, and made famous in the early twentieth century by William James and John Dewey. Pragmatism in the broad sense locates meanings and knowledge in the context of social action; if somebody's theory or idea has no implications for what we should do, it means nothing. If somebody claims to "really, deeply" love you while betraying and destroying you, they are lying. Pragmatism was connected to the theory of evolution. Human beings are animal actors first—they have to be. What we mean and know functions to guide our conduct. As we will see, a strain of analytic philosophers throughout the second half of the twentieth century have been either open or closet pragmatists, including Carnap, Quine, White, Hilary Putnam, Nelson Goodman, Richard Rorty, and Donald Davidson.

The relevance here is that pragmatism *must* reject the fact-value dichotomy. If action is always driven by purpose or value or evaluation, and what is "true" can be decided only in the context of action, the truth of facts is related to values. This does not mean pragmatists think that whatever I want to be true really is true, or whatever purpose my action serves is right. But it does mean the two cannot be utterly separate. All this led some of the great analytic philosophers of the second half of the twentieth century, like Putnam, to declare by the turn of the millennium that the fact-value dichotomy had actually "collapsed," that it had always been misguided and now we know it.

Putnam had the right idea but was wrong in applying it. There has always been something fishy about the fact-value dichotomy, and a pragmatically oriented analytic philosophy inevitably noticed this. But people will keep eating fish that smells if they can find nothing else to eat. Reports of the collapse of the dichotomy are greatly exaggerated.

Where the Dichotomy Came From

The history of the fact-value dichotomy is usually said to begin with the great eighteenth-century Scottish empiricist and skeptical philosopher David Hume. But his theory was itself responding to a view of the world already in place in the seventeenth century. Yes, the nature of The Good had of course been an issue at least since Plato in what we misleadingly but usefully call "Western" thought. But before the modern period one cannot find, except perhaps in the most extreme skeptics—who applied their skepticism to facts as well as values—the view that knowing, rationally judging, or finding values in the natural or human world was uniquely suspicious. It was common throughout the ancient and medieval world to regard things as having "natures" and natures as implying or containing purpose and value, most famously, Aristotle's "final causes" that had been taken up by the medieval Scholastics.

The scientific revolution of the seventeenth century ended that. It was primarily a physics revolution that eventually impacted medicine, biology, and chemistry. Newtonian or classical mechanics understood phenomena as the deterministic result of interactions of (ideally) rigid bodies moving under forces acting with respect to a small number of properties of those bodies (mass, velocity, location), often in a mathematically simple fashion (like proportionality of force to the inverse square of distance between bodies). Today, "mechanism" or the machine analogy is often criticized, and it is true that twentieth-century physics—both microphysics and the theory of spacetime—have had to regard mechanics as a limited phenomenon inside more basic field theories. But there *are* machines in the world, and our theory of microphysics is not called quantum "mechanics" for nothing. Mechanism is not wrong, just limited; it fruitfully applies to some phenomena, or more precisely, some aspects of some phenomena, and not to others. You really do need your heart to pump blood like, well, a pump.

The central task of philosophy in the seventeenth century was to figure out how to reconcile the new mechanical physics with our understanding of human mind, will, soul, and values. Of the multiple answers one was dominant. Descartes and Locke, who famously disagreed on epistemology, had more or less identical metaphysics, which was also adapted by Spinoza: excepting human minds, all nature is material objects operating mechanically as modern science claims. The properties of those objects are "primary qualities," namely, mass, volume, shape, location in space and time, and velocity. Humans alone, besides having material bodies, have minds identical to their immortal souls. All the other perceptible qualities we find in the world—color, taste, sound—are "secondary," not primary, meaning they are in our heads and do not resemble anything actually in the objects causing them. This doctrine is the inevitable result of confronting mechanistic physics with a personal consciousness that doubles as an immortal soul. In this scheme, the value of a thing is certainly not primary, nor even secondary; it might be "tertiary" (although Locke already used that term for a real thing's power to affect other things). So the stage was set for claiming that any value cannot be a property of a thing or fact, but solely lodged in the human mind.

The new dualism also had a devastating effect on the theory of knowledge and perception. The seventeenth-century philosophers, especially Locke, created *representationalism*, which holds that we experience, and directly know, not independent existences but their representations. Everything of which the human subject is conscious, every experience and cognition whatsoever, is a property or process of mind, and mind is individual and nonmaterial. Strictly speaking, I don't perceive the house; I have a mental image in my head caused by the house. The mental image is what I perceive. Representationalism created a host of problems, including the so-called "problem of knowledge," the "problem of the external world," and the "problem of other minds." For it meant that, literally, whatever a human mind is immediately aware of is a property of itself, not the world, and we must then inquire into how we can be sure of a mind-world relationship, of the valid representation of parts of the world in and by those representational states. Ancient and medieval thinkers never combined all functions of the human psyche into one—sensation, perception, emotion, thought, reason—or asked how, from *inside* the former, we could be sure that our perceptions and cognitions can be shown to be true of the "external" world.

The only way to respond to such problems was to seek a *foundational* solution. Philosophers now sought some proof of the existence of the world, some self-evidently true knowledge, which could be used to infer the at least partial validity of all human cognition and perception. Descartes's attempt to ground all knowledge in "I think therefore I am" is the most famous, but by no means the only example. "Foundationalism" meant that most of our daily empirical beliefs are epistemically dependent on the truth of much more fundamental beliefs or principles, and unless there is a self-evident anchor, the former cannot be secure. The foundations must be recognizably true without inference from something else—any such inference would be circular reasoning. Instead of the inquiries into different subject matters having their own distinctive bases, as in Aristotle, all inquiry needs one global defense, one link to attach it to the world that "causes" our representations.

It was in this context that Hume turned to the question of facts and values. The famous statement, from his 1739 masterpiece *Treatise of Human Nature*, is as follows.

> In every system of morality, which I have hitherto met with . . . the author proceeds for some time in the ordinary ways of reasoning, and establishes the being of a God, or makes observations concerning human affairs; when all of a sudden I am surprised to find, that instead of the usual copulations of propositions, *is*, and *is not*, I meet with no proposition that is not connected with an *ought*, or an *ought not*. This change is imperceptible; but is however, of the last consequence. For as this *ought*, or *ought not*, expresses some new relation or affirmation, 'tis necessary that it should be observed and explained; and at the same time that a reason should be given, for what seems altogether inconceivable, how this new relation can be a deduction from others, which are entirely different from it.[7]

This was called "Hume's law." Calling it that implies more than was in Hume's characteristically historical ruminations. He arguably meant only that one cannot infer moral norms or "oughts" from statements of what is, without additional argumentation. But this seemed to mean that a value statement can be derived only from another value statement, there being no way to crossover from one to the other. Human reason, he separately argued, could provide just two kinds of knowledge, of *matters of fact*, or what others would call synthetic judgments, like "That is a YIELD sign" or "John is a bachelor," and of *relations of ideas*, or analytic judgments, such as, respectively, "Triangles have three sides" and "All bachelors are unmarried." Taken together, "synthetic" statements of facts and "analytic" statements of what is true-by-definition are all of human knowledge, all that human reason can hope to grasp or validate. This means value judgments can't be judgments of reason. Hume was not arguing that reason could never contribute to judgments of morality or beauty or value; indeed, some of his best work is in ethics, history, and human affairs. But such judgments always had to be based in natural passions, in sentiments, which were not open to rational validation, even while we have no choice but to obey them. Morality is crucial, but reason by itself is impotent in morality.

After a nineteenth century dominated by idealism and utilitarianism, owing above all to Hegel and John Stuart Mill, the counter-reaction against these at the start of the twentieth century brought Hume's distinction back. The landmark 1903 *Principia Ethica*, by Russell's Cambridge colleague G. E. Moore, made a related logical point based in the analytic-synthetic distinction. It is a beautiful example of the new method of linguistic analysis Moore and Russell were inventing.

Moore's target was Mill's utilitarian attempt to say that the moral good *is* pleasure, or pleasure is identical to The Good. But his critique would apply to any claim that goodness is identical to any of the usual suspects: happiness, benevolence, love, beauty, et cetera. He argued in effect that the utilitarians were worse than wrong: they didn't even know what they were talking about! Moore wrote:

> propositions about the good are all of them synthetic and never analytic . . . Nobody can foist upon us such an axiom as "Pleasure is the only good" or that "The good is the desired" as on the pretext that this is "the very meaning of the word" . . . definitions which describe the real nature of the object or notion denoted by the word, and which do not merely tell us what the word is used to mean, are only possible when the object or notion in question is something complex.[8]

The reasoning is this. Definitions are stipulations of meaning, made true just by the meanings of the words. But such analytic statements are not discoveries, do not yield any information about the world. A definition or statement of identity makes the two sides of the equal sign (actually, the biconditional) the same, so either should be substitutable for the other in any sentence without changing meaning or truth. "John is a bachelor" and "John is a married male" mean the same thing, and you should be able to switch "bachelor" and "married male" around in sentences without changing their truth. So "All bachelors are unmarried men" would then have be logically equivalent to "All bachelors are bachelors," which tells us *nothing*. It just repeats. Moore is claiming that if the statement "the pleasant is the good" is supposed to be a definition, hence analytic, it would be logically equivalent to saying "the pleasant is the pleasant" or "the good is the good." Which says nothing.

Moore buttresses the point with his famous "open question" argument. If the question of what pleasure is, is "open," if is a real question, it has to be synthetic, and that must mean "pleasure" and "good" are *not* identical. Moore makes clear that this does not mean that the predication of the word "good" to this or that—say, "love is good"—has no use or no meaning; he wrote, "If I did think so, I should not be writing on Ethics."[9] His objection is not to any statement of the form "X is really good," but to statements of the form "Goodness is X," that is, goodness equals X. The claim "Most people mean 'makes me happy' when they say 'good' " is also fine—it's just a report on common usage. Likewise, "Pleasure is one of the things that is good" is fine. What is thrown out is the identity claim, "Good = X."

Moore called the error that people make when they violate his principle the "naturalistic fallacy." One cannot infer that X is good from X's natural properties. It may be pleasant, and it may be good, but the goodness is not deducible from the pleasantness. Some people have glossed the fallacy in simple terms as "Just because something is natural doesn't mean it's good." That would be acceptable to Moore if "something" includes not just entities but also properties, activities, states, et cetera. But neither is he claiming "X is good because it is natural" is absurd or contradictory, only that a further argument is needed. A natural property is always by itself insufficient to establish goodness. But the implications of this, given our broader understanding of the world, could well be momentous. For what kind of argument could we ever give for something's goodness, other than citing that a natural property is obviously or in itself good?

This has something to do with reduction (and as we will see later, emergence). For Moore, to define something is to say what are the parts that compose it. If it has no parts, it can't be defined, like "yellow." You can point at something yellow and say the word, but you can't define yellow because it has no parts. He accepts that some things are "organic wholes," in which the whole has a significance that is not the sum of the meanings of its parts. But goodness can only be a simple, indefinable, intuitable, nonnatural property. Just like "yellow," which is real but cannot be reduced to or identified with a frequency of light vibrations. For

> light-vibrations are not themselves what we mean by yellow . . . The most we can be entitled to say of those vibrations is that they are what corresponds in space to the yellow which we actually perceived . . . a mistake of this simple kind has commonly been made about "good." . . . far too many philosophers have thought that when they named those other properties [i.e., light frequency] they were actually defining good; that these properties . . . were . . . absolutely and entirely the same with goodness. This view I propose to call the "naturalistic fallacy" . . .[10]

Moore was at this point a Platonic realist, believing that certain universals, like yellow, exist or subsist independent of their particular manifestations. Good must be one of them.

While many thinkers have criticized Moore's analysis, his view serves as an anti-naturalistic spine running throughout twentieth-century analytic ethics, right up to the present time. (Just as everybody rejects Descartes's mind-body dualism today but still has a hard time getting past it.) Some positivists, like C. L. Stevenson, accepted Moore's rejection of naturalism, turning to the solution that moral sentences like "murder is wrong" are not statements or assertions at all, not true or false, but expressions of emotion, as noted earlier. The Oxford philosophers of the 1950s argued instead that moral utterances are commendations or commands, but still rejected any hint of naturalism, as we will see. As Michael Ruse points out, Moore himself deliberately opposed early forms of evolutionary ethics found in Darwin and in Herbert Spencer.[11] Twentieth-century philosophical ethics was born to be anti-naturalist.

But there is another side to the fact-value dichotomy. We now turn to a thinker whom philosophers often neglect: Max Weber, the greatest sociologist in an era where philosophical questions still riddled that field. Weber is famous for, among other things, claiming that science, including social science, investigates facts only and is *wertfrei* or "value free."[12] Weber's doctrine has been harshly criticized by sociologists and philosophers who admire a critical, political, value-laden social theory.

This criticism is unfair. Especially in his famous 1917 lecture "Science as a Vocation," the point of Weber's claim was simply that social scientists have expertise only in finding and describing fact (Weber 1949a, 2004). When they turn to endorse or reject a political position, they are moving from the scientist's role to the stance of a concerned citizen or political activist, for which science lends no authority. In the midst of a nationalistic Germany during an unprecedentedly brutal, stalemated war, Weber was warning his students and the German public not to transfer political value-authority to the professor, historian, economist, or legal expert. Those decisions are for society at large.

This claim went along with Weber's more general analysis of the modern age. Modernity has been created by modern science, modern capitalist markets, and modern bureaucratic organization, all of which embody "rationalization," or "intellectualization." Rationalization is the breaking down of complex traditional practices into specialized procedures and claims meant to achieve some calculable end. What makes industrial production rational and progressive, its achievement of higher output for lesser input, is its exclusion of extraneous factors, especially the cultural values of earlier modes of production. What makes science rational is its exclusion of considerations other than fact as leading to truth. It is the isolation of the end, the value that is being sought, that allows rationalization and hence progress. None of these activities can validate the ends they seek; capitalism cannot prove profit is good, science cannot prove truth is desirable, medicine can only presume life is worth saving. Only religious faith can validate those ends, and we moderns now live in a "disenchanted" world. We will return to this.

There is one more powerful motivation for the fact-value dichotomy, the notion that value claims are dependent for their validity on social valuations and hence on culture. Human beings come in historical kinds called "cultures" that have distinctive rules for living and their own value "systems," some say. In the twentieth century, the notion that culture acts as a basis for knowledge and judgment was especially promoted by the cultural anthropology of Franz Boas and his students Ruth Benedict and Margaret Mead. Remarkably, these anthropological views played a role in the linguistic philosophy of the 1950s in the so-called "rationality debate." The new linguistic turn in philosophy made anthropology relevant. Peter Winch, for example, argued on Wittgensteinian grounds that rationality itself is a linguistic feature, that each language as practically deployed in its cultural context has its own standard of rationality (Winch 1974a, 1974b). The Western "rationalist" anthropologist has their own, as does the tribal

Samoan or Nuer who endorses magic. Neither is more or less rational by any culture-independent standard. In a world recovering from fascism and dealing with the end of European imperialism this was an attractive view.

Now cultural relativism has many forms, some easily refutable and self-defeating, such as, "The validity of any statement is limited to the culture in which it was pronounced or to which its utterer belongs." That is self-negating. But others are not.[13] Its relevance here is that if the validity of value judgments is dependent on the validity of the value-perspective of a culture, then it seems no noncircular argument can be made for the validity of those value judgments. The young Alasdair MacIntyre, later a prominent ethicist, and the young Ernest Gellner, who became the most famous analyst of nationalism, each made important, albeit controversial, responses to Winch's relativism. For MacIntyre, the very idea of discussing the existence of God in a modern idiom means that the discussion takes on a different meaning than it had in medieval times (MacIntyre 1974). Similarly, Gellner argued that, *contra* Winch, logical coherence and social coherence can be different, and modernity, unlike traditional societies, must treat them differently (Gellner 1974). We will return to these issues later. The current point is that the philosophical turn to ordinary language and culture added yet another reason to doubt the general validity of value claims.

The "Collapse" of the Dichotomy

So, the hard form of the fact-value dichotomy softened after 1950 through a combination of the decline of positivism, rise of linguistic philosophy, and finally a surprising renaissance of pragmatism in the 1980s. Revisionists argued that the is-ought dichotomy was overblown and fraught with exceptions, claiming that there are in fact some "is" claims from which we *can* infer "ought" claims. This turn was encouraged by Hilary Putnam, one of the most prominent analytic philosophers of the second half of the twentieth century. Like Richard Rorty, with whom he had an ongoing debate over the plausibility of philosophy itself in the 1980s and 1990s, Putnam had been early influenced by American pragmatism. As he aged, his pragmatic strain reasserted itself.

Putnam's *The Collapse of the Fact/Value Dichotomy* is a fine review of the issue (Putnam 2004). He points out that the "trichotomy" of analytic statements versus synthetic statements versus value statements was undermined in the late 1940s and early 1950s, as students of the positivists promoted a pragmatic turn inside analytic philosophy. Putnam correctly recalled that this very point had been made by Morton White, colleague of Quine (White 1956). Putnam claimed that we can now see there had never been any true "dichotomy" of fact and value in the first place. What was his argument?

First, Putnam points out that our cognition of fact is not what many once thought it was. Observation is theory-laden. That is, whenever we linguistically express an observation it has already been influenced by prior concepts and learning, by theory. Hence, there is no absolutely objective knowledge of fact to which a merely "subjective" knowledge of value can be opposed. Second, perception is already conceptual, already informed by meanings and concepts, and with that we *perceive* values. For linguistic creatures, perception of fact has already been sorted and organized by concepts, and these concepts have been influenced by values, by pragmatic programs of action. We *taste* that "the wine is full-bodied" and *see* that "Fred is elated." Third, in ordinary language there are clearly lots of thick factual judgments that "entangle" fact with value.[14] We make and accept these all the time. We say that was a "great" decision, a "bold" conjecture, a "beautiful" insight. Is the statement "that was a great catch" in a baseball game an unjustifiable inference from "is" to "ought"? Last, Putnam notes, there are epistemic values that guide inquiry itself, such as coherence, rationality, simplicity, and beauty. Theory selection in inquiry, even scientific inquiry, presupposes values, some aesthetic (e.g., simplicity) but some practical (e.g., fruitfulness). Ockham's razor, the notion that in inquiry we ought to accept the simplest explanation, cannot be justified as "true" but as a practical or aesthetic limit on what should be asserted as true.

Now, let us investigate Putnam's points systematically, moving from the most trivial to the most important. Is he right that the fact-value dichotomy has collapsed?

First, some acts or events are wrong or bad by *definition*. There are terms that describe something as good or bad, so merely asserting them is a legitimate, rational assertion of value. "Murder" is arguably one of them: to call an act a "murder" and not just a "killing" is to say the act was illegitimate. One might say "cruelty" is always illicit; the question is whether a particular act of harm *is* a case of cruelty as opposed to being, say, justifiable punishment. If "cruelty" and "murder" aren't obvious enough for you, when something is called "evil" it is claimed to be bad. Likewise, Putnam mentions other judgments—"One ought to do what is right" and "Virtue is good"—that seem if not purely analytic then pretty close.

Second, some "ought" statements can be inferred from "is" statements, either deductively or inductively. Suppose I argue that, "Murder is wrong. Fred murdered Jane. Therefore, what Fred did was wrong." That argument is valid. We have derived a value or "ought statement"—Fred did something wrong—from two "is" statements. Now, advocates of the dichotomy would retort: okay, the inference is valid, but surely this is not the point at issue. The problem is, how do we *justify the first premise*, which is an "is" statement with value hidden in it, hence simultaneously an "ought" or value statement? Fair enough, the first statement, while it looks like a simple predication of fact (murder has the property "wrong" like water has the property "wet"), is actually a value premise that would need its own justification. But that is not an unbridgeable barrier in itself; it is a question of a missing justification.

Third, and more crucially, there is a class of natural language predicates that arguably entangle fact and value, and which we assert all the time: *functional predicates*. "The desk is messy," "The car is running well," "That fish you caught is delicious." These statements refer to how some activity or practice is supposed to go, or to the purpose some entity is supposed to have. As MacIntyre liked to pointed out, the knife is supposed to be sharp; the batter is supposed to get a hit; the cook is supposed to make a tasty meal. Failure to play chess by the rules—moving the rook diagonally—is bad chess, or not chess at all. Role performances are functionally describable. We will return to this.

Finally, as Putnam points out, inquiry into truth and fact, like any human activity, is likewise normed. Science can be done well or ill, an experiment or paper can be "beautiful," a solution "elegant," and so on. We do value science; in fact, pretty much the only people doing science are doing it because they value it. And parsimony can be a criterion we use in choosing among papers or theories or accounts.

So Putnam's revisionist response to the alleged dichotomy is correct. The putative dichotomy was always riddled with important exceptions. In fact, one might wonder, who could have believed such a silly idea—"no ought from is"?

Or maybe it wasn't so silly; perhaps Putnam's examples just undercut the easy cases. For it remains true that "you punched Fred" has a different evidentiary burden from "you shouldn't have." Philosophers of value do, after all, have endless arguments about what the rules of right, good, beauty, and justice are. Stating truths about values has a different burden than stating that it is rainy or sunny; saying someone was harmed is easier than saying that it was good or right that he was harmed. Neither Putnam nor others who question the existence of a "fact-value dichotomy" actually show us how, in what sense, values and principles of ethics, politics, or aesthetics can be rationally adjudicated within the context of our best view of human beings and their place in the world.

Sometimes when landscapers clear trees they bury the stumps underground to avoid hauling them away. Homeowners learn this a decade later when the stumps rot and create sinkholes. Those who have tried to clear away the fact-value dichotomy have left some buried stumps. The sinkholes continue to warp our movements. The best that can be said is that the distinction has become blurry. But the issue remains: how can statements of value be rationally advanced and adjudicated? A broader treatment may be required.

What in the World is a Value?

This is a metaphysical question, so its answer depends on what things are. It is arguable that the majority of the Western philosophical tradition from Aristotle to the eighteenth century had a largely functional view of its most ubiquitous metaphysical entity: *substances*. The independent entities composing the world had final causes or functions. But since Galileo, Descartes, Locke, and Newton, all nonphysical properties of anything have to be mental events, the physical entities having the "powers" to cause those. Nature in itself is value-neutral; values are solely human projections.

Now, we are no longer Newtonians today. But it remains the case that the dominant metaphysical view today is physicalism—the view that what has the greatest claim on constituting "reality" is the objects of fundamental physics and their causal interactions. There are two problems this causes for values.

One is that everything is physical, has mass and spatial location, for example, and is a particular. What is real, or most real, or the basis of everything real, is *actual physical particulars*, like me and the computer I am working on. If objective reality independent of the judgments of individual human subjects is constituted solely by physical particulars, then lots of things would be unreal: the past, possibilities, properties (which are universals holding of many particulars), numbers (which aren't physical), meanings, and ideas, not to mention minds (unless you equate mind and brain). All these are either unreal, or real but enormous complexes of little actual physical bits, or play no causal role in what happens. I am not saying all philosophers, or even most, accept this. But there is a strong tendency to think any departure from physicalism has a heavy burden of proof. And if redness or being a dog or the Holocaust or five or my future death are not "real," because they are not currently perceivable physical particulars, how might "goodness," "beauty," "truth" or even "fairness" fare?

A different but related issue is that philosophers mostly presume that the objects of physics, hence ultimately real things, are what they are *intrinsically*. The actual particular is what it is, and the accumulation and interaction of such particulars make up reality. But showing that X is good or bad seems a very different bowl of fish from showing that X exists as a particular. *Values seem relational by nature*. Ever since Aristotle, ethicists and others have distinguished between things that are "instrumentally" valuable, like tools, and things that are "intrinsically" valuable, like pleasure or love or happiness, and have thought that the value of the former must be grounded in the later. Intrinsic value plays the role in philosophy of value that "sense data" once played in the theory of knowledge. But if "intrinsic" means nonrelational, means that something is valuable *even if everything else were different*, what could have such value?

Lastly, what kind of justification for value norms or value claims would be acceptable for philosophers? The attack made by Richard Rorty in the 1980s against foundationalism, the attempt by philosophers to give a self-evident justification of all our valid claims, had an ethical side to it. It was applied to ethics by Bernard Williams, another one of the new linguistic philosophers of the 1950s. Williams called the modern Western notion of morality, as embodied particularly in the major competing modern ethical views, a "peculiar institution" (Williams 1985). He pointed out that the search for an ultimate, rationally justifiable rule that would provide decisive and valid guidance throughout our lives, independent of questions of success or luck, was a uniquely modern and problematic search. What is "peculiar" is the combination of: (a) a foundationalist urge that seeks an ultimate justification for moral norms to defeat skepticism and relativism; (b) a modern universalism that hopes to apply the same set of norms to all humans regardless of culture, historical period, social convention or even social role; and (c) a morality strictly distinguished from any concerns other than the rightness of a choice, like practical success or "prudence" or aesthetic value. Could anything ever satisfy such criteria? Or are the very criteria wrong?

We will see that this approach to ethics has much to do with modernity, the new form of urban, bureaucratic, capitalist, specialized life that replaces the local, agrarian existence that dominated all societies for millennia. Progress required that key institutions, processes, and their characteristic modes of judgment had to be differentiated and segregated from others, for example, truth claims and technological and economic improvement from cultural tradition. Weber regarded this modern "rationalization" as a two-edged sword, one edge of which he even called "the devil." Commenting on whether science is an objectively valuable vocation, speaking to the romanticism of the German students of his day, he said: "I personally by my very work answer in the affirmative, and I also do from precisely the standpoint that hates intellectualism as the worst devil, as youth does today . . . if one wishes to settle this devil, one must not take to flight before him . . . one has to see the devil's ways to the end in order to realize his power and limitations."[15] For Weber, the way to deal with modern rationalization is not to abandon or suppress it—which would be impossible anyway—but to think it through, and reconceive the context in which it functions. That is what we must do. We are going to have to deal with a host of problems. To avoid some of these problems we need a way of talking about things in general that does not privilege, or disadvantage, either judgments of facts or judgments of values, which does not think "entities" are more real or basic than relations and processes. We need a more neutral but nonfoundational language for describing both the natural and human worlds. This is the task of the next chapter.

Chapter Two

An Objective Relativism

> I believe that few habits would be more useful to philosophy than the habit of refusing to discuss whether certain entities exist, unless we ask *exist how? or in what kind of a system?*
>
> —Morris Cohen, "The Distinction Between the Mental and the Physical"[1]

If you believe in a real world then you believe many of the things of that world continue to exist whether you experience them or not—or even whether you *exist* or not. That is "realism." The old saw, "If the tree falls in the forest and nobody hears it, does it make a sound?" was always a bad example because sound could be defined as something heard by an animal. Better would be, "Does it make a dent on the ground?" Realists say yes. "Relativism" sounds like the opposite view, the claim that whatever there is or whatever I experience depends on me, or on my culture. But there is a kind of relativism that is compatible with realism: *objective relativism*. All it says is that each thing is relative to some other things. You and I might be some of those things, but we might not. Nothing is totally independent of relations. This does not mean everything is relations or everything is related to everything. It means each thing is related to, relative to, some other things.

If you search for the term "objective relativism," you will find that it was a minor view in ethics or in value theory generally (Allan 2008; Hickman 2013). Paul Kurtz, the famous secular humanist, endorsed the term as designating human moral principles that have an empirical, "transactional" function rooted in human experience. He probably got this from John Dewey. Hilary Putnam's influential *Reason, Truth and History* (1981, ascribed the "objective relativity" of values to Dewey and claimed this was akin to his own "internal realism."[2] A number of philosophers regarded C. I. Lewis's *An Analysis of Knowledge and Valuation* (1962) as an objective relativist theory of values. Lewis claimed that to say an object has a value is to say it has the potentiality to result in some value-experience. Saying the bread is nutritious means eating it will keep you alive. Objective relativism even came to be discussed in aesthetics (Stolnitz 1960).

But objective relativism started out having nothing to do with ethics, aesthetics, or values in general. Herein lies another tale. The tale matters because while objective relativism is not by itself an answer to the questions of value, it is the basis for an approach that will make those questions tractable. This chapter and the next suggest that one can have a systematic philosophical language that avoids claims to being foundational or self-evident, yet funds an approach to values that is naturalist and realist. A relativism that is objective, not subjective, is the first step. For this we must return to the year 1900.

The New Realism

In one of the best accounts of the development of twentieth-century philosophy John Passmore characterized the break of that century from the nineteenth. He suggested, "The main tendency of nineteenth-century thought was towards the conclusion that both 'things' and facts about things are dependent for their existence and their nature upon the operations of a mind."[3] That was *idealism*. It had two running mates, *psychologism*, which claimed the validity of logic is psychological, and *historicism*, which claimed truth depends on history. For all three, realism is naïve; what is true depends on the relation to human mind or history. But right around 1900 there was a widespread reaction inspired by the cumulative effect of the four different scientific revolts, if not revolutions, of 1859–1905.

First was Darwin's 1959 *Origin of Species*. For religion and culture, the shock of Darwin may have been that humanity was not specially created, but for philosophers and psychologists more important was that mind and consciousness must have evolved from creatures that had neither. Second was the mathematical logic of Boole, De Morgan, Peano, Peirce, and Frege, which culminated, for philosophers, with Russell. Most of the new logicians believed logical-mathematical truths held *of something*, of objects neither mental nor physical, and that relations are as real as anything else, not second-class realities for which there was no clear logical expression. Third was Wilhelm Wundt's experimental psychology lab in Leipzig, founded in 1879, the beginning of an empirical and naturalistic approach to human mind. William James would quickly establish a second lab in Cambridge, Massachusetts. Last was of course Einstein's theory of relativity, which not only rejected "absolute" space and time and simultaneity at a distance but made spacetime measurements objectively relative. That is, an event, such as an object's trajectory, has as many different equally valid measurements of speed, time, and displacement as there are reference frames from which it can be measured. This has nothing to do with the experience of any subject; it holds equally for cameras and watches. All these developments put pressure on idealism, psychologism, and historicism. Russell later wrote that experimental psychology had made mind more like matter, while the new physics made matter more like mind.[4]

Realism exploded on the scene in 1895–1905, one of those decades where a host of innovators attack the same thing albeit from different directions. Passmore again:

> In the early years of the present [twentieth] century, it could no longer be presumed that Realism was intellectually disreputable, a mere vulgar prejudice. What a mind knowns, Brentano and Meinong had argued, exists independently of the act by which it is known; Mach, and James after him—if they were still, from a Realist point of view, tainted with subjectivism—had at least denied that what is immediately perceived is a state of mind; and then Moore, seconded by Russell, had rejected that thesis which Idealists like Bradley and phenomenalists like Mill had united in regarding as indisputable; that existence of objects of perception consists in the fact that they are perceived. The "New Realism" brought together these converging tendencies; it owed much to Meinong, more to Mach and James, and it acknowledged the help of Moore and Russell in the battle against idealism.[5]

"Realism" was the new battle cry. It was commonly understood to claim, against idealism, that mind is not everything, that the objects of knowledge do not depend upon being known, that logical or mathematical entities exist or "subsist," and that we experience things directly rather than mere mental representations of them. (Quite different claims, as we shall see.) It was sparked simultaneously by thinkers that, from today's perspective, seem utterly unlike: Ernst Mach (1897), Edmund Husserl (1900), Bertrand

Russell (1903), G. E. Moore (1903), Henri Bergson (1903), and William James (1904a, 1904b). In England, Russell and Moore invented analytic philosophy to defend realism. Husserl would invent phenomenology, one of the core methods of continental philosophy, to return us to "the things themselves." The American pragmatists stood ambiguously between the idealists and other realists, depending on the issue, but James's late essays, collected as *Essays in Radical Empiricism*, inspired the 1910 manifesto of his students, "The Program and First Platform of Six Realists," matched by the English Realism of T. P. Nunn, Lloyd Morgan, and Samuel Alexander (which in turn created British Emergentism). Russell found himself "in almost complete agreement" with the American New Realists (Russell 1911). In Lovejoy's terms, all this was a "Revolt of the Twentieth Century against the Seventeenth." J. H. Randall could write, "Modern philosophy, thank God, is at last over."[6]

It is not too much to say this eruption invented twentieth-century philosophy. The founders of what would become all the major schools of twentieth-century philosophy were simultaneously moving in a realist direction. But the issues were complex, and the battle cry "realism" hid differences the realists themselves did not recognize. Realism meant at least four different things, even exempting concerns about values (e.g., moral, aesthetic, or political realism). *Metaphysical realism* claimed that things exist independent of mind, that mind is part of a larger nonmental reality, in opposition to some kinds of idealism. *Epistemic realism* claimed that what we know is in some cases true of things as they are independent of our minds or experience, versus some idealisms but also what would later be called antirealism or relativism. *Perceptual realism*, or "direct" or "naïve realism," held that we perceive real things themselves, repudiating representationalism. The claim that universals like "red" or "two" exist independently of particulars, such as two particular apples, we can call *logical realism*, versus nominalism and the psychologistic interpretation of logic and mathematics. Central to this was the notion that relations, crucial to the new logic, are objectively real and not "secondary."

Each thinker accepted one or two of these and called it "realism." The driving forces of the discussion were actually logical-relational realism on the one hand, and perceptual realism on the other. This formed two overlapping groups. The first fought for logical realism against nominalism and psychologism. Some claimed logical objects and meanings "subsisted" as a "third realm" distinct from the mental and the physical qualities (e.g., the golden mountain of Meinong). So Idealists like Josiah Royce could be logical realists, and since psychologism could be a consequence of naturalism, logical realists could be anti-naturalists, like Husserl. The second group argued that perception directly presents real things, like Mach and James. If the perceived objects are members of the "third realm," they subsist like meanings. However, for naturalists or monists who accept no division between a realm of essences or meanings and physical things, perceptual realism became "naïve" realism. All this was being sorted out in the Roaring Twenties when Bergson, Husserl, Heidegger, Broad, Lloyd Morgan, Alexander, Dewey, Whitehead, Russell, Wittgenstein, and Carnap produced monumental studies. Much of twentieth-century philosophy was a series of footnotes to the 1920s.

Most relevant for us are two early realist doctrines whose distinction only later became clear. First, if objects are conceived as relational, then the difference between "real" and "apparent," "subjective" and "objective," even "physical" and "mental" can be analyzed as two relational functions of the same thing. Is the pencil dipped in water bent or straight? Representationalists said the pencil is really straight, but its appearance is bent. But Mach said the very same fundamental content or elements "in their functional dependence [on the perceiver] . . . are sensations. In another functional connexion they are at the same time physical objects."[7] The pencil is both but in different relations. This was *neutral monism*, a view both James and Russell supported.[8] The train tracks are parallel *and* converge for they only occur in relations, yielding two separate but equal occurrences, the "tracks-in-relation-to-the-train" (parallel) and "tracks-in-relation-to-vision-when-standing-on-them" (convergent). As James student E. B. Holt wrote, "things *are* just what they *seem*." For Holt, all things "physical, mental, and logical . . . subsist." This includes error, illusion, and hallucination: "every content . . . real or unreal, subsists . . . in the all-inclusive universe of being . . . this being is not 'subjective in nature.' "[9]

Second is objective relativism, which arose in the work of long-forgotten philosopher Morris Cohen, the first Jew to hold a regular faculty position in American philosophy. He left Harvard with his PhD in 1906, having been more influenced by Royce than by James, who he feared was a nominalist regarding logic and mathematics. Unable to achieve his dream of a Columbia position, at City College of New York he taught virtually all Jewish philosophers from New York City from 1912 to 1938 (e.g., Justus Buchler, Lewis Feuer, Albert Hofstadter, Sidney Hook, Milton Munitz, Ernest Nagel, Joseph Ratner, Herbert Schneider, Paul Weiss, Morton White, and Philip Wiener). He was also a famously difficult person, at least for his students.[10] In 1923, Cohen published the first collection of Peirce's writings. For fifty years, all collections of Peirce were by Cohen or Cohen's students.

Cohen's earliest work, in the 1910s, was in support of perceptual realism against A. O. Lovejoy, who would become one of the "critical realists" (Drake 1920). Cohen is in contemporary terms an odd duck, a Roycean-Russellian realist about logic, and on the other hand a perceptual realist like Mach and James. In a 1913 essay, he rejected Russell's term "subsistence" as "makeshift." If mathematical facts, incorporated into physics, serve as constraints on physical events, then there is no reason to ascribe them a lesser form of existence. The fact that "abstractions," such as triangularity, do not occur by themselves but only along with other things—for example, matter—is no stranger than that Jack being a brother cannot occur without Jack also being a human being, a male, et cetera. Triangularity exists as fully as brothers do. And this applies both to the realities of perception and mathematics. Logical realism and perceptual realism can be combined only if each thing is relational. Cohen wrote:

> The world of existence is thus a network of relations whose intersections are called terms. These termini may be complex or simple, but the simplicity is always relative to the system in which they enter. . . . Even the mathematical point is . . . simple . . . only in point geometry. In line geometry a point is a complex formed by the intersection of two lines. . . . The metaphysic here suggested starting with the relational structure of things avoids the ontologic ills that beset things in themselves.[11]

Our fixation on what "exists" or "is real" should be dropped. Rather, Cohen argued, instead of discussing whether certain entities exist, we should ask "*exist how? or in what kind of a system?*"[12] These views of Cohen's had little influence outside the circle of his students (we will return to that later). Nevertheless, he foresaw something that became a central idea for naturalist philosophers at Columbia. Rejecting both idealism and materialism, he endorsed neutral monism but offered that it "may as well be called . . . [neutral] pluralism."

In 1927, Arthur Murphy, briefly a colleague of G. H. Mead's at Chicago, was the first to name "objective relativism."[13] He claimed to find it in Dewey and Whitehead, although it was more true of Mead, whose paper "The Objective Reality of Perspectives" appeared the same year.[14] Murphy wrote: "The objective facts of . . . nature . . . are the very apparent and relative happenings . . . disclosed in perception. . . . Such relativity is hence an ultimate fact about the objective world."[15] Lovejoy, one of the critical realists, made objective relativism famous by his lengthy critique in *The Revolt Against Dualism* (also calling it "pan-objectivism"). Charles Morris, another student of Mead, maintained all his life that objective relativism was the proper metaphysics for pragmatism.[16]

Most important for us, later the threads gathered at Columbia, home of two former Cohen students, Nagel and Buchler, and a Cohen admirer, Randall. Randall referred to objective relativism by name repeatedly in the late 1930s and 1940s. In 1947, Ernest Nagel described what he thought was "beyond question America's most significant contribution to philosophical intelligence."[17] Strikingly for a student of Dewey's, Nagel did *not* say it was pragmatism. He wrote that it was alternately named "objective relativism, functional realism, contextual naturalism, and process philosophy." This view accepts, first, "the essentially incomplete but fundamentally plural character of existence" in which contingency and qualitative discontinuities are "ultimate." Second, "every quality and event is a genuine occurrence in some . . . process or context," but "no one context . . . is relevant to the occurrence of everything," so "there is no absolutely privileged context." Third, it is antireductionist, holding that "the world contains at least as many qualitatively distinct features as are disclosed in human experience." The human "is as much an integral part of nature . . . as is any of [nature's] other sectors."

After the 1950s, objective relativism virtually disappeared amidst powerful imported movements: in analytic philosophy, the new Oxford ordinary language approach, which impacted the students of positivism; and the importation of continental philosophy in the form of major European emigres. Murphy himself would later write an essay, "Whatever Happened to Objective Relativism?" (Murphy 1963). But there was to be one more inning: in 1966, Justus Buchler, student of Cohen and Nagel, and colleague of Randall, formulated the most precise version of objective relativism in his *The Metaphysics of Natural Complexes* (1990), although without using the term.[18]

Reformulating Objective Relativism

What to make of all this? Here we will need to do some metaphysics, but it will be worth the effort. What follows is my reconstruction of objective relativism. I am not claiming it is true, or even that it is the right way to begin philosophizing. But it is a least determinate language for discussing things, allowing the issue of what is the best way to understand those things to remain a subsequent question. For philosophers, it performs the role of an ontology, albeit without an account of being *per se*. My claim is that this odd approach will yield dividends for understanding values.

The first hypothesis is the core idea. (1) *Each being is characterized by relativity and hence is complex.* By each being I mean anything discriminable whatsoever, including entities, kinds, properties, meanings, universals, events, experiences, relations, perceptual images, or feelings. For "being" we could substitute "complex," the short form of Cohen's term "a complex of things-in-relation." By relativity I mean that *what the being is* depends on some relations—"internal" relations, philosophers say—to what is not itself or a part or property of itself, not merely "external" relations to beings that make no difference to what it is. This does not mean each being is dependent on relations to everything, just to some things. Each being functions in sets of relations to other discriminables. Nothing fails to be dependent or contextual.

This is partly illustrated in figure 2.1. X is something, a complex. On the one hand, X is related to a variety of contexts in which it functions, Y. X has an integrity or function in $Y_1, Y_2 \ldots Y_n$. At the same time, X is itself a context in relation to which other complexes, Z, function. X is a context for $Z_1, Z_2 \ldots Z_n$. The same can be said of each Y and each Z because all are complexes. (The figure is misleading in that none of this has to imply encompassing spatial relations.) In each context in which X functions there is the possibility that some of those relations are, in Buchler's terms, "strongly related" to X, meaning they are relevant to what X *is in that* context, others "weakly" related. Thus the distinction between what philosophers call *internal*, or identity-related, and *external*, or not-identity-related properties, is, as Cohen pointed out, itself contextual.

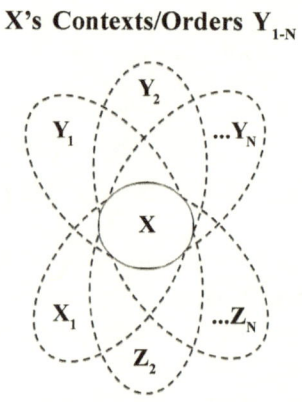

Figure 2.1. A complex. (Author created)

This approach is strange in two ways. First, objective relativism is a *distributive* rather than collective approach to things, separately suggested by James, Cohen, and Randall.[19] It provides a language for describing each, not all. It does not characterize beings collectively or present an exhaustive list of types of being. It just says any complex x functions in relation to other complexes y, which may serve as a context or "order" for x. Likewise x functions as a context or order for its own properties and/or parts z. The same holds of y and z. A baseball game is a complex, but so is each player and each pitch, the tempo of the game, the stitching on the ball, as well as the city and the culture in which it occurs. This is not an attempt at what Thomas Nagel called a "view from nowhere," nor a view from "everywhere," but a *view from anywhere*.[20]

Second, objective relativism accepts what Buchler labeled "ontological parity."[21] As Cohen and Randall had separately put it, the question is not, "Is something real?" but "How is it real?" or "In what context does it function?" There are no degrees of reality or existence among discriminables. Ontologically, the opposite of "real" or "existent" would have to be "unreal" or "nonexistent," and it makes no sense to deny reality or existence to anything that must be accounted for. ("Actuality" is another matter; its antonyms include possibility and the past.) That something is more independent, or causal, or important than something else does not mean it is more "real" or "existent." The real-versus-unreal distinction is here captured by distinguishing the orders in which something functions. The unicorn is as real as the horse, one in the context of literature, the other in biology. Minds too are somethings. They are a kind of something to which others can be related in a special way, called "intentionality" or "experience." A human being's experience is an historically evolving activity into which somethings enter by way of these relations.

Objective relativism has a rather heterodox implication. Because it makes no use of terms that imply that the analysis of any complex ends, or a referent's character is unaffected by what is outside itself, it abjures reference to simples as noted. But for the same reason it refuses foundations, a highest reality, the Whole, or the One. As Ernest Nagel put it, "no one context . . . is relevant to the occurrence of everything."[22] We will return to this.

The second hypothesis, which was implicit among the objective relativists, is that (2) *Our knowledge of any complex is never certain or complete.* That is just Peirce's doctrine of fallibilism. All objective relativists were influenced by Peirce. He insisted that we have knowledge of objects as they are independent of our knowing, but such knowledge is never complete or certain. We never have adequate reason to say there is nothing more to know about *anything*, and we cannot know that the "more" will not recast the context in which the known is located. Recontextualization does not disqualify prior knowledge; that Einstein was more right does not mean Newton knew nothing. And fallibilism too is fallible. The denial of certainty is not certain. But, there being no pragmatic difference between accepting a belief due to high likelihood and due to certainty, no truth is lost. The "lack of certainty or completeness" condition applies to itself.[23]

Fallibilism has a corollary that deserves mention. It denies that the validity of knowledge in a given context is *necessarily* dependent on the validity of knowledge of more basic or more inclusive contexts, hence transitively, the most fundamental or most inclusive. We cannot hold our local knowledge hostage to knowledge of the first or the last, the Foundation or the Whole. As Peirce wrote, "Philosophy ought to . . . trust . . . the multitude and variety of its arguments rather than . . . the conclusiveness of any one. Its reasoning should not form a chain which is no stronger than its weakest link, but a cable whose fibers may be ever so slender, provided they are sufficiently numerous and intimately connected."[24] The philosopher of biology William Wimsatt has called this *robustness*, a robust claim being one for which we have multiple independent sources of evidence, argument, or experience, as we will see later. For any judgment about fundamental or comprehensive contexts will have to be tested against our judgments of the more local and robust.

Objective Relativism and Metaphysics

That's it. That is the core of objective relativism. But we can't go further without locating this strange, minimal view with respect to some major metaphysical topics, and dealing with some objections not definitively but plausibly.

First, objective relativism removes the question of "reality" and "existence" from the domain in which we discriminate and describe. The world we know and live in is sufficiently subtle that we cannot deal with it if we can only speak and make true statements about what is "real" or what "exists," which exclude past or fictional objects or possibilities. We need a broader language that is less prejudiced conceptually. Secondary qualities are as "real" as primary qualities; fantasies, hallucinations, and dreams are as "real" as the sun's warmth. Numbers, universals, and meanings are as discriminable as rocks. The metaphysical question is, what are their properties in the contexts in which they function? We must be able to talk about them before we try to discern that.

Likewise, the project of trying to decide what are the smallest number of kinds of "beings" or "substances" or "realities" or "properties" required to account for the world is banished, not from inquiry in general, but from our list of what we need to account for. We must start with whatever is discriminated, experienced, thought, claimed, and then ask what role each plays, what is dependent upon what. Objective relativism denies that the fact that something is dependent on something else, be it a temporally prior cause, a simpler kind of thing, or an encompassing context or order, fully dictates what that something is. The reductive project is rejected from metaphysics (not from science). We do not seek fundamental simples or an all-encompassing Whole, thinking that what depends on them is *nothing but* what the two determine.

A prominent consequence of objective relativism is that neither the *actual* nor the *physical* nor the *particular* have any ontological priority. Some of the things that actually hold or obtain are possibilities. An actual thing must have possibilities. Possibilities are as real, as necessary, as unavoidable as actualities. A near accident leaves you rightly shaken because you recognize your possible violent death. In science, many systems are defined partly by their possibilities (e.g., a chemical substance by its boiling point, an immature organism by its potential adult form) or their pasts (what did occur, or must have occurred, for them to be what they are now). Possibilities can come to hold and cease to hold without being actualized. My playing in the game establishes the possibilities of my winning or losing, which never arise if I do not play. But winning and losing cannot be actualized in the same order at the same time: I can't win *and* lose (Rosie Perez in *White Men Can't Jump* to the contrary). In terms of the naturalism to be explained later, possibilities are not space-occupying or energy-possessing, which arguably means their causal role cannot be material or efficient, but can be formal or final, given the right conditions. They are part of the structure of a situation.

What philosophers call "universals" or properties can be understood quite naturally as possibilities. Suppose a red apple and a red ball. Each is actually red. So they are similar with respect to one property: they are red. *Similarity* holds between complexes in some respect if they have the possibility of sameness in some respect. Redness is a discriminable complex; whatever else it is, it is that with respect to which some things (e.g., apple and ball) can be similar. This is Buchler's formulation (Buchler 1990). Having the property, as some would say, "justifies" the common predication of redness, in the sense that if it does not have the property, it would be wrong to call it red. It does not "ground" the predication, it is not "exemplified" by the ball and apple, and it is not simple. The red apple and red ball are actually red, but redness considered independent of them is a possibility of many complexes (not all).

The past is as real as anything. It had better be. It was, we know something about it, and it had effects. The Holocaust occurred. That is our fallible judgment, at least as well supported as my birth. But neither are actual now; they are past. Pasts are discriminables, and we discriminate them not only through our experience in the form of episodic memory— what each of us remembers—but through a host of historical and scientific techniques. We can take this further: nobody knows what a "fact" in the present is at all without cognition or memory of the immediate past. None of this implies that the past is actual now, but it was actual before. What occurred has a lot to do with certain kinds of causality. It is what led to now, and if it is not real, neither is now. How we account for pasts in our description of reality and its structure is a subsequent matter.

These issues connect to the thorny question of the metaphysical status of *time*. This is a huge topic, but we can at least say how objective relativism approaches it. The contemporary philosophical debate over time is largely between *presentists* who accept what John McTaggart called an "A," or tensed conception of time, and *eternalists* who accept a "B," or tenseless conception (McTaggart 1908). The tensed conception holds that the comparative relation to the now, in phrases like "before today" and "after today," is critical, hence the present is real and distinct from the past and future. The tenseless conception holds that while statements of dated events can be true—"John Kennedy was assassinated in 1963"—any talk of "before now" and "after now"—like "John Kennedy was assassinated long ago"—reports mere appearance, a secondary quality, not reality. That is, "nothing is really past, present, or future."[25]

Objective relativism must obviously reject the tenseless prejudice that secondary qualities are less real. Pastness, presentness, and futurity are, at the least, discriminable traits of events. Some somethings are tensed. Kennedy was killed in 1963, which was six decades ago *now*, as I write this. But objective relativism must also reject the tensed view that the present has an ontological priority. Actualities are tied to *a* present, but not necessarily to our present now. The 1967 Red Sox actually lost the World Series, but were potential, possible, winners then. Some things actually happened in the past; some events were actual for some complexes, but function now only as precursors to current events, and in each case there were likely other possibilities not actualized. Somethings are *not* tensed, like some universals—such as some objects of logic and mathematics. And while anything actual must have possibilities, a future is not the same as possibility. A future is possibilities that will be realized—about which we can and will make our fallible guesses. When those are right, that still does not mean the future contingencies are "actual" now. Whatever has played a role in a history, like the life of a living creature, perhaps one with memory, may later play a role in a future. Lastly, any naturalism that takes contemporary science seriously must accept that there is very robust evidence from multiple quarters that our physical and material and biological universe is the product of evolution over time. It began. And until the second law of thermodynamics is repealed, natural processes, including my own life, have a temporal direction toward unstructured equilibrium. Things fall apart over time, some quickly, some slowly.

Meanings too are possible traits of natural complexes as real as any other. They exist, we can know, use, and manipulate them, they are publicly recognizable, and they can make a difference in our behavior. That meanings may be, or frankly are, relative to human activity makes no difference. They may not have existed before human minds and language, although the possibilities *referenced by* the meanings often have. Flints could have been struck to make fire before humans evolved. On the other hand, food and behavior did not exist before organisms, and verbs did not exist before humans. As possibilities, meanings cannot be efficiently causal by themselves. But they may make a causal difference to events when they play a role in the determination of the teleological behavior of complex animals, as we will see.

Some will object to fallibilism that the claims of logic and mathematics are analytic or necessary, hence certain. We may note Peirce's simple response: mathematicians make mistakes too.[26] A fallibilist can say that the principles of first-order predicate logic and certain areas of mathematics are among the most trustworthy principles of our thought, and we are pragmatically *right* to believe them. But this does not mean they are incorrigible. We cannot know that our understandings of logic and mathematics will not be improved, as they have been in the recent past. Others may object that physics does assert simples, that is, in particle theory, quarks and leptons are currently simplest of all fermionic particles. But in quantum field theory, they are also quantized intensifications of energy fields, and whatever fields are, they are not simples. We can claim something is simple in the context of a theory, but a noncontextual simple would have to maintain its character *even if everything else were different*. A fallibilist cannot know what that means.

Other philosophers may object that to drop the Whole or the One from consideration is a deflation or even renunciation of the task of metaphysics. The objective relativists did deny that the Whole or the One could be a discriminable something. But our explicit fallibilism helps to clarify this. For fallibilism, the Whole, or any noncontextual first or last term of analysis, is unnecessary for the metaphysical intelligibility of what we discriminate, but not forbidden. The term "everything" in its collective sense is intelligible. We can always make inferences from any sample to any population containing it. But the character inferred to any such population must be probabilistic. In the case of "everything," that population includes indefinitely many unknown orders of complexes! So any hypothesis regarding its character, while legitimate, must be *highly* tentative. What fallibilism cannot abide is using any such an hypothesis to deny the validity of apparently robust, local knowledge that is inconsistent with it. The global is known through the local.

Now to a more technical difficulty. Russell and Lovejoy raised a problem with objective relativism, specifically against the American New Realists. Suppose x is something that functions in relation to two different orders, R to y and R to z, and exhibits at least some different properties in each case (e.g., the penny may be elliptical, not circular, from my point of view). If x's identity is not independent of xRy or xRz, that seems to imply that the x of xRy and the x of xRz are two different xs or that Ry and Rz change x into a new complex, *not-x*. If y and z are the perceptions of two agents, *Yael* and *Zachary*, that implies perception changes the perceived. Those implications would destroy realism (the first two points doom metaphysical, the third perceptual realism). How can x be identifiable and re-identifiable as something x while owning nonidentical xRy and xRz, each of which is *another* something, as it is for objective relativism?

Buchler solved most of this. All that is required is to distinguish *identity* and *integrity* and hold that to identify a complex is to ascribe it an identity potentially functioning in multiple contextual integrities (Buchler 1990). X is a something with an identity that includes relations to some other somethings, hence alternate integrities; all the ellipses and their integrities in figure 2.1 are relevant to the identity of x, some complexes strongly ("internal relation"), some weakly ("external relations"). Xavion is an individual who can become a brother to Yael and a friend to Zachary, all while remaining Xavion, however much those relations may alter him. As Cohen argued, the relation between "essential" and "accidental" properties is itself context-dependent.[27] Some properties of *xRy* may be essential to *x*'s identity, while others are not; "essential" now means applying to many or all contexts, rather than fewer. But what then is the criterion for *x*'s identity? What is the line between a new integrity of *x* and *not-x*? *That is a question for the fallible methodology of the local subject matter, not ontology.* There is no reason to believe identity conditions for photons, gods, events, properties, histories, bacteria, possibilities, and art works should be the same. They are empirical hypotheses about subject matters, not an *a priori* metaphysical decision.

Objective Relativism and Values

For objective relativism, values *are*. We can discriminate them—good, bad, contemptible, beautiful, sublime, just, true or false, as well as high, low, tall, short, pasts, possibilities, fictional characters, et cetera. The value placed on something plays as much of a role in human experience and culture as pain or pleasure, or any possibility, hence, any predicate we can imagine. The inability to ascribe value to things would upset our understanding of the world as deeply as the inability to ascribe possibilities or pasts to things. The recognition that the jaguar has failed to take down the antelope, not merely that it and another creature ran around and the creature went away, is a recognition of what drama just occurred—two animals were trying to do something, and one succeeded. As C. I. Lewis pointed out, if we can't know anything about the validity of any values, we can never have reason to believe one action is better than another. But we can.

The point is that values are relational, but for objective relativism *so is everything else*. Dependence on relations does not make something less objective or real. The rock is only solid because temperature is low and pressure is high—enough heat and it is a liquid or even a gas. Objective relativism denies that anything has its properties independent of *all* relations to anything besides itself. One might say that the painting or moral act is only good with respect to some people who perceive it or are affected by it; but even if so, I am a father only because of the historical appearance of my children. "Relational" does not mean "subjective," still less "unreal." Rather, it holds those properties over some contexts of relation, a larger set of contexts, or a smaller set of contexts. The rock indeed maintains a larger percentage of its current properties over a wider range of contexts than I do. It remains the same on Earth or in a vacuum. I do not. This is a matter of degree. What is "intrinsic" cannot mean what is independent of *all* relations.

This will have a major impact in how we think about values. For example, instrumental value is not necessarily opposed to intrinsic value. This is because "intrinsic" value cannot mean "valuable even if everything were different." What is intrinsically valuable, valuable as an end in itself rather than as a tool or means to an end, is still valuable to or for something. If love is intrinsically valuable, it is so because complex animals exist; if an apple is tasty, it is because there are creatures who can eat it. The acorn is objectively valuable food for the deer, but not for the coyote. Something can also be *objectively instrumentally* valuable, like money. If Plato's "Good" holds, it presumably does not hold for bacteria, the oceans, or asteroids. We will return to this.

What Is Missing in Objective Relativism?

But there is one thing that objective relativism does *not* do for us, something big: it is not an adequate metaphysics, and definitely not an adequate naturalistic metaphysics. It provides us with a language in which we can discriminate complexes and the orders in which they function. Period. That is an important job. But the question remains, is there anything to be said about the relations among those orders?

Let us return to the train tracks. For the objective relativist, the train tracks are parallel and convergent, with no contradiction as long as the contexts are specified. That is, as long as we know what context is relevant to us at the moment (building the tracks, riding the train, looking down the tracks, making a drawing of what we see), each comes out right. But what then is the relation between those contextual integrities? *Objective relativism does not say*. But any naturalism must regard the parallelism of the tracks as prior to their convergence in some sense.

Cohen, Morris, Randall, Nagel, and Buchler regarded objective relativism as naturalistic. But it is not; it is pluralistic. Objective relativism is too thin an account to be naturalistic. Naturalism is indeed the best metaphysical candidate for accounting for what we discriminate through objective relativism. I cannot here explore the justification of that claim, except to say that, rightly understood, naturalism provides an adequate explanatory background for key areas of evidence, including the modern natural sciences, the logical analysis of concepts, the pragmatics of human social agency, phenomenological accounts of experience, and semiotic analyses of culture (Cahoone 2013a). Objective relativism without naturalism is an inadequate metaphysics. Naturalism without objective relativism is the wrong kind of naturalism for values.

We are seeking a merger of objective relativism and a naturalism hospitable to modern science. They are compatible. But how? This is what we must explore next.

Chapter Three

Emergence in Nature

> I do think that science has taught us a lot about the evolving universe that bears in an interesting way on Paley's and Darwin's problem of . . . design. I think that science suggests to us . . . a picture of a universe that is inventive or even creative; of a universe in which *new things* emerge, on *new levels*.
>
> —Karl Popper, "Natural Selection and the Emergence of Mind"[1]

What is naturalism? At the very least, it denies the "supranatural," refusing to speak of anything beyond nature. Consequently, it wants to see not only matter, but life and mind, as well as meanings and ideas and culture as "natural." Contemporary philosophers, though, mean something more modern: naturalism holds that the conclusions of the natural sciences have priority in understanding reality. For some of these philosophers, "naturalism" is just another word for "materialism" or "physicalism"—everything is matter or a property or instantiation of matter, or everything is physical or a property of or instantiation of the physical. (Many philosophers don't make much of a distinction between materialism and physicalism. But they should.) Then there are some philosophers who use "naturalism" instead of physicalism or materialism because they are "nonreductive" or "pluralistic" or even "liberal" naturalists, meaning that nonphysical or nonmaterial properties do exist, and the human or social sciences too have explanatory power.

The naturalism I propose seeks to join the latter. But it has some special characteristics. I will call it "ordinal" naturalism, a term Beth Singer applied to Buchler's metaphysics.[2] As argued in the last chapter, objective relativism was pluralist, not naturalist. But it can be the language in which a novel kind of naturalism can be defined, one fully compatible with natural science and realism. That is, we can accept the rootedness of human culture, morality, art, and knowledge in biological and physical nature without reducing their norms to something non-normative. How? There is a way. It starts with the concept of emergence.

Emergence

Emergence arose in the early twentieth century in the controversy over how to explain how living organisms can appear to avoid obeying the rules of inorganic matter. They maintain complex equilibrium states, or *homeostasis*, not to mention they grow and reproduce, all of which would seem to violate the second law of thermodynamics. That law describes the fact that in closed systems, structure cannot spontaneously increase. Things fall apart rather than together, or in the fetching phrase of J. Willard Gibbs, they increase their level of "mixedupedness." But living things heal and grow and reproduce. They grow more structured over time. Now, because they vent disorder or entropy into their environments, the second law isn't violated, but still their behavior is different from anything else. At the end of the nineteenth century those taking a mechanistic view claimed that biology and perhaps mind could be fully reduced to and eventually explained by chemistry and physics. Their opponents, the "vitalists," claimed that there is a special life force or process outside the ken of physics and chemistry. (We will return to their disagreement in the next chapter.)

Emergence took a middle path: the whole (e.g., the cell, the organism, the mind) can have properties not present in any of its parts, or more precisely, not derivable from aggregating the parts' properties. Inspired by a comment of John Stuart Mill's, his countryman George Henry Lewes invented the term, and it was promoted by the British Emergentists, Samuel Alexander, Conwy Lloyd Morgan, and C. D. Broad in the early twentieth century. Among the North Americans it was adopted by Mead, his colleague Charles Morris, the entomologist William Morton Wheeler, and Roy Wood Sellars, father of Wilfred Sellars.[3]

After the 1920s, for fifty years, very few philosophers or scientists explicitly discussed the idea of emergence. But it came back with a vengeance, arguably in response to the rise of scientific work on complexity, chaos, and critical point phenomena, and the philosophy of biology. By now the literature on reduction and emergence can hardly be explored at less than book length.[4] There are "strong" and "weak" forms of emergence, and these compete with various forms of reductive physicalism or reductive materialism, particularly "ontological" reductionism of systems to components (i.e., the system is "nothing but" its components), and "explanatory" or theoretical reduction of our explanations of higher level phenomena to lower level science (i.e., biology reduced to chemistry). I have discussed emergence and reductionism at length elsewhere (Cahoone 2013a). In this context all we can do is present the most useful analysis of the idea, from the philosopher of biology William Wimsatt. His key point is that emergence and reduction are *not* in conflict.

We commonly explain the dent in the fender by the impact of the other car. This is explanation by means of comparable systems and their properties (two cars). Let us call this a *systemic* explanation, an explanation of what happens to system N at the level of comparably scaled, N-level systems. But sometimes we find a more useful explanation at the scale of the car's components, like the density of the materials in the fender. Such *reductive* explanation derives a system property (N) from the properties of the system's parts and their interaction rules (N-1). We could look at how mechanical and heat energy impacted the chemical bonds among the molecules in the fender. Sometimes that is relevant—your car could be made out of lousy materials. Third, we sometimes employ a *functional* explanation that derives a system property (N) from its role in an encompassing system's activity or structure—like local traffic patterns, or a faulty traffic light (N+1). It might be that a missing road sign was a cause. Note that these explanatory levels don't necessarily conflict—they might all apply.

For Wimsatt, reductive explanation tries to show a system or property to be "mechanistically explicable in terms of the properties of and interactions among the parts of the system."[5] In actual scientific practice, reductive explanations are introduced to turn a more complex problem into a simpler one, by modeling the system in question in terms of more easily understandable and mathematically treatable parts, like point-particles obeying linear dynamics, or little pumps or oscillators vibrating in an easily describable way. That is *the point* of reduction. Scientists then aggregate the behavior of those "parts" to see if this correctly predicts the relevant properties of the system as a whole. Wimsatt points out that a reduction typically explains: (a) *only some* properties or performances of a whole system; (b) on the basis of a perspectival (hence selective) decomposition of the system, that is, a particular way of cutting it into parts; and (c) by using an *idealized model* of the parts and/or their interactions (point particles, pumps, oscillators), resting on or employing significant approximations.

When the endpoint of a complete reduction is achieved, justifying the claim that a system property or performance is entirely explicable as "nothing but" its part properties, we can say that the system properties or performances are *aggregations* of part properties or performances. Wimsatt suggests four conditions of aggregativity: *intersubstitutability* or invariance of the system property under rearrangements of the parts, so serial or aperiodic ordering does not play a role (there is no difference between xyz and zxy); *qualitative similarity* under scaling, where addition or subtraction of parts leaves the property only quantitatively changed (bigger or smaller); *reaggregativity*, or invariance of the system property under decomposition and recomposition (so it will be the same if we take it apart and rebuild it); and *linearity*, where change in output is proportional to change in input, with no feedback, either cooperative amplification or inhibitory damping.

For Wimsatt, only when *all* these hold can we say the system property is "nothing but" the aggregation of decomposed parts and their interaction rules. Full reductions are very powerful explanations because they apply regardless of higher-level conditions. But Wimsatt points out that they are rare. In reductions it is entirely common for us to succeed in explaining some properties of a system out of several, but not all. Mass is one of the few properties of physical systems that is fully reducible, just the aggregation of the same property of the components. This is why there is a law of the conservation of mass. My mass equals the sum of the mass of all my organ systems (including liquids and gasses), which is equal to the sum of all my chemical substances, which equals the sum of the mass of all my molecules, all my atoms, and so on. But most of my properties are not like that; for example, volume is not, because in some chemical reactions volume changes. This shows how fundamental, and yet how narrow, the band of aggregative properties is. *Reduction explains something about almost everything, but everything about almost nothing.*

Emergence can simply be defined as *non-aggregativity*. It occurs when a true explanation of an event at level N cannot be reconstructed as a causal sequence of entities, processes, and/or forces of level N-1 without employing reference to processes, structures, and entities at the N or N+1 levels. In systemic explanations, as we saw, explanandum and explanans are at the same level (N). Most explanations are systemic. Functional explanations explain a system's properties by reference to higher level or encompassing systems at N+1 (or higher, +2, +3, etc.). The desideratum is to what extent the structure/processes of the whole system are caused by more or less isolable, environmentally uninfluenced properties of parts and their simple interactions, usually meaning no more than two-body interactions. To the extent that the former holds, we have a more complete reduction. To the extent it does not, we are saying the whole properties are the result of part properties and interactions *plus* properties of the whole or an encompassing system, requiring reference to the latter to fix or explain (systemically or functionally) the causal contributions of the parts. The effect of the parts on the whole has been influenced *by* the whole.

Let's look at an example. What is informative and what is misleading in the claim that "the mill pond is quarks and electrons governed by their interaction rules"? (electrons and quarks being the most elementary fermions). It is true that the pond has quarks and electrons in it; it is dependent on them, indeed, the parts of its parts of its parts . . . are quarks and electrons; they are the smallest "entities" we can identify in the pond. All good. But it is *not* true that (a) there is nothing else in the pond (even the pond *water*) beside quarks and electrons; (b) the interaction rules explaining quark and electron behavior explain the pond's behavior; (c) the state of the pond is entirely determined by what happens to its quarks and electrons; or, (d) what happens to the pond happens to its quarks and electrons. For there are spacetime structures, relations, processes, and events characterizing the system that are not "in," not "properties of," nor "explained by" the quarks and electrons plus force laws. Concomitantly, things can happen to the pond that cannot in principle happen to its quarks and electrons; for example, the pond can freeze, but its quarks and electrons cannot because freezing cannot happen to something smaller than a collection of molecules. There are regularities governing the pond system that are inapplicable to its elementary particles *by definition*.

There is nothing mystical here. It just means reduction must be supplemented by other kinds of explanations. Reduction remains a crucial component of our explanatory practice. We understandably keep trying to decompose systems and idealize their components' interactions in just such a way as is likely to yield workable reductions. There is nothing wrong with this, as long as we recognize its merely partial success most of the time, and do not presume it is the only or the ideal form of explanation, or worse, our definitive ontological criterion.

The fact of reduction's success and limits teaches important metaphysical lessons. For our most successful explanatory practices must be a major clue as to the composition and processes of the universe. Wimsatt points out that the relative dynamic autonomy of higher levels "is a general fact of nature." Across not only mental, but biological and material systems, macro-state stability often rests on micro-state flux. Again, there is nothing mystical here. It simply is the case that "the [relative] stability of macro-states . . . further entails that the vast majority of neighboring (dynamically accessible) micro-states map into the same or (more rarely) neighboring macro-states." Macroscopic systems, like the pond, a cloud, me, or the Earth, must be organized in such a way that the microstates of their components are mostly irrelevant, leaving higher levels statistically unaffected. This is *multiple realizability*. For the tree in the forest, the minerals and water it absorbs, and the atmosphere surrounding it, stable macro-states must be "tuned" so that the chaos at lower levels does not lead to deviation-amplifying effects that would destroy macroscopic stability. While the macro-properties must be sensitive to certain kinds of micro-changes, "it is crucial that most differences [at the micro-level] do not have significant [macro-level] effects most of the time."[6] This has a simple but powerful consequence: there cannot be purely micro-level explanations for most stable macro-level properties.

Nature thus appears to be hierarchically arranged. The description of nature requires that it be understood in terms of *levels*, as described by hierarchical systems theory (Simon 1969; Ahl and Allen 1996). Wimsatt is able to define natural levels rather objectively as "local maxima of regularity and predictability in the phase space of different modes or organization of matter."[7] As such, levels are real complexes of the world; we perspectivally select them for description, explanation, and prediction because *that is where the explanations are*. The range of entities with which an entity interacts is a nonarbitrary and informative fact about that entity; levels are collections or orders of interacting entities. Size or scale is a common, not always sufficient, indicator of level, for "size is . . . a robust indicator for many other kinds of causal interactions." Entities are generally at levels; levels are "where the entities are," ranges of scale where one finds the greatest "density of types" of entities, such as atoms, molecules, organisms, macroscopic material objects, and so on. There are processes and phenomena between levels, but levels naturally act as "attractors" for entities. Wimsatt summarizes: "Levels of organization are a deep, non-arbitrary, and extremely important feature of the ontological architecture of our natural world, and almost certainly of any world that could produce, and be inhabited or understood by, intelligent beings. . . . They are constituted by families of entities usually of comparable size and dynamic properties, which characteristically interact primarily with one another, and which, taken together, gives an apparent rough closure over a range of phenomena and regularities."[8]

So there appear to be levels or strata of natural complexes where things similar in size and dynamic properties largely interact with each other, constituted and funded by lower-level entities, in a context imposed by higher strata characterized by irreducible, or as Wimsatt puts it, "non-aggregative" properties. That is why we need multiple sciences. Integrating these stratified phenomena is a search for the unity not of *science*, but of *sciences*.

An Ordinal Definition of Nature

Now, instead of endorsing physicalism or materialism, we can define naturalism in a distinctive way using the language of objective relativism. But how can that be? How can any modern naturalism, cognizant of four hundred years of a modern natural science upon which we are highly dependent, exclude claims that all is physical, or realized by or based in the physical, or that the physical sciences are the privileged knowledge of nature? In the following way.

First, consistent with objective relativism we can say that nature is an ensemble of orders in which complexes function, where no set of members is causally isolated from all others. This merely excludes metaphysical dualisms like God versus Nature, mind versus matter, forms versus matter, idealities versus actualities, and the like. We also do not have to say "nature is everything" or "everything is nature"—since we do not and are unlikely to know "everything." We do not have to refer to what we will never imaginably know.

Second, we add a trait from the preceding section: it appears to be a nomological fact that among the complexes functioning in nature some kinds *asymmetrically depend on others*. "Nomological" means an empirical, not *a priori*, law or generalization. We have strong evidence that there is chemistry without life but no life without chemistry, that minds appear to require neurology, and that cultural meanings depend on rare linguistic animals. These dependencies are empirical, *a posteriori* facts, derived from experience of the natural orders we discriminate. We are recognizing that nature possesses a hierarchical structure of asymmetric dependence, and part of that structure is the dependence of things like culture and mind on the biological, the chemical, and the physical. Such a naturalism accepts that in the nature we know, other identifiable natural strata directly or indirectly depend on the physical, understood as the objects of fundamental physics.[9]

This formulation shares with physicalism the claim that the nonphysical seems dependent on the physical. But it does *not* endorse the ontological priority of the physical, nor grant epistemic superiority to physical explanation. As fallibilists, we presume the *prima facie* approximate but fallible validity of all contemporary "sciences," in the broad German sense of all *Wissenschaften*, all rational inquiries, regarding their objects. Both natural and humanistic studies are due this respect. But naturalism must grant *one* limited priority to the natural sciences: the objects of the human sciences are one species and its products that obtain among and on the basis of the objects of natural science. The mental and the biological are dependent on the physical and cannot contradict the laws of the physical where those laws are applicable.

Thus, naturalism need not—indeed ought not—say the objects of human and biological sciences are solely physical or realizations of the physical. Indeed, emergent naturalism must reject "the causal closure of the physical," the claim that only physical things and properties can cause changes in physical things and properties. This does not mean, as some think, an endorsement of "ghostly" influences! For if the physical is defined in terms of the unique objects of physics, as I have argued it must be, then the unique objects of other sciences can *downwardly* cause changes in the physical (Cahoone 2013b). Once in existence, the living organism manufactures organic compounds; the location of the lobster's elementary particles is the result of the animal's learning; the chemical structure of bronze is an artifact of human history. Dependent orders can, under the right conditions, causally alter the orders on which they depend.

Thus the definition of a naturalism compatible with objective relativism is this. (1) *Naturalism claims that whatever is discriminated functions in one temporally enduring ensemble of complexes called "nature," where no set of members is causally isolated from all others, and in which some natural kinds, like the objects of the human sciences, asymmetrically depend on other kinds, like the objects of the natural sciences.*

Is everything discriminated, or discriminable, capable of inclusion in that ensemble of natural orders? As far as we now know and hence predict, yes. That is, we don't seem to have robust knowledge of something that cannot be so included. That makes one a naturalist. The complexes of these orders are now "natural complexes."[10] To be a naturalist is to claim nothing heretofore discriminated cannot be a natural complex, and to believe that the same will likely hold in the future. This could turn out to be false, like any other of our claims. But to this point it does not seem to be. A view based in objective relativism can be naturalist if it satisfies this definition. It does not say that everything is physical or material, or an instantiation or realization of something physical or material. We have a "nature" composed of complexes, including entities, processes, relations, possibilities, actualities, universals, properties, et cetera, none of them causally isolated and some of them asymmetrically dependent on others.

Now, let us get a bit more concrete. We can provide a set of more determinate concepts for analyzing nature, consistent with the foregoing. We add the following hypothesis: (2) *Natural complexes can be understood as systems, with their kinds and properties, which are (a) constituted by structures, processes, and subaltern systems; (b) of varying degrees of entification; and, (c) locatable in at least five emergent orders, the physical, material, biological, mental, and cultural.*

That is, among all the equally real discriminable complexes of nature we may term what are usually considered entities *systems*. Stars, planets, atoms, clouds, organisms, books, and societies are systems. Hydrogen, mammal, oxidation, fear, and death are not: "mammal" and "hydrogen" are classes of systems; oxidation, fear, and death are properties or states of systems. This may appear to be a systems theory version of Aristotle that substitutes systems for Aristotle's key metaphysical category, substance. That is true, but it departs from Aristotle in other respects.

First, Aristotle makes "substances" independent entities that cannot be predicated of (i.e., properties of) or part of anything else. But for us, the parts and environments of a system are themselves systems. Most important, systems have no ontological primacy: *there is ontological parity between processes (hence events and states), structures (hence relations), and systems (hence components)*. If there is no *a priori* reason to privilege entities there is also no *a priori* reason to privilege processes or structures. That is, each system or entity is simultaneously a structure of relations, a set of components, and a process by which those components remain in that structure. Lastly, there are degrees of entification or "being a system." The peak of entification seems to be *individuals* like atoms, molecules, planets, rocks, organisms, and persons, which are all components undergoing processes maintaining them in a structure. But systems or entities need not be so well formed. In addition there are *ensembles*, such as volumes of gas and liquid, clouds and swarms, which are components in negligible structures undergoing processes, as well as the *fields* of the basic forces that are spacetime structures of a quantity undergoing processes but lacking the aggregative, fermionic components of normal matter.

Now to the bigger picture. Systems, processes, structures, and their properties and kinds occur in at least five orders important enough for a philosopher to distinguish: *physical, material, biological, mental, and cultural.* By "physical," I mean the objects of the part of physics called "fundamental," the smallest systems studied by quantum field theory, the largest structures of general relativity and cosmology, and the processes of energy transformation governed by thermodynamics. Many aspects of physical reality are not material, such as energy, gravitation, spacetime, and electromagnetic fields. From these emerge normal (fermionic) matter, the objects of chemistry, astrophysics, and the Earth Sciences. Science tells us that matter *evolved.* Then there is life, a set of activities characteristic of the complex material organisms studied by the biological and ecological sciences, and the macromolecules, societies, and ecosystems that come with them. Minds are something some animals do, integrated sets of intentional activities performed by the neurologically gifted (as we shall see). Culture, the manipulation of social meanings expressed in narrative, artifact, and ritual, at present seems characteristic only of *Homo sapiens.*[11]

Why these five orders? Couldn't the pie be sliced differently? Yes. But these five are particularly robust because they both correspond to a set of distinctive sciences and seem to have evolved in serial order in the history of our universe. In the contexts of the relations among the basic forces of our expanding universe, certain thresholds of scale and energy (e.g., temperature) yielded major changes in the content of the universe: atomic matter arose only after sufficient cooling; stars took billions more years to form; all heavy elements, like those that constitute planets, came billions of years later after stellar nucleosynthesis performed its magic, seeding galaxies with those elements—eventually making some dense, rocky planets at the right temperature the possible home of the incredibly complex systems we call life, which itself underwent several billion years of evolution, eventually creating animals with minds and the possibility of human selves with culture. The nature and relations of these orders is contingent and open to endless inquiry. No claim is made that they are the only ones—just that they are at present the only ones we know.

Finally, emergence repairs a problem left by objective relativism. Let us return to the train tracks for (I promise) the last time. We saw that for objective relativism the tracks are convergent and parallel in different relations or contexts; neither status is prior. Emergence allows us to say more: *the order in which the tracks converge emerges from the order in which the tracks are parallel.* The convergence of the tracks is a real visual, psychological phenomenon whose occurrence depends on both the tracks' material construction and the evolution of animal binocular vision. Our physiology forms a retinal image of the tracks as convergent in order to recognize their parallelism; that is how we evolved. For naturalism, the material order in which tracks are parallel is the basis for the psychological order in which they converge. This is ordinal naturalism.

Values in an Ordinal Nature

What will all this do for our inquiry into values? Quite a lot.

First, we gain freedom from a tenacious philosophical, and to some extent scientific, aim: the belief the rules governing either the "whole" of nature, or nature's "foundation" or simplest parts—hence the most inclusive or most fundamental contexts—explain everything. Physics uniquely studies the smallest and largest; all other disciplines study the "in between." Emergence means that we can expect some relatively more complex systems to manifest properties not exhibited by their parts. This explains why we need multiple sciences, not just one. And it shows why objective relativism and emergence, while very different kinds of theories, cohere. For both deny that objects of inquiry are utterly determined by the most fundamental or the most comprehensive level of analysis. Physicist Richard Feynman asked which end of the continuum of nature is nearer to God, microphysics or the human ideals of Beauty and Hope. He answered himself: "I do not think either end is nearer to God . . . To stand at either end . . . hoping that out in that direction is the complete understanding, is a mistake. . . . The great mass of workers in between, connecting one step to another . . . are gradually understanding this tremendous world of interconnecting hierarchies."[12]

Then there is the distinction between realist and representationalist theories of perception, hence between primary and mind-dependent secondary qualities. For ordinal naturalism, the difference between "primary" and "secondary" is not a difference between objectivity and subjectivity, but between the breadth of the domains in which properties function. Ordinal naturalism accepts the realist view that normal perception directly captures its objects. But it is still "representational" because representation is not a thing but rather a function some emergent psycho-biological processes have. As we will see, the state of that process we call the "perception" is the functional integrity of the object in the working of the organism, such as the convergent train tracks.

This also impacts the theory of knowledge. For as we will see in chapter 7, ordinal naturalism can employ *evolutionary epistemology*. One might think that anybody who is a naturalist, and who accepts Darwinian evolution, must accept that human cognition evolved in natural environments from the cognitive processes of nonhumans. Objections are made because "epistemology" is regarded by many as a normative discipline, which descriptions of fact cannot help. However, in an emergent naturalism, norms arise from the very processes which they then norm. Emergence will allow us to use evolutionary epistemology in a more effective way.

This same idea applies to values other than knowledge and truth. For values, while relational, can be objective as anything else. We will see that such objectively relative values, as well as purposes and norms, are evident throughout the biological order. Emergence means that norms like "healthy" or "successful" or "good" can be dependent on but irreducible to the processes from which they arise.

This will be particularly important in trying to understand human agency. Philosophers sometimes ask, do *I* go to the store, or do my *legs* go to the store? Did the man murder the woman, or rather did his gun, or his finger on the trigger? Do I perceive the tree or only its electromagnetic pattern on my retina? Going to the store, presumably to buy food, is the act of a human agent—so is murdering. Perceiving is an animal activity, and what is perceived is the environmental state (the tree). All of these are objective and relative psychological processes emergent upon physiological processes involving organs and bodies in motion, which themselves emerge from chemical and electromagnetic interactions. Any event or process at a higher scale depends on processes at a lower scale. In such a nature, just as cultural, mental, biological, chemical, and physical processes and structures are as real as each other, so possibilities, pasts, meanings, minds, universals, and particulars are as real and potentially explanatory as anything else. If humans are by nature social, self-conscious, collaborative learners, the stage will be set for the claim that human values like truth, moral and political rightness, and aesthetic value *emerge from, and can downwardly restrict, our psychological and biological processes.*

In the first stage of our journey we have picked up some conceptual tools. We are now ready to look for values in nature. We will have to traverse many areas, climb some hills, get some perspective. We will begin by describing purpose in biology (chapter 4); minded animal agency, which we humans share (chapter 5); the unique features of human agency (chapter 6); and how this defeats the "naturalistic fallacy" (chapter 7). Then to prepare for part III we'll need an account of human value judgments (chapter 8) and how modernity revolutionized the landscape in which they function (chapter 9).

II

Nature and Human Judgments

Chapter Four

The Feud over Purpose

> The biologist should have no inferiority complex vis-à-vis the physicist, for although the latter can predict . . . the trajectory of a planet, the former can reliably predict that the hen's egg will hatch only into the chicken's tiny sector of an immense phase space.
>
> —Laszlo Tisza, in Shimony, "Some Proposals Concerning Parts and Wholes"[1]

We believe we know some things about nature in a very broad sense. It involves an expanding ensemble of matter, energy and spacetime, stars and star systems, in galaxies and clusters of galaxies. These can be described with physics, certain areas of chemistry, and inferences from the Earth Sciences like geology. The question of whether this layer of natural reality can be ascribed values is highly speculative; I have discussed it elsewhere (Cahoone 2013a, 2016). But it is one of the points of our kind of naturalism that the question of whether the objects of physics, hence the smallest components and largest contexts we know, exhibit values does *not* determine whether more complex, middling systems made of and operating in the context of those objects do. The middle need not be determined by the smallest or largest. Indeed, *the middle is where the complexity lies*. In our cosmic locale there is something special. It might occur in innumerable other places in the universe—we don't know. Our own Earth allows something amazing to flourish: *life*.

Living things have a number of relatively uncontroversial characteristics. They metabolize to garner energy from the environment. They are homeostatic or auto-regulating, that is, their internal milieu is controlled to reestablish certain parameters in response to changes. They are auto-making or -remaking as they must rebuild their own bodily structures. They maintain cellular walls and other barriers to the outside, but must be sensitive and responsive to their environment. Organisms reproduce, a complex activity requiring the storage of information in specialized macromolecules, which must be preserved and maintained. A living organism must remain in ongoing transaction with its environment, taking in chemicals and energy, and voiding heat and waste. But at the same time it must maintain its distinctiveness from environment. Loss of separateness is *death*. Organisms need, do something about their needs, and die. When they die, all their materials are recycled by the environment. Lastly, over many generations, a kind or species of organism can change, can go extinct, or new species or kinds can evolve from them. Life is not an entity but a process or activity (or as time interval approaches zero, a state).

As far as we know, cells are the smallest parts of organisms that are alive, and the smallest things that can be alive in relative isolation, that is, unicellular organisms. Organisms both undergo events and do them, and it is entirely legitimate to call them *biological agents*. It is true that scientists sometimes speak of "chemical agents" and the "behavior" of an iron molecule or an asteroid. But organisms do or behave in a different sense. This applies not only to mobile but to sessile or stationary organisms. Plants are still agents, acting internally, and they do move roots, branches, and flowers, just not much. Even unicellular organisms, like bacteria, are irritable, respond to changes in temperature or light or the chemistry of their environments, and move toward or away by means of tiny flagella. The core of biological agency is ceaseless, manic internal chemical activity, with no comparison in the nonliving world.

It was recognized by many in the nineteenth century that while the physical and material orders of reality must be the basis for the construction of living organisms, the laws of physics could not explain the functioning of those organisms. For contrary to the second law of thermodynamics, organisms gain structure or complexity and maintain it over long periods. Biology also seemed to be wedded to purposiveness in some way. Darwin's theory of natural selection did not deny this; it denied only that the process by which novel species appear is purposive. Rather, that appearance is the result of competition over scarce resources, heredity, and mutations. But nothing in Darwin denies that phenotypic features of a species are purposive. Whether the giraffe's elongated neck arose by inheritance of acquired characteristics (as Lamarck thought) or by nature's killing off those lacking the long neck mutation (our modern view), its adaptiveness is not in question.

The philosophical conception of life, and of biological explanation, generated two opposed trends from the late nineteenth century to the present day. For the sake of simplicity, we can call them by the somewhat unfair terms "mechanism" and "organicism." In fact, each was a family of related philosophical ideas, one promoting the application of physical science methods to life, the other attacking the former in any way possible.

The Reaction against Mechanism

Mechanism can be understood in a narrow way as the application of the metaphor of a machine. A machine is a device with parts connected in such a way that force or energy at one end (input) automatically and deterministically yields a consequence at the other end (output). Strictly speaking, such a notion of mechanism does indeed reject "finalism," or any use of telic or teleological explanation *at the level of the working of the mechanism*. A thermostat has a purpose; that is why we built it with the structure it has. But the explanation of how it does what it does—how the efficient cause of its input generates its output need only refer to the components, their connections, how force or power is transferred through the system—is not purposive. The thermostat has a purpose but is not purposive in its workings.

Some say the whole approach of modern physics, chemistry, and engineering, from Newton through most of the nineteenth century, was mechanistic. Einstein himself called it that in his 1938 book with Leopold Infeld, *The Evolution of Physics* (Einstein and Infeld, 1967). He had in mind the classical mechanics that understood phenomena as the deterministic result of ideally rigid bodies bumping into each other under forces, as we saw earlier. Einstein believed the turn to field theories in electromagnetism was the turn away from mechanism; then relativity and quantum theory put nails in mechanism's coffin. But as noted, this is a bit unfair. Machines do exist, and the mechanical model is fruitful for understanding some of the behavior of systems that are not machines.

In fact, in the sciences and philosophy there is a family of terms, or "isms," that often went along with mechanism, including "reductionism," "materialism," "atomism," "empiricism," "associationism," "nominalism," and "behaviorism." While each is distinct and can be combined with nonmechanistic views, all of the above were trying to understand phenomena in ways like physics and engineering. For this approach, (a) any complex system, like an organism, can be explained through the properties of its smallest components (atomism) and their rules of interaction (reductionism); (b) organismic behavior is the product of links between units of input (empiricism) and output (associationism); and (c) causal factors and their effects must be actual particular (nominalism) external phenomena (behaviorism), as opposed to any deep, medial process or structure of the organism.

It so happens that the German and French traditions in the early twentieth century were particularly concerned to combat this approach. This was a reaction against not only the tendency to reduce biology to physics but also against the new "conditioned reflex" account of learning championed by the Russian Ivan Pavlov and promoted in America by J. B. Watson, which seemed to promise that simple relations of stimuli (S) to motor response (R) could eventually account for all animal behavior. The German traditions of *Lebensphilosophie* promoted by Max Scheler and Wilhelm Dilthey and Husserl's phenomenology, as well as German *Naturphilosophie*, along with the French thinkers influenced by the vitalism of Henri Bergson, combined to forge an "organismic" approach to life and behavior. For many of them, Kant's philosophy played a special role; they are part of the Neo-Kantian or "Back to Kant" movement in early twentieth-century Germany, the German wing of the realist rejection of Hegelian idealism.

The first giant was French. Henri Bergson was a precursor of German phenomenology, affirming that the abstract space and time framework of physics could not do justice to a human experience accessible in raw form only to "intuition." Among his many contributions, two are important for us. Bergson criticized mechanics for analyzing time as if it were an infinitely divisible geometrical line composed of extensionless points. He insisted a temporal interval must be a unit of change, an "indivisible mobility," which Bergson famously labeled *durée*. For example, a transverse wave does not "exist" until at least one full cycle has occurred. Waves come in quanta that cannot be arbitrarily divided. Likewise, time is also intrinsically creative of novelty; the current moment must overlap with and contain part of the preceding moment, so cannot be either identical to it, nor completely external to it. To analyze time in geometrical terms is to destroy its unique nature. Both biological life and mind are intrinsically temporal phenomena—the organism has an historical career, and mental experience is organized by time, not space. The geometrization of time as an infinitely divisible line makes a science of life or mind impossible.

Second was his Bergson's notion of *élan vital*, vital impetus or force, which unfolds through time as the essential feature of life and mind. This force fuels creative evolution, in which the essence of change is novelty. Evolution by its nature creates the novel (Bergson 1998). It should be noted that, while Bergson's *élan vital* linked him with later vitalists in biology, Bergson explicitly claimed that any vital force applies only to life as a whole, not to individual organisms or species.

Bergson was the most famous French philosopher for a generation, and had a strong influence on James and Whitehead. But his vitalism, called "teleologism" or "finalism" by some, would be rejected by the English, Americans, Germans, and eventually even Bergson's compatriots after his famous 1922 public debate with Einstein (Canelles 2016). Bergson was then forgotten by the French, and regarded as "irrationalist" and "anti-scientific" by Anglo-Americans. This was deeply undeserved, as Miliĉ Ĉapek has shown (1971).

The organicist torch was taken up by a series of Germans. In the nineteenth century the Germans already had a holistic tradition, expressed in the work of Husserl, Dilthey, and Scheler. But our interest lies in later, more scientific developments, particularly in psychology, psychiatry, and medicine.

First of all, the Gestalt theory in psychology had a very wide impact. It began with the experimental work on perception of Czech-born Max Wertheimer (1923) and was continued by his students Kurt Koffka and Wolfgang Köhler. *Gestalten* are wholes the behavior of which is not determined solely by their parts or individual elements, but rather "the characteristics of the parts is determined by the whole." Perception exhibits *Gestalten*. The process of perception formation certainly receives bits of information, but the whole thereby produced is not solely a sum of those bits. The percept is actively formed out of bits by organismic processes. Wertheimer even remarked in an article on the physical sciences that "An aggregate of 'parts' or 'pieces' is a genuine 'sum' only when its constituents may be added together . . . without thereby causing any alteration in any of them."[2] Where there are such alterations, we find Gestalt effects.

Kurt Goldstein was heavily influenced by the Gestaltists. His *The Organism* (*Aufbau des Organismus* 1934) presented a holistic approach to human pathological phenomena, into which we have more insight, as a key to the organization of "lower" organisms. The observer's identifications of simple processes are abstractions from the more complex. Every pathological symptom must instead be understood in the context of the organism as a whole dealing with its environment, as the answer the organism gives to a problematic situation in its attempt to restore equilibrium. This is the opposite of the behaviorist approach of considering reflexes in isolation. Goldstein makes clear he is not restricting his holism to the phenomena of experience or perception, or to any one field.

But perhaps the most widely influential of the organicists was Jacob Von Uexküll, who created an "interpretive" biology in *Theory of Biology* (1926; *Theoretische Biologie* 1920). His most famous work was his *A Foray into the Worlds of Animals and Humans* (1934). Von Uexküll had a major influence on continental philosophy; his concept of *umwelt*, the surrounding world of the animal, was the source of Heidegger's concept of *welt* or "world" in *Being and Time* (Buchanan 2009).

Von Uexküll's first point is that for any animal, the recognition of a stimulus is an act of selection dependent on its anatomy and needs. Vast numbers of events take place without selective notice. The organism's *Bauplan* (body plan) dictates that certain *Funktion-kreisen* or functional cyclic processes take place, one for each relevant interaction (e.g., food, sex, defense/flight). The key to each function circle is a *Merkmal*, a perception mark or feature, that the animal *projects onto* the stimulus, leading to an effector response, which projects its own *Wirkmal*, effector mark or feature, onto the object, thereby "erasing" or replacing the former, ending that cycle so another can begin. The tick's body selectively responds to carbon dioxide from a passing animal, triggering it to fall on the creature; then it crawls until it senses the right temperature (e.g., less hair) and attaches itself. The physical phenomenon (carbon dioxide, movement, temperature) causes electrical impulses in the tick that serve as signs (*zeichen*) or sign processes. Von Uexküll writes, regarding auditory animals: "In the ear the airwaves are transformed into nerve impulses that encounter the perception organ of the brain . . . Then the perception cells and their perception signs (*Merkzeichen*) take charge and transpose a perception mark (*Merkmal*) into the environment."[3] This marking happens *outside* the perceptual organ and the body of the animal since; after all, the tick does not perceive its own electrical impulses—*it perceives the other animal* "in units that become qualities of the object that lie outside the animal subject."[4] We can understand the tick's behavior only if we understand the *umwelt* of the tick.

While only animals have meaning "carriers" that they project into the world, all life, all plants and single-celled organisms, still have meaning "indicators," or selected stimuli, and hence a world. Consequently, in *his Theory of Meaning*, Von Uexküll writes: "The question as to meaning must therefore have priority in all living things."[5] He ascribed signs to all life, down to the bacterium! For the biologist, "there are as many worlds as there are subjects," and the elements of those worlds are intelligible only in that subjective context. Thus the biological domain of factors that enter into behavior and perception must be distinguished from physical/material factors, both inside and outside.

Von Uexküll is here applying several features of Kant's analysis of human cognition from the latter's epochal *Critique of Pure Reason* (1781). First of all, the organism's own internal processes alone can explain the relation of input to output. The inside *does something to* the input. Second, the forms imposed by such processes are not derivable from impressions or associations; they are not mere aggregations of particulars. But Von Uexküll goes further: the notion that there is "one world" of space and time is an illusion! There are multiple worlds, not only for each organism, but for each sensory-effector modality of each organism. Indeed, "without a living subject there can be neither space nor time." This is right out of Kant. The insight that animal perception is organized by an internal process is applied *to science itself*, to us, the ethological observers of the animal. Our own world is likewise organized in space and time by our own perception signs, in terms of which we then describe the tick's world. Germanic organicism, for which inner experience or life actively dictates to and is irreducible to particulars or sensations, and from whose activity science's claims to objectivity are not exempt, is central to much of the continental philosophical tradition.

We should note that Von Uexküll was colleagues at Hamburg with the neo-Kantian philosopher Ernst Cassirer, as well as the developmental psychologist Heinz Werner. All influenced each other. Cassirer, the great historian and systematic philosopher of science and culture, is not usually associated with the organicists, but his thought was comparable, particularly his conceptions of linguistic development and mythical thinking (Cassirer 1953). Werner's "organismic-developmental" framework for comparative psychological development interrelated biology, language, child development, and psychopathology. It resulted in the "orthogenetic principle," professed by him and his student Kaplan, as the claim that developmental changes in the biological and psychological domains are characterized by "increasing differentiation and hierarchic integration," as well as the retention of earlier modes of activity in a subordinate form occasionally reasserting themselves in pathological states (Werner 1957; Werner and Kaplan 1964).

Merleau-Ponty was influenced by all of the above. Like many French philosophers between the world wars, he imbibed recent German phenomenology. Among them Merleau-Ponty has the distinction of pushing the limits of the Husserlian phenomenology as far as possible in the direction of naturalism. This is most obvious in his early work *The Structure of Behavior* (1942) and in his later essays, including the unfinished *The Visible and the Invisible*, rather than his most famous book, the masterful *Phenomenology of Perception* (1945).

In *The Structure of Behavior*, Merleau-Ponty's opponent is the reflex circuit of associationism and behaviorism, which analyze the organism "from periphery to the center." He argues the organism's active transformation of sensation into action has to be presupposed, Kantian fashion. There is always a form, structure, or "field" projected by the organism with respect to which any element gets its significance. Behavior is not situated either in the *en soi* (in itself, mere thing) or the *pour soi* (for itself, consciousness): "It does not unfold in objective time and space like a series of physical events; each moment does not occupy one and only one point of time . . . behavior is detached from the order of the in itself (*en soi*) and becomes the projection outside the organism of a *possibility* which is internal to it."[6]

Like Von Uexküll, Merleau-Ponty continues the Kantian or "critical" analysis to the point of applying it to the scientific observer as well. Our observation and analysis of the nonhuman organism presupposes our "world" of projection. Merleau-Ponty is stretching his phenomenology toward a kind of critical naturalism: "[O]ur analysis has led to the ideality of the body . . . Nature, as we said, is the exterior of a concept."[7] In his lectures on nature from the 1950s, he refers to Whitehead as well as Bergson and Von Uexküll. "The animal body," he writes, "is a relation to an Umwelt circumscribed by it (Uexküll), but without its knowing."[8] Further, this process seems to hold wherever there is life: "There is everywhere an unfurling of an umwelt."[9] This leads to Merleau's fascinating but unfinished *The Visible and the Invisible* (1968). Seeking the most primordial reality where subject and object cannot be distinguished, he proposes an intermediary, the "flesh" (*fleich*). As feeling-availability (*Empfindbarkeit*), the flesh touches in being touched and vice versa. This is the "Chiasm" or interlacing (*entrelacs*), the reversibility of subjectivity and objectivity, like the warp and woof of a textile. He is trying to touch the primordial meeting point of objectivity and subjectivity.

At the same time, Hans Jonas—like his friend Hanna Arendt, a Jewish student of Martin Heidegger—was pursuing an "existential" biology. In *The Phenomenon of Life*, originally published in 1966, Jonas's main purpose was to oppose the tendency of all modern metaphysics to regard either matter or mind as the basis of reality. For life cannot be derived from either, or both. Living things, he claimed, are uniquely characterized by "needful freedom," possessing a degree of autonomy foreign to inorganic existence. The existence of living things is based on their ability to maintain boundaries from the environment and control their internal distinctiveness. "The point of life itself," he writes, is "its being self-centered individuality, being for itself and in contraposition to all the rest of the world, with an essential boundary dividing inside and outside . . . Profound singleness and heterogeneousness within a universe of homogeneously interrelated existence mark the selfhood of organism."[10] With autonomy, there must be *identity*, or else there is no "auto" to be the "nomos," the law or governor, of its activity. The organism remains a unity, with an inside and outside, and the difference matters. A lot.

But this autonomy has nothing to do with independence! Living things are *more* dependent than their nonliving precursors; they remain invariant over only a tiny bit of their phase space. Simply, organisms need and die. Jonas writes: "The privilege of freedom carries the burden of need and means precarious being . . . living substance . . . has taken itself out of the general integration of things in the physical context, set itself over against the world, and introduced the tension of 'to be or not to be' into the neutral assuredness of existence."[11] Precisely because they are so distinct, they are precarious. The price of life is death. Life is "hazardous being" because it forms an identity that can and will end. Death is complete, rather than controlled, openness to environment. It is fought off by ceaseless metabolic, and in some cases behavioral, activity. Every cell is running in place. Jonas writes, "The organism has to keep going, because to be going is its very existence . . ."[12]

Adapting Aristotle, Jonas points out this is enabled by something unique to life: *form*. The relation of the organism's structure to their components is more independent than that of nonliving things, for the structure remains the same through a virtually complete exchange of token molecular components. DNA and its characteristic set of structuring activities are utterly foreign to nonliving matter. The organism is a not a form; it is a member of a natural kind. But it is *formal*; it contains or is characterized by a form and shares most of it with others of its natural kind. Cells and organisms are *designed*. This does not mean designed in every way, nor that there is a designer. There is design nonetheless.

Across the pond, the Americans, starting with Peirce, James, and Dewey, had always been sensitive to the new experimental psychology and animal ethology. It was the distinctive fate of the Americanist philosophical tradition almost entirely to coincide with this period of naturalist reinterpretation after Darwin. And indeed, with the exception of Royce, the Americans were nonreductive naturalists, as well as anti-Cartesians and anti-dualists. Peirce, ostensibly a panpsychist—believing everything has some rudimentary mental features—nevertheless incorporated human mind in nature. James was arguably phenomenological in regarding experience as his ultimate category, but he remained, as we saw earlier, a neutral monist. His extra-philosophical associations were with social, rather than natural, sciences. The same was true of Dewey. Dewey's "The Reflex Arc Concept in Psychology" (1896) had argued that the S and R of stimulus-response must be understood as phases of a continuous circuit of organismic adjustment, each setting up the other. The "activist" Kantian perspective was not lost on him. Dewey became the most prominent nonreductive naturalist of all the Americans, describing life and mind as part of an evolutionary sequence. Dewey was familiar with the term "emergence," which would be endorsed by his Chicago colleague G. H. Mead, but rejected it, regarding it as absurd and even "feudal."[13]

Like many new ideas in the nineteenth century, emergence was born in England. As noted, George Henry Lewes first used it in 1877. British ethologist Lloyd Morgan adopted Lewes's term in his 1913 *Spencer's Philosophy of Science*. This was before Samuel Alexander's Gifford lectures of 1916–1918; Alexander later cited Morgan as the source for his use of the term.[14] Morgan argued that there are three different "modes" of relation among natural phenomena, the physico-chemical (A), the organic (B), and the cognitive (C). In each case, the latter is asymmetrically dependent on the former but has "new and distinctive properties which are not merely the algebraic sum of the component things prior to synthesis. We may speak of them as constituents of the products at a higher stage of relatedness . . . the related things are progressively more complex . . . I do not say more real; but I say emphatically as real."[15] The emergence of novelty, a kind of nonlinear change or "jumpiness," was an application of the "saltation" hypothesis in evolutionary theory, which believed the otherwise smooth and piecemeal course of evolution might have been punctuated by major leaps.

G. H. Mead, Chicago colleague and friend of Dewey's and inventor of social psychology, was more involved with the natural sciences than either James or Dewey. While it is not clear from what source Mead acquired the term "emergence," he reviewed an earlier book of Lloyd Morgan's and so was most likely familiar with the latter's formulation (Mead 1895). In the lectures that constitute the posthumous *Mind, Self, and Society* (1934), Mead explicitly claims that two related but distinct principles constitute the whole basis of his approach to nature: *relativity* and *emergence*. "Relativity" means the relativity of the objective characteristics of an organism's environment to the organism: the acorn is food, but only because certain creatures can eat it. What is emergent is "[a]nything that as a whole is more than the mere form of its parts has a nature that belongs to it that is not to be found in the elements out of which it is made."[16] He uses the common chemical example of the properties of water being something "over and above" the oxygen and hydrogen atoms which make it up: "Emergence involves a reorganization, but the reorganization brings in something what was not there before. The first time oxygen and hydrogen come together, water appears. . . . emergence is a concept which recent philosophy has made much of . . ."[17] But Mead's clearest statement is from *Philosophy of the Present*:

> The thread of the physical scientist is reduction and that of the biologist is production. The biologist cannot investigate until he has got a life process . . . He must, however, have physical means for this process . . . If he reduces the reality of the life process to the means . . . he becomes a mechanist. If the life process appears to him a reality that has emerged out of the physical world . . . he is a teleologist. These two attitudes . . . conflict . . . only if on the one hand he . . . refuses to recognize that the process that he is investigating is a reality that has arisen, or if, on the other hand, he states the physical and chemical things that enter into the process solely in terms of the process . . .[18]

For Mead, there is only a conflict between accounts of the telic, complex, self-organizing behavior of living organisms and the mechanical processes of physics and chemistry, if one side refuses to recognize the reality and necessity of the relations and processes employed by the other. That is, if the reductionist claims the emergent properties are not realities, or if the teleologist claims the physico-chemical phenomena are dictated by a higher end. But if each is given its due, then, "What for Aristotle is formal and final cause is coming back as an emergent."[19]

Teleonomy

In June 1874, Darwin's friend Asa Gray wrote in *Nature*: "Apropos to these papers . . . let us recognise Darwin's great service to Natural Science in bringing back to it Teleology: so that, instead of Morphology *versus* Teleology, we shall have Morphology wedded to Teleology."[20] According to his son Frances, Darwin responded, "What you say about Teleology pleases me especially, and I do not think anyone else has ever noticed the point. I have always said you were the man to hit the nail on the head."[21] Unfortunately, today the popular arguments of science versus religion have made all this obscure, even worse, injected politics into the mix. Some regard "purpose" as a stalking horse for a teleological view of nature as a whole, even for religious conservatism. (On the contrary we must accept that modern biology is an equal opportunity offender of all political views.) Purpose, teleology, meaning, goals, ends, design—all these get muddled up, even in the work of prominent thinkers—as do materialism, mechanism, associationism, reductionism, and empiricism, by their opponents.

Purpose is not an enemy of reason and science. We may take a famous case. Jacques Monod's *Chance and Necessity: Essay on the Natural Philosophy of Modern Biology* (1972) is often described as an attack on teleology. That is partly right. Monod specifically criticized the process philosopher and archaeologist, Teilhard De Chardin, who did have a teleological conception of nature as a whole. The teleology which Monod criticizes was the claim that evolution itself, and the arising and success of novel species, serves some objective purpose. He opposed vitalism and the "scientific progressivism" of Teilhard.

But that does not mean Monod rejected purpose. For the analogous case of cybernetic mechanisms allow us to see how "in a very real sense the organism does effectively transcend physical laws—even while obeying them—thus achieving at once the pursuit and fulfillment of its own purpose."[22] Monod endorses, not teleology, but *teleonomy*, the fulfillment of a genetic program (unfortunately interpreted by some to this day as the mere "appearance of purpose"). Organisms are hierarchically organized, and the activities at a lower level of organization can be "selected," constrained by higher levels, all in accord with the action of a genetic program in the context of adaptation to environment. Not all is chance. There is biological necessity too; it comes from the inside of the organism but is highly constrained and objective, not a mental choice or vital impulse. Monod even refers approvingly to the experiments of the premier emergentist in neuroscience, R. W. Sperry (whom we will see later). Monod has no problem describing teleonomy as endowment with a purpose:

> Every artifact is a product . . . which . . . expresses . . . one of the fundamental characteristics common to all living beings

without exception: that of being *objects endowed with a purpose or project* . . . Rather than reject this idea (as certain biologists have tried to to) it is indispensable to recognize that it is essential to the very definition of living beings . . . which we shall call *teleonomy*. . . . By examining nothing beyond the finished structure and . . . its performance it is possible to identify the project, but not its author or source.[23]

The "morphogenetic structure" of the organism is autonomous, and executes its program, which is purposive. It is mechanical, but cybernetic, with an autonomous control mechanism. For Monod, "All the structures, all the performances . . . contributing to the success of the essential project" of living and reproducing "will hence be called 'teleonomic.'"

The term "teleonomy" originally came from Colin Pittendrigh to mean "a physiological process or a behavior that owes its goal-directedness to the operation of a program . . . [hence] depend[s] on the existence of some endpoint or goal which is foreseen in the program regulating the behavior."[24] Natural selection creates teleonomic systems. The heart has a purpose; it doesn't think or know it, and no one designed it, but it is as purposive as a shovel and was created by natural selection. After Monod's adoption of teleonomy, biologist Ernest Mayr, in a 1974 paper, made a very useful distinction between teleology, telonomy, and "teleomaticity." Mayr's point was to separate most teleonomic biological processes from teleology understood as mental intention. Teleology is presumably restricted to neurally complex animals, who may be said to have *minded agency*; for example, the wolf desires, sees, pursues the elk. But all life is teleonomic in the sense of being genetically committed to maintain states amidst internal and external perturbations. As Mayr put it, in biology we do not merely say the wood thrush migrates in the fall and "thereby" escapes the northern winter. Such a statement misses a crucial bit of information: the wood thrush migrates *in order to* escape the winter, albeit an "in order to" that does not presume minded intent.[25] The fixed action pattern serves a purpose. Mayr explicitly endorsed the notions of emergence and hierarchical organization as inescapable for biology.[26]

One way of schematizing the factors involved in purposive explanation in living organisms comes from Wimsatt. When we say something has a function, we are saying: "According to theory T, a function F of behavior B of item I in system S in environment E relative to purpose P is to do C."[27] The P variable is *purpose*, and is essential for it picks out criteria for an "intensionally defined class of state-descriptions of the system and its environment," that is, a set of conditions of which the behavior B "promotes the attainment." In explaining something's behavior it is entirely justified scientifically to say that the something is organized is such a way as to do what is necessary to achieve a state within certain parameters—like sweating or releasing more or less of a chemical or altering sensitivity to stimuli. Indeed, "purpose and teleology are correlative concepts" (although here "teleonomy" would be better).[28] The functional consequence is "causally responsible for the selection and presence of the functional entity . . ." It answers the "why" question, "giving a causal answer to a causal question." If this view is correct, then, Wimsatt concludes, "the usual disputes over reduction in biology have no bearing upon the status of teleology in biology. . . . Only by denying that evolution has occurred as a result of selection processes or that it is of any scientific interest could teleology [i.e., teleonomy] be eliminated from biology" (my interpolation).[29]

Nothing here implies intent or design or mind. Some things or properties have functions; the function is a contribution to a capacity or achievement of a process of the system. Just as in a cybernetic system, like a thermostat, there is a governor which senses deviations from a state that is to be maintained, and responds to regain it. In living organisms such systems are not only far more complex because constructed out of living cells and tissues, but also multiple systems may be called into play to regain the homeostatic norm: heartrate changes, endocrine system release of chemicals, neurological alterations, et cetera. Natural selection constructs purposiveness. Which does not mean natural selection *itself* is purposive.

We may then say the property of the organism's form serves *a final cause*. No claim must be made here that a final cause suffices to accomplish an event—only that, without the final cause, the function or value of the complex in question, it would not occur. As I have argued, there is no good reason to restrict the meaning of "cause" or "causality" to efficient causality, that is, to events or happenings, or even further, events or happenings for physics. We can relax the notion of cause while yet retaining the distinction between efficient and other causes. That is, a cause is something without which, all other things being equal, *something else would not have come about*. That such an attribution is contextual is no problem for ordinal naturalism.

The heart pumps blood. That is its main purpose. The heart is a cause of things—a good test being that if you remove it, bad things happen. It is also caused by a long chain of circumstances including random genetic changes, natural selection in various environments, and a host of conditions that keep it functioning. The "function" of the heart does not efficiently cause or make anything happen. But if the heart did not serve that function for the organism, it would not be there.

Things That Matter

What kinds of things have value in the biological domain? Most fundamentally, organisms. Organisms evaluate. They have preferred states of their own, pursued homeostatically. They have norms; they are living or dying, healthy or sick, succeeding or failing. They evaluate parts and states of the environment; they turn toward the sun, stretch their roots for water, explore for resources, chase prey, seek secure locations. "Evaluate" does not mean thinking, ruminating, imagining, or deciding. Indeed, the species itself can be said to evaluate, not as a collective agent but as a biological "form" that presses its case genetically. The bird is supposed to have two wings.

Environmental philosopher Holmes Rolston rightly characterizes the organism as an evolved "valuational system" (1988). That it values things the way it does is genetically coded by natural, hence environmental, selection. He notes that there is "nothing extraneous or accidental about the food value in a potato." If the potato has food value, its chemicals have value too. The chemical value was there, evolved in concert with the evolution of animals who eat it. When a predator eats its prey, or a herbivore eats vegetation, they are "capturing the value" of the organism eaten. Value circulates through an ecosystem. Rolston writes: "Value is not apart from the whole; it is a part of the whole."[30]

Rolston completes his discussion with a rejoinder to the eighteenth-century moral philosopher Joseph Butler's famous remark that "Everything is what it is, and not another thing." Rolston retorts: "To turn Bishop Butler on his head: everything is what it is in relation to other things."[31] But ordinal naturalism allows that both statements are part of one truth. The value is a fact about the acorn. It is true that it is relative to the species that can eat it: if they all ceased to exist, the acorn would have no more food value than sand. It would have a set of chemical traits that did not in fact potentially serve as food. Indeed, fruits and nuts evolved in concert with the animals that eat them. Each living thing is what it is depending on key relations to others, and *is thereby not another thing*. So with the existence of living biological organisms, many things acquire objective value, like food, mates, offspring, resources.

Some species develop a further novel mode of conspecific organization, which, like animal mind, will extend to humanity: they are *social*.

What I mean by "society" is rather special. The parent-offspring pair is crucial to many species, until the offspring attains sexual maturity. Many species in local populations group around favored watering holes or mating sites. Communication is widespread. Simple animals, like corals, exist in colonies, and some pass chemical influences back and forth. Some writers want to claim that societies of organisms are themselves "super-organisms." However useful and helpful such language may be in a particular inquiry, ordinal naturalism makes this point something less than groundbreaking. Every entity, at least every individual and ensemble, is a system of parts and obtains in other systems of varying degrees of coherence. If the colony of corals is one kind of unity, its ecosystem is another, and so is the biosphere as a whole. Having abandoned the notion that real things are unrelated particulars, this is not surprising. We may call some of these cases "proto-social."

But some species are social in a stronger sense. They exhibit a *social organization* into which members are born, usually spend their entire lives, and play different *roles*. Such societies assign roles to individuals and subgroups, requiring interlocking practices or institutions. Such roles are an essential condition of the individual's existence. Mammals with permanent troops or herds, where key individuals are dominant and others subservient, are an example. Where this holds, explanation of the individual member's behavior requires reference to the structure and process of the society. The most extreme case is eusociality, or "true sociality," in which multiple generations are organized by means of a genetically inherited "altruistic division of labor," most famously studied by E. O. Wilson (2013). It can be argued that this development has occurred only a few times in evolutionary history, producing the hymenoptera (ants, wasps, and bees), termites, and just a couple of species of mammals, such as mole rats. In these cases, all members are kin born from a single queen. (We need not explore the controversy over "group selection" here.[32]) Wilson himself repeatedly calls this sociality "emergent"—unsurprising since the emergentist William Morton Wheeler was his "intellectual grandfather" (Gibson 2013, 607). Such sociality adds an entirely different dimension of valuation. For now, animals value their own roles, conspecific's their partnerships, et cetera. Not only are social phenomena valued by the individual social member, but the society itself is now capable of valuing. This means *society is teleonomic*.

Among species capable of recognizing particular individuals (unlike hymenoptera), individuals can also be valued in accord with their *perfor-*

mances. The dominant male is supposed to ward off potential usurpers; the emperor penguin is supposed to carry eggs on its feet; the subordinate member is supposed to defer. None of this is a moral "supposed to" in the human sense, but it all has value in the perpetuation of the social group. A performance or practice is a series of coordinated social behaviors meant to achieve a goal. Performances have beginnings, middles, and ends. It is perfectly acceptable to ascribe practices to nonhumans (as long as we don't think of them in human, cultural terms.) The performance may have a value, and a norm; it is supposed to achieve something—chase down food, avoid a predator, court a mate, find or build a nest—and these practices can be performed better or worse. One individual may perform it better or more efficiently than others, and this might make a social difference.

Then there are what we might call *tools*. All organisms and societies of organisms alter their environment, construct a "niche." But some organisms do more: they select and preserve some environmental supplies, even make up some novel structure with them. Many animals construct nests to lay eggs or hatch offspring, or make mounds or warrens. Termite mounds and beaver dams are particularly marvelous examples. Some select bits of the environment as an aid in accomplishing necessary tasks, like sticks to dig insects out of holes in trees. While it is stretching the term a bit, we can regard all these selective constructions as tools. Tools have functions, which is to say, purposes. They are good for something. The ant colony is supposed to have water traps; the bird nest is supposed to hold the eggs and keep the residents safe from predators. Hence some are good or bad, well done or inferior, successful or not. An appreciation of instrumental value is genetically programmed into numerous species. This does not mean they "think" about such value; but their behavior cannot be explained without it.

Lastly, organisms are dependent on the *ecosystem*; if they have value, the ecosystem must have value, both as an ensemble of such entities and as that whose processes of interaction make their lives possible. And this fully includes the variety of other species and the inorganic features of the ecosystem that are crucial to its continuation. This likewise involves what Rolston calls the "dialectical" or conflictual relation of species value (1988). The continuation of the ecosystem, hence its inhabitants, depend on harming and killing off members. This does not mean there is no cooperation or symbiosis; it is just to say that wild nature in any locale operates on a circulation of valuable energies and substances through species, populations, and organisms, and that circulation is both that on which individual members depend and often what kills them. The hawk snatches a snake, and then drops it; this saves the life of the snake but may kill the hawk's hungry chick. Ecology recognizes that organisms live at each other's expense. Not only predators, but scavengers, fungi, fruit-eating animals, and even plants eliminate competitors by monopolizing resources. Plants may not usually kill to eat, but their eating can kill. Ecological ethics recognizes that this is a good, a positive value for the ecosystem on which all future generations depend. One may argue this holds for the biosphere itself, even if that is a value only humans can recognize.

Living Values

So, at least among living things, we have some examples of value more fundamental than human evaluations. This allows us to make a guess about value. What is it?

Value is not an entity, nor an activity. It is a status something has in relation to something else. But what? An activity or process of some system. Whatever else it may be, *value is a characteristic of a thing's functional integrity which, in relation to some other system, has a positive or negative effect on—advancing or inhibiting—a process characteristic of that system.* Value seems to be "bivalent," up or down, good or bad, appealing or repulsive, successful or not. Something has that status in relation to something, and in particular, to some process characteristic of the latter. This does not mean all value is like this—how would we know? But much of biological value seems to be. This is our starting point.

We saw that the naturalistic fallacy, originally from Moore, says that no natural property, state, or event can, in itself, justify that it or anything else is good. We can now say *that is false*, and crucially so. It claims that a true judgment of some complex without an additional ascription of value cannot by itself have value implications. In the biological realm there are states of affairs that are teleonomically valuable and objectively so. Further, the organism, especially the minded organism, is specifically designed to experience evaluation in the form of pleasure, pain, stress, comfort, and emotional states. Those phenomena are *factually evaluative*. They can be affected by learning, and sometimes the minded experience can diverge from what is objectively good for the organism.

We must distinguish objective from subjective value, intrinsic from instrumental value, and both distinctions *from each other*. The distinction between valuing something as an end versus as a means is important because as tool users we humans are familiar with the fact that context of use can utterly change some kinds of value. The stone is useful as a hammer until I have a hammer, and then its value disappears. Humans can value something noninstrumentally, as an end, like our loved ones. Likewise, nonhumans can value and cease to value an environmental resource. On the other hand "subjective" value means idiosyncratic valuing by an agent; "objective" means value not dependent on an individual agent's behavior. That I value water is objectively characteristic of my species, but my fondness for old movies is personal, even if it is shared by some others. But all four kinds of value are *relational*.

The individual we call an acorn has the property of being food, having food value, objectively, regardless of what anything thinks of it. But only because of the existence of species who can eat it. It is food for deer and turkeys but not for wolves. This is the acorn's objective value as an end for or in relation to the species that eat it. Its objective value is intrinsic as opposed to instrumental. What else can food be but an end in itself? Likewise, instrumental value may itself be valued objectively. If anything is intrinsically valuable, money is. It is designed and *defined as* something with value; if it ceases to have value, it ceases to serve as a medium of exchange and is no longer money. And yet it is clearly instrumental, a means to other ends (see figure 4.1).

Did the acorn have food value for a particular species *before* the later started eating it? Take our species: humans can and do eat acorns, but only when cooked, so it is likely no hominins ate acorns before they learned to control fire. It seems natural to say that hominins thereby *discovered* food value that was already present. Otherwise we must say hominins endowed or

	Intrinsic Value	Instrumental Value
Subjective Value	Particular agent values it as an end	Particular agent values it as tool/means
Objective Value	Kind of agent values it as an end (acorn for deer, not coyote)	Kind of agent values it as tool (money, handaxe)

Figure 4.1. Values in relation. (Author created)

conferred food value on the acorn. Certainly, humans do endow or confer values on some things, like baseball. But acorns were already here, and we discovered their objective value for us. A previously undiscovered spring in the desert that saves a thirsty traveler, human or not, was objectively valuable for, and merited valuation by, living things.

One might say that all these forms of value and valuation are related to function: if something has a function then what fulfills the function is a *value-fact*. It is an objective fact that it has value. This will hold of all social performances and tools of any species. Once we know something is a soldier ant, or a queen ant, or a submissive member of a chimpanzee troop, or a human baker or brewer, we will know *prima facie* what it ought to do, or try to do, in certain circumstances, and that a superior performance is better than an inferior one. All these are facts, *normative facts*, albeit not moral. Indeed, in many cases the phenomenon or fact would not exist without the value; this applies not only to human performances and tools (money, the hand axe) but to biological value-facts whose evolution involved its value, for example, apple trees.

All this will lead philosophers to ask two questions. First, even if some things or states are relatively valuable, valuable to or for an organism or species, are these goods *really* good? That is, should *we* value them as goods? Now what could that question mean? Presumably, either they are good absolutely independent of all relations (good even if everything else were different), or good in light of the Whole of, or Foundation of, or Purpose of Nature, or good to or for the only creature that can bestow value, namely *us*.

Would any of those alternatives make any sense? How might they address the question as to whether the beaver dam is *really* good? The beaver ought to value and build its dam; the dam is good for the beaver. Maybe the dam is good for some fish, or for the ecosystem (or not, it depends on what equilibrium one thinks is best for the ecosystem). But beyond that, to seek some other standard is like asking *whether beavers ought to exist*, whether a world with beavers is better than one without. How could that be answered? Anthropocentrically, it may be; many of us enjoy seeing beaver dams. But surely there is no other (especially moral) good involved. There is of course a real and practical question, with genuine moral import: "What parts of the nonhuman world ought we humans value, respect, preserve?" Should we avoid destroying beaver dams? But if the answer is yes, that answer would arise in a subsequent inquiry: "What ought members of the human species morally do about beaver dams?" That is a perfectly good question for human morality, for example, in environmental ethics. That the beaver dam has objectively relative value to the beaver is an independent fact to consider in that inquiry.

Second, some will say all this biology will be irrelevant to human norms and particularly ethics. But that too has to be false. *Human ethics cannot be conceived in total independence of the kind of creatures we are.* For example, if a philosopher decides what is the highest good or greatest moral rule, should it be applied to nonhumans? Should we expect the beavers to seek or obey our notion of the chief good? Our theories of value must presuppose a human versus nonhuman distinction, hence some conception of what humans are like. Suppose we did not have a standard life cycle and then die (as some plants do not), did not have to and could not forage for food (like coral do not), did not give birth sexually to live young that are utterly dependent for years (like fish do not), did not have large brains capable of complex learning (like reptiles do not), were not social animals (like cats are not)—would that not affect human ethics or whatever norm should govern our lives? We must start by seeing what humans are like before we can consider what human norms are or ought to be like.

So we have made a beginning. Living things value and have value. They are teleonomic agents. The vine has needs and values things and states. But it does not have, as far as we can tell, *wants*. It does not perceive nor feel pain and pleasure, desire, rage, fear, and so on. That requires a mind. Even the most positivistic defender of the fact-value distinction argues that values are mental, are qualities of the experience of minded creatures. To understand human valuing we have to understand minded valuing, or teleology. But before we get to our favorite topic, ourselves, mind is not uniquely human! Many animals have minds, and with minds, perception, cognition, desire, pleasure, pain, fear, rage—even shame and other "social" emotions. And however different we are, our minds have evolved from theirs. The place of value changes once we move from the teleonomy of bacteria, unicellular organisms, fungi, and plants to the kind of creature who feels, perceives, and acts. So before we examine uniquely human values, we have to explore the teleological values of the kingdom we belong to, the kingdom of minded actors: *animals*.

Chapter Five

Animal Minds, Theirs and Ours

[T]he generally problematic, equivocal nature of man's relationship with animals shines through . . . man has never really known exactly what an animal is. . . .

—Jose Ortega y Gasset, *Meditations on Hunting*[1]

When we describe animals, we are describing ourselves. As Aristotle knew 2,300 years ago, we are animals, albeit special "rational" ones. What kind of agency do we have in our status as, and inheritance from, the animal world? By no means can we here summarize the vast subjects of our genetic inheritance and the fields of zoology and ethology, which are continuously modifying our views of what nonhumans can do. But the reason we have neurons, forage for food, mate, care for young, learn, live in social groups, hear, see and taste, feel pain and pleasure and rage and fear, is that we are a kind of animal. When we talk about perception and emotion, motivation and learning from experience, raising offspring, foraging for food, communicating, and performing social roles, we are talking about things animals do. A theory of values for humans that did not take those capabilities into account would be a theory of . . . what? Disembodied spirits? Or very noisy, demanding plants?

This requires that we give a basic, doubtless contentious, account of mind and consciousness, which we share with a host of nonhumans. The field called the "philosophy of mind" should by rights be called "philosophy of human mind," for with rare exceptions it gives little recognition to ethology or animal psychology (Andrews 2020). To speak of human minds by rights presumes a long history of evolution and lots of other "kinds of minds," as Daniel Dennett puts it (1997). Once we accept evolution, and that we humans have minds, we must either ascribe mentality to all life, including plants, fungi, protists, even bacteria, or accept that at some point in evolution creatures with minds evolved from creatures without minds. Mental abilities arose. In what follows we need at least a rudimentary philosophy of animal mind.

Nobody knows for sure when mind first arose in evolution, but there are guesses, and we will endorse some of them. Wherever animals have neural structures and corresponding behavior similar to ours, we have no good reason to deny their mindedness. This is clearly true of the most cognitively advanced and behaviorally flexible nonhumans, like great apes, cetaceans, canines, elephants, and corvids, maybe the warm-blooded vertebrates—mammals and birds—maybe vertebrates in general, or perhaps more. Fortunately, what matters for us is less *when* did mind arise than *what* is the legacy of the minded animal agency we have inherited. To understand the role of values in human experience requires that we know something about feeling, emotion, motivation, and their relation to perception and cognition. These are animal processes. Our human distinctiveness operates on the basis of, and within the bounds of, animal life, even if we have something built on top of it.

What Are Animals?

Aristotle had a pretty good, if incomplete, conception of what makes animals distinct from plants, namely, that they *desire, perceive,* and *act.* Today we can be more precise. Animals or metazoans are motile, multicellular "heterotrophs," meaning unlike plants they have to eat other living things. For two billion years after life began on Earth, there were only single-celled, ocean-going prokaryotes (cells without a nucleus), both bacteria and archae. For another billion years, there were single-celled, ocean-going eukaryotes (cells with a nucleus). Only then did single-celled eukaryotes combine into colonies and then into multi-celled protists that differentiated into the precursors of all later kingdoms of life: heterotrophs (animals); decomposers of organic material (fungi); and autotrophs (plants). In the Cambrian Explosion, 565 million years ago, a sudden efflorescence of large numbers of distinct and complex animal phyla (the largest classification below kingdoms) occurred: annelids (e.g., worms), arthropods (e.g., crabs), mollusks (e.g., clams), echinoderms (sea stars and urchins), cnidarians (jellies), and the chordates that soon became the first vertebrates, fish. Far later, after many fits and starts, and then crawling onto land, some fish became amphibians, later reptiles and then birds, and finally mammals.

We can make some generalizations about the novelty of animals. They mate, so a new kind of sex arose, different from the sexual reproduction of plants. They are motile, or move around a lot, again unlike plants and fungi. They mostly have definite bilateral body plans, with a fixed number of appendages or limbs, and a high degree of organismic centralization, unlike plants' phenotypic plasticity in response to environmental conditions, which allows them to lose or shed parts and limbs—not just skin, feathers, or exoskeletons—while remaining one living organism. Animals have a relatively definite life span, again unlike many plants. And animals grew a new kind of cell: *neurons*. Neurons transmit information, particularly from sensory organs to response organs, like limbs and muscles. Enough "interneurons," balled up between sensory and afferent neurons, collecting and sending information to each other, is a brain. As far as we can tell, only animals have minds. If creatures without brains have minds, we have no idea what they are like. The mentality we can understand is dependent on brains and central nervous systems.

Much of this may be connected to the new lifestyle animals invented: *foraging*. Most organisms metabolize whatever is around them, whatever current or wind or sunlight deposits on them. Simple animals, like barnacles and other filter feeders, either open a mouth or extend feelers to receive particles of food that happen to bump into them. An instructive example of a pre-foraging animal is the sea squirt, which has a brain for the first stage of its life, when it seeks a rock to which to attach itself. But once it is attached and begins to filter feed, it digests its own brain! Foragers do something different; they go in search of food and mates. Most complex animals spend their lives moving around in search of food with distal senses (smell, hearing, sight, etc.) while trying to avoid danger, that is, predation, injury, and illness. Those tasks are in direct conflict: the best way to get eaten is to move around. So you have to move at the right time, in the right way, in the right direction. For animals, what you do matters. Action is animal property. You can say plants dropping pollen or seeds is an "act" if you stretch the term. Bacteria move too. But it is only among relatively sophisticated animals that of a number of possible actions or action patterns of which the animal is capable, one gets selected for the moment (i.e., search, float or rest, eat, fight, hide, display, mate, pursue, get lost, etc.).

Action can be simple or complex. Animal *reflexes* (e.g., blinking and swallowing) are automatic multi-body-part responses to stimuli that utilize the immediate connection of receptor and effector neurons with minimal processing in between. It would be perfectly reasonable to deny that those are "acts," something an animal does rather than undergoes. *Instinct* is more complex, an innate "fixed action pattern" (FAP), a coordinated series of acts for which the stimulus only needs to be present to begin, not to guide or maintain, the action. Then there is *learning*, the acquisition of a new behavioral pattern. The simplest form is *classical conditioning*, pairing a new stimulus with an unlearned reflex, which appears to be available to any creature with neurons. *Operant conditioning*, or trial-and-error learning, is the next big step, selective retention of successful spontaneously produced actions in response to a problem (like hunger). This requires memory and a centralized brain (Lorenz 1973). Dennett calls this "Skinnerian" mind, which engages in roughly blind variation and selective retention. Beyond this, Dennett distinguishes "Popperian" intelligence, the ability mentally to process alternative courses of action or test hypotheses "in the head" rather than in reality before making a selection (Dennett 1997). Popper called this letting hypotheses "die in our stead"(1987), but in Dennett's hands it applies to any minded evaluation of options, for example, affective ranking of remembered action possibilities (Dennett 2018, 147).

One of the very few philosophical attempts to trace the origin of mind in the animal world is Tyler Burge's masterful 2010 *Origins of Objectivity*. It is an account of animal perception and its validity. Perception is generally regarded as the most fundamental form of cognition. Some distinguish "sensation" as the most primitive kernel of information reception, saving "perception" for a more holistic, cognitively rich version, but this is a matter of degree across very different species. Burge argues that animal perception provides objective representations of environment that can satisfy "veridicality conditions." He calls such perception "representation-as . . . of," meaning representation *of* particulars (tokens) *as* falling under kinds with properties (types). He argues that this is already a normative achievement in the sense that "a generic notion of 'should' . . . applies to functioning well."[2] He claims animal perception is objective sensory representation of an object or state in the world via proximal sensory stimulations, which functions well or badly. Its norm is "a level of performance adequate to fulfill a function or a purposiveness, and that constitutes an explanatorily relevant kind, independently of any individual's having a positive or negative attitude toward the function or the norm."[3] Such animal perception, which he finds beginning with arthropods (crustaceans and spiders) is not epistemic, for Burge, but it is an "ancestor" of human epistemic norms. (We will return to this later.)

In terms of intelligence and behavioral flexibility we can distinguish many different levels of animal life. There are the nonforaging animals with minimal neurons and "neural nets" like oysters, corrals, siphon feeders, and some limited foragers, like snails. Then come the arthropods, an enormous group including insects, spiders, and crustaceans, who have very substantial brains with over one hundred thousand neurons, who must seek and trap or ambush to make a living. Many of them exhibit trial-and-error learning (you can train a lobster). Then are the vertebrates with central nervous systems of millions of neurons, starting with fish, amphibians, and reptiles (and that great outlier among invertebrates, the cephalopods). The homeothermic or "warm-blooded" vertebrates, birds and mammals, with fifty or more million neurons, are capable of more complex learning. Mammals alone have a neocortex, although some birds have alternate structures that seem to enable mammal-like learning. Finally, there is a select set of highly intelligent mammals and birds with neurons in the billions, including primates (especially the great apes), cetaceans, canines, elephants, corvids (crows and jays), and parrots. These creatures sometimes exhibit remarkable problem-solving abilities.

So we are now going to proceed backwards, you may say, trying to base our tentative definitions of mind and consciousness on fallible guesses as to what kinds of creatures have them. As I have suggested elsewhere, "having a mind" means the performance of mental processes. Following Burge, it seems to be correlated with (a) a single centralized brain of at least one hundred thousand neurons; (b) a lifestyle of purposive foraging with at least some distal senses; and (c) the capacity for trial-and-error learning. The flower turns toward the sun, the protist reflexively withdraws from touch or heat or the wrong chemical gradient, cnidaria digest what falls into their tentacles. They are not robots; they are need-driven, homeostatic, living, teleonomic agents. But the minded animal can do more: it can *feel* hunger and *image* objects in the environment in relation to its own body, and *cognitively* combine that information with memory, permitting learned action sequences. This may be wrong; perhaps mind in any practical sense came later, with fish, amphibians, or reptiles (plus again, the cephalopods). But what matters now is to get some characterization of what it means to have a mind, and even *what good is* a mind, hence what allowed mentality to be naturally selected.

What Good Is a Mind?

Following Franz Brentano's classic statement, a mental act is "intentional." He defined "intentionality" as a state that contains its object in a certain way (Brentano 1995, 68–70) That is, an intentional act, versus any nonmental act, contains an "intentionally in-existent" object within itself. Thinking has a thought, perception an image, remembering a memory, and so on. Many philosophers parse intentionality as "aboutness," claiming the mental act is about something, in the way belief ("x believes that p") and desire ("x wants p") states seem to be "about." The problem is that some mental states do not seem to be "about" in the way belief and desire states are "about." It is standard to regard simple conscious qualities, like the feeling of pain and sensing the color red, as nonrepresentational and therefore nonintentional awareness of "qualia." But this is much too narrow for dealing with non-linguistic, nonhuman minds.

Intentionality is a kind of act performed by an animal. An intentional act is *of* something, not necessarily *about* something. The sensation of red is of red, the feeling of pain is of pain. The memory or thought of pain may be about pain, but the feeling is not "about." Brentano agreed with this; intentional acts present something "without exception." The function of that presentation is *representation*. That does not mean redness or pain *are* representations; they are mental presentations that function to represent. Some processes in nature serve to represent; mental processes are one kind. As natural processes, they take time; as time span approaches zero, they provide states. So when we speak of "a" representation (idea, feeling, percept, imagination, etc.), we are speaking of a selected state of a process that is by its nature related to something and functions to represent it—whatever that something may be.

If so, then at a minimum a mind is *a suite of intentional activities*, activities with intentional content. These activities are sometimes divided into the cognitive (sensation, perception, memory, imagination, thinking, problem solving); the affective (feeling and emotion); and the conative, "conatus" being an older term for "will to live" (desire, motivation, or will).[4] We will have more to say about these below. For the moment, we can just say that *a* mind is an integrated subset of those activities performed by an organism in virtue of its embodied neurology; not all of them are required for a mind to be active or present (i.e., nonhuman minds have only some of these abilities). They are intrinsically intentional; that is, without the intentional content, we could speak of a somatic or neurological act *but not a mental act*. Most of what my brain does is not involved with generating mental states at all but rather with regulating things like heartbeat and breathing. My liver is essential to my existence, but unless it is damaged I will never perceive or feel it. I can exhibit reflex actions without recognizing it, which are hence no more "mental" than the functioning of my liver. But if a neural process functions mentally it generates intentional content.

Now, how can a natural, biological and neurological, system generate intentional states? My response will be no surprise: *emergence*. We have had an emergent theory of mind since the pioneering work of neuroscientist Roger Sperry in the 1960s (which actually helped inspire Wimsatt).[5] It may be put it this way: the feelings of hunger and pain, and the sensation of red, are how certain neural states feel to a creature capable of feeling them. Nicholas Humphrey suggested that consciousness is the state of a feedback loop in which one efferent neural pattern, caused by stimulus from environment or soma, is monitored by, read by, a second pattern and the emergent property of that reading is a feeling.[6] The nervous system is so constructed that a change in a neural signal is read (as if semantic) by other neural processes as the *qualē* we call "cold," or "pain," or "hunger." The feeling is the feeling of (not about) the organismic state, given background neural and endocrine activity, long-term dispositions, and learning. The central nervous system (CNS) represents the pattern as a feeling to itself. This is the emergent property of "being mental." There is no way to reduce this content to something else, or to construct it out of a physical, material, or biological description. It is emergent, just as life emerges from complex macromolecules, or normal matter from electromagnetic fields.

Connected with this is a somewhat technical philosophical question, almost never applied to nonhumans, of what mental content "supervenes" or depends on. The term "supervenience" was invented by Lloyd Morgan as a synonym for emergence. It was redefined by analytic philosophers to mean a form of dependence of mental states on physical (e.g., neural) states in which no change can occur in the former without a corresponding "subvenient" change in the later (Davidson 1974). *Internalists* then claimed the human mental contents or meanings supervened on brain states alone, while, arguing on the basis of the philosophy of language, *externalists* like Putnam argued they supervene as well on the organism's relations to environment. For ordinal naturalism this is not a deep problem, since everything depends on relations to other things, and the question is only which, how many, how often. It could well be that some animal mental states depend on only internal states without external reference (perhaps the feelings of nausea and pain), while more complex mental states (e.g., the coyote's representation of *x* as/of a turkey) are externalist. This may have to do with whether the mental state depends on past learning. But even if externalism is mostly right, this cannot mean that *no* equivalence classes of neural states are necessary for a mind to entertain a content, that it is realizable with just *any* neural state.[7] There is no reason the breadth of dependence cannot vary among species and mental acts.

What about consciousness? Neuroscientists think of consciousness in terms of the global quality or degree of attention. More attention, more consciousness. The organism can have mental contents characterized by different levels and qualities of consciousness of them. In his *The Feeling of What Happens: Body and Emotion in the Making of Consciousness* neuroscientist Antonio Damasio analyzes all consciousness as the monitoring of soma and/or environment, contributing to behavior control (Damasio 2000). It comes in three kinds or levels. *Proto consciousness* is rudimentary feeling produced by monitoring an organismic state, for example, pain, hunger, fear, spatial disorientation, disgust, et cetera. Feelings are non-analogical or non-iconic representations of organism state; they do not "resemble" but are expressions of the body state. (I am using Peirce's term "icon" here, which we will encounter later.) *Core consciousness* is the ongoing mapping of such feelings onto a perceptual images of the body-in-interaction-with-environment. By "images" Damasio means not only visual, but any sensory analogical or iconic representations of environment that resemble their causes in some way. Core consciousness uploads somatic monitoring into an ongoing soma-environment map. Many nonhuman animals have both.

Then there is a third kind of consciousness that will only become important in the next chapter because it appears to be unique to humans: what Damasio calls *self-consciousness*. It is the reading of the contents of core consciousness as possessions of an historical, narrative self. It makes possible the "I know that" which accompanies much of our experience.[8] It uploads core consciousness into, or in relation to, a narrative, autobiographical self. It seems to be linked to episodic memory, language, and enhanced "mind-reading" of the experience of others. In unusual states, like epileptic seizures, this can be switched off while we remain core conscious. Self-consciousness will be explored in the next chapter, but it is important to recognize it now, because it is our tendency to understand nonhuman mind *through* our narrative kind of self-consciousness (which you are using to read this).

We have little insight into the kind and degree of consciousness non-humans possess. But it may be that, at least in warm-blooded vertebrates, core consciousness is the mind's advanced scout in its exploratory state. This does not mean it is primary, or most behavior determining, or most necessary. On the contrary, it seems to be the slowest and least directly connected to the organism's motor and sensory systems. Evolution endows reflexes, and organisms acquire fixed action patterns, to deal with commonly met absolute necessities. It may be that most minded species have *at least* proto consciousness, but this consciousness might in invertebrates and some vertebrates be limited in scope and/or intermittent. It may be that many species remain mentally active but without core consciousness much of the time, as long as needs are being adequately fulfilled by hard-wired, past-acquired FAPs, and perceptions register without much attention until something special arises. But core consciousness seems to perform a crucial function for complex animals, as a front-loaded attention system while more vital activities are maintained without it, serving opportunism and learning, especially in exploration of novel environments.

We face one final issue: *mental causation*. This is a deep philosophical problem, and a precursor to the human problem of free will. If, as we assume, any mental content of an organism supervenes on a neural state, and if one neural state is naturally the cause of the next, *what causal difference can the mental state make*? Imagine that mental content M_1 arises from and happens at the same time as neural state N_1. Then comes M_2/N_2, then after that M_3/N_3, which is the cause of a motor response, an action. A famous argument is that the M's cannot possibly make a different to this process, because if M_2 depends on or is caused by N_2, then M_2 is "redundant," meaning N_2 does all the work in producing N_3 (Kim 2000). We can accept with most scientists and philosophers that an intentional content, like the *qualē* of pain or redness, cannot push or pull a neuron or release a chemical by itself. That is, intentional contents are not *efficiently* causal for neural, physical states. If so, how otherwise could M_2 be a non-redundant difference-maker in the process whereby M_1/N_1 leads to M_3/N_3? How can M_2 matter?

As I have argued, it could matter if in response to M_1/N_1, the central nervous system produced N_2 *because* N_2 yields or codes for M_2 (Cahoone 2013a, 2018). Then all else being equal, N_2 would not have occurred if it did not yield M_2, and not occurring, could not cause either N_3 or M_3/N_3. The intentional object or semantic content of the mental state would thus be a causal difference-making part of the ensemble M_2/N_2 and hence the series $M_1/N_1 \to M_2/N_2 \to M_3/N_3$. For this to happen, the relevant CNS systems must have learned, or been trained, to produce a neural state *because* it codes for a mental content, hence the latter plays a causal role in guiding the ensuing sequence of states and hence behavior. The brain learns that some mental phenomena serve as indicators of success or failure, so the brain selectively produces the neural patterns that code for them in response to similar stimuli in the future. Using philosopher Fred Dretske's distinction of "triggering" and "structuring" causes, the brain is capable of utilizing "information-carrying structures for control duties *in virtue of the information they carry*" (Dretske 1988, 99). Through learning, the semantic representation or mental content M_2 becomes part of a "structuring cause," such that the brain next time produces a neural content in response to a stimulus *because* its produced neural pattern codes for, represents, an intentional content.

When I touch a hot stove, a reflex causes me to begin to withdraw my hand before I consciously feel a pain. But the brain's continued production of the conscious feeling of pain leads me to put my burned fingers in ice water, which I have learned previously will minimize the damage. Without the feeling of pain I don't do that. As the famous James-Lange theory of emotions held, I may indeed start running from the bear before feeling fear, but the fear makes a difference to how fast and long I run. What matters is that the brain can (a) produce neural states that have associated mental properties (e.g., a feeling or image); (b) recognize the mental properties; and (c) learn to produce some phases in a sequence of neural states *because of* those mental properties. If the actions that result are adaptive, this ability of the central nervous system could be naturally selected. As Dretske pointed out, our ability to predict that a conditioned rat will complete the maze and press a bar that releases food is not the ability to predict its precise trajectory or sequence of muscle movements.[9] In each trial the rat moves different muscles in difference sequences altering its course. What is reinforced is the molar, emergent, purposive activity of reaching the bar, not its piecemeal reflexes or movements.

If this is plausible, it would mean that *biological teleonomy has found a way to produce mental teleology*. Minded organisms have gained the capacity to organize behavior through M content; a series of M's becomes the way the central nervous system organizes a sequence of N states, hence behavior. The nervous system found a way to make M's matter. The combination of feeling, perception, learning (hence memory), and cognitive processing, is relevant to the resultant act. Mental states and properties can play a causal role. For just as it is very hard to imagine that conscious mental activity could be independent of neural activity, it is equally hard to believe that evolution went to the trouble to produce and maintain, and over time intensify, costly conscious mentality across thousands of species for millions of years for no behavioral gain.

Teleological Agency

The great majority of organismic behavior is teleonomic, including inherited fixed action patterns. But the ability to learn means that acquired memories, cognition, affect, and perceptual states can play a role in behavior regulation. Whenever a mental state plays a regulative role in behavior, like foraging/seeking or defense/avoidance or mating/childcare, we have *teleological agency*. And here we can distinguish kinds of mental activities and their relevant contribution, as they bear on the question of values.

Among complex animals, the cognitive function becomes more sophisticated and additional functions are indispensable to it. Especially memory; any organism capable of trial-and-error learning must store successful and unsuccessful trials. It seems that among the most intelligent of animals—primates, cetaceans, some others—there may be at least a rudimentary form of imagination, particularly in cases of "insight" or "one-trial" learning. Given sensations that might come from multiple sensory modalities, plus memory, in a creature with complex foraging possibilities lots of different information must be "processed," or interrelated, and a selected bit of information made determinative for a specific action. "Thinking" is too lofty a term here. I will use "cognition" very broadly to mean *information processing*. The point is not to introduce digital metaphors, but that we have to imagine all organisms with multiple senses, felt motivation, memory, and evaluation, as requiring the integration of information. Action without such integration means death in any situation of consequence.

This integration must include the valuative information that, as Damasio suggested, is rooted in monitoring the soma. Conation or motivation or drive leads to action. One could say motivation is the felt mental representation of certain teleonomic activities, promoting the behavioral conditions for continued life. Hunger, nausea, pain, bodily disorientation, and sexual desire, and pleasure are drive-related or drive-representative. As organisms evolve more complex abilities, they then develop affect, which is a direct evaluation of sensed circumstances in relation to those somatic conditions.

Motivation and the evaluation of body and environmental state mentally present as *feelings*.

At the basic level, "sense" or "sensation" is not much different from "feeling." "Sentience" in fact comes from the Latin *sentiere*, to feel. We say we "feel" a lot of things: the coarseness of fabric, hungry, happy, embarrassed. Interoceptive sensations of my body state can scarcely be discriminated from feelings, at least phenomenologically. Following Damasio, feeling and emotion are expressions of the self-monitoring, meaning the body-monitoring, of the organism's state in relation to its environment. One might say it is the experience of conatus coming up against the salient features of the organism's body state in relation to its environment, an organismic evaluation of a situation.

Jaak Panksepp, a long-time student of animal emotion, distinguishes between (a) homeostatic interoceptive feelings, or feelings of body state, such as hunger or nausea; (b) surface sensory feelings, including pain or nociception; (c) primary emotions, which for Panksepp are Seeking/Appetitive (learning/exploring), Fear/Escape/Freeze, Rage, Lust, Maternal Care, Offspring Separation/Panic/Grief, and Play; and finally, (d) secondary social emotions, like shame and guilt. Feelings, and then in more sophisticated cases, emotions, tell the organism what is good/bad with what is going on in relation to its state. Affectivity is for Panksepp the primal form and organization of subjectivity (Panksepp 2005).

Panksepp disagreed with Damasio's book title, "The Feeling of What Happens." He retorted, "Emotions are NOT just 'the feeling of what happens,' but more 'by God, I am going to make this happen!!!' " or action-urges.[10] Feelings are intrinsically motivational. Hence, it is a mistake to separate emotion as action system from mere feelings as subjective valences; the two are connected in the upper brain stem. Feelings of body state that are linked to needs can be classified as motivational or conative, while emotions, both primary and secondary, are more sophisticated forms of monitoring the relation of body state to exterior perception. In either case feelings may then be called "valenced phenomenal qualia," or "affective intentionality." Felt motivations, like desire or hunger; felt disequilibrium states like nausea or dizziness or shivering due to cold or panting due to heat; pain states like the feeling of a wound; and affective states like fear or aggression—these are intrinsically evaluative, value-laden representations of the state of the organism-in-its-situation, and cannot be conceived otherwise.

Panksepp correctly points out that feeling and emotion therefore also serve as a means of reward and punishment to reinforce behavior independent of external events. Neurochemical events can after all cause pleasure. There has to be a reward mediate and prior to the completion of tasks that bring external reward (food, mate, escape). The brain evolves to be able to learn to reward/punish the organism itself to reinforce or inhibit actions short of their "ultimate" external goal. These are motivational, in short. Feelings are in this sense the valenced dimension of the Popper-Dennett notion that complex animals are able to allow our hypotheses to "die in our stead."

When any combination of intentional iconic imagery or perception, affective evaluation of somatic and environmental states, memory-stored learning, not to mention complex cognitive problem-solving, fund and regulate action we have teleology or minded purpose. If the image of a predator or mate, a feeling of hunger or fear, a remembered association of some environmental condition linked with benefit or harm, plays a causal role, that is teleology.

Animals and the Fact-Value Distinction

Now, ever since the decline of positivism philosophers have been recognizing that perception has not only a receptive but an active component. The recognition that perception is normally "loaded" or funded by cognition—so observation statements are not fully independent of theoretical statements—and by conation or need, affect, and past habit and behavior, is a central achievement of the second half of the twentieth century. The organism's *umwelt* or perceived environment, the parts of the physical environment that the sensorium and needs pick out as important enough to perceive at all, what J. J. Gibson called "affordances" or perceived objects with intrinsic value, are all examples.[11] Likewise the pragmatists placed perception and cognition within the circuit of action, hence tied it to need and affect.

But the holism, the interconnection, of these functions must not be exaggerated. Conation and affectivity are intrinsically evaluative, but perception and cognition are often not. The more complex perception becomes, the more it must be able to receive and process information about the environment irrespective of its affective/conative significance. It might be true that the spider or lobster never senses anything that is not directly relevant to satisfying its needs: water temperature, sunlight, chemicals indicating food nearby, pressure, and so on. But information reception and action have to be separated for more complex animals. If not, it would have to mean that (a) motivation-affect could not be restrained from dictating action, and/or

(b) nothing would ever be perceived that is not directly related to prior need. Certainly for even the most neurologically sophisticated animals, intero- and nociceptors, are intrinsically value-laden; the more fundamentally important the information, the less can it be value-neutral. However, a mind that permits a forward-aimed workspace for exploration, downloading novel if-then patterns to less focal and faster mental reactions, must permit perception that is not always in the service of need, while continually pressing the organism in the somatically required direction with varying intensity. Simply: smart animals must be able to perceive and remember stuff that wasn't important when they perceived it.

Part of the logic of evolution seems to have been that a bigger brain is often worth the energy cost, because it allows greater learning, exploration of novel sensations, only *some* of which will prove profitable. The foraging/hunting creature notices things it doesn't "have to," some of which later turn out to be correlated with something good or bad. This is precisely what exploratory learning requires: the organism must notice what it was not already directed to notice, to learn new important stimuli that signal danger and opportunity. An organism that could not perceive anything that was not tied to its past successful pursuits of the attractive and avoidance of the dangerous would be in trouble in any novel situation or environment. That is, the perception of advanced animals can be *value neutral* perception of what hasn't been valued up to now but might be later.

This is a strange lesson: the ability to separate the cognitive from conative/affective is the evolutionary basis of the fact-value problem. I do not mean the modern fact-value distinction of David Hume, G. E. Moore, and Max Weber is a biological or evolutionary fact. Nor that nonhumans have a fact-value problem! I mean only that the fact-value problem presupposes evolutionarily acquired abilities. Most wild animals do not consume much more than their basic energy needs, for good reason: exploration is costly and risky! The best way to get in trouble is to wander about when you do not have to. But the most sophisticated nonhumans do show an increase in curiosity, play, willingness to explore and learn what has no pre-given affective-motivational value. This allows cognitive advance and novel learning, beyond whatever the organism has found to satisfy its needs.

Humans take this to a new level. Many species are physiologically capable of seeing the stars, but no normal, self-respecting nonhuman would waste their time on it. Indeed, even more striking, humans have displayed a remarkable ability to overcome negative affect, genetically programmed repulsion, to perceive facts that can lead to novel learning of the most important kind. The greatest example is one of the oldest: no healthy terrestrial nonhuman ever considered overcoming their natural fear of flames to reach into a fire, capture flaming wood, and use it as a tool. All this may be connected to what Valerius Geist called the "exploratory" phenotype, in contrast to the "maintenance" phenotype.[12] During periods of scarcity, when a species population in its local ecosystem has come near carrying capacity, a minimum use of resources and activity is favored by natural selection; when the species breaks out into a new environment, a more robust phenotype is favored. The oscillation between the two is common to many species.

Geist argued that *Homo sapiens* were somehow able to maintain "an exploratory phenotype under maintenance conditions." How? How can the robust, exploratory phenotype be maintained even when no breakthroughs to new environments pay off with sudden nutritive gains? Perhaps if the population finds a way repeatedly to *explore while staying in place*. That means exploratory gains in exploitation of the current environment. Such could only have a cumulative impact if it can be passed across generations independent of changes in genotype. Novel learning cannot change social conditions into the future without *culture*.

So we will now turn to a very strange species: an animal, still dependent on mating, sleep, food, security, social relations, foraging, like so many other species, with all those inevitable, crucial valuations to keep them alive—but with utterly new capabilities for learning and valuing.

Chapter Six

Dimensions of Human Agency

> I tapped to the guy next door and I said, "Gosh, how I wish Descartes could have been right, but he's wrong."
>
> —James B. Stockdale, *A Vietnam Experience*[1]

In an April 10, 1964, episode of the pioneering American television talk show, the *Jack Paar Program*, Paar handed comedian Jonathan Winters a stick. Over the next four minutes, Winters proceeded to do fourteen miniature comic skits using that prop as a hunter's spear, handle of a lion tamer's whip, a flute, a violin bow, a giant beetle's feeler, a fishing rod, a magician's wand, a teacher's pointer, an oar, a golf club, a matador's sword, a pillory for a prisoner (Winters misnames it "stocks"), and a witch's spoon. Winters was famous for this kind of spontaneous innovation. The clip is hilarious.

Now, many animals communicate, some make things, a few play. But what allows a creature to take an object, treat it *as if* it were an entirely different object, get others to share the same attitude, verify that they "get it," all the while recognizing with them that it is *actually still* the same thing with which he began, a stick? Certainly Winters was engaging in comic play, and maybe a form of artistic expression—acting. Many philosophers have examined both. But something more profound and even crazy was occurring: animals communicating about an x, acting as if it were many different, incompatible things, *all the while recognizing it as x*. That makes no sense. But it made us human.

Every animal species is different, unique. To ask what makes a species "special" is usually to ask how it differs from other species in its genus (or family, order, class, phylum, etc). In our case, all others of our genus—and there were many—are extinct. We are naturally interested in what distinguishes us from our nearest evolutionary ancestors and their living descendants, which means the great apes. But we must begin by recognizing that we did not evolve from them.

Homo sapiens evolved, we currently believe, about three hundred thousand years ago from earlier members of our genus Homo, likely *Homo heidelbergensis* or *Homo erectus*. It was they who conquered fire. Some of them left Africa to explore the world, leading not only to us but our older cousins, the large-brained European Neanderthals who originated four hundred thousand years ago, and perhaps also a bit later the Denisovans of central Asia and the recently discovered *Homo longi* of East Asia. *Heidelbergensis* and/or *erectus* themselves evolved 2.5 million years ago, the beginning of the Paleolithic or Old Stone Age, early in the Pleistocene Ice Age, from the first of our genus, *Homo habilis*, who in turn evolved from earlier hominin species, like *Australopithecus*, four to six million years ago. It was they who diverged from the lines of the other great apes. That is, five or six million years of hominins separates our origin from the lineage of existing great apes (hominids).[2] And because *Australopithecus* walked out of primate forests on two feet for the savannah, our lineage evolved in an environment unlike that of any other great ape. They are forest creatures; we evolved in the world of grass-feeding foragers, like deer and their predators.

Some of us *Homo sapiens* may have early exited from Africa 120,000 years ago but mixed with other hominins or died out, but the larger, more successful exit from Africa was only about seventy thousand years ago. Brain growth achieved its peak around then, and with it behavioral modernity, also called the "Great Leap Forward," marked by cultural artifacts, jewelry, burial rituals, and cave paintings. Up until twenty thousand years ago we cohabited the African/Eurasian megacontinent with the other hominins in a kind of real world "Middle Earth": tall thin *Homo erectus*; short *Homo florensiensis*; and robust *neanderthalis*, with whom we sometimes mated. They are all gone. Only we are left.

Humans have a huge brain, the largest for body size of any existing animal. But we are weird in many other ways as well: large mammals with opposable thumbs, an omnivorous gastrointestinal tract, teeth good for grinding and tearing, feet good for quiet stalking (we can stand on one foot), the ability to climb trees, run long distances and swim (the other great apes cannot), daylight color vision from a head held aloft by an upright stance leaving hands free, a larynx capable of nuanced vocalizations more like a bird than a primate. Humanity's achievements are barely conceivable without these.

But here we are naturally interested in our unique mental and hence behavioral abilities. How to characterize them, or the root from which they come? Some of the most famous hypotheses for our mental and behavioral distinction are tool use and tool making, language, free will and moral agency, self-consciousness, and reason or rational problem solving. All these answers are partly true but limited. Our present goal is to find a small core of capacities that would have impacted all of them. Recent comparative psychology, paleoanthropology, and primatology have suggested some partial answers. Based on this work, I will claim that, whatever else is unique to us, and whatever may later be discovered, a core and powerful human characteristic is *joint intentionality*. Joint intentionality was then expressed and operationalized in *language* and eventually *culture*. Whether Erectus or Neanderthals had one or two of these abilities, the complete package of joint intentionality, language, and culture seems to have been unique to *Homo sapiens*.

The Logic of Joint Intentionality

Remarkably, the prehistory of the concept of joint intentionally traces to the American pragmatist George Herbert Mead. Mead and the other Americans suggested against the current of modern philosophy that social communication is logically and temporally prior to human mind. A human mind is a set of activities that arises through social interaction, rather than the other way around. The notion that the human mind is social had been suggested by David Hume and his countryman Adam Smith. But in the twentieth century, G. H. Mead added the claim that humans alone engage in *significant gesture*.[3] Many species produce communicative behaviors to enhance the process of mutual adjustment. One organism responds to another's act by a movement that changes the situation communicatively: Fido, rather than biting Rover, barks or growls; rather than being attacked, Rover shows a submissive posture. Bees do a waggle dance that shows others where the pollen is; cetaceans have elaborate social cries.

But Mead claims humans alone can treat gestures *as signs*. What allows humans to treat a gesture as a sign is that the gesturer responds to its *own gesture from the perspective of the recipient*. It does so implicitly—we might say, "out of gear"—rather than explicitly. I can only send you a sign if I implicitly respond to the sign just as I expect you to respond explicitly. I can do that only if I know what it is to experience the sign from your point of view. That is, the gesturer must regard herself as an object from the viewpoint, or attitude, of the other. The gesture and its meaning are then *objective*. Each social member eventually then internalizes a "generalized other," the perspective of the group. A shared language must presume the generalized other.

As we noted earlier, Frans de Waal, Raimo Tuomela, Michael Tomasello, and others have argued that humans are uniquely social or "prosocial," far more so then even our great ape relatives.[4] Humans develop a cognitive and emotional ability to take the perspective of others, making it possible, when multiple agents attend to the same object, to share a mental state. This has been called "joint attention" and even "joint intentionality." It is expressed in our remarkable "mind-reading" abilities, allowing us to recognize the mental states of others. A neural basis for this has been suggested in the discovery of *mirror neurons*. The brain areas that fire when I engage in an activity or undergo an experience also partially fire when I observe another person engage in such an activity or undergo that experience. Our joint intentionality funds cognitive and affective *empathy*, from the German *Einfühlung*, or "feeling-into," the cognitive/affective apprehension of another's mental state, experiencing into another's point of view (Stueber 2006). If the individual mind is social, that means its activities include the basis for affective and cognitive empathy as well as collaborative rule-governed activity.[5]

Take a simple example. A human caregiver introduces an initially distressing object, for example a wind-up monkey toy, to a year-old infant. Initially, the child looks at the toy in fear, and then looks at the caretaker. She smiles, amusedly handling the toy, exhibiting her attitude of enjoyment rather than fear, and then turns it toward the child. The child smiles and handles the toy itself. The point of joint intentionality is that this is not merely the child imitating the behavior of the caregiver; the object has become acceptable by virtue of the child's *taking up* the caregiver's attitude toward the object, which of course requires first that the child "read" that attitude.

Peter Hobson calls this early identification and transference of attitudes the "Copernican Revolution" of human mind.[6] Incorporating and retaining the perspectives of others complexifies the self and the perspectives it can take. Adopting others' attitudes sets up different optional perspectives for the individual. Mary Warnock suggested that "the possibility of taking up different perspectives is essential . . . to having a thought about something."[7] When I think, I switch among perspectives on what has happened or might happen. Thinking is social and cannot be otherwise. As such, joint intentionality would be the basis for a host of core mental capacities.

The human child is hardwired to be motivated to engage in joint intentionality. Very young infants are constantly scanning the faces of caregivers for clues to the caregiver's attitudes and intentions. While nonhuman primates are capable of a limited form of mind-reading, such as attributing perception or knowledge and goals to another, Tomasello argues that the full mind-reading of shared intentionality is uniquely human.[8] Our joint intentionality, doubtless dependent upon brain size, seems also to grow out of our uniquely helpless childhoods and intensive pair-bonded "allo-parenting"—whereas others contribute to providing resources and help to child-rearing mothers, often other females, for example, grandmothers, which is *almost* uniquely human—as well as a provisioning father.

The point is that human mind-reading of the attitude of the other has a unique intensity. There seems to be a kind of social relating, with both cognitive and affective features, that forms a key difference between ourselves and our closest living relatives. The human mind does not merely involve or require communication in the coordination of activity but is itself communicative. The human individual's very thought process are social. My mind represents what others say and think; I incorporate and think from their perspectives, take on their roles, converse with them internally, exchange signs with them that arouse the same response in myself, a self that emerges from out of my relations to them. The others are *in my head*, like it or not.

We can analyze the achievements of joint intentionality diagrammatically (see figure 6.1). Imagine a baseball diamond with X at home plate, I at first base, W (for We) at second, and Y (for You) at third. X is some object; I and Y (you) are two agents, which constitute or are part of W (we). We is the combined perspective of you and me and others, hence public or social

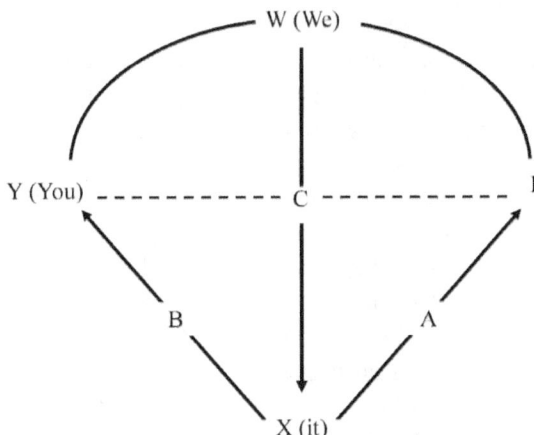

Figure 6.1. Logic of joint intentionality. (Author created)

objectivity, what is recognized as common.⁹ The I understands itself in relation to You, to We, and all three are understood in relation to the objects of our mutual concern, *X*. This makes it possible for the I to recognize that *X* can function as *A* with respect to I, *B* with respect to You, and *C* with respect to We, all while remaining *X*. In joint intentionality we acquire the ability to cognize the fact that one thing can have multiple functions in different relations. My claim is that the logic of these relations, all derived from joint intentionality, fund a variety of humanity's cognitive uniqueness.

First, the I comes to know itself by knowing You and We. The ability to take your perspective on me is the ability to regard myself as an object. This makes me into a different kind of subject: one that is *self-conscious*, in Damasio's sense as we saw in the preceding chapter. That is, the ongoing monitoring of soma and environment, core consciousness, which we share with nonhumans, is taken up into and read as the ongoing narrative of a self that routinely takes the perspective of other conspecifics on itself. Humans alone, I argue, have what we call a "self" because having a self entails being capable of self-consciousness and is social.

Nonhuman animals feel, have minds, are conscious, and have characteristic behaviors and dispositions. They can love and be loved. They can create new solutions. They are minded agents. But not selves.[10] It is quite true that some few nonhumans have passed the famous "mark" or mirror self-recognition test. In these tests, experimenters place a mark of tasty material on the forehead of an animal, and then allow it to see its image in a mirror, to see if it will touch its *own* forehead and maybe eat the treat. Elephants, dolphins, and magpies have occasionally passed the test, but only the great apes consistently pass. Even then, more than half fail.[11] I do not think that success on the mark test by itself indicates possession of a self. Certainly, it indicates a recognition of one's own body, an important cognitive achievement, but one more akin to causal reasoning, as in recognizing that the movements of the mirror image are causally related to one's own felt movements. Possession of a self is different and tied to extended or autobiographical consciousness as possession of a historical narrative self among others. My claim is that shared or social intentionality permits both a new level of prosocial identification and cooperation, and a new kind of individuality—that of an intrinsically social self.

Second, this leads to great possibilities for collaboration. Other primates certainly share and help foraging partners, and collaborate on group hunts. But in those hunts they follow a dominant member, and when the hunt is successful, the dominant takes its share, then others scramble in a free-for-all. There is no such thing as equal allotments. Among humans, I relate to you through taking your perspective; you do the same. From this, *I-with-you* comes to take the perspective of a social *we* collaborating in our joint attending to some object, X. Each of us, while remaining literally the same individual organism that must have its own single biophysical perspective—my hunger or injury are really mine, not yours, and I do experience them as such—nevertheless adopt and enact the perspective of the *you* or *we*, and juggle the meaning of the object X for each of these while recognizing its continuing identity. X can function as A and/or B, serially or simultaneously, in different contexts, perspectives, or relations, and still be X. The stone or patch of fur or stick can serve in one function for me today, and in another function for you tomorrow. Likewise, you can drive the deer today while I hunt them, and we can switch roles tomorrow. That is the magic of joint intentionality. Something can be identifiable and re-identifiable as itself, by you and me, while simultaneously functioning in a distinctive fashion in relation to you, and another distinctive fashion in relation to me, which we can switch.

Third, all this implies joint intentionality is the source of *sign relation*. X stands for A to I, or B to You, or C to We; A, B, and C are alternate meanings of X. For to recognize A and B and C are different, is to distinguish the function or meaning of X from X itself. The stone can be a hammer one day, a grinding stone the next. The same is true of human agents occupying and switching roles. *This is the birth of meaning.* The ability to use or make signs is dependent on the joint intentional capacity to recognize that X, while remaining an identifiable and reidentifiable X, can function differently in different sets of relations, can serve as something else, even as more than one something else, in those different relations.

Fourth, the relations of the diagram above are an analogue of the logic of *temporal* and *causal* relations. Imagine for a moment that in the figure above I is not a person but an event or a goal we want to achieve. Think of X as fulfilling or functioning in role A, hence leading to I. Recognizing that A, a function of X, is distinct from X makes it possible to substitute other acts or steps or things for X to get to I, as if A were an event or stage on the way to I. Suppose a hole needs to be dug, I. Yesterday we used a flat rock, A. But if the rock is not here today, we might use a spear. Different but functionally equivalent causal intermediaries can be substituted for X on the way to I. This is inherent in the notion of multiple realizability of function or meaning; multiple complexes can serve the same function. This cognitive recognition is crucial to production processes, like making a hand axe, which require a necessary ordering of steps resulting in an end. Tomasello points out that the other great apes, who are capable of remarkable feats of problem solving that require some recognition of causal relations, do not recognize the intermediaries of intentional or causal relations; they do not understand that the relation of antecedent and consequent, or stimulus and response, may entail an intermediate causative force or agent intention, hence that the same result might be preceded by a variety of antecedents (Tomasello 1997). X can get to I by way of A, but a functional equivalent of A will do as well. Causal, temporal processes have a logic into which the entities fit.

Fifth, this applies as well to the spatial construction of a *whole from parts*. The hogan can be made of deer or buffalo hide; the patch of fox fur can contribute to a dwelling or to a piece of clothing or perhaps a bag for carrying. It also applies to social members who switch roles in collaborative endeavors: the last time you drove the prey, I speared it; this time I will drive the prey, you kill it. Just as X can serve different functions with respect to different agents, and a different action with the same function can be substituted in a series of steps leading to the same conclusion, the same X can serve as a part in the construction of different wholes. This is central to the human ability to plan, to construct (not merely use) tools, and to innovate during a collaborative effort.

Language

The most remarkable sign medium is of course language. We do not know when and how language evolved among *Homo sapiens*, nor to what extent other hominins, like Erectus and the Neanderthals, had language, or what kind, or how much. There could be great variability here—manual and verbal language, and different parts of language, arising at different times. But we do have very good evidence that spoken linguistic ability as we know it is partly anatomical (our larynx) and neurological (Broca's and Wernicke's areas) and hence genetic. We *Homo sapiens* at least are born with the cognitive and performative hardware for verbal language competency, and with the joint intentionality that will help to fill it with a historical, learned language, as long as child-rearing conditions are favorable. Perhaps we humans always had more robust linguistic ability than our ancestors, or perhaps we developed it. Regardless, my claim is that the use of language we are familiar with arose in, and functions in the context of, joint intentionality.

It is true that nonhumans collaborate and communicate, some in remarkable ways, like the bee waggle dance, bird vocalizations, and the calls of cetaceans. In recent decades, humans have taught a remarkable amount of American sign language to certain great apes.[12] But very simple human sign behaviors—like pointing with the fingers—do not occur in the wild among nonhumans. And certainly the ability to recombine words using grammar permitting the production of a literally infinite number of speech acts or sentences, called "recursivity," is unique to us. Nobody claims nonhumans have recursivity. Finally, the language that some great apes have learned, while impressive, is acquired only via human teaching. The question of whether language is uniquely human is actually the question of how much linguistic complexity is uniquely human. The current answer is still quite a bit.

Human languages are repertoires of learned, artificially produced "symbols," meaning conventional signs. Here we need to say something preliminary about the theory of signs into which our analysis of language must fit. This will be important later.

For Charles Peirce, the inventor of semiotics, a sign is anything (the "ground" of the sign) that stands for something (the "object") to someone, where that someone understands or interprets the sign (the "interpretant"). The triadic structure is crucial, for Peirce is claiming that signification occurs only where the relation of one thing (the ground) to another (object) determines the relation of a third thing (interpretant) to that *same* other (object). Peirce had many categories of signs, and kept revising the list, but three sets of categories will be particularly useful for us. In terms of the way the sign relates to its object, it can be: an *icon*, which resembles its referents (like a photograph); an *index*, which represents what it is causally related to (like a wind sock); or a *symbol*, whose ability to represent is based on social convention ("tree" means the tall leafy things because we agree that it should). Peirce eventually added the term "hypothetic icon," or "hypoicons," for alternate kinds of grounds that represent their objects differently: *images* resemble the quality of the object; *diagrams* present the relations of the object; and *metaphors* represent a parallelism with the object. (All of these will be important later.) Lastly, Peirce distinguished three types of interpretants: the *emotional*, a feeling; the *energetic*, an action or process; and the *logical*, or the idea the sign stands for (Peirce 1935, 5.467–91).

Many thinkers continue to use "sign" and "symbol" in disparate ways. Some want to interpret "signs" (or symbols) in the broadest possible way, so as to include symptoms (e.g., fever) or "natural signs" (e.g., clouds, tracks on a trail), or even anything that means, or can be taken to represent, or carries information or is interpretable (bee dances, whale songs). There is a field called "biosemiotics," echoing Von Uexküll, that interprets all life in terms of signs. Peirce himself considered symptoms "natural signs."

Without any prejudice regarding those attempts, the kind of signs extensively used by humans deserves a unique term. In this book, by "sign" I will mean a *learned, artificial, communicative (hence public) vehicle of meaning*. My claim is that the signs we use arise in and acquire their function in the context of joint intentionality, as described above. So my notion of sign excludes (a) the communicative gestures of other animal species, from the bee waggle dance to mammal and bird calls to cetacean vocalizations (which are genetic and not learned); (b) so-called "natural signs," meaning any phenomenon correlated with another that serves as an indicator or symptom, such as a rash, fever, dark cloud, rumble of thunder (which are not made nor communicative); and (c) indicators that humans admittedly treat *as* signs, like clouds or animal tracks (not artificial, learned, or communicative). These cases may be called sign-like or proto-semiotic, but here I will be concerned only with signs that satisfy Mead's notion of significant gesture. So I am using Mead to limit Peirce's definition. Signs in this narrow sense are learned communicative creations.

Now, back to the familiar symbolic signs we call human language, which again must have referents and interpretants, as Peirce said. It makes sense to regard the logical interpretants of natural language expressions—manual or spoken or written, words and pictograms and sentences—as equivalent to Frege's *Sinn* or "meaning" in the narrow sense of "intension," while the object is the referent, *Bedeutung*. Famously for Frege, the phrases "the morning star" and "the evening star" have the same referent, Venus, but two different meanings; the two meanings pick out the same thing in the world, as do "six" and "half a dozen." The referent for Peirce could be anything, not only an entity; it could be a process, relation, feeling, category, structure, or property. So, combining Peirce and Frege, "the morning star" and "the evening star" are grounds, or signs themselves, both standing for the object Venus, each of which has a different intellectual meaning or logical interpretant.

Natural languages are historical systems of fixed symbols in a vocabulary, endlessly combinable under given rules of grammar. As Susanne Langer—whom we will meet again—pointed out, linguistic signs or "discursive symbols" are characterized by: (a) a rule-governed vocabulary, shared among a social group; (b) syntactic rules of sentence formation, or grammar; (c) statements that are translatable; and (d) nested in a linear fashion in terms of meaning, a "logic," as we will see. The meanings of these words, their logical interpretants, are given in dictionaries, and all but proper nouns (names) have meanings that are universals, that is, complexes with respect to which things can be similar or different (e.g., "red" stands for a universal or predicate with respect to which the apple and stop sign are similar). It is entirely reasonable to regard the meaning of a word as its contribution to the meaning of a sentence, which is how words function in practice. Then, if the sentence is assertive, like "dogs are mammals," its meaning can be parsed in terms of truth conditions. Truth is but one function of linguistic utterance (of assertions or declarations), but the contribution of the word remains mostly constant across the different speech acts in which it can be used.

Given ordinal naturalism, we can understand these meanings more broadly, which will have a definite relation to human evolution. The meaning or logical interpretant of a word can be understood as *a perspectivally selected, coherent set of possibilities*. Most can be logically parsed as class terms; only proper nouns (e.g. James), or indexicals (e.g. "that boy") cannot be. The meanings of all other words are possibilities, in terms of which complexes exhibit similarities, and mean properties and kinds of things, hence universals (as described in chapter 3). The recognition of meanings, as opposed to referents, allows us to break up events and objects into many properties, cognize the properties, hence the similarities in terms of which almost anything can be like and unlike anything else, while remaining the same thing, just as we can recognize multiple uses or roles of each thing and of ourselves. The meanings of expressions ("the King of France") and sentences ("The King of France is bald") then gain their meaning through their use in speech acts, to which words are contributing elements (about which more later).

As we shall see, all cultural complexes mean, including human art, practices, rituals, narratives, and more. But language has a special relation to meanings: it provides a way by which *meanings can be treated and manipulated as objects*. Language provides a device for labeling, handling, and storing them in memory. Meaning manipulation allows us to objectify and communicate about meanings that are non-actual, that are in the past or the future. For Mead "The [human] mind holds on to . . . different possibilities of response . . . and it is [this] ability to hold them there that constitutes his mind."[13] In the broad sense, as we will see below, any entity, event, or property which indicates to an agent something nonpresent, an alternate function that is not now being perceived, has "meaning" in the broad sense and can be handled by expression in language.

This links into other uniquely human cognitive abilities. For example, humans famously are capable of a unique degree of "time traveling." That is the name cognitive scientists give to the ability to think about past and future. Nonhuman animals clearly have memory, and learn. Their most obvious forms of memory are *procedural*, which is remembering how to do something. That a task can be learned, then reproduced more efficiently or very quickly later on, is procedural memory. *Semantic* memory, remembering a fact or state of affairs, is more rare. That an animal can find an acorn, or some other treat, that it once hid or saw hidden and find it again is semantic memory. Rarer still is the ability to recall the sequences of events by which something happened, the narrative of what happened over a discrete process or chain of events. That is *episodic memory*.

Whatever nonhumans can achieve in this way is far surpassed by humans. It is central to what goes on in and with the self, the narrative self-consciousness. Thought itself is a time-traveling conversation—a conversation in which participants move between present, past, and future, among socially acquired and imaginatively recombined perspectives. It seems that episodic memory, while of course supported by specific neurological structures, cannot go very far without signs, without the ability to flag a perspective. Episodic memories, which require step by step causal recounting, and possibilities and planning, require the ability to communicate. Joint intentionality rests on the ability to take the perspective of others on the self. But to trace the self's history in causal steps, just as to record or relate the set of perspectives that the self adopts, would seem to require a way of holding evanescent events, or memories, that would be recognized by others in a series. This almost certainly requires language.

Consequently humans can plan, can practice a task before it has to be performed, can mentally rehearse what can or should happen, can carry a bag of tools or "possibles" to a location where they might or might not be needed. This is already evident in children by the age of four. And planning is made possible by a new level of imagination. Some very sophisticated nonhumans show evident of implicit or one-trial learning. That is, some primates, faced with a problem to solve, seem to ponder it, and then, without trials, solve the problem, as if they were entertaining imaginations or hypotheses. But only with human language to capture and hold possibilities could the conscious version of cognitive processing of which humans are capable be shared.

Finally, this connects to what Thomas Suddendorf identifies as cognitive "nesting." It is connected to linguistic recursivity. I can think and say "Robert lied to Xavion." But also, "Sebastian believes Robert lied to Xavion," or even, "Ivan knows that Sebastian believes Robert lied to Xavion." This can be applied to all manner of scenarios. "Today Lucinda will hunt deer so we can eat." Then imagine a modification: "Sebastian could help (Lucinda hunt deer)." Then new information comes along, "Ivan says hunting a possum would be better than [Sebastian helping (Lucinda hunt deer)]." So then "We all agree that Sebastian could help (Lucinda hunt possum)." This allows the mind to represent a host of alternative possibilities in the handling of any situation. It is very unlikely that an animal could cognize and remember these sets of contexts without language. Consequently, and amazingly, for the joint intentional, self-conscious, linguistic animal, *the past and possibilities for the future now stand equal as components of the situation with actualities.* This is a different kind of creature.

This logical, cognitive achievement of language is, however, only one side of the coin. Because its root is joint intentionality, there is also an affective side we are far from understanding. The acquisition of language seems to change experience in an affective way because it is intrinsically interpersonal. One of the most compelling examples here is a passage from Helen Keller's autobiography. It is the famous scene where, with her hands under the water pump she realizes that the signs for w-a-t-e-r mean the cool liquid in her hand. (Depicted in the 1962 Arthur Penn film, *The Miracle Worker*.) The quotation is long but worth our time.

> One day, while I was playing with my new doll, Miss Sullivan put my big rag doll into my lap also, spelled "d-o-l-l" and tried to make me understand that "d-o-l-l" applied to both. Earlier in the day we had had a tussle over the words "m-u-g" and "w-a-t-e-r." Miss Sullivan had tried to impress it upon me that "m-u-g" is mug and that "w-a-t-e-r" is water. . . . I became impatient at her repeated attempts and, seizing the new doll, I dashed it upon the floor . . . Neither sorrow nor regret followed my passionate outburst . . . In the still, dark world in which I lived there was no strong sentiment or tenderness . . . We walked down the path to the well-house . . . my teacher placed my hand under the spout. As the cool stream gushed over one hand she spelled into the other the word water, first slowly, then rapidly. I stood still, my whole attention fixed upon the motions of her fingers. Suddenly I felt a misty consciousness as of something forgotten . . . and somehow the mystery of lan-

guage was revealed to me. I knew then that "w-a-t-e-r" meant the wonderful cool something that was flowing over my hand. That living word awakened my soul, gave it light, hope, joy, set it free! . . . Everything had a name, and each name gave birth to a new thought. As we returned to the house every object which I touched seemed to quiver with life . . . On entering the door I remembered the doll I had broken. I felt my way to the hearth and picked up the pieces. I tried vainly to put them together. Then my eyes filled with tears; for I realized what I had done, and for the first time I felt repentance and sorrow.[14]

Every object which I touched seemed to quiver with life. Whatever that packed phrase indicates, it at least signifies that the perceptual experience of the thing was now supplemented with a new emotional significance because potentially shared by self and another. The word drapes the object with the emotional charge of joint intentionality. The understanding of the transmitted symbol means that you and I are thinking the same thought, sharing a perspective. *For the first time I felt repentance and sorrow.* Only now is the shattered doll a gift that mattered to you and me, thus to we. But this brings sorrow. Eating of the fruit of the tree of language gives us meanings, but not only happy meanings. Feelings are now more intense, the pain and the joy. The acquisition of language has provided a new medium for the relation of self and other in which the perspective of the other is quite precisely represented by my own brain.

Culture

Language probably preceded, made possible, then came to be part of culture. Some claim culture is not uniquely human. This is because some scientists define culture as learning passed across generations by a local population of a species. Such transmission is indeed extremely rare. Populations of an animal species are not especially different in their behavior. Even where a local population has learned something unique, they have no way of passing it on. Transmission is by the genetic lottery plus natural selection, period. There are a few nonhuman populations that seem to have something like culture. One of the most famous cases is a troop of macaques, a kind of monkey, in Japan who alone among their species wash their sweet potatoes in salt water before eating them. The point is, they teach their offspring this behavior. Some scientists call this "culture."

But we must distinguish culture from society. A vertebrate society is a group of not-solely-kin conspecifics who live together and are interdependent such that belonging to the society makes a difference to individual behavior. In intelligent species, society may entail rules of behavioral propriety and intelligibility. But culture is not society; it is something society *has*. If society and culture were identical, no society could exhibit major cultural change—it would no longer be the same society. Nor could there be "multicultural" societies, societies with more than one culture. When the population of macaques acquires potato washing, its society has indeed changed and it has passed on social learning across generations.

Culture, I suggest, is something different: it is *learned construction of things that mean*, things that function communicatively. More elaborately, it is (a) a learned ability to construct public practices, artifacts, or narratives; (b) that are valued intrinsically as ends in themselves; and (c) which realize shared meanings in terms of which social life and the world are understood. The termite mound is a social product. Like the dances of honey bees it is unlearned, a genetic fixed action pattern. The hominin hand axe and bow are invented, learned social technologies, passed on generationally. They are still not necessarily cultural (again unless every social fact is cultural). But the cave paintings of Lascaux, or the ornamentation of bodies and clothing, ritual dances, and narratives told around the campfire, are different additions to reality: they are valued in so far as they *mean* something for members that contributes to their orientation in the world. They are cultural things. Evolutionary anthropologists note the distinctiveness of behavior in ritual versus mundane, customary, everyday social coordination (Chase 1999; Watts 1999). During ritual, sign use becomes narrow, loud, intense, highly structured, and repetitive. As of now it appears that we *Homo sapiens* alone developed such constructions seventy to fifty thousand years ago. Everyday spheres of communicative social behavior were augmented by what some call "symbolic" culture. Taking the lowest-hanging fruit, art and religion are human alone. No other animal tells stories around the campfire, paints caves, or worships an icon of King Kong.

Culture is clearly a social product, a product of the *We*. It presents a new interpretive environment for the understanding and valuation of the world (or X), the I and You, and the We itself. Humans began to root their social order in a dimension of intrinsically valued, made icons, myths, and rituals. This doubtless adds to the already existing social bond. As Tomasello argues, the cultural era develops what the great social theorist Emile Durkheim called "group mind." As Ernest Gellner writes of Durkheim's conception of archaic society, "We cooperate because we think alike, and we think alike thanks to ritual."[15] The affective dimension of culture is remarkable. The ritual is capable of provoking ecstasy. At the least it provokes solidarity, the feeling that what the We does, and the I does, is what they *ought* to do. The degree of integration of the agents is emotionally charged. As evolutionary psychologists have noted culture intensifies the social bond. This creates the problem of tribalism, to which we will later turn.

But with culture comes more. For the first time *something is intrinsically valuable because of its shared meaning*, rather than being edible, sexual, or comfortable. Intrinsically valuable things have been created in terms of which much of the world is understood as meaningful for human life. A totemic animal embodies the spirit of me and my ancestors. The stars depict human scenes. My life and death take place in a normative circle of the four winds. Now my fertility expresses the order of the world, the circulation of manna and power and value. Only with culture do humans organize their lives according to an understanding of the meaning of human life, an understanding of its function within the wider nonhuman world.

It should be noted that this highly prosocial picture I have painted is not anti-individualistic. There is no contradiction between our sociality and our individuality. We are indeed more individualistic, that is, more individually distinct and capable of novel, unique action, than any other animal. *But we are more individualistic because we are more social.* I cannot think about myself and what I want to do with my life without having learned a socially invented language. Knowing who you are and how you are unique is a socially acquired ability. It is probably true that modern human societies, especially deriving from what we call Western civilization, are more individualistic than earlier human societies. But that is not because the species has changed—it is because culture changed. We have a shared, inherited culture that make us individuals. Either way, individual selfhood is enabled by sociality.

Free Will or Something Like It

We have to confront one last potentially deal-breaking anthropological issue for any value theory that takes natural science seriously. There are many philosophical problems regarding free will, but the one relevant to the present inquiry is its apparent conflict with science. "Free will" usually means an event of will, or choice, that is spontaneous and uncaused. But natural science requires that events have causes. An event not causally related to other events couldn't be connected to any phenomena, external or internal. If "free will" were uncaused, science would have to say there is no such thing. How then could we make sense of moral responsibility?

In 1985, Benjamin Libet asked subjects to, without planning, flick their wrists while simultaneously noting the precise moment when they felt the impulse to do so.[16] The reported impulse preceded the flick by about half a second. But he also found that a "readiness potential" in the cortex (or RP) preceded the reported impulse by another third of a second. It appears that when I voluntarily act, even before the brain activity that is my *knowing I am about to act*, my brain has already begun preparing the act. My brain starts the act before I am aware of what I am about to do. Libet's work and that of many subsequent researchers appear to put "you" or your conscious self "out of the loop" of decision making, as an epiphenomenal accompaniment. Is it?

The initial question is a purely philosophical one: what does "free will" mean? What is the thing whose existence is being denied? First, it's not "the will" that is supposed to be free. This point was made by John Locke in the seventeenth century:

> *Is man's will free or not*? This has been long agitated, but I think it is unreasonable because unintelligible. . . . the question itself is as . . . meaningless as *Is man's sleep swift or not?* and *Is man's virtue square or not?* because liberty no more applies to the will than speed does to sleep . . . Liberty, which is a power, belongs only to *agents*, and cannot be an attribute of the will. . . .[17]

So it is the agent, the person, that is the subject of freedom. But what does "free" mean? Many seem to imagine it means purely spontaneous, uncaused choice or action. That notion indeed can make no sense in naturalism or science. But the notion of freedom as *self-determination*, well known to philosophers, accepts that free acts are caused or conditioned *by the self*. This was the view of Rousseau and many within the German philosophical tradition, sometimes called the "positive" notion of freedom as *freedom to*, versus freedom *from*, absence of obstacle to choice. An individual's free choice is not undetermined; it is determined by the "self" as opposed to being determined by something else. All of this of course hangs on what counts as the "self."

Daniel Dennett points out that the recent neuroscientific critique of free will assumes the "uncaused will" notion and in a very particular way: it makes a weird assumption about time. If we try to locate one unanalyzable instantaneous moment of decision as the sole precursor or cause of an act, we will never get to it—or if we do, it will not be integrable into either our neural or mental life. Such a simple moment could not be causally related to the continuous activity of the central nervous system. After all, the mere fact of dependence of mental events and contents on neural events must imply that a decision, a product of a neural process, *takes time*. The decision or impulse must emerge into consciousness *after* the neural state has already begun to evolve. Dennett writes, actually echoing Bergson: "[W]e can see that our free will, like all our other mental powers, has to be smeared out over time, not measured at instants. . . . You are not out of the loop; you *are* the loop. . . . You are not an extensionless point."[18]

Libet himself later recognized that while RP initiation of an act starts before the conscious impulse, the act can be consciously "vetoed" just a couple hundred milliseconds before motor neurons are fired. He called this, instead of free will, "free won't."[19] Many acts based on prior learning, habit, and discipline cannot be initiated by a conscious act because it would be too slow. Dennett points out that the tennis player consciously decides beforehand how to respond to a later possible shot—"the next time she lobs, I am going to . . ." Such "pre-commitment" makes a great difference in reaction time, in effect creating a reflexive or reflex-like response, so that a later conscious decision will be unnecessary. This is the same thing that Velmans has called "preconscious free will."[20] Is such an act not consciously caused? As Damasio puts it, "nonconscious control is a welcome reality," indeed indispensable, and "can be partly shaped by the conscious variety" of control.[21]

While a mental state can arise only after the beginning of the neural process that creates it, it can also be maintained simultaneous with it and be causal thereby. As noted earlier, I may start running from a grizzly before I feel fear, but the continuing fear may *keep* me running. I am partly constituted by the mechanisms that handle input automatically. I depend on and even train such mechanisms consciously. They are part of the self. But so are the processes that train them. At each waking moment my organism, through its brain, is maintaining homeostatic parameters, and my conscious mentality has nothing to do with it. Some of my behavior is guided by core consciousness without self-consciousness; I shift from one foot to another, change my posture, maybe even scratch an itch. I have no *self*-consciousness of the movements of my tongue and larynx as I speak—although I am capable of uploading them to the autobiographical narrative, if something odd happens or they become intense enough. Generally, once I have learned a complex behavior which has become habitual for me, like driving to work, my organism and core consciousness carry it out, with my self-consciousness acting only as *monitor* and *memoirist*, not as *motor*.

In everyday social life we can legitimately say the self-conscious social agent named Larry Cahoone *did* my acts, even if it/he was not the motor driving them. For pragmatic and moral, social purposes we may say that to be self-determining means to have self-consciousness turned on, as it monitors, records, adjusts and occasionally vetoes acts. Dennett calls this self an ambassador or public relations agent, rather than a CEO. A coach of independent athletes, like a Davis Cup team, might be a better analogue.

We may be able occasionally to talk of self-determination in a fuller sense. As Mary Midgley suggested, freedom is the action of "the whole" of the self in the context of clashing desires, purposes, or behavioral patterns. She wrote: "human freedom centres on being a creature able, in some degree, to act as a whole in dealing with its conflicting desires. . . . The more clearly that being is aware of the clash and the more it can, on occasion, distance itself from any of its impulses, feeling itself to be a whole that contains them all, the freer it becomes."[22] Sometimes the self of self-consciousness is more than monitor and editor, sometimes it comprehends and makes a decision for the whole that certifies a single perspective as dominant and thereby guides action. The self is deciding or affirming what the self is to be. But such moments are probably rare.

Conclusion

With humans we have an agent of a new kind: one that is both more social and more individual than any other teleological (minded) or teleonomic (living) agent on Earth. Humans are still animals who must recognize a series of value-facts, and as social creatures, must preserve their social group or die. Nothing can be more evolutionarily basic than that. Many things must be done: care of utterly dependent offspring, pair-bonding and allo-parenting, instruction of the young, collaborative foraging, maintenance of cooperative relations, political participation and obedience, and transmission of a variety of cultural practices, artifacts, and narratives.

And it is this cultural animal alone who *makes history*. Only creatures with culture can have a history where their current lifeways are different from past lifeways while still the same species. What appears "unnatural" about us is that we can learn new things, objectify them in culture, and pass them down so each generation does not start over from zero. We are naturally historical, and history is our apparent departure from "nature." Later we will examine how history has changed the context of human values. But first we will see that joint intentionality allows us to conceive of the relation between human and animal norms in the realm of knowledge. Thus to go beyond the naturalistic fallacy.

Chapter Seven

Beyond the Naturalistic Fallacy

Epistemology is a branch of ethology.
—Marjorie Grene, *A Philosophical Testament*[1]

When a philosopher and a dog play Frisbee, do they perceive and cognize the same Frisbee? Is the dog a "naïve realist," while the human "socially constructs" the Frisbee? Is Fido subject to the "myth of the given"? The questions are not silly. Marjorie Grene's quip about epistemology being a branch of ethology may appear false on its face, since most would say epistemology is a fundamentally normative, not merely a descriptive inquiry, as the study of animal behavior presumably is. But *that* is what is in question. If humans are animals, and evolved from other animals, then so did our perceptual and cognitive abilities. Cognition is an animal, not merely a human phenomenon. There is a distinction between the animal and the human, and between the causal and the normative, but for naturalism they must be related as genus to species.

Any naturalism that employs the work of modern biology must accept that human knowledge and its norms arose in the context of the evolution of the activities they norm. For cognition, that must mean the successful guidance of action. Further, those human capacities must be continuous with like capacities of other animals. A view called "evolutionary epistemology" attempts not merely to describe human cognition in the context of evolution, but to derive normative, epistemic consequences. This coin has two sides and each side sports a large philosophical question. First, how can we claim that nonhumans have anything comparable to, continuous with, the human capacity to know what is true? Second, is it possible that human norms of truth, objectivity, and rational justification of knowledge are true of real objects independent of human interests, if they are nothing more than a natural adaptation satisfying survival? What is good for an organism to believe needn't be true, after all. Some philosophers believe a naturalistic view of human cognition and behavior would have to undermine normativity.

In the twentieth century, logical positivism raised problems with any "realist" view of perception as grasping objects independent of our experience, while happily endorsing empirical science as the most valid form of knowledge of reality and recognizing that such knowledge was wholly dependent on cognition of "sense data." After the Second World War, the offspring of the positivists, like Quine, argued against traditional logical empiricism that there is no epistemically dispositive perceptual knowledge, no way linguistically to represent sense data without use of other terms, the meanings of which have to depend on their location in a framework of belief or theory. Concepts, hence theories, are embedded in any description of sense data. Hence the choice among conceptual frameworks must be pragmatic, what fits with other beliefs and works best in guiding action (Quine 1951).

Objections to realism have since been formulated in this context. Michael Dummett proposed that "being true" means "being verified" (Dummett 1978). Hilary Putnam asked, could our best possible account of the world be false? Antirealism says no. Putnam said yes, but his work in model theory argued that any logical construction can have an endless number of different consistent models that cohere with it (Putnam 1980). So, Putnam argued that "metaphysical" realism, the claim that there is only one true account of the world, must be false. Whatever realism remains must be "internal" to our language. Donald Davidson, who applied Alfred Tarski's insights—which we will see later—to natural language semantics, endorsed "correspondence through coherence" (Davidson 1986). Belief for Davidson is by nature veridical because we cannot translate or interpret the meaning of a speaker if we do not attribute to her or him mostly true beliefs. Nevertheless, he insisted, there is no possible "confrontation" of belief with nonbelief, with sense-data or things. Rorty agreed but took the lesson that our best verification practices can never be justified with respect to what obtains independent of them, hence the whole inquiry into the validity of justification procedures is vain (Rorty 1991).

One of the most influential contributions to this tradition was made by Wilfred Sellars, son of the philosopher R. W. Sellars, in his discussion of the "myth of the given." Sellars rightly saw that his own argument was linked to G. E. Moore's attack on the naturalistic fallacy. For on this issue, the problems of morality and knowledge are analogous. The question of how the norms of "good" or "right" or "ought" could be derived from natural facts raises the same issues as how the norm of "true" could be derived from facts about animal perception, instinct, and action. Whatever holes there are in the naturalistic fallacy, as we discussed in our first chapter, it still stands in the way of a naturalistic account of human norms in general. No fulsome theory of knowledge will be given here (we will explore a naturalist notion of truth in chapter 11). For now, my only goal is to show that some major objections to a realist notion of knowledge can be handled by naturalism, when rightly conceived. Fido will play a crucial role.

Evolutionary Epistemology

The major progenitors of evolutionary epistemology were four thinkers of the second half of the twentieth century, the philosophers Karl Popper and W. V. O. Quine, the ethologist Konrad Lorenz, and the psychologist Donald Campbell. Others have followed them (Kornblith 1985; 2002; Shimony and Nails 1987).

Konrad Lorenz's remarkable essay "Kant's Doctrine of the A Priori in the Light of Contemporary Biology" (1941) went to the philosophical heart of the matter. He argued that the twentieth-century neo-Darwinian synthesis of natural selection and genetics provides an answer to the philosophical problem of knowledge! Human knowledge involves, Kant had claimed, an active process of construction. That led Kant to posit an unbridgeable gap between known appearances and unknowable things-in-themselves. We know how things appear to us, indeed how they *must* appear to us—because we know how cognition structures appearance—but we have no reason to believe that our mode of cognition is true of things in themselves independent of human experience. And we never will.

Lorenz's claim is that Darwin provides the answer to Kant. The subject's construction of appearances has itself been selected by things in themselves. Cognition is a natural capacity naturally selected, an adaptive mechanism produced by evolution. Things in themselves have a causal relation to the cognitive abilities by which we know them. Lorenz later produced his *Behind the Mirror*, a systematic account of cognition's evolution, in a sense a precursor to Dennett's *Kinds of Minds* (Lorenz 1973; Dennett 1997). He argued that we cannot doubt the limited, perspectival, fallible but real and objective validity of the judgments of the naturally selected cognitive apparatus. An utterly inaccurate cognitive system would mean death. The organism "constructs" its hypothesis, meaning its exploratory heuristics, but under the pressure, and through the selection, of an unconstructed world. Things in themselves edit our "appearances."

None of this means that cognitive powers must be right or true all the time or mistake-free. Lorenz writes:

> This central nervous apparatus does not prescribe the laws of nature any more than the hoof of the horse prescribes the form of the ground. Just as the hoof of the horse, this central nervous apparatus stumbles over unforeseen changes in its task. But just as the hoof of the horse is adapted to the ground of the steppe which it copes with, so our central nervous system apparatus for organizing the image of the world is adapted to the real world with which man has to cope. Just like any organ, this apparatus has attained its expedient species-preserving form through this coping of real with the real during a species history many eons long.[2]

But it was Donald Campbell, to whom Lorenz and Popper both admiringly refer, who invented the term "evolutionary epistemology" and provided the most telling suggestions as to the evolutionary methods and mechanisms of human cognition (Campbell 1988a).

Campbell hypothesized that the foraging organism moves in space until it bumps into favorable or unfavorable objects or chemical or temperature gradients. But among more complex animals there are "vicarious selectors," internal mechanisms which substitute for or replace the external event of moving-and-bumping-into, allowing selections short of injury or death. Whereas the paramecium's blind search could as easily make it food, distance receptors allow a higher organism to scan until it finds a representation of beneficial conditions. These are Popper's hypotheses which "die in our stead." Vision plays an especially useful role as substitute for locomotor search, even if it is always presents "fringe imperfections" requiring tactile checking. The point is, distality matters, and so does objectivity understood as invariance across organismic states and orientations. As Campbell wrote, "Continuing the evolutionary paradigm, we can note that the higher the level of development the higher the degree of distality achieved . . . and the greater the degree to which external events and objects are known in a manner independent of the point of view of the observer."[3] This independence is relative; there is no utter independence of all observer perspectives. The more active this process—one might say, the more Kantian rather than Lockean—the better. Intelligence makes this possible.

Nature's editing is often, Campbell admits, "indirect."[4] He writes, "we should expect a gap between scientific beliefs and the physical world comparable to that which we find between animal form and ecological niche."[5] The historical evolution of knowledge, as of anything else, works with the resources available. Nothing is designed all at once for perfect fit; what adapts at any moment is the cumulative product of a particular history of past adaptations. Campbell points out the intriguing case of "monitor-modulating" systems which generate perceptual judgments that conflict with the data *in service of* objectivity. When an unchanging object is seen against differently shaded backgrounds, humans perceptually judge that there is a change in the object's shade when there is none. This shows a bias in our visual recognition system toward positing stable, enduring objects rather than discrete images. To localize holistic alterations, the brain artificially constructs a likely ontology. As Campbell writes, "These features make our experienced image of the world more vividly real and complete, but do so by an artificial reconstruction of that world."[6] Knowledge needs to make yes/no decisions sometimes when sensation finds a fuzzy situation, and often those decisions achieve a higher level of recognition of objective conditions.

It is quite true, however, that adopting evolutionary epistemology requires abandoning a foundationalist approach to the theory of knowledge. The totality of human cognition can never be justified in a noncircular way; only some kinds of knowledge can be justified by other kinds. Quine himself made this point in his famous essay, "Epistemology Naturalized":

> I shall not be impressed by protests that I am using inductive generalizations . . . and thus reasoning in a circle. The reason . . . is that my position is a naturalistic one; I see philosophy not as a priori propaedeutic or groundwork for science, but as continuous with science. I see philosophy and science as in the same boat—a boat which, to revert to Neurath's figure as I so often do, we can rebuild only at sea while staying afloat in it. There is no external vantage point, no first philosophy.[7]

Naturalistic or evolutionary epistemology thus makes a limited claim: while nothing whatsoever can justify human cognitive capacities' representation of reality *per se* or as a whole, if those capacities evolved we have very good

126   THE EMERGENCE OF VALUE

reason to believe they are in general objectively true of the natural environment with which humans interact. But the general objection to naturalism in dealing with cognitive norms remains, "Isn't all this causal and descriptive, not normative?" Here Sellars's argument was crucial.

The Myth of the Given

Wilfrid Sellars's critique of the "myth of the given" played an outsized role in analytic philosophy. It informed the work of Hilary Putnam, John McDowell, and Richard Rorty, and through Rorty, continental and Americanist philosophers as well. Sellars delivered the famously complex lectures "The Myth of the Given: Three Lectures on Empiricism and the Philosophy of Mind" in London in 1956, later published as *Empiricism and the Philosophy of Mind* (Sellars 1997). His attack on the empiricism of the positivists denied, not that sensational content exists, but that it can *function epistemically*. Sellars argued that the normative "order of reasons" in which beliefs are adjudicated is discontinuous with the causal order of sensation or perception. The former cannot be grounded in the latter. My claim will be that Sellars was half wrong.

Sellars's scheme (see figure 7.1) distinguishes several stages or, given his reference to Hegel, "moments" of the process leading from sensation to belief.[8] At some point in the process of a human coming to know, there is, say, a physical object causally interacting with a sensorium. Call that stage A. This interaction generates a sensory content had by the sentient being, B. At stage C there results a *noninferential perceptual belief*, such as a recognition that "there is a red rose," which is a kind of sapience or "knowing," not merely sentience. This is the key moment. Then C leads to or funds D, all subsequence inferences, arguments, reasons, hence the rest of the web of human belief, e.g., everything I believe or know about the rose in front of me in relation to everything else.

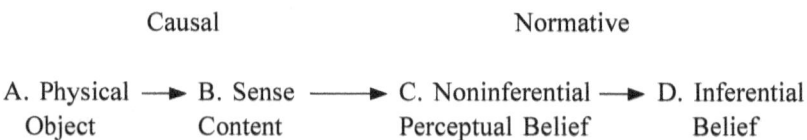

Figure 7.1. Sellars on sensation and belief. (Robert Brandom)

Sellars's point is that we cannot epistemically ground C in B, sapience on sentience, because they are different in kind: C is normative and linguistic, located in the space of reasons, whereas B is a causal result. As others have since put it, an object or event cannot justify belief, only an object or event "under a description." Sellars in fact claims that philosophers posit B in the attempt to ground C in a causal relation. That is the "myth of the given." He rightly noted that his argument resembles G. E. Moore's critique of the naturalistic fallacy: the normative cannot be derived from the causal or the natural, and no "intermediary" or third thing sharing the qualities of both can tie them together.

Now, Sellars was right that human belief cannot be reduced to sensory input, meaning, it cannot be recast as a summation of such inputs. Nor can linguistic beliefs, which express relations among universals ("the swan is white") be adequately derived from such inputs, unless the inputs are already described in epistemic terms. He was also right, as we shall see, that humans cannot discover and cite the un-interpreted data of their *own experience*. That is, the normative epistemic space is linguistic and human, and it cannot be reduced to or adequately derived from the causal-sensory. We are "trapped" in the linguistic, and can't "know" our sense data without the interference of language. (We might call this linguistic Kantianism.) But it is not the end of the story. For following Sellars's model, if perceptual belief C is linguistic, then nonhumans must *not* have it. Differently put, the human linguistified recognition of the fact or object in C must not be the product of, nor justified by, nor continuous with, human prelinguistic sense content B, and hence nonhuman nonlinguistic sense content B. Here is where Fido has his say—or bark.

But unless evolution is false, that cannot be right. There must be some continuity between nonhuman and human cognition, and hence between prelinguistic human sensation and linguistic human perceptual belief. The human B and the B of say, some other mammals at least, must overlap. It must be the case that nonlinguistic animals can perceive many of the same things or states of affairs as the linguistic animal, unsurprisingly since the latter evolved from the former and can interact with, even collaborate with, the former! Like playing Frisbee with Fido. The sensory, perceptual, and "alethic" (truth-relevant) levels must be in interaction, hence "confrontation" *in some sense must occur.*

Of course, where the line is between "sensation" and "perception," and to a lesser extent between perception and cognition or recognition, is debatable. For complex nonhumans, sensory/perceptual products must be integrated with memory, hence learning, leading to a cognition, or recognition of some relevant state of affairs, which, combined with feelings, emotions, or motivations, result in a behavior. One might try to segregate all valid or objective perceptual content to a higher level of the sensory-perception process, thereby denying it to nonlinguistic creatures. That would mean Fido never objectively cognizes the Frisbee or anything else.

But that is just what Burge's *Origins of Objectivity*, which we saw in chapter 5, denies: we cannot restrict nonhuman sensation-perception to a process that fails to identify objects and factual situations. Like humans, nonhumans perceive objectively, which is to say, veridically. In homely terms, a human playing Frisbee with a dog, whatever their cognitive, interpretive, and motivational differences, cannot be explained unless the human and dog cognize the Frisbee as an object having many (not all) of the same properties. Simply put: *if a human and a nonhuman can cognize and collaborate in handling the same object Sellars must be wrong about something*.

Let us reinterpret Sellars's diagram (see figure 7.2). Say A is an interaction of organism and environment in which objects (broadly understood, including states of affairs, events, conditions) causally affect the organism's sensory organs, and D is the world of human sociocultural inferences and arguments. In effect, A and D remains as in Sellars. But B and C are more complex than he allowed.

It is arguable that B has at least two subphases: B1 is the informational content of some object's causal effect on the sensory-neural apparatus of the animal. Something changes in the organism's sensorium and neural activity because of the object. Now, for animals with what Damasio called "core consciousness," B2 is the cognitive processing of that impact into an ongoing representation of the environment that includes the results of past learning. Unless no nonhumans perceive, *B2 must be "perception."* Fido must have it, and we must have it, or something very like it, as well. At some level of analysis of human cognition, a similar process with overlapping content

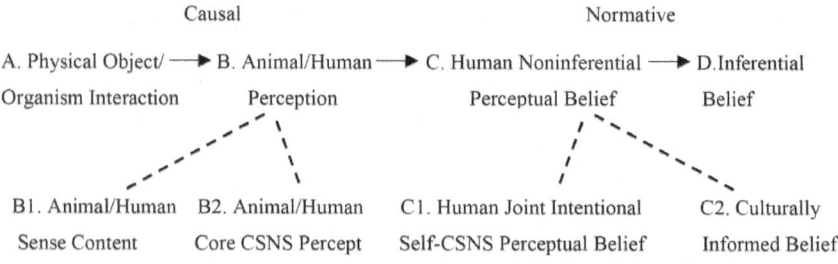

Figure 7.2. Sellars revised. (Author created)

must be occurring, however it is altered or recontextualized, or taken up by higher-order, uniquely human capacities. If my dog and I can perceive the same Frisbee, that must be true.

C for Sellars is human noninferential belief, and it is informed by language. We can agree. But that means it is also characterized by Tomasello's joint intentionality and Damasio's self-consciousness. Hence it is *social*. C1 is the joint-intentional, social, linguistic but noninferential cognition that would operate with any linguistic human being of normal endowment. That is, C1 would be the content of perceptual belief shared by any normally endowed and socialized human. To this we can add C2, the particular linguistic meaning of C1 in a particular social and linguistic context, but still noninferential, that is, the kind of "seeing as" and "seeing that" that may differ among socio-linguistic groups. Inferential cognition and the rest of social belief and cultural history then remain in D.

My point is that *C's normative character is emergent upon its social character*. And while C is inherently normative and B is causal, B must be part of the content of C, taken up, as it were, into C's functioning, like the contents of core consciousness are taken up into human self-consciousness. When the human plays Frisbee with the dog, the human's B sensory/perceptive content of the Frisbee must be similar in most salient ways to the dog's B sensory/perceptive content of the Frisbee, thereby providing cognition of the single object of their joint play. By all means, we can restrict "belief," "assertion," "normative," and "logical," maybe even "knowledge" or "knowing that," to the human linguistic moment, to C, but we *cannot* restrict veridical perception or objective cognition to that moment, unless nonhumans do neither.

So, is perception B "true" in human or nonhuman cases? Sellars was right that "true" properly applies only at the level of C. At the B level, "validity" can mean only *functioning properly* in responding to objective conditions by consistently presenting those conditions and particularly, its objects of interest. There is a teleonomic function that B may or may not fulfill, and that is normative but not linguistic. If it succeeds within tolerable limits, it is veridical or accurate, as Burge asserted. The question of whether and to what degree B is "conceptual" depends on the species and perhaps also on individual learning. We alone have linguistic means of expressing classes and properties and handling them. But the dog can clearly recognize the token (particular) as-of a type with its properties. The dog may never have a C because the dog doesn't have human joint intentional self-consciousness, and is never in the position of having to socially adjudicate the validity of one representation against another. That is, the dog's great sociality is still not the kind where he *argues with another dog about what is true*. Our noninferential perception, C1, when functioning properly, is "true" in the normative sense, true of its objects in representing those objects on the basis of, in part, sensory content. Our only way of reporting our perception is to say, "That is a Frisbee" or "*Das ist ein Frisbee*," which are enculturated statements, C2, that express, whatever else they express, the human cognition of C1.

At the same time, it makes no sense to deny, as antirealists like Rorty denied, that there are "intermediaries" between my true belief C and that of which it is true, A, or A's causal impact, B1. The problem is not that we can find no intermediaries or "third thing." *It is that there are too many!* The process by which sensation becomes cognition can be divided as many times as you like depending on the scale of examination, as any process can. When I eat an apple, the process of eating is "mediated" by my desires, hands, saliva, and enzymes, serially interacting with the apple's pulp, fructose, cells, and atoms. However many intermediaries there are, it is still the apple I eat. Likewise with perception. A finer-grained analysis does not throw the reality or validity of the process into question. Perception is *direct*, but not immediate or unanalyzable, because no process is. The "true," which is inherently social, emerges from the (animal) perceptual process as it takes place in the human case.

But Sellars was right about something else: we cannot *phenomenologically* discriminate B from C. My analysis of my own sensations, perceptions, and cognitions, cannot reach back to a point where there is only causal impact from an object, and no normative contribution from my social, linguistified self-consciousness. That is because self-consciousness is not core consciousness. My social self-consciousness, imbued with joint intentional norms, cannot phenomenologically describe the portion of my experiential process unstructured by it, any more than it can phenomenologically describe my liver. But we can study it scientifically and philosophically.

Lastly, there is a further characteristic of D that Sellars of course knew, but did not emphasize. The world of inferential beliefs among humans is cultural. And that means it is historical. This recognition is entirely compatible with realism, and is relevant to the advance of knowledge.

Putnam Evolving

Hilary Putnam, whose analysis of values we saw earlier, spent much of his life arguing about realism and pragmatism. His twists and turns are instructive, particularly in that his career is in one sense a long journey to a naturalistic realism. Putnam began, like Ernest Nagel, as a child of positivism and pragmatism both. The early Putnam was above all a realist about the explanatory objects of science versus phenomenalism. Partly under the influence of his work in model theory, he formed an "internalist" kind of realism, opposed to "metaphysical realism," or a "God's eye view" of reality. While our best possible account of the world might be false—a nod to realism—there is no one true account for which there is "fixed set of language-independent objects"—a nod to antirealism.[9] In this period he rejected naturalistic epistemology as incoherent (Putnam 1982). Later he would refer to this view as "pragmatic realism" or a "realism with a human face," reminiscent of William James's line, "the trail of the human serpent is thus over everything."

But in 1994, under the apparent influence of John McDowell and a rereading of J. L. Austin, Putnam switched to a direct perceptual or "natural" realism (Putnam 1994a). He came to believe that a mistaken representationalism, holding that percepts are of mental effects rather than their real-world objects, was at the core of the attack on realism. Perception was now the lynchpin for defending commonsense, scientific, and even moral realism. Putnam maintained this view for the last twenty years of his life, eventually calling it "liberal naturalism," a term borrowed from McDowell, which means a "nonrestrictive" naturalism as opposed to a naturalism that takes science to be the sole arbiter of truth.

A Jamesian example, on which Putnam wrote, is relevant here. In a 1907 letter complaining about the anti-realist misinterpretations of his famous book *Pragmatism: A New Name for Some Old Ways of Thinking*, he wrote:

> I am a natural realist. The world per se may be likened to a cast of beans on a table. By themselves they spell nothing. An onlooker may group them as he likes . . . so long as he takes account of them, his account is neither false nor irrelevant. If neither, why not call it true? It fits the beans-minus-him, and expresses the total facts of the beans-plus-him. . . . Whereupon we are accused of denying the beans, or denying being in any way constrained by them! It's too silly![10]

Now we must say first of all that James must be wrong. Neither the human nor Fido sees an undifferentiated set of identical objects. But he is right that their perceptions do not uniquely determine one and only one valid linguistic description or belief. If we can produce equivalent accounts that cohere with other knowledge and verify as widely, then these are all true as far as we can tell. This is exactly what Putnam had argued about models on the basis of the Lowenheim-Skolem theorem, that there is no one true description of anything or all things as a whole (Putnam 1980). Inquiry seeks and validates *a* true account, not the one and only true account, which he rejected as metaphysical realism. But in a late paper, Putnam softened, taking "metaphysical realism" as the claim that our most ideal theory might still be false, and hence truth is independent of warrant or verifiability. He could write in his final decade, "I am a liberal naturalist, but I am also a realist in my metaphysics and a realist with respect to the normative."[11]

While, as noted, Putnam had always rejected evolutionary or naturalized epistemology, at this point his view was directly affected by Burge's theory of the validity of nonhuman perception. He places his liberal naturalism on a biological basis, in the process noting Sellars again:

> I am not turning my back on "liberal naturalism" and opting for "scientific naturalism"; I am rather opting for a *liberal naturalist understanding of what natural-scientific explanations are* . . . There *is* a difference between linguistic reference, which presupposes complex cognitive capacities, and primitive perceptual representation, but the idea that organisms cannot discriminate objects prior to acquiring those cognitive and linguistic capacities is misguided. Linguistic reference grows out of perceptual representation, as Burge rightly argues, and if we can accept that, we need not be frightened into denying that truth of linguistic representations is a form of *accurate representation*. Moreover, if we see reference as growing out of perceptual transactions between organisms and things in their environments, we also won't be tempted to deny that reference *is* a relation between words and things, as Sellars at times did.[12]

An Ordinal Naturalist Conclusion

Now, how might ordinal naturalism shed light on these twists and turns? First, as to that canonical realist vs. antirealist question, "Could our best possible account of the world be false?" ordinal naturalism replies "Of course!" We could never know that there is only one complete and true account of anything. Assertions and their validity are objectively contextual, hence local, holding over some range of the functioning of their objects. As to the "our best possible account," that is an attempt to label the whole of all possible humanly accessible cognition. If we did know what it means (we do not), the best we could say would be, "as far as we can tell, we would have to accept that the best account we can ever come up with or understand, is mostly, probably true, as far as we can tell." Could it yet be false? Yes.

Second, how can we know that what we say is true is true independent of ourselves and our cognitive capacity in the broadest sense? We *cannot*. Evolutionary epistemology cannot justify human knowledge *per se* or as a whole—because nothing can. If we let A stand for the totality of human cognitive capacities, including perception, the question "Can we know that A accurately represents reality as it is independent of A?" cannot be answered, because such "knowing" would be part of A itself. But that does not undermine the perfectly reasonable questions, "*How* do we know what we know, *what* do we know when we know, and *which* knowing is more reliable?" Because humans alone have a variety of ways of knowing, evident in human culture and history, making them capable of improving knowledge over time. We are alone in this, at least on Earth. Humans are perfectly capable of learning "I know it looks like there is water on the horizon, but we have walked there and there is none. Something about looking at a dry place on a sunny day from far away misleads us. Don't trust it next time."

Objective relativism allows us to say more. For our judgment does capture something about the function of things with respect to us, and that "with respect to us" *belongs to the things* in question. The object functions in multiple contexts, with integrities in each, and among these contexts are the multiple modes of human cognition. The integrities of the object are "real," belong to it. Some of them continue to characterize the object in contexts that do not involve us. And humans have the remarkable ability to vary perspectives. We can know the relation of some of our knowledge to some its objects, and we are able to separate *some* of our contributions to the knowing from some of the object's contributions to the known, by multiplying perspectives, inquirers, contexts, and pragmatic tests to show which known features of the known are more invariant. That is, we seek more robust cognition. Our science and experience, and evolutionary epistemology, give us a very good reason for rejecting the idea that we are massively in error. We have lots of sources of evidence that our species is not utterly misperceiving the world. One of them is that Fido and I share a veridical recognition of the Frisbee and many of its properties.

Third, our normative notion of knowledge emerges from the uploading of animal capacities for veridical perception—a capacity that was edited by the world in evolution—into a joint intentional, linguistic, social self-consciousness, which formulates and can say beliefs and share them with others. This serves a new norm, and the norm matters: *truth*. Truth must have been crucial for any linguistic, collaborative human social group. A true assertion represents something with which the group must deal. When a member of the foraging party announced, "there is food over the next hill," it was offered or understood not as an act that modified the world, nor as an aesthetically compelling construction or personal expression, but as a claim meant to be true of its objects so as to guide group behavior. The opposite of a true assertion is either a lie or a mistake, with hallucinations or delusions being pragmatically equivalent to very bad mistakes. The truth of statements had to be socially adjudicated. Collaborative linguistic animals must be able to decide which descriptions of the world, or of social events, of personal history, are valid. No claim is made here that their validity is always solely a matter of truth, as opposed to being also socially or aesthetically normative. But sometimes it does matter whether the food is really over the next hill.

The layer of normative judging in the human sense is emergent, hence derivative from and a species of the causal and biological, but not reducible to it. Human cognitive, moral and aesthetic norms are intrinsically part of human social, joint intentional, linguistic self-consciousness, but emerge from animal perceptual-affective-cognitive core consciousness.

Now, what about Fido? Does he perceive the Frisbee? Clearly. Does he "know" it? We can say yes as long as we don't equate this with human knowing. Does Fido have "true beliefs" about the Frisbee? This can't work because we don't know what "belief" or assertive judgment and truth mean for a nonlinguistic creature. Can we say that human cognition of the Frisbee is or can be "more true" than that of the dog? That is stretching "true" out of shape in applying it to nonlinguistic Fido but also because *true is true* (as we will see later). The statement "2 + 2 = 4" and "baseball involves pitching" are both true, equally so, and it makes no sense to say one is more and the other less. Indeed, the things Fido "knows" about the Frisbee, he knows just as well as I do.

But I know more. I can know where the Frisbee was manufactured, and how the dog perceives it, and even that the dog can smell it but I cannot. Because I can (a) perceive and cognize not all, but important features of the phenomenon which Fido perceives and cognizes; and (b) often connected with instrumentally mediated perception, cognize what Fido does not and cannot, including lots about the past of the Frisbee and its possibilities; and (c) cognize the relation between Fido's cognition and my own. The reason I can know more is that I am always simultaneously viewing from perspectives beside that of my own organism, and collaboratively testing them with language. Human knowledge is social, linguistic, and cultural, therefore historical. As a view called "critical rationalism" has argued, the superior account or theory is the one that (a) explains everything that its predecessor explained as well or better; (b) explains what the earlier view could not; and (c) explains why the predecessor could not (Popper 1963; Bartley 1984; Radnitzky and Bartley 1993).

None of this is a definition or analysis of truth (that must await chapter 11). It is a modern conception of how human knowing and inquiry advance. Inquiry is a very important, but not the only, means of acquiring and improving knowledge. The realist view of truth and of human knowledge holds as long as one accepts fallibilism, objective relativism, and the emergence of human cognition from animal cognition, to which it is not thereby reducible. But given emergence, naturalism can deny that such norms are thereby reducible to those processes. The normative system piggybacks on and must have evolved from the causal system, and yielded downward causal benefits that were naturally selected. Fido and I are pretty smart social mammals, and without my inner social mammal I could not exist. But having eaten of the fruit of the tree of knowledge, I have some special abilities and problems. None of which makes me a better friend than he.

Chapter Eight

Values in Judgments

> Language is not merely rooted in ritual; it is a ritual. . . . Most uses of speech are closer in principle to the raising of one's hat in greeting than to the mailing of an informative report.
>
> —Ernest Gellner, *Plough, Sword, and Book*[1]

Before proceeding, we need to put value judgments and judgments of fact in a common context, where we can evaluate their respective meaning, their rationality, and their cognitive significance. That is, we need to consider them as two versions of something. That something is, naturally, *judgment*. This doesn't mean equating fact and value judgments, any more than understanding baseball and football as sports means that you can hit a home run with a football. They remain fundamentally different, but different within a context both inhabit.

This is important for several reasons. First, while we often think of fact judgments as linguistic, value judgments are often not linguistic at all—they are usually acts. Going to a political demonstration, embracing a loved one, and driving to work are value judgments. Second, some philosophers in recent decades have tried to interpret propositions, truth claims, as acts or constructions to be evaluated politically or aesthetically. To critically analyze such work in terms the authors must accept, we have to evaluate their work under a broader category than truth claims because they refuse to stand before that bar. Last, as we will see in the next chapter, the modern age has crucially altered the relation among our various kinds of value judgments. We can discuss none of this without a theory of the different functions of human judgment.

It so happens that this is another novel feature of ordinal naturalism, coming from a little-known theory of human production from the American philosophical tradition. It was created by Justus Buchler, one of the Columbia Naturalists. Buchler provided a way to regard truth-functional statements, actions, and arrangements, or in effect, science, ethics and politics, and art, as equally cognitive, meaningful, potentially rational and valid, while nevertheless qualitatively distinct. All are modes of judgment. When we act or make things, when we run for a bus or choose what to make for dinner or arrange furniture or decide how to help a sad friend, we are judging, and that judging can involve knowledge, rationality, signs, and method, as much as any informational report or treatise. The point is that we must cease to regard saying, asserting, describing, claiming, and propositions as the archetype of human rationality, meaning, or validity. Meaning, rationality, and validity apply just as much to action and construction as they do to science or philosophy. Because all are judgments.

For G. E. Moore and consequently much of twentieth-century analytic philosophy, "judgment" was simply the act of believing or uttering a proposition, which expresses some state of affairs. But that usage is somewhat anomalous in our philosophical tradition.

The concept of judgment is old. Often it refers to something done by a person with a special adjudicative role, a judge in a law court or an authority deciding a dispute among citizens. In philosophy it has had a variety of meanings. In ancient Greek, *krisis* meant to distinguish, discriminate, or decide among options. For Aristotle, it referred to a determination made by an agent on a matter that is not merely "given" in experience, but requires inference and/or comparison. Kant's use of *Urteilskraft* (power of judgment) excluded both theoretical reason regarding facts and practical reason regarding morality: whereas moral or practical reason makes rules, and understanding imposes rules on events, judgment for Kant is required to find the appropriate rule for the case. Generally "judgment" (*krisis, iudicium, jugement, Beurteilung*) was used for a cognitive act of discrimination as opposed to either the passive reception of causal information or a deductive inference that applies a given rule mechanically. Hard cases "require fine judgment," or show "good judgment." We will broaden this notion of judgment in a way continuous with its historical uses.

As noted earlier, with complex animals it is useful to distinguish among all the things that happen with an organism, those *undergone* from those *done*. I undergo a blow to the stomach; I do not "do" it. Neither do I "do" my heartbeat: it is something that my organism does, even when I am asleep. As Alicia Juarrero asks, what is the difference between a wink and a blink? A wink is something I do; a blink is not (1999). To be sure, doing and undergoing are commonly intertwined in a circuit, as Dewey saw (1896). Animals are almost never not acting or maintaining a place and posture, and almost never not experiencing. Every doing or "active" phase of the circuit sets up an undergoing or "receptive" phase, and vice versa. I don't see anything unless I turn toward it. Nevertheless, once I turn my head and open my eyes I undergo, and cannot forgo, the sight. And scale is involved here. "Walking to the store" is my doing, which cannot occur without my muscular leg and arm movements, neurological events, and so on. But a description of the latter is not the description of a human doing or act. No deep theory of the distinction is needed here. We can just say that that our experience of the world, and ourselves, has phases of both undergoing and doing, and they are not identical. In what follows, whatever we do, as opposed to undergo, involves judgment.

A Tripartite Theory of Judgment

Pragmatism certainly had something to do with doing, since it located cognition, assertions, and meanings in the context of purposeful human activity. As a Columbia Naturalist, and scholar of Peirce, Buchler inherited that approach, but then deviated from the pragmatists. He wrote, "The pragmatists, emphasizing the active character of belief, neglect the judicative character of action, and even more, the judicative character of contrivance."[2] While it was a genuine advance to recognize that judgment, understood as something cognitive and potentially rational, could be seen in the context of action, a further step would be to recognize that action *in itself* is judicative, just as propositional statements are. Grabbing a life preserver when drowning is as much a cognitive and rational doing as saying "That's a life preserver. I should grab it." Arranging furniture in a room to be more appealing is also judicative, endorses a policy, and can be more or less valid, albeit not in terms of "truth."

Buchler distinguished three kinds of judgment: actions or "active judgments," makings or "exhibitive judgments," and sayings or "assertive judgments." More simply: acting, making, and saying. The tripartite categorization was not new. Buchler was recontextualizing Aristotle's three types of wisdom, theoretical, practical, and productive, and perhaps Kant's three applications of reason, theoretical, practical, and aesthetic. For Buchler, each kind of judgment is "an appraisal" and makes a promise of validity that hopes to be useful for future judgment.[3] Each is a product of selection, embodies a policy, and enacts a perspective. The philosophical significance of Buchler's claim is that all three kinds of judgment are equally and indifferently capable of being characterized by *meaning, communication, cognition, evaluation, validity, method*, and *rationality*, albeit in distinctive ways. That list is explicit. That is the basic point, the parity of the three modes of judgment with respect to processes that philosophers often restrict to assertions. This means the communicative, cognitive, and rational character of an act or an exhibition need not be understood in terms of or translated into assertions.

But the three kinds of judgment remain fundamentally different. Assertive judgment is normed by *truth*; action by *rightness or success*; exhibitive arrangements by *aesthetic compulsion* (beauty, sublimity, etc.). Each of the three can be methodically elaborated, in what Buchler called "query," the exploratory, cohesive ramification of a judgment by a series of judgments. Fixing a door and composing a poem are forms of rational, methodic query, as are conducting an experiment or a debate. Assertive query is *inquiry*; active query, for Buchler, is *morality*; exhibitive query is *art*. Nothing about this scheme implies propositions, assertions, inquiry, or truth are indistinguishable from actions or constructions. It is also true that our judgment and query can cross these lines, and often does: we find a conclusion in inquiry "elegant" or "useful." We will discuss this later. But the three modes are nevertheless distinct. Buchler remarks, "we may formulate in the briefest terms a distinction which is of the utmost importance. None of the modes is translatable *into* any other. Any of the modes is translatable *by* any other. . . . if 'translation' means 'achieving an interchangeable equivalent' [it] is not possible. If . . . [it] means 'articulating in another order of utterance,' mutual translation is possible. The modes . . . though not reducible, are relatable . . ." (my emphases).[4]

While only some of our judgments are linguistic, J. L. Austin's distinction of speech acts is useful here.[5] In saying "Shut the door," we are simultaneously performing a *locutionary* act, namely *producing* the sounds and words "shut the door"; an *illocutionary* act or mood, in this case *commanding*; and lastly, a *perlocutionary* act or what is meant to be accomplished by the illocutionary act, in this case, *getting the door shut*. This helps to clarify Buchler, as long as we stop using "act" for all modes. Buchler's modes of judgments are kinds of *functions*; what determines a judgment as one type or another is how it functions in a context. If the perlocutionary act is what is relevant in the context, we are dealing with the active functioning of judgment and not its assertive function; a picture or hand gesture may function as an assertion, rather than as an exhibition or act. And one judgment might function differently in different contexts. A diagram in a technical manual is a picture that functions to say or assert. But placing it on the cover of a book employs it as a work of art. Saying "I do" in a wedding serves as an act, writing it in a poem or play serves as an aesthetic exhibition. Judgments always actualize or enact a perspective, a selective ordering of traits of some set of complexes. Hence they also characterize or disclose the judge, as well as what is judged, while only the latter is usually the function.

Judgment and Language

Because we must wean ourselves of the habit of regarding judgments as all linguistic, some clarification is in order. All judgments mean, but assertions and exhibitions are intrinsically communicative and significative, that is, function as signs. *Actions do not need to.* Of course, as noted, we can interpret any judgment by considering it in alternate contexts, contexts other than that of its production. So your action, when an historian describes it or a psychiatrist interprets it, can be taken as a sign of your era in history or your psychic pathology. But the point of the act in question, the function of the judgment, was probably not communicative. Assertions communicate, represent, and signify in one way, exhibitions communicate, represent, and signify in another.

There is representation in nature prior to the arising of human language. Animal perception and cognition represent, as we have seen. We can speak of representation at the point at which a minded organism with dedicated sensory organs and motivation is capable of neurologically constructing an image or feeling which constitutes part of its experience. But communicative signs, as I have argued, represent in the sense of saying or showing. To the extent that something functions as a sign, it functions as a saying or assertive judgment, which *says* its meaning (where we are concerned normally with its logical interpretant), or as an exhibitive making that *shows* its meaning (as to what that interpretant entails, we will leave to a later chapter). Of course there are other and muddier cases.

Language can occur in any function of judgment. We can "act" with words, as Austin noted. The most common categorization of the illocutionary force of speech acts comes from John Searle (1970) He lists five categories: *assertives*, which commit the speaker to belief in the truth or falsity of a proposition; *directives*, which try to get other agents to commit to an attitude, like suggestions, requests, and prescriptives or commands; *commissives*, which commit the speaker to some act, like promises; *declaratives*, in which the speech act accomplishes some modification of the world, like saying "I resign" or "I pronounce you husband and wife" (these were Austin's original performatives); and last, *expressives*, which show the speaker's attitude, such as congratulations, excuses, apologies. I would add one more category Searle does not consider, *constructives*, in which what is said or written makes something with exhibitive properties, like speaking a poem or making a joke. These are not the same as his expressives or declaratives because they are not aimed as revealing the speaker's own attitude nor accomplishing an act.

Searle's "assertives" are assertive judgments in Buchler's sense, and what I just called constructives are exhibitive makings. The rest—commissives, directives, declaratives, expressives—are all related to active judgment, each in different ways. Declaratives are literally acts which modify the world—"I do" in a wedding ceremony *gets* me married. Commissives are promissory acts, redeemable for the action. Directives are in a sense acts themselves, but serve to guide or cause or prevent some other act. Expressives, we should note are not autobiographical assertions, for example, "I feel sad," but statements that show, rather than say, an attitude, but not aesthetically. Certainly all these can overlap in the sense that what matters is ultimately the usage in context, so we will always have border crossings. We may remember the most famous American philosophy joke of the twentieth century (personally witnessed by Joseph Margolis). In response to Austin's claim during a lecture that in English a double negative can mean a positive—"It's not true that I'm not sick" means I am sick—but a double positive cannot mean a negation. The New York philosopher Sidney Morgenbesser from the audience: "Yeah, *yeah*."

Kinds of Judgmental Validity

To judge is always to attempt to judge rightly, validly, well, or successfully, as future judgments by self or others will confirm. The motivation toward "valid continuance," as Buchler put it, is inherent in judging, which is to say, doing. All modes of judgment are capable of methodic, exploratory rendition, meaning lengthy projects constituted by a series of such judgments: the making of an elaborate cave painting or totem pole, the composing of a narrative, the description of many discoveries on a hunting trip, a communal dance, the building of a dwelling, the negotiation of a dispute, the skinning and butchering of a large animal.

In the complex action sequences of human social life, I and others are engaged in query, in a series of coordinated, exploratory judgments. If the function of the whole series is to modify the world, to make conditions different from what they otherwise would be (if I/we did not act), they are active, and normed by right/wrong, successful/unsuccessful, etc. The series could be all acts, but assertions might well be a part of this purposefully active query. Or we may have nothing but a discussion aimed at truth, an inquiry proper, in preparation for an action. Even here many other verbal statements that are not descriptive or assertive can play a role. And our exhibitive dance may require reminding another with assertions how it is to be done. My point is: a query whose overall aim is exhibitive, or active, or assertive, may be populated by judgments solely of that type (all exhibitive, all active, all assertive), or may include the other types of judgments within its process.

There is a norm that applies to all three types of query, and to judgments in general. When organized properly, so as to be capable of leading to a valid conclusion—capable, not actually—a query is *rational*. "Rationality" refers to a character of the organization of steps or parts, which are themselves judgments made in some series, such that they aim at a valid conclusion. Rationality is typically *successful method*, best practice in ordering judgments. One could say for simplicity's sake that all query, all methodic judgment is normed at least by *consistency*. No train of judgments working toward an end can afford mere, pointless, unproductive inconsistency. The novel, the inventive, the unusual can be valid and validated, but no query is valid in which one builds and burns down a hut, repeatedly draws and erases a picture, asserts then denies and asserts again the same claim. Rationality is first of all coherence, which in this case, means coherence of meaning. Rationality is usually a necessary, but not a sufficient norm for validity. While the three forms of judgment have this in common, their kinds of coherence are different, as we will see.

Assertive judgment seeks to be true. It is some linguistic or sign behavior that is constative or descriptive. Assertions are truth functional, which means their meaning is, as R. M. Hare suggested, determined by a combination of syntax plus truth conditions (1952). The meaning of its judgments as assertions can be exhausted by propositions. They typically are, but do not have to be, linguistic; deictic gestures like pointing or holding up an object can function to assert. Their most basic norm is true/false, but nothing about the present theory requires restriction to a two-valued logic; there can be degrees of probable truth or falsity. Validity in assertive judgment must be true, and truth is to say of what is that it is, and what is not that it is not (as we will see later). Judgments of truth *per se*, *qua* assertions, are nonpractical or nonproductive and non-exhibitive in the sense that they do not directly alter the conditions of experience nor are they valued in their presentation as such. They are *cumulative*, as the next truth claim takes place on the basis of or in the altered context of the earlier truth claim. The rationality of inquiry is the coordination of assertive judgments. A rational inquiry, whatever exhibitive or active components are included, is a series of mostly assertive judgments that serve to assert or declare or come to a conclusion. Its rationality is normed *by logic*.

There are, as Putnam pointed out, other norms used in inquiry, like reasonableness, usefulness, reliability, simplicity, and even elegance. Again, we combine the modes of judgment, often with one mode as the "leading edge" or primary function, with others in a supporting role. The current view is not that such combinations are illegitimate, but that they are combinations of different judgmental functions. And that may have effects.

Action is in a sense, as Buchler points out, the most difficult of the three modes to characterize. As noted, judging is something we do; all judgements are doings. "Action" and "active" must be saved for one of the three modes *of* judgment. Actions actualize something, and in doing so modify the world directly in the sense that they alter the worldly conditions to which they are addressed from what they would have been otherwise. This holds even for a decision *not* to speak or move in a circumstance where doing so makes a difference. The rationality of actions is the fittingness of steps to a goal, even if that goal is mere repetition of a state. Components of an act, or a series of acts, bear a linear relation very like temporal moments, because actions are temporal. They are evanescent, as Hanna Arendt noted, meaning need not by themselves make anything lasting, and are specific to the context of their occurrence—although of course they may have effects that persist.[6] When I am done cleaning the room, my cleaning is finished, only the effect remains, whereas when I finish a painting, the act is done but the painting remains, and is not merely an "effect" of my making. But the effects of acts are cumulative; each changes the playing field for the next, at least in the short run (the dishes have to be washed again tomorrow). Consequences, at least within the purview to which the act is addressed, matter to acts. Anticipating deontological theories of morality, one might worry that this rules out acts done for duty's sake. But surely the obligatory act is *an act*, a direct difference-maker in its occurrence in any social situation. "She did it" remains different from "she said it" or "she showed it."

Actions for humans are judgments, and hence involve reasons and purposes. We do not need to explore the complex analysis of agency here. But we can say that actions are not mere movements. As noted, a "blink" is not an action, but a wink may be (Juarrero 1999). Philosophers wonder, when one flicks a light switch which startles a prowler, which is "the act," flicking a finger, turning on a light, startling a prowler, or are they all one act? (Davidson 1963). For our emergent naturalism, just as for Austin's theory of speech acts, there are simultaneous levels of description, for example, the physiological motion (finger movement), the molar purposive achievement (turning the light on), and a host of possible consequences for a variety of agents and contexts (e.g., startling prowlers). Intentionally pulling the trigger while pointing the gun at Steve *is attempting to shoot* Steve, at the level of human agency, with its purposes and acts: as a social action which humans can decide to do or not, it lies between the level of physiology where it is merely moving a finger, and its place as one among innumerable social phenomena yielding a statistical result. A socially recognizable human act is an emergent phenomenon not reducible to the bodily movements of the agent. As a manifestation of the judgment of a joint intentional agent, it is a process of modification of the world that has meaning for human social agency.

In terms of norms, it is basically true that "moral" norms are primarily norms of social action, or more precisely, social interaction, as we will see. But certainly not of all. Success and fealty to convention are the most common norms, whether moral or not. We will return to these distinctions later. But for the moment we can say that while "good" is so vague as to be applicable to any form of validity (truth and beauty being "good" too), in the case of action the most generically applicable norms are "right" and "successful." Active judgments, like all other judgments, are normed by a particular kind of good, which in the case of action we can call "right" or "rightness," but this comes in two kinds: success, or successful rightness, and moral rightness. We will be interested in moral rightness later, but we have to remember that the two can overlap.

Regarding exhibitive judgment we must make some clarifications. Many things, many experiences, many doings exhibit or show qualities. Aesthetic experience can be described as an experience of aesthetic qualities, or manifesting aesthetic qualities. (We will return to this in chapter 14.) But making need not be exhibitive at all. Many actions are constituted by making something where the only concern is with determining some effect, as when I configure straps to hold up a piece of wood, or make a sandwich. But the made artifact is only "art" or "exhibitive" in function to the extent that it was made to be experienced as such. Thus the third mode of judgment is the meeting of making and exhibiting: *exhibitive making*. So while Buchler uses "making" and "exhibiting" more or less interchangeably, he means that something is both: a *made exhibition*. His most complete depiction of this form of judgment, in his theory of poetry, is that it rearranges materials into a constellation that is "assimilated as such."[7] The constellation or arrangement of elements, the structured piece, we might say, has some quality that is crucial and is perceived, or assimilated in the perceiving.

Such makings do not have one norm, but rather one *kind* of norm. In terms of its validity or value as a work, exhibitive making may produce something remarkable, beautiful, striking, harmonious, sublime, pleasing, interesting, displeasing, disgusting, frightening, soothing, disturbing, exciting, and so on. We may say in general that their exhibition is supposed to be *compelling as such*. It is little harm to use one kind of positive compulsion, like beauty, as an exemplar and stand-in for the other aesthetic values. And unlike both assertive and active judgment, the product of exhibitive making is *not* cumulative. The value of the work is not its place in a series. One may object that there is such a thing as the history of art, and the historical development of artist and audience! But no one told Shakespeare, "Wait, you already wrote a play about princes!" or tells Picasso, "This painting does not follow from your last painting!" Artworks start at zero, are framed to be experienced as a particular, like sporting events.

Whereas active judgments modify the states of affairs *being* judged, resulting in a new situation that must be responded to by future judgment, exhibitive making introduces something for the sake of being experienced which may or may not be experienced. When I mow the lawn, as an action, the lawn is no longer the same and it will play a modified role in the experience of anyone who happens to walk on or see it. When I paint a painting of a mowed lawn, no one who walks by need pay any attention; their feet don't undergo a different state of affairs. The viewer, or audience, must give themselves over to the commentary on lawns that I have created; this may then alter their experience of other lawns. The rationality or consistency of an aesthetic product is the fittingness of a part to a whole, the coherence of some element with the art work as such. A rational exhibitive query is a series of coherent exhibitive judgments that lead to an arrangement of materials that achieve an exhibitive character.

Naturalizing the Modes of Judgment

From a naturalistic or evolutionary point of view, the modes of judgment are not equal. They cannot be. Acting is more fundamental and was historically prior. This is not Buchler's view, indeed, he tried to avoid it because it would tie him to pragmatism, which he thought limited. From a naturalist perspective, however it is a virtue of pragmatism that it has always seen human cognition in the light of biology, and hence in an animal context. We have seen that action is an animal, ethological category. The things that act are animals.

I do not mean nonhuman acts are just like ours, that they judge actively in the same way we do. *Homo sapiens'* action—and perhaps some other hominins—is certainly different from nonhuman action. Nor am I claiming that action is the "least human" mode of judgment. But action is that mode of judgment that is most continuous with nonhuman judgment. Vertebrates, and some invertebrates, are foragers. They must perceive their environment, evaluate directions of movement, positive or negative, seek food, avoid predators, find mates. There is a moment of indecisiveness, then a major sustained effort: attack, retreat, mating, and so on. There is attention, tension, selection, muscular movement. At the very least, we must say the most intelligent, learning-capable, behaviorally flexible nonhumans (e.g., cetaceans, great apes, etc.) adopt a policy, select an alternative, and thereby modify the world or what would otherwise be by moving in such a way that is an "act" at some level of description.

But nonhumans *neither assert nor exhibitively make*. One might claim there is evidence of "saying" and "exhibitive making" in nonhuman species, but the cases are controversial, limited, and very different from their human versions as we have seen. Certainly the nonhuman world is full of communication, verbal and nonverbal, but as we saw, not human language. And even the most sophisticated of nonhumans, in the wild at least, never use their social communicative apparatus for assertion, to declare or constate, as opposed to call, warn, command, express, intimidate, etc. As for exhibitive arrangement, there is no evidence of artifactual culture outside human society. Many species, even invertebrates, "make" nests, anthills, dams, etc. Birds sport beautiful plumage. A few sophisticates, some birds and primates, use tools. But none decorates, makes cave paintings, or builds what functions to "show." As already noted, some claim nonhumans pass distinctive social learning across generations. But, as I have argued, culture is making things that mean.

If so, then the evolutionary use of the tripartite account of judgment allows us an interesting insight: human being has created two wholly additional functions of judgment, assertion and exhibitive making. To put it in evolutionary terms, at some point hominins ate, slept, learned, worked, foraged, hunted, mated, fought, courted, communicated, nurtured children, even made simple tools. All these were actions, some very sophisticated. Nonhumans also did all these things, if differently. But then at some point saying or asserting was invented, for example, deictic pointing and showing, maybe drawing diagrams with a stick. Eventually as manual and verbal language became sufficiently complex, they also reported, agreed, disagreed, discussed. The advantages for collaborative foraging must have been enormous: we are talking about the most remarkable device on Earth for the discovery of what is true, *social, communicative, linguistic inquiry.* Then, perhaps a mere seventy thousand years ago, we invented *exhibitive making*. We danced and sang, decorated our bodies and possessions, dyed our clothing, arranged our hair, buried our dead, painted cave walls, arranged hogans to conform to sacred directions. Action feeds, fights, mates, preserves life, and more, but it was supplemented and organized by assertions and by exhibitive arrangements.

For ordinal naturalism, or for any adequate contemporary naturalism, active judgment is biologically, anthropologically prior, both temporally and in terms of necessity or survival. Not metaphysically or logically prior; assertion and exhibition are just as real, as valid, make just as much sense. But they cannot occur without a living animal, and without active judgment the animal ceases to live.

Judgments of Facts and Values

Now to the main point: *all three kinds of judgment are cognitive, evaluative,* and *disclosive*. By "cognitive," I mean only that they are dependent upon, and manifest, information about the object of the judgment and its context. By "evaluative," I mean they manifest an appraisal. By "disclosive," I mean they are expressive of the state of the judge, the agent. This does not mean, however, that each of these properties are equally the aim or function of the judgment—if that were true there would be only one mode of judgment. The primary or illocutionary functions remains distinct; the judgment has a leading edge or function. The "fact-value" problem is not hereby solved, but repositioned.

In what sense is an assertive judgment evaluative or disclosive? First it is an evaluation of possible assertions, of potential claims about what is objectively true, and true in a sense available to the social we. It selects, affirms, and makes a claim in a context that is relevant. It is implicitly a claim that what is affirmed in the assertion is dispositive for the relevant contexts of experience and judgment. Truth is very valuable; we do call *true* and *false* truth values for a reason. Second, it is both a disclosure of the perspective of the agent making the judgment, and again, implicitly certifies that perspective as valid, as useful, and usually, objective. Its evaluative and disclosive secondary functions were central to the analysis of Jürgen Habermas, as we will see (Habermas 1985).

Active judgment, the modification of the conditions of judgment from what they would otherwise be, is clearly appraisive and disclosive. That an act is needed or called for or valid is itself an evaluation on the part of the agent. It appraises its objects and situation. It discloses the agent in multiple ways: the actor's motivations and interests, her evaluation or appraisal, and her cognitive state or the character of her recognition of conditions. But it is also clearly cognitive. The action is a deployment of knowledge or know-how, regarding what ought to be done and how it is to be done. Especially among social humans, it is almost always the deployment of learning. This is why, as the pragmatists and philosophers of language in the last fifty years have pointed out, behavior or action is a crucial means for testing interpretations of the meanings of an agent's utterances.

Exhibitive making is primarily an exhibition of the properties of the object, and secondarily, but always, a disclosure of the attitude of the agent. As we will see, the exhibitive judgment has to be recognized as the intention of the maker in order to be regarded as "made" at all (this does not mean endorsing a particular aesthetic theory, as we will see). And it is created to be so regarded, as the assertive judgment is made to be understood by others. But it also deploys not only know-how but a perspectival appreciation of its object, and serves to impact the understanding of its audience. This does not presume the artwork is "mimetic" or representational; some artworks are, some not. But it presents itself as an occasion for interpretation that potentially will affect cognition.

The functions of assertive, active, and exhibitive judgments all involve appraisal and disclosure as well as cognition, but do so in different ways and to differing degrees. While the illocutionary functions of assertion, action, and exhibitive making remain qualitatively distinct, we will now be able to relate and compare the three *as judgments*, all being both cognitive and evaluative, all having meaning, seeking validity, and capable of being rational. The "fact-value" problem is thus no longer a dichotomy of cognitive-descriptive-rational judgments versus noncognitive-evaluative-irrational judgments.

Omnivalence

But we have one last concept left to complete this account of judgment. We already know that the three modes of judgment are commonly interwoven and contribute to each other, and to the ongoing judgment and query that are parts of the life of the human individual. But further, it is possible simply to fail to distinguish the modes of judgment, or to choose not to distinguish them. By "omnivalence," I mean the condition in which the modes of judgment are *not* distinguished by the agents who combine them. That means their validity is undifferentiated as to whether they are true or assertive, right or successful, or aesthetically valuable. I am merely giving a name to something entirely familiar to us. For the highest values and concepts of human cultures, like the divine, are often omnivalent in just this way. The sacred is often the unification of the true, the good, and the beautiful.

Sometimes this is blatant and explicit. Here the norms of the different functions of judgment and query are merged; that is, when the true is not distinguished from the right or the aesthetically compelling. The fullest omnivalence would regard what is "true" and what is "good" or "right" or "successful" and what is "beautiful" or "sublime" or aesthetically compelling as *equivalent*, in effect, as "valid" without further distinction. An example would be John Keats's line "Beauty is Truth—Truth Beauty." More commonly, we may find that while a judgment or query is claimed to be devoted uniquely to one or another of the three norms, occasional use of the other norms is made, sometime surreptitiously, sometimes explicitly, to validate it. Indeed, much of what we call "reasonableness" in everyday life is the balancing of a number of different norms in one query. When a group must make a decision about a public works project, they balance practical success with aesthetic concerns and moral-traditional norms. Also, while a series of judgments have one dominant function and norm—for example, assertion and truth—other functions of judgment and their norms will be imported to bolster a conclusion, validate a result—for example, when aesthetic elegance or practical usefulness occur as reasons for accepting the truth of an argument or conclusion. Omnivalence is a matter of degree.

In that sense, one could say that human life, judgment, and culture are fundamentally omnivalent. The restriction of a human activity solely to one or another of the three modes of judgment and norms of validity is probably the exception rather than the rule. Humans judge in all three ways, life cannot be lived solely through inquiry into truth or practical-moral success or aesthetic construction, and culture likewise is composed of science or assertive knowledge, social and moral practices, and aesthetic making. Except for a small number of persons and occupations, we cannot say that any one of the norms "truth," or "the good," or "the beautiful" is the sole aim of anyone's life or any culture.

But human social institutions and activities are often defined by their segregation and restriction to one or another mode. Indeed, we will see that it is one of the unique characteristics of modernity to enforce the differentiation of the three modes of judgment thereby to enable unprecedented progress in each. This creates an entirely new historical situation for the adjudication of values. And to that recent and monumental story we must now turn.

Chapter Nine

What Modernity Did to Values

> Rationalization has thus far been successful because it has not been completely successful.
>
> —Edward Shils, *Tradition*[1]

When we ask today about the rational basis of human values, of morality, aesthetics, politics, and truth, we are presuming something. *We are modern.* We live in a very unusual time of human existence, which colors how we pursue such issues. What the question of values means today is different from what it meant for thousands of years. Some of those differences make the question clearer, others make it more obscure.

    Of course modernity did not change everything. As of now we still live not much more than three score and ten years, if we are fortunate; breathe, drink, and eat; rub two bodies together to procreate; are born of woman; raise our children; cope with natural and social necessity; work; create; and die. The desire for "meaning," in the sense of purpose, was always present. But society, culture, art, economy, inquiry, and politics have changed in such a way that forces us to recognize the form and manner in which we pursue answers is not like the form of earlier times. Without broaching the endless controversies in understanding modern society, we can at least say it has something to do with market economies, science, industrial production, novel technologies, liberal republicanism, rational organization of collaborative activities, a shift in the role of religion in society, and mass communication. We can imaginatively debate Aquinas and Confucius and Aristotle on important questions of value, and we should. But they had no idea of the kind of society in which we would apply their conclusions. This does not mean they were wrong or are irrelevant, but it does mean we cannot judge how right or wrong they were without judging the relation of their societies to ours. And our modern theories of value, if they presume a modern society, may be in principle inapplicable to other kinds of societies or the past. So we need some historical perspective before, in the next part of this book, we give our hypotheses of specific human norms.

The Stages of Human Culture

A historical, and pre-historical, picture can be offered based on the scheme of anthropologist and philosopher Ernest Gellner. It is not unique to him, but he presents it in a particularly useful way (Gellner 1990). Gellner divides the human sojourn into three eras: the hunter-gatherer, the agro-literate, and the modern industrial. Or we can say, *foraging, cultivating,* and *fabricating*. One can hardly quibble with this categorization, even if there are exceptions. Pastoral herding societies, which in the middle ages dominated Asia, have some characteristics of the hunter-gatherer society yet are capable of achieving wealth and territory, making them competitors to, and potential conquerors of, agrarian communities. Culturally, however, they tended to become absorbed by the farmers they conquered. Then there have long been coastal trading cities, which had the opportunity for certain commercial aspects of modernity before all others if they were self-ruling. There were also marauding cultures who exploited their military prowess to periodically raid other societies without conquest and thus supplement their hunting and/or pastoral economies. But it remains the case that most human beings have lived in one of the three main circumstances Gellner cited: our "original" condition, foraging for sustenance, including hunting; getting food from planted land and domesticated animals, invented about ten thousand years ago; and systematically making things that continually increase productivity, which is less than three centuries old.

We can use Gellner's distinctions to understand culture and even reason itself. Following our account of human judgment and query, in all eras of human history and prehistory humans have been characterized by rational query. But in that process, human societies are commonly in the position of having to decide among competing judgments. They must adjudicate. Reason is the characteristic of query by which humans investigate and adjudicate other judgments, whether those judgments are active, exhibitive, or assertive. When we adjudicate methodically or systematically, according to rule-governed practices we develop, that is "reasoning." Reason is in effect *methodical meta-judgment*. This is actually relevant to the "rationality debate" of the 1950s, to which Gellner, Hare, and MacIntyre all contributed, where anthropologists and philosophers disagreed over how to interpret the "primitive mentality." Some argued that the most ancient societies exhibit a lack of rationality, saying irrational, contradictory things (e.g., magic); others claimed that "rationality" is just a name for the adequate deployment of a language, so all cultures are equally rational. But it is also possible to say that while all indeed are rational in the sense of needing consistency in judgment and engaging in methodical meta-judgment, the procedures of adjudicating judgments have evolved. What we call reason is part of a cultural transmission of knowledge acquisition and modification. I have argued that reason is emergent from culture (Cahoone 2006). That is part of what follows.

Foragers

For the great majority of their existence *Homo sapiens* lived in small, mobile bands of twenty-five to fifty members earning a living by finding stuff, foraging. They made stone tools and culture, but they survived by hunting and gathering. The bands were usually linguistically and culturally related to a network of similar bands in a region, constituting a "tribe" of several hundred, which was crucial for exchanging potential marriage partners, to avoid excessive inbreeding. But all existed at extremely low density. Hunter-gatherers were one form of "segmentary" societies. This term, invented by Durkheim, refers to organization of society through similar unilineal (usually patrilineal) descent units, in which subsets function as "coherent autonomous corporate groups."[2] This term will apply as well to small subsistence pastoral and agrarian societies.

Hunter-gatherer social and cultural lives were rich, they possessed great expertise in exploiting local environmental resources, and were, given the negligible ability to accumulate property, highly egalitarian. This was coupled with the inability to store or make food, absence of written records, and the mostly narrative transmission of cultural knowledge. Hunter-gatherer religion was not pagan or polytheistic, nor doctrinal; it was typically animistic and ritualistic. Select animal species and natural forces embodied sacred power. They were not soteriological; individuals didn't need "saving" because religion was so intermixed with society that a social member could hardly fail religiously. They arguably endorsed an ecological metaphysics of power or value circulating among natural forms, for example, "mana."[3] This was the exclusive condition of all *Homo sapiens* for more than 96 percent of our time on Earth.

Gellner claims that foraging culture is characterized by the undifferentiated normative governance of cognitive activities; each act is beholden to a multiplicity of value constraints that actors do not differentiate. In our terms, that means exhibitive, active, and assertive judgment, and their norms, the beautiful, the good, and the true, are mostly undifferentiated—all are social, or if you will, beholden to the active judgments of social members. As Gellner remarks of the vast majority of human existence, "Language is not merely rooted in ritual; it is a ritual. . . . Most uses of speech are closer in principle to the raising of one's hat in greeting than to the mailing of an informative report."[4] The villager may approve the statement "It is raining" because the village shaman predicted it would rain, even though it is not raining. The point is not that she lacks rationality, or even fears the shaman, but that propositions, including "It is raining," serve not one illocutionary function but several; they are as much a reaffirmation of a social tie, or ritual performance, as a truth-functional report. This means "truth" and "rightness" have not been fully differentiated as norms.

This does not mean foragers lacked knowledge. They had vast empirical knowledge of plant and animal species and their seasonal locations and activities; they were the true Baconian empiricists and Linnean taxonomists. While omnivalent or multifunctional judges, still in their mundane practical activities they were excellent empiricists. We must imagine that their cognitive and cultural norms developed to be consistent with uncountable generations of useful empirical observation in cyclically stable habitats. So their ritualistic propriety rarely had to be trumped by their traditional empirical knowledge. The shaman did not often claim it was raining when the sun was shining—not in tribes that survived, anyway.

Gellner calls the type of reason characteristic of such societies *Durkheimian*. Durkheimian reason is the consideration of plural values through analogy to narrative exemplifications, deployed with minimal differentiation among the norms of judgment. It is exemplified in storytelling. The reasoning used to decide amongst judgments is pluralistic, entertaining multiple considerations, without our hard and fast distinctions of irrelevance (e.g., our belief that argument from authority is a "logical fallacy"). In foraging life, *society and culture are everything*. This does not mean nature is nothing, for we are speaking of a form of society that existed in direct contact with its natural environment with a minimum of novel artifice, and with sacred characters multiplying along the border between the two. The human and the nonhuman are in a reciprocal, ecological relation (which does not mean they were always "good environmentalists"). Wisdom in this context is the ability to interpret narrative tradition, to reason from a variety of historical and narrative cases expressed in practices, in order to adjudicate current disagreements or problems. Society is highly unified or integrated, but it is not codified.

Note here that society, politics, and culture, including religion, are virtually inseparable. A human society is a geographically continuous association of humans who live together, open to a high degree of interaction and interdependence. To collaborate they must share some grammar of intelligibility and propriety—this may or may not be provided by a dominant language and culture. If the society is relatively independent, it must have some "politics," meaning processes of group decision making and decision enacting. Their culture, which could be shared with other nearby societies, is a set of practices, narratives, and artifacts that express shared ends or values, in terms of which the meanings of social facts are interpreted.[5] In foraging societies there is hardly a distinction between the moral rules by which social members interact, their shared cultural practices, narratives, and artifacts, and the manner by which political decisions are made.

Lastly, it must be the case that no distinction was made between validity in light of social convention and validity with respect to its nonsocial objects. If one wants, one may say hunter-gatherers are naturally moral and epistemic conventionalists. They did not *assert* that truth was "relative" to the conventions of cultures, including their own. It is better to say that no notion of a truth separate from the truth recognized in social adjudication had yet arisen. There may well have been exceptions to this, as we will see later, but if so they were rare and concerned either social exiles or spiritual leaders capable of breaking with the historical truths of the tribe. My suggestion is not that in the Durkheimian period all truth and prescription was conventionalist, and later was not. It is that culture did not make a distinction between what is real independent of social judgment and what is particular to my culture.

CULTIVATORS

The development of agro-literate civilization took a long time and proceeded differently in different parts of the world. The revolution came in two large pulses. Farming and animal domestication began in many desirable locations nine to ten thousand BCE, the Neolithic or New Stone Age, at the end of the Pleistocene Ice Age, eventually creating sedentary, subsistence villages. The human economy gradually centered on husbanding vegetable and animal sources of food in a favorable location, while continuing to supplement with hunting, fishing, and foraging. As tribes became sedentary, they developed clan-based political organization, usually patrimonial (Fukuyama 2011). While still tribal or descent based, larger societies first developed "chiefdoms," where chiefs were able to pay off tribal and clan members with resources and protection. Chiefs, usually distinguished as rulers of a people or tribe, sometimes grew into kings, ruling over a territory, hence "kingdoms." But it took until approximately 3000 BCE during the Bronze Age for this to yield cities in prime riverine valleys, first in Mesopotamia, hence the beginning of the agro-literate states that have dominated human history.

Agrarian states were stratified, with a division of labor between peasant commoners, warrior-land holders, and scribes or literate preservers of religions and/or legal information, pithily expressed by Gellner as those who *work*, those who *fight*, and those who *pray*. Such societies are based in *storage*, the storage of grains (agriculture) and information (writing). Both technologies led to social hierarchy, for food now depended on land and grain stores, or herds and prime season grazing lands that required defending by a martial elite. Warfare became more important. Writing was invented at least three times, in Sumeria and Egypt around 3000 BCE; in China during the second millennium BCE; and in Mesoamerica sometime in the first millennium CE. Politically, cultivating societies oscillated between feudal decentralization and empire building.

Once there is farming, writing, metallurgy, engineering and cities, we begin to have a new social unit: *civilizations*. There were no civilizations for the vast majority of human existence. This is not an insult—civilization is a good thing, but it brings a lot of trouble too. Pretty much all humans have lived in societies, and since the Great Leap Forward all humans have had cultures. But civilizations are different. They can be regarded as families of ethnic groups that share some cultural characteristic based in literate, architectural urban centers, sufficiently important to make a difference in local society and culture over a far-flung area. The ones we know are all about agricultural productivity, a strong military, writing and building things that last, and often sharing one of the "great" organized, doctrinal world religions.

Crucial to centralized states is Edward Shils's important distinction of "center" and "periphery." The powerful urban civilizations extend at least nominal political control over vast areas populated by far-flung rural, and perhaps nomadic, communities whose daily workings are mostly unconnected to the center (Shils 1975). Political power, commerce, and learning was in the hands of urban elites. In some cases this leads to the circulatory phenomenon cited by the world's first sociologist, Ibn Khaldun, in which martial tribes cyclically conquer the urban center, becoming sophisticated and decadent, to be conquered by the next generation of religiously inspired rural tribes (Ibn Khaldun 2015). And with the center-periphery, and the existence of literate scribes, there is now another new distinction: *high and low culture*. High culture is literate and urban, while low or "folk" culture is illiterate and rural.

To this description of the agro-literate epoch we can add a conception that Gellner notes but does not fully exploit. German philosopher Karl Jaspers coined the term "Axial Period" for the remarkable global explosion of philosophical-religious genius that occurred within three hundred years before and after the midpoint (or "axis") of the first millennium BCE, including the Hebrew Prophets Isaiah and Jeremiah, the Persian Zoroaster, the authors of the Hindu Upanishads, the Buddha, Confucius, Lao-Tzu, and the Hellenic Greek philosophers (Jaspers 1953). The Axial Age brought, in southwest Asia, the flowering of monotheism of a personal God, in south-central Asia an impersonal pantheism, in east Asia belief in a divine process of balanced creation, but in each case a transcendent conception of the sacred along with a need for salvation, calling the individual to confess fealty to or harmonize with the Ideal. Once the religious task has changed from performance of ritual to belief in textual doctrine and obedience to authority, religion becomes something to which social members can be re-called by prophets and periodic revivals.

The Axial age simultaneously developed the momentous perspective of *logic*. By this I mean something wider than, but including, the treatises on normative thinking produced by Aristotle and by Hindu and Buddhist philosophers. I mean that the standards for human belief, formerly narrative, now are based in the capacity to adjudicate judgments via explicit rules supposed to be society-and-culture-transcendent. The model of validity is Platonic. The observed particular and the practical decision are valid because they embody or participate in a transcendent model in logical pursuit of truth (as in formulation of and obedience to coercive law). This is also the beginning of the major civilizational traditions of philosophy and mathematics.

To use yet another handy term from Shils, Axial civilizations introduce the division of the transcendent from the primordial (Shils 1957). Shils wrote that human societies typically seek legitimation in two directions at once: down and from the past, up and toward the future. The former is the primordial, a normative relation to the particularities of kin, locale, and past inheritance; the latter is the transcendent, a normative relation to an ahistorical, universal ideal which grants future redemption. Relation to the transcendent valorizes the individual in their universality, for which all humans are equally unencumbered souls in the sight of God or sacred law. But nothing in transcendent religion makes intelligible why it was right for me to be born with *this* body, to *these* parents in *this* place, to *this* culture, a child of *this* blood and soil. That is the job of primordiality. Ancestor worship is very old.

Taken together, this heralds a new form of reason: *Axial reason*. One might say, with a nod to Jacques Derrida, that Jasperian or Axial rationality is an exploitation of the implicit possibilities of writing. Reasoning must relate worldly events and possibilities to rules independent of the processes and society in question, must apply the Ideal to the Real. Normative models, now textual, can only be known by those with special knowledge—that is, literacy. They carry high culture, and argue their doctrinal disagreements with logic. Low or folk culture remains in many ways still Durkheimian. The hierarchy of reason nicely matches the hierarchy of caste and power. Just as now there is religious (hence metaphysical and spiritual) doctrine, there is also law, written and explicitly worded, legislated and judged by specialists. For the first time, a traditional or ethnic practice can be criticized for failing to meet transcendent standards.

Fabricators

After nearly five thousand years of agro-literate civilization, the third era of human history started a mere four centuries ago in central and western Europe and soon after in North America, but affected all rungs of those societies only in the late eighteenth century. It has in the past seventy years spread around the world in some of its manifestations, but not equally in all. When and what was the starting point depends on what one thinks is most crucial of the family of changes that constitute the modern world: modern financing of trade and global commerce in the late fifteenth century; the Protestant Reformation of the early sixteenth; the advance of political republicanism from the sixteenth (Holland) through seventeenth (England) to the late eighteenth centuries (the U.S. and France); the emergence of modern science in the seventeenth century; the extension of the market economy into the industrial capitalism of the late eighteenth and early nineteenth century, which materially transformed most classes; and finally the years 1870 to

1914, which saw the "new" imperialism of European powers, the "second" or chemical-electrical industrial revolution, modern art and the beginnings of mass culture.[6] There are many accounts of modernity, but it is at least inconceivable without a new way of directing economic activity, a novel form of knowledge of nature, permanent technological innovation, centralized national organization of practical affairs and a new post-aristocratic social, political, and cultural order. All this involves a continuous fabrication and refabrication of social media by *Homo faber*, humanity as maker.

We will not even attempt to summarize the various explanations of the modern world and its arising (which is still unfolding before our eyes). But many accounts converge on a central process of modernization directly relevant to our concerns. The classic sociology that arose in the later nineteenth century, present in Henry Maine, Emile Durkheim, and in all the great German social theorists, from Karl Marx, Ferdinand Tönnies, Max Weber, George Simmel (Weber's friend), to Arnold Gehlen and eventually Niklas Luhmann and Jürgern Habermas, agreed on this: modern society and culture are marked by *increasing differentiation*. This doesn't mean modern society lacks centralization. Durkheim brilliantly recognized that modern society is both more unified *and* more disunified than traditional society. In terms of the traditional unity of society through similarity of social units (kin and locale) organized under a common view of life (religion) we are less unified; in terms of the functional interdependence of social members in interlocking economic and political institutions, we are far more unified. The division of labor in a modern society integrates us into functional systems *by* differentiating our roles.

Differentiation impacts social activities and institutions across the board. Key modern institutions, processes, and their characteristic modes of judgment have had to be differentiated and segregated from others. The most conspicuous examples are three: science, economy, and technology, but eventually others, like government, law and art, followed suit. The lesson is ubiquitous: progress in any of these areas hinges on the segregation of the purpose at hand—be it discovery of how magnetic fields work, the cheapest way to produce pins, the advancement of mathematics, the re-engineering of a town's water supply, or artistic invention—by putting aside all other cultural and value concerns as extraneous. Each activity must become *unifunctional*.

This is virtually the dividing line between the traditional and the modern. The ancient village's irrigation system may be inadequate for current needs in the current climate. But because that system is connected in a hundred ways with the cultural and social life of the village—in the Spring it is blessed in a religious ceremony, we honor the ancestors who designed it, the sluice and gate keepers have a special status in the village, homes have been built in precise spatial relations to it and the fields according to magical significance—it cannot be changed. But to the Western engineer who comes on a mission of mercy there is only one question: how to regularize flow at a higher level? Nothing else matters. That is how progress happens, like it or not. Western modernity has come to accept that progress in truth claims and in practical improvement of material processes are each achieved only when they are segregated from all other value concerns.

Rationality itself thereby changes: it is now a contextual relation among intramural statements or acts. We may follow Gellner in labeling this form of reason *Weberian*. Weberian reason is the instrumental rationality by which practices and claims achieve justification in the context of goals and explicit premises internal to them. It is modular, unifunctional, and contextual. That is, there arises a purely procedural notion of rationality, which applies in the realm of inquiry (definitions and presuppositions or axioms, implying or inferring conclusions), successful action (the efficiency of a process being judged by its output), and social collaboration, both private and governmental (facilitated by bureaucratic offices performing piecemeal tasks and recording them under rules of equality and fairness). Truth, moral goodness, success, beauty, and salvation are utterly separable, both in theory and in their institutional embodiment.

This was reflected in the most systematic philosophical account of modernity and the contemporary world: Jürgen Habermas's monumental *Theory of Communicative Action* (1985). This work has been often criticized but never matched; no one else has provided a comparably interdisciplinary, social, and philosophic vision of the dynamics of the modern world, along with a diagnosis of the problems, and promise, of our current condition. Modernity is characterized by Habermas as the differentiation of economics, law, politics, and art from cultural tradition. Employing Searle's speech act theory, he distinguishes: imperatives and perlocutionary effects characteristic of strategic, or instrumental action oriented toward success; the constative (truth claims) of discussion oriented to reaching intersubjective understanding; "regulatives" of normative or ethical action that govern interpersonal relations in terms of rightness; and the self-expressive statements of what he calls "dramaturgical" action. In modernity, the institutional action systems coordinated by these different speech acts are released from cultural tradition (i.e., omnivalence), hence free to pursue their "inner logic."[7] Cognition in the form of science, industrial technology and its economic deployment in bureaucratic systems, democratic political rightness, and finally art were all released to pursue distinctive aims. The only concern in making shoes is how to make the most number of shoes at lowest cost; the only concern in science is to advance a research program without concern for religious belief or cultural tradition; political authority will now be decided by liberal republican or democratic methods independent of religion; and, art can be made for art's sake, following the lines of creativity of the artists themselves.[8] Incommensurability *between* norms of each institution or sphere permits commensurable judgments *within* the discourse of each norm.

Modernity's New Values

But modernity also created new values, and these deserve to be noted. That is, it introduced new conditions which people have come to value, and which affect the philosophy of value. I do not merely mean modern societies have novel or different moral values from premodern ones, nor that modernity changed what people value. I mean that wherever modernity goes it brings some values with it that are new because they were not possible before.

First and most stunning has already been noted: *progress*. Modern societies are intrinsically progressive, by which I neither mean "good" nor politically liberal, but rather capable of improving the conditions of human life. Indeed the conditions of social life are now *supposed to* improve. Progress now serves as a social norm for the first time, for the continual improvement of the material conditions of social life, which was not possible in the past, is now a part of the legitimacy of any ruling class or sovereign authority. The notion that the present and future are supposed to be different from the past is antithetical to most cultures in human history. Far more common is the view that the present is debased and inferior to the Golden Age of great heroes, the ancestors who created society and spoke with the gods. Religious and cultural legitimacy are tied to the past. Deviation from the past is bad, not good. To take one example, as Fukuyama points out, in many traditional societies the fact of reverence for ancestors, and consequently their burial plots, made migration for labor or building projects culturally and religiously impossible (Fukuyama 2011). Traditionally, all societies remained in the "Malthusian Trap," where population increase (good times) were followed by starvation and disease (bad times). The state of the commoners was assumed to be awful, and always would be. That might be unfortunate, but it did not mean religious, cultural, or political leadership was failing in its job.

Today, which portions of traditional society are allowed to be changed by modernization differs from society to society; Saudi Arabians and the Dutch take alternate approaches. But whatever forms of technical, economic, educational, scientific improvement are available, very, very few political movements—one thinks of the Khmer Rouge and the Taliban—advocate avoiding progress. There are of course states where there is little material progress, or where what improvement there is, is restricted to elites. But until recently nobody thought that mass illiteracy, poverty, and pestilence among huge numbers of peasants or laborers was necessarily delegitimating for political leadership or the basis for a moral indictment of society. The effect of material progress is both unprecedented and irrevocable.

Second, just as stunning and more relevant to value inquiry is *equality*. The great Axial civilizations were aristocratic at least until the eighteenth century and many into the twentieth. Stratification was their hallmark. Not just economic and educational, but legal inequality among the classes was the norm in all large scale political states. Today, in contrast, virtually no state openly declares that its lower classes or racial or religious minorities are subhuman; that there are rightful legal distinctions among full adult male citizens, and in many modern states, among all adult citizens, including women; or that one set of laws holds for one ethnic group or class but not another. The United Nations Declaration of Human Rights, applying equally to individuals, is universally accepted, if variously interpreted and violated. That is, it is no longer possible openly to endorse what were entirely traditional, virtually universal denials of equality for five thousand years. I am not claiming that universal equality and rights are now everywhere practiced, but in 1750 they were not even preached.

Equality was essential to what we call "democracy," or better, "modern republicanism," which arose against various forms of monarchy, aristocracy, and eventually colonialism. Republicanism is the better name, meaning a political society where the power of government rests with the people considered as one great equal mass of citizens (with, of course, gender, property, racial and even religious restrictions). "Democracy" is best used to mean "majority rule," and indeed, each republic has to have some kind of majority rule ("direct" or "indirect," that is, elected) legislative body in it. In the West, republicanism was often "liberal" meaning it had constitutional limits on government granting a large degree of individual liberty, partly out of concern for property rights. That does not mean equality trumps liberty or material progress or preservation of communities and cultures, or any other value. Nor does it mean the political expression of equality in democracy or liberal rights is universal. It is not. But it does mean the almost universal demolition of traditional legal aristocracy wherever modernity has gone, even in autocratic states.

All this reflects a new and modern notion of society itself. Equality *per se* is not new. Almost every member of even very hierarchical societies did in fact live in some *intramural* (sometimes called "isonomic") sphere of equality. That is, while aristocrats ruthlessly ruled the peasants, the peasants were equal to other peasants, under a set of laws. The aristocracy too, while exhibiting a pecking order, was subject to a common code of behavior and rules. My point is that rough equality within some milieu or caste is normal and virtually ubiquitous in human societies. The agricultural civilizations of the past five thousand years hierarchically stacked these orders or classes or castes one on top of the other. The modern political revolution of equality was as much as anything a change in the definition of "society" itself. What now counts as a society politically, in terms of sovereignty, is a massive state of (in principle) equal citizens subject to equal law.

This has something to do with nationalism. The traditional tribalism and ethnic homogeneity of segmentary societies is not nationalism. Nationalism is the creation of a single people over a large territory whose culture legitimates its state. It was crucial to the achievement both of democracy and the equality of citizens in the West, in that it helped to destroy aristocracy. The fact that nationalism was crucial to modernity does not mean globalism or cosmopolitanism is impossible or undesirable (as we will see in chapter 13). My current point is that modernity *redefined the social unit* to which any politics or morality may be applied.

Last is the value of *individuality*, or individual rights and liberties. Individuality is related to equality, because legally in most countries (even autocratic ones) what is equal is the individual, not a group or class or ethnicity. In some cultures and societies this comes in the form of guaranteed individual rights, and an ever increasing degree of personal liberty, particularly in the West; in others it does not. But in all societies it presents the novel possibility that the individual is not defined by inherited class, ethnicity, and social position. By individuality, I mean respect for the distinctive perspective and hence some degree autonomy of individuals in relative independence of social role, as Peter Berger has argued.[9]

However much the quality of a modern individual's life and fortune is directly linked to job or career, in the premodern period that social role dictated far more: one's moral worth, legal standing, political power, and rights. Nothing in this world (or perhaps even in the next) was separate from social role. And role was fixed: birth status defined the permanent nature and worth of the person. Modern individuality was perhaps embedded Renaissance culture, applied only to the few, and it certainly informed the triumph of the conception of individual rights in the seventeenth and eighteenth centuries. But it is really a Romantic, eighteenth- to nineteenth-century notion. With it comes the value of "diversity," the idea that individual differences are good. Wherever equality holds, there is some kind of valuation of individuals, since it is the individuals that are equal to each other, and wherever there is a modern economy, individuals have to be able move among social roles. However, different modernities, that is, modernization in different cultures and civilizations, have famously differed on just how free the individual is permitted to be. The West is at one extreme; communitarian forms of East Asian modernization have been noted; the restrictions on liberty by religion is clear in many Islamic countries; and some populations are more comfortable with autocracy.

What Have We Learned?

As we come to the close of part II of this book, what have we learned? The fact-value distinction has not collapsed, nor can it. *For the fact-value distinction was crucial to modernization and is inherent in it.* It is inevitable in the unifunctionality of modern development. Modernity, which has given us scientific knowledge, political equality, unimaginable material progress, and individual liberty, has also caused us to recognize the distinctiveness of these modes of validity, and at least officially reject omnivalence. That is, assertive, active, and exhibitive judgments are distinct, these unifunctional values cannot be reduced to or founded in a single omnivalent source that society or culture must rationally accept, and the contextual Weberian reason we inevitably use in in our institutional lives makes progress possible. The benefits of science (truth), equality, law, and freedom (politics), industrial and technological and economic gains (progress), the expansion of moral norms (ethics), and relative freedom of cultural creativity (art), come at that price, which we cannot abjure without cataclysmic suffering. In a modernized society the methods by which institutions, and the members operating in them, make their normative, value decisions, are now largely unifunctional. The degree of unifunctionality, like the division of labor itself, is inherent in modern society.

Weber saw much of this. His remark on the Biblical Abraham is to the point. Regarding life in an inherently progressive society, he gave a caution:

> Abraham . . . died "old and fulfilled by life" because he was part of an organic life cycle, because in the evening of his days his life had given him whatever it had to offer . . . he could have "enough" of life. A civilized man, however . . . inserted into a never-ending process by which civilization is enriched with ideas, knowledge and problems may become "tired of life," but not fulfilled by it. . . . what remains in his grasp is always merely provisional, never definitive. For this reason death is a meaningless event for him. And because death is meaningless, so, too, is civilized life, since its senseless "progressivity" condemns death to meaninglessness.[10]

But it is the point of this book that we need not follow Weber's stark conclusion. Because we have learned some things he did not recognize.

First, we have learned that at the very least in its living dimensions, the natural world exhibits values, including objectively relative values, both among all teleonomic organisms, and those teleological values pursued by minded animals. These processes are dependent upon but irreducible to nonliving processes and systems. The Earth's evolution created living nature and living nature embodies value and purpose. Second, we have learned that human beings are socially self-conscious sign users, meaning to have a self they must take the perspective of others and share intentional states, which are then infused with linguistic and cultural signs, making possible human rationality and creativity. Third, we have learned that humans judge actively, assertively, and exhibitively, but rationally, all on the basis of this social, linguistic, and cultural membership. These normatively governed modes of judgment and query fund human ways of living well, that is, social reproduction in a human form. Humans socially adjudicate among their judgments using the fallible rationality of collaborative learners.

How does this impact the philosophical understanding and justification of the value spheres we will explore in the remainder of this book? A few anticipatory words can be said about each.

Truth. The achievements of science, not just the natural but all the social or human sciences, or learning in general, are of course monumental. The unifunctional ability to apply inquiry without traditional cultural inhibition has yielded a new world of knowledge. But this also led, as Gellner and others have noted, to the "critique of Enlightenment," or the criticism of standards of objectivity and truth that no longer could be supported by a cultural or religious tradition they themselves had called into question. Unfettered inquiry can devour itself.

That has been happening since the dawn of the twentieth century, and arguably defines that century's philosophy. It is most evident since the 1970s as the sociological and philosophical side of the movement called "postmodernism." Sociologically, postmodernism claimed that Western society after the Second World War had passed into a "postmodern" era, where any encompassing "metanarrative" or cultural unity of society—a shared worldview, for example—was neither present, nor necessary, nor even welcome. Whether in its, we might say, leftist version by Jean-François Lyotard or its conservative version by Niklas Luhmann, the claim was that advanced societies do not require, and cannot use, narrative unity (Lyotard 1984; Luhmann 1982). They are collections of institutional language games progressing internally, monadically in their own rational, instrumental growth. In Luhmann's figure, modern society is "a whole that is less than the sum of its parts."[11] No" metanarrative" or world view about the sense and significance of human existence guides social organization or regulation. Such a shared cohesive view is neither required nor possible. This was represented by postmodernism, but more widely by the rejection of "foundationalism," or the belief that human knowledge as a whole could be justified, grounded, or unified, in analytic as well as continental philosophy. In a sense, the twentieth century witnessed the burning off of the *ancien regime* fog, the forms of doctrinal unity and hopes for certainty characteristic of premodern Western civilization. My current point is that this situation puts post–World War II value theory in a brave new world, where either it stays in touch with the *aporias* of general philosophy, or ignores them through a specialization that never brings the subject up.

Art. The effect of modernization on art, at least in the full flowering of the twentieth century, was to set it free from any external restrictions. It is striking that the very notion of "aesthetics" as a field is an eighteenth-century creation. Some have argued that the aesthetic movement of early modern art sought a new degree of objectivity, by which art was believed uniquely to capture the character of either the outer world or the inner. But this was abandoned in the twentieth century. The years 1890 to 1950 brought epochal revolutions in all the arts—painting, music, dance, theater, literature, and architecture—associated one way or another with the term "modernism." The notion of art as a non-ideal commentary on social reality by an artistic advanced guard became common. Art was to explore new territory, sometimes to shock. Eventually, radical modernists and later postmodern forms of art broke down the very distinction between the art object and everyday objects. The whole notion of the aesthetic, of a special kind of experience or taste, came to be rejected by "anti-aesthetic" conceptions of art. If freedom means absence of restraint or obstacle, art was set free. But with this freedom came of course a great uncertainty as to the meaning of its norms, or even what constitutes a work of art.

Politics. Here we find some of the greatest achievements of modernity. One can wholeheartedly approve these norms, even when honored in the breach. The view that all humans, of every society and culture, are in some sense equals, deserving of moral treatment and some degree of political power (popular sovereignty), possessing universal "human rights," and that each people or society or culture has some kind of right to self-determination—these are uniquely modern ideas, and have been put into at least limited effect in public policy, international law, and various international organizations.

But at the same time, with the collapse of foundationalism, no philosopher accepts that liberal republicanism can be philosophically justified by a rational, noncircular argument. Its defense depends on both certain "liberal" cultural traditions, and on practical success, which itself is subject to differences in cultural evaluation. Clearly, some societies prefer autocracy or theocracy, and many endorse a nationalism hostile to local minorities. The modern state is the most powerful entity in human history. And its concerns often diverge from morality. The modern attempt to impose civic ethical rules on political behavior (especially internationally) is surely salutary, but also dangerous. For the twentieth century saw both attempts to constrain political power by ethical rules, and to unleash political and military power *in service of* ethical rules.

Ethics. Modernity altered the function and place of ethics in social life. That stratum or scale of "society" to which morality applies has fundamentally enlarged. Today, whenever philosophers in the contemporary world debate moral questions, they seek what rules rightly apply to either all fellow citizens, all members of "our civilization," whatever that is, or all human beings. This has tended to focus the attention of ethicists on those areas of ethics that may fund social regulation and politics. It is perhaps why the dominant theories of ethics for almost two centuries have been theories directly applicable to law, justice, and social regulation: Kant, Mill, and Rawls are examples. There is a tendency to believe that the norms of politics and the norms of ethics are the same.

There has also been a tendency of a now politically employed ethics to fill the place of religion as the domain of matters of "ultimate concern."

This is why Bernard Williams was right to call twentieth-century Western morality a "peculiar institution." Whereas art has been freed of the demands that other cultural regions had traditionally made on it, ethics has oddly been left as the zone for answering questions such as how ought society be structured, how should government behave, and even "how then shall we live?" It is true that one can find that aim in ancient Greek, pagan thought, but only in largely monocultural and aristocratic societies. For ethics to attempt that task in a modern, open, multicultural, secular society is a remarkable burden.

If modernity is based in the rise of unifunctionality, then it is must restrict multi-functionality or omnivalence, human judgment understood as governed by undifferentiated validity. Since the most prominent institutional representation of socially accepted omnivalence is religion, secularization is the most famous example. It would be wrong to say that modernity entails the simple erosion or displacement of all religion. It clearly does not. However, it is true that modernity involves a shift of the importance of religion. In the twentieth century, large areas of social life came to operate without religious oversight or interference. There is then a tendency for other kinds of institutions to fill the role of absent religion. Totalitarianism arguably tried to do so in the mid–twentieth century. History since 1945 has been far kinder, but it is always tempting for ethics or politics or some combination of the two to fill the vacant throne.

The next five chapters will each suggest an account of morality (chapters 10 and 12), truth and logic (chapter 11), politics (chapter 13), and art (chapter 14) consistent with our ordinal naturalism. They do not claim to provide *the* one, true, or right account of each norm, whatever that might mean. The attempt is merely, as I said, to free up a traffic jam. But to see how to do that we have more ground to cover and slopes to hike. To illustrate a way of offering realist, normative claims made available by having relocated the fact-value problem in an ordinal concept of nature, so that modernity's conception of values may no longer be restricted by the accidents of its birth.

III

Emergent Norms

Chapter Ten

Objective Morality

A man alone is a waste of good firewood.

—Erazim Kohák, *The Embers and the Stars*[1]

Now it is finally time to return to the evolutionary psychology I mentioned in the Introduction. Do we have reason to accept that there are moral values and norms that are natural for human beings? The answer is yes. Of course they are interpreted differently, and most important, they can and do conflict. How we might rationally adjudicate those conflicts is the subject of chapter 12. The current chapter seeks a naturalistic account of basic moral values. For a long time it was presumed by many thinkers that any use of Darwinian evolution to explain human morality would be a fool's errand. Not anymore. The question, is what, does the argument for the evolution of human morality give us and what does it not?

We should first recognize that the task is not new. Indeed, in *The Descent of Man*, Darwin speculated,

> It is possible, or, as we shall hereafter see, even probable, that the habit of self-command may, like other habits, be inherited . . . The imperious word *ought* seems merely to imply the consciousness of the existence of a persistent instinct, either innate or partly acquired, serving him as a guide. . . . We hardly use the word *ought* in a metaphorical sense, when we say hounds ought to hunt, pointers to point, and retrievers to retrieve their game.[2]

T. H. Huxley joined his contemporary Darwin in such speculations. And in the mid–twentieth century, Conrad Waddington, the "father" of epigenetics, wrote on the evolution of human ethics.

But it is in the last few decades that evolutionary psychology, cognitive science, and primatology have led to a kind of renaissance in evolutionary ethics, including the work of Frans De Wall (2009), Jonathan Haidt (2013), Mark Johnson (2015), Philip Kitcher (2011), Mary Midgely (1994), Michael Tomasello (2016), E. O. Wilson (2013), David Wong (2009), and Robert Wright (1994). The best of this work makes it very likely that early hominins inherited at least some prosocial patterns of behavior from nonhuman primates, shared to some extent by current great apes, especially chimpanzees, but then expanded these in novel ways, leading to a small number of crucial moral patterns that are likely built into our species. Evidence suggests that these moral values are extremely widespread across human societies, despite being applied and prioritized differently. Simply put, the notion that Darwinian evolution must inevitably lead to an amoral egoism has been rejected.

Humans need morality. Mary Midgley argued that morality is what humans assert to impose rules and purposes on themselves because, as a cognitively sophisticated animal, we cannot endure the recognition of the inconsistency of our multiple, conflicting fixed (and acquired) action patterns. Unlike other creatures, we know what we do, remember what we have done, and imagine what we may do. This requires the self as a social member to direct and choose among aims. In discussing Darwin's speculation above, Midgley wrote: "He is insisting that no creature with inner conflicts of this gravity can avoid taking sides somehow. This is what makes morality necessary . . . Once you realize that you are constantly wrecking your own schemes in the way that the migrating swallow does [abandoning her nestlings], you are forced to develop some sort of priority system."[3]

The phrase "objective morality" is used by Tomasello in his account of the evolution of human morality (Tomasello 2016). For him it refers to the fact that in the cultural stage of human evolution people acquired the ability, and habit, of adopting the Durkheimian "objective mind" perspective of the group as the privileged perspective on issues of truth and value. For him this is the second of a two-stage process, the first being the acquisition a largely dyadic, "second person" morality of collaborators based in joint intentionality, as we saw earlier. Tomasello may be right. But it seems to me that the "we" intentionality is already present in the collaborative hunting parties of earlier hominins, and some form of language use far greater than what we see in nonhuman primates must have been involved as well. It is reasonable to believe that the combination of pair-bonded allo-parenting over long periods, as well as the demands of truly "obligate collaborative foraging," as Tomasello puts it, which demanded brain growth and supplied the protein to achieve it, were essential innovations, along with teaching the young to make shelters, tools, clothing, and—the greatest tool of all—to control fire. Collaborative hunting involved language of some kind, and it may have been present in some way already at the peak brain growth of *Homo erectus*. The creation of cultural symbolism could indeed have come much later.

Moral Foundations Theory

Jonathan Haidt and his colleagues famously argue that all human societies exhibit a small set of fundamental moral values. This is their *moral foundations theory* (Haidt and Joseph 2007). The claim is that humans naturally or as a species exhibit a plural set of irreducible values or goods that are exhibited in, and serve to regulate, behavior in their social groups. Haidt originally listed these as five values or value systems, each paired with its antithetical "disvalue," but he later added a sixth.

Haidt's general view in moral psychology is "social intuitionism," partly inherited from Hume and Smith. Morality is based in empathetic sentiments, feelings or intuitions, which only subsequently are rationalized, rather than being primarily a product of rational thought. Our current interest is less in his meta-ethical position than his thesis that humans are generally endowed with a small number types of moral "taste buds," as Haidt calls them. The metaphor is apt, for taste buds provide both a receptor of information and an evaluative motivator for response; each registers a type of event that tastes good or bad. These evolved sometime in the development of *Homo sapiens*, playing some role in enhancing adaptive fit.[4]

We can begin by listing Haidt's six positive values, with their opposing disvalues. First is *care/harm*, care being empathetic concern for the welfare of another conspecific. It was partly inherited from other primates but then greatly expanded in humans. Second, is *fairness/cheating* in the sense of reciprocity and in some cases equality, meaning each of two or more collaborators get equal benefit or share. Third is *loyalty/betrayal*, meaning loyalty primarily to one's group against others, but also loyalty to coalitional partners in intragroup competition. Fourth is *authority/subversion*, which means above all deference to established authority in dominance hierarchies. Fifth is *purity/degradation*, the self-control of the bodily integrity and avoidance of "taboo," concerning contamination, poison, parasites, filth, the soiling of the body or social character or even the soul. Haidt later added one more, *liberty/oppression*, referring to both the desire for liberty and the resentment of extreme forms of dominance. This was rooted in the separate claims of Christopher Boehm and Richard Wrangham, who noted the tendency of the members of a male primate/human hunting group to remove domineering "bullies" or those who violate egalitarian distribution of spoils (Boehm 1999; Wrangham 2019). Haidt's claim is that we can find elements of these six in all, including early, human societies.

On this basis, Haidt makes a telling political point: that contemporary American progressives and conservatives equally express moral values, but different ones. Progressives prioritize care and fairness (especially fairness as equality or equity), whereas conservatives affirm loyalty, authority, and purity. The difference reflects the "ominivore's dilemma," defined by Paul Rozin (1976). Omnivores might eat anything. As early humans traveled to new environments, they must have met constant dilemmas in deciding which new items could be eaten and which could not. The price of not being open to novelty may be starvation; the price of being open may be illness and death. So Haidt's list is arranged such that we can distinguish those values more concerned with the preservation of safety and order—who then tend to express authority, loyalty, and purity, in addition to the other values—versus those more open to novelty, leading them to focus on care, fairness, and liberty. *Homo sapiens* oscillate between, and communities must balance, those two.

Philosophically, the best way to understand Haidt's moral foundations is through the work of Englishman Sir David Ross. One of the great philosophers of ethics, Ross claimed that there are a small number of "prima facie duties."[5] He meant that there are several obligations we can call moral: nonmaleficence (nonharm), fidelity (promise keeping), reparations for harm done, gratitude for benefit, and promotion of maximum aggregate good. The claim is that nobody doubts certain obligations are moral, and morality must consist in some not very large set of considerations. From Ross's perspective, anyone who could fulfill a promise, or refrain from harming someone, or provide repayment or gratitude, or act to promote general benefit, without incurring any cost or undermining any other obligations, would be morally wrong not to do so. If that were not so, then we could not agree on *any* examples of morality. Ross was certainly not a naturalist; he was a "rational intuitionist," believing humans rationally intuited his *prima facie* duties. Haidt's evolutionary psychology gives us a naturalistic and anthropological account of a comparable set of basic moral values.

Following Haidt, I will suggest that early humans, at the least *Homo sapiens*, acquired through natural selection, in tandem with their joint intentionality and linguistic ability, a set of moral receptors/motivators. These may have been repurposed versions of cognitive-affective social capabilities of the great apes from which our hominin ancestors evolved. But they are now human, rooted in the social-self-consciousness, unprecedented forms of human linguistic collaboration, and reinforced through culture.

We should note what this naturalistic, evolutionary approach to morality does not and cannot do. It is not an adequate normative ethics, or what some call an "ideal theory." It cannot by itself provide any rational justification for any particular application of the norms given, ranking of norms, or adjudication of the conflicts between the norms. What it does provide is a very plausible account of the natural, human sources of universal moral complexes or constituents. Nor, some argue, does it give a rational argument that these six values are *right*, that they constitute the values and norms humans *ought* to obey. That objection, however, ignores the fact that the natural basis for human existence must inform and put limits on any discussion of morality, of what humans ought to do.

Moral Foundations Revisited

I will use Tomasello's term "objective morality" more boldly than he does. I claim that Haidt's moral foundations describe a family of values and rules that fund an objective morality for humans in the sense of a *Homo sapient* moral way of life. These values are applied differently in different geographical conditions, and in different balances or prioritizations, but as a family they constitute the objective common morality of the human species. I mean this descriptively and normatively: these values are the basis of what *is* done and *ought* to be done. As Haidt puts it, they are the most basic colors on the human moral palette. These values must be stated in intentionally vague terms, for the specification of the terms is just what individual societies in particular historical periods do. Conflict among the moral constraints has always been present, and adjudication can differ greatly.

Given my purposes, I will suggest some alterations to Haidt's list. Haidt is an empirical social scientist with evidence for his list of values. My suggestion can only be an attempted clarification of his conceptual tools, which would have to be borne out empirically. It is a particular philosophical interpretation of his moral foundations theory.

Two emendations will be suggested. First, liberty for Haidt is based in the reactance of submissive primate males against a bullying alpha, which Boehm called a "reverse dominance hierarchy." I do not believe what we call "liberty" can be an inherited, evolutionary moral foundation at all. Haidt may be trying to give a basis for a third "liberal" value in his scheme, and one that indeed plays a great role in modernity. But history shows little evidence of it; agro-literate civilization is a testament to the willingness of members to accept aristocratic dominance. Certainly there was always, and will always be, individual self-interest, and when the self-interest of members runs up against the bullying of a dominant figure, rebellion of some kind can result. But is that evidence of a *moral* value? Not everything good or bad is a moral phenomenon. The list of moral taste buds cannot be expected to account for all behavior, or even all socially normed behavior. It seems to me the self-interested revolt of submissives is not a moral taste bud. So it ought not be on the list.

Second, it seems to me that "duty" needs to be on the list. This threatens major misunderstandings. "Duty" is usually a synonym for "obligation," hence perhaps for moral norms in general. But I am suggesting the need for a narrower meaning. The positive performance of certain actions linked to the social membership of the individual deserves its place on the list. Haidt does not deny such, but either regards social duty as a synonym for moral obligation in general, or distributes it among other norms (e.g., a duty to care, a duty to be fair, etc.) But the duty to perform a social function or task within the group seems to me a crucial, distinctive component. Indeed, "cheating" is as much an antonym of duty as fairness, very close to "not doing one's duty yet expecting a share anyway." In any collaborative scheme, doing one's job is the usual basis of any desert or merit, and this must matter morally.

These alterations are connected to a more general point. For Haidt, loyalty, authority, and purity are "traditional" or conservative norms, the others "liberal" or nontraditional. While that may be true in contemporary, modern, liberal societies—which are very unusual in historical terms, as Haidt knows—tradition is more or less *everything* in premodern societies. *Traditum* is what is passed on, culturally inherited. All societies seek to preserve. Modernity is indeed ambiguous in this way—not a society without tradition, but a society with a tradition that is to some extent antitraditional. Care, fairness, and, for me, duty, are not by themselves "liberal" but *nonhistorical* values. They are moral obligations that would hold for members of a collaborative group without history, for example humans thrown together by a disaster, like survivors of a plane crash in the wilderness who are forced to collaborate. Haidt is right in suggesting that human society inevitably must balance caution with exploration, like Rozin's omnivores. But the difference between the two sets of moral receptors is not that one is traditional and the other not. *All must be traditional.* But one set of traditional receptors are made to be historically sensitive, and others relatively neutral regarding history.

My amended list of Haidt's moral foundations follows.

1. *Care* (vs. harm). Care is concern for another's good. It is based in empathy and benevolence, or the desire to benefit another. It may well have its original home in the intimate family, especially in the care of young, but it fuels collaborative partnerships too, potentially expanding from the intimate to the local to beyond. Care is meant to have results, improvement in the well-being of the other. In philosophical terms, it is consequentialist or teleological. It is also inevitably linked with success: to try but fail to benefit someone is not to be a very good caregiver. This is probably continuous with primate care and sympathy, but greatly increased by human joint intentionality, language, and culture.

2. *Fairness* (vs. cheating, fraud). Fairness I take to be the basis for justice, and justice I take to mean "*to each what is owed,*" or "*to each their due.*" (We will return to this in chapter 13.) While justice is clearly related to social and political life, here we are talking about the fairness or justice of a person in social interaction. Its origin appears to be a novel human arrangement of obligatory equality regarding certain situations, like sharing the results of collaborative foraging. Haidt takes this especially from the work of Robert Trivers on "reciprocal altruism," characteristic of beings who can remember and honor agreements in the past, involving a "delayed return" (Trivers 1971). To be sure, there are cases of nonhumans sharing, and offering food to non-offspring; cases (and videos) of primates becoming upset when they do not receive the same treat as another; cases of reciprocity when the failure to return benefit leads to conflict. But most primate mothers do not distribute food equally among their offspring, and collaborative chimpanzee hunts end in a free for all after dominant members take their share.

Reciprocity concerns equality of obligation but not an obligation to equality. The aristocratic landowner and his peasants had reciprocal but unequal obligations. Human fairness may require that I must accept less because you deserve more. Equality can be regarded as a limit case of desert. In distributive justice, desert has been criticized by John Rawls and others. We need not dwell on such issues. To each their own, to each what is owed, in effect means to each what is deserved—for desert need involve neither special activities nor special moral worth. In the minimal case, equality is the deservedness of all members by virtue of being members—members of a collaborating party, a society, or even of the human race. As Haidt recognizes, contemporary progressives and conservatives each value fairness, but they think of fairness in different ways, the former as equality or even equity of outcome, the latter as proportionality, implying reward ought to be proportional to merit. By "fairness," I mean the underlying commitment that is then actualized differently in each of these.

3. *Duty* (vs. negligence). Unfortunately, there is no better term; commonly one could use "responsibility" or even "fidelity" (a term Darwin liked). I will mean by "duty" not moral obligation in general but *persistence in the performance of social role*. It includes duties I hold as a father, a teacher, a clan member, an office holder, or as a citizen or member of my society, or even as a human being. Particularist or "agent-relative" duties are as fully duties as any more universal ones. We have to imagine that the differentiation of such duties is a phenomenon of agro-literate civilization and, even more, of modernity. My notion is meant to capture, but not be restricted to, the notion of duty offered in 1876 by F. H. Bradley's "My Station and Its Duties" (Bradley 1988).

The paradigm case is actually performing the task or role one is supposed to perform in a collaborative scheme. Notice this can certainly overlap with promise keeping, care, fairness, loyalty, and authority; to fulfill one's duty to a child, for example, is to care for the child. But duty is distinct enough to deserve its own place. Care is open ended in a way duty is not; this is why one may go "above and beyond the call" of it. To loyally perform one's duty is just to perform one's duty; to obey authority when one is supposed to is just to perform one's duty. The dutiful collaborator must have been highly prized in all epochs of history. Like fairness, duty is central to what would later be called "deontological" notions of morality, except that it can be particularist. And it may conflict with considerations of fairness and care or benevolence; my duty to my partner or relative may outweigh other concerns. The complaint that someone has acted as a free-rider might not involve cheating or thieving but rather failing to do one's duty, such as falling asleep during a hunt. My point is that actually performing a task as one is supposed to needs a place on the list.

Care, fairness, and duty share the trait of being nonhistorical, not past-oriented. Of course any moral value whose obligation is based in a past relation can be said to be "past" oriented in some way: to care for an old friend or parent is to share a history, to honor a promise is to honor a past agreement. Nevertheless, care, fairness, and duty are not intrinsically tied to maintaining or restoring a status *quo ante*. They could apply in a group of utter strangers thrown together in a disaster, as political theorists have noticed (Nozick 1974). They are Haidt's progressive or "liberal" values in the sense that they are capable of being indifferent to history.

4. *Authority* (vs. disobedience). Authority is another matter. Authority has to mean both deference and obedience to those of higher social status. It must begin with filial obedience to parents, extend to other elders, and to those in more commanding positions in a collaborative scheme, eventually to religious and political offices. Authority is important in all societies, even relatively egalitarian hunter-gatherer communities. For obeying elders is crucial. One can say authority is the remnant of primate dominance. Primate deference to the alpha male or female is crucial to avoiding continuous conflict in many primates, but what is being obeyed is the dominance, which is rewarded by first choice of mates and food. In the human case, the prevalence of equality means deference can be limited or undermined by lack of group success. Authority is the human, moral version of dominance. It must be legitimate and *deserved*, meaning the behavior of the authority figure can be self-delegitimating. The feeling toward the authority figure can include loyalty but does not have to. The soldier that disobeys an order is criticized by his peers, both for failing to follow a moral code they have imposed on themselves, hence for being "selfish," but also for putting them in danger. Authority cannot mean merely fear. It must mean there is both a felt obligation and a satisfaction in proper obedience to the socially higher, even if it is not always to one's individual benefit.

Here we have to recognize an historical change. *Authority was greatly magnified in the Axial Age*. The replacement of hunter-gatherer bands and tribes by agro-literate civilization generated concentrations of power in very distant castes and social specializations, which lasted for thousands of years. I make no claim here that this was connected to biological evolution, but merely point out that the decline of certain forms of authority in the modern world is largely a move away, not from all prior human society but from the stratified Axial religious cultures that constituted what we call "civilization."

5. *Loyalty* (vs. treachery). Haidt is certainly right that loyalty is a basic, distinctive, moral receptor and motivator. But it is easy to conflate with others. We think of it above all as loyalty to the group, which is on display in competition or, in the extreme, war between groups. Patriotism and nationalism seem to fall under loyalty. But for an isolated human band

half a day's walk from other bands of the same culture and tribe, is disloyalty to the group even possible? There would have to be conflict with other nearby groups (probably cousins) and the possibility of betrayal of one's own, but that condition must not have been constant. Nor can we take loyalty to mean just social fidelity, socialization, or "groupification" because that is the root of *all* moral values, just as fealty to tradition cannot be one of the colors on the moral palate. We cannot confuse part with whole.

Loyalty is historical. It is a differential obligation to individuals or groups to which one has had a relation of historical dependence. One owes a *debt* to the family and collaborators of yesterday. Loyalty is the down payment on that debt. When two strangers from distant villages meet alone in the savannah, they certainly can mobilize their care or sense of fairness, or some other value in dealing with the stranger as a basis for collaboration—but not loyalty. However, after foraging together for three days, when other strangers arrive, the first two now retain a special bond, and that is loyalty. It is not only because they have evidence of trustworthiness but that they have engaged in mutual dependence. To care is one thing, and to be fair another; but to be uniquely concerned with the welfare or with obligations or duties toward those with whom one shares a history, is loyalty. Loyalty can directly conflict with care and fairness; as Freud wrote, the problem with "universal love" is that it is a betrayal of my family (Freud 2010).

6. *Purity* (vs. *Degradation*). There is no great word for this. "Purity" works well enough. Sometimes Haidt uses "sanctity." It must be connected to excellence; not that all excellence is purity, but purity must be excellent. Haidt reasonably understands this value dimension as rooted in the fear of toxins and parasites, and perhaps sexual mores, or touching something poisonous, or violation of the body's integrity. Doubtless this is basic, and the feelings of nausea and other illness connected with touching or eating or smelling the wrong thing had to color experience. Keeping food, especially on special ritual occasions, "pure," as well as bodies and costumes, must have been a chore. Feces, urine, blood, saliva, and water should each be where they are supposed to be, and not everywhere. It may also be that this generalizes to something broader: fear of and distaste for absence of a certain kind of order. The anthropologist Mary Douglas described dirt as "matter out of place."[6] But not sheer chaos; rather, it is the kind of disorder indicated by the presence, within what is supposed to be entirely X, of *not-X*. One might say purity is *qualitatively unmixed goodness*. Its violation is a protrusion or incursion of what should not be there. Purity is related to order, or rather the avoidance of what Buchler called "alescence," the

introduction of contrary traits. This then may have expanded into a way of emotionally experiencing and evaluating a class of social experiences in terms of high and low, fine and gross, pure and disgusting. In the Axial Age it probably coalesced with and helped to fuel Edward Shils's notion of "transcendence," "refinement," and "high" culture.

Morality and Its Neighbors

Human persons and societies value many things. Values include kinds of food, mates, clothing, social status, love, preferable resting and living areas, ancestors, totems, the gods, and so on. "Having an intact body" is certainly a great value. Some of these are functional and biological. Members of the segmentary societies, hunter-gatherers or subsistence villages and herders, as well as residents of urban centers of agro-literate urban centers, are all socialized. They live together and collaborate. Just as the hunter-gather band, the herding tribe, the subsistence farming village, or the chiefdom did not separate its religion from its art, politics and its moral norms, we have to explore the inevitable degree to which the "moral" has always been entangled with other spheres.

One could say the primary behavioral norm of every member of human society is best described as *propriety* (which was an important notion for Adam Smith). Societies are people living together over time, relatively independent of others, who share a horizon of intelligibility and propriety (Cahoone 2005). Propriety is what every child is taught. But that is only to say that the norm of behavior is to behave as social members want you to behave. Propriety can then be broken down into at least three related, distinguishable, but mutually supporting kinds of values, hence norms: *efficacy*, *morality*, and *aesthetic quality*. Morality is distinct but related to the other two, and its distinctiveness can vary historically. The term "excellence" captures the connection of the moral to the efficacious *and* the aesthetic.

Humans live collaboratively, which means they can also die collaboratively, for if the society dies I will too. Therefore, at all times in human society existence is dependent on efficacy or success. Successful performance matters. Whether we like our cousin or not, however much we must force him to share the fruits of his activity with others, however improperly he behaves, if he is most often successful in the hunt, he is crucial to our survival. The child-rearer who keeps more of her children alive, the gatherer who finds the best nutrients and builds the best fires and huts and clothing—all this is essential. Success is always in itself a *prima facie* good. This carries into social relations. The kind of person who habitually says the wrong thing is not as "good"—in the general, not merely moral sense of the term—as the person who says the "right" thing. Our notion of morality is not equivalent to efficacy, but overlaps with it. Even in our modern society, which tends to want to segregate the moral and the successful, we are especially praiseworthy of the hero who actually does save the drowning child over the one who tries but fails. And if care is especially prized, that entails successfully benefiting the other.

Suppose one task we teach our young people is to care for the infant, another to feed the hogs in the morning. The failures of right action can fall into two categories according to the way the community remedies them. If the infant care is done poorly, and the infant fusses for hours, or if the big hogs push out the small so not all get fed, the good of "success" was not achieved. The same result occurs if the youth goes to sleep instead of watching, forgets, acts surly and indifferent with the infant, complains bitterly while feeding the hogs, et cetera. But the first set of failures lead us to either teach the youth to do it better or to get someone else to do it. Their actions are not right by virtue of being unsuccessful. The later forms of failure lead us to berate the youth for failing to do a duty or to manifest the right attitude. Those are *moral* failings; the act is wrong, not right, *morally*. In the doing of the practices required for social life, including those that the individual may be free to choose for themselves, a character, rules for how to do the act, and the norm of success are almost always present.

At the same time, propriety and praiseworthiness had to include an individual's display of the proper, the pure, the beautiful. These became significant for social status. As moral care and duty overlap with efficacy, moral purity overlaps with *aesthetics*. Disgust is aesthetic, in this case, a morally mobilized sense of revulsion. I am claiming that the aesthetic and the moral overlap. The revulsion at what the tribe considers taboo, what will violate the moral functioning of the social order, is partly aesthetic.

This applies as well to the morally or civically "high," hence status. It doubtless matches to some extent social hierarchy whenever it is expressed in costuming, manner, or bodily presentation. The chief will likely look great, fine, exceptional, high, not low or common. And those with the resources for such a presentation will often seek to avoid certain things—it could be feces, or mud, or blood (under some circumstances). Animals must be butchered, human offal must sometimes be dealt with on a more than individual basis, and refuse must be taken away or burned. The chief, the elders, the aristocracy will not be doing these things. In more "civilized" times, the description of moral and civic greatness normally takes on aesthetic character. So both purity/degradation and authority often overlap with the aesthetic. But as with success/morality, there remains a line between them. The failure to wear the proper clothing to the wedding ceremony or religious ritual is wrong, in the first instance, aesthetically wrong, wrong in aesthetic presentation. It is a moral wrong when the failure was heedless or rebellious or a deliberate insult (which of these it is will be the subject of gossip around the fire, the well, the coffee station, the courtroom).

The six moral values are primarily concerned with providing norms for the *interaction among members*. That is morality's home, its central issue, however much it may have implications for private behavior or the moral visions of exiles and recluses and the political relations among societies. Morality must be understood first of all as a social phenomenon regulating interactions among you and I and we. The immoral is a blameworthy violation of the entitlements, interests, or proper expectations of others in the six zones of moral value. That is the primary function of morality, its basic evolutionary point. It thereby makes it possible for narratively self-consciousness, joint intentional animals—the only species on Earth that maintains large, non-kin societies over time—to live together (Baeten 2012).

This brings us lastly to a special term, and tradition: *excellence*. It is the better translation of the Greek term *arête*, commonly rendered as "virtue," which played a central role in Aristotle's ethics. Excellence covers both moral and nonmoral value, whether efficacious or moral or aesthetic. Excellence was the social term for the best, *aristos*, in aristocratic, Axial civilization. I am using it here as in the virtue ethics tradition, as at least partly a judgment of character, of the agent, not merely of the act. We will discuss virtue ethics later; the current point is that excellence of the agent may include moral, efficacious, and aesthetic features. In different eras and societies, excellence of character may be more connected to the purely moral virtues above, in others more to success and aesthetics. "Prudence" came to be the name among some philosophers for rational choices of actions that mix moral and pragmatic considerations, the overlap of the moral and the efficacious. It is connected with Aristotle's "*phronesis*" or practical wisdom. Aristotle's notion of moral virtue was, famously, a disposition to deliberately choose the mean between excess and deficit—like courage between foolhardiness and cowardice. The virtuous person is the one who gets it right or hits the mark. In all ancient societies it must have been common to judge people as excellent for their behavior but also for their skills, appearance, and character. There can be no strict line between excellence, reputation, and status—especially in a premodern world with a narrow set of roles or "job descriptions." As De Waal emphasizes, most primates are obsessed with rank and dominance. This is also very human; it is largely true that once a human being has enough to eat, their fancy turns to social status.

To summarize: *homo sapien* societies were able to incorporate and control the individual organism's conative pressure to stay alive and protect its young through the six moral evaluators described. Care for the closest relatives, but extending to unrelated collaborators; fairness, especially to collaborators and/or potential collaborators; performance of duties that exceed individual immediate needs; deference to authority; loyalty to those to whom one is indebted; and treasuring purity while avoiding degradation—however locally, culturally interpreted, these nodes of moral sensitivity and motivation make possible the moral living together and collaboration of joint intentional complex learners. The claim is, for the continued existence of a highly dependent, almost neotenic animal, with joint intentionality, social self-consciousness, and language, which must care for its offspring, collaborate, and pass on learning of technologies and practices, all understood through a distinctive linguistic-cultural set of rituals, narratives, and icons, it seems to be required that the group maintain itself via some distribution and application of the six moral receptor/motivators. Without morality, society begins not to be human; and without a society, there is no morality to practice.

Too Social to Be Moral?

The new evolutionary psychologists performed the great service of demonstrating how human moral values could be compatible with Darwinian evolution. The story used to be that we are too selfish to be moral—even our genes were selfish. The new approach says we evolved to be prosocial. But this very success creates a new problem. Doesn't the new view make us *too social to be moral*? That is, prosocial human nature may not provide the kind of morality most modern Western educated people want. This is partly—but only partly—accurate.

Morality is intrinsically "groupish," as is said. This must mean the evolutionary account of our prosocial nature implies loyalty to locals against strangers. It is not cosmopolitan. This is the tribalism problem. It is the great fear common to the students of the new evolutionary naturalism in ethics. To the extent that humans evolved to become group members, have they not been programmed to be intrinsically hostile to outgroups? Are external relations a moral-free fire zone where anything goes? Some even wonder if a world of intragroup loyalty is actually a good one. Robert Wright in *The Moral Animal*, while generally extolling the bright side of the evolutionary story, notes the dark side: "evolution should produce a strong and well-targeted strain of benevolence . . . And it has happened, to a great extent, with us. Maybe the world would be a better place if it hadn't. Brotherly love in the literal sense comes as the expense of brother love in the biblical sense."[7] Meaning kin, blood, soil, nation—loyalty to these seems a barrier to empathy for the Other.

But this problem is less troublesome than is often thought. First, "tribe" is too narrow a metaphor, particularly in modern times. In terms of size, tribe comes after band, before chiefdoms, and way before nation-states. Nation-states, which are uniquely modern, are far, far larger than any tribe could be—our current world population of eight billion is divided into about two hundred nation-states. One can of course argue that the nation-state was based on a spreading of tribal feeling to a large population through a lot of effort, standardizing a language over a large region into a new kind of "national" society, with some vague cultural inheritance similar to the tribe. But if so we are very massive, bureaucratic impersonal tribes. The very recent achievement of this unprecedented ability to say "we" in reference to hundreds of millions of strangers is no more than three hundred years old. Perhaps it ought not be condemned because empathy has not yet reached eight billion.

At the same time we must accept an unavoidable fact: *the very things that make us human makes us different from each other*. Because we are semiotic animals, our deeply social nature is expressed in languages and cultures. We accumulate knowledge and technique group by group, and pass it on using a natural language, which others humans will not share. My dog can be airlifted to Eurasia and dropped in a kennel. While an unknown stranger, doubtless distrusted, he can communicate with the other dogs as well as any local. But I will be unable to talk with the owner of the kennel because the owner and I each depend on linguistic learning to communicate. Language and culture, our human glories, must separate us into groups.

As born collaborators, we must both be sensitive to who is a potential collaborator and also loyal to present and past collaborators. Not only do I trust my past collaborators more than the newcomer, I *owe* my past collaborators, and my life is partly based on that debt. Loyalty need not be a hostile ignorance directed toward the Other, but it begins as a debt that is ignored at one's peril. Progressives who argue for high levels of communal provision or distributive justice base many of their arguments precisely *on* such debt. Rawls in particular argued that no one "bootstraps" themselves to success without the public schools, hospitals, paved roads, and general security provided by the community. And therefore, by Rawls's "principle of fairness," all are indebted to the pre-existing "cooperative scheme."[8] Debt to one's community, which is a debt to those people who implicitly acknowledge mutual obligations, is morally crucial. However much racism and ethnic or national bigotry might someday be transcended, there is no imagining human partnering that does not valorize collaborative, communal history. How else could it be? Only if humans had no episodic memory, no ability to pair and bond or to recognize individuals as narrative histories.

So human sociability, while not intrinsically universal, is *open and not closed*, ready to interact with and collaborate with any promising conspecific. But being finite learners, we must be socialized and acculturated in some language, community, and culture. This need not lead to hostility; indeed, the traditional moral codes of many societies includes norms of hospitality to travelers and foreigners. Probably more blood has been spilled between people who look alike and speak the same language than between those who do not. But the theorists frightened by tribalism are correct in noting a theoretical problem: there is no reason to believe a modern, liberal, egalitarian, cosmopolitan ethics of universal rights and obligations is somehow intrinsic to or justified by the nature of human morality. It is not. You cannot get our modern Western cosmopolitanism out of evolutionary psychology. For that you need additional argument.

Conclusion

We have evolved to value some things in certain ways, and one of the most obvious ways is our valuing of certain basic human forms of relationship. Just as there is an evolutionary theory of knowledge, which does not justify all knowledge or give us strict limits on what we can or cannot know but explains the sensitivity of basic cognitive capacities to environmental conditions, there is an evolutionary theory of value, which does not justify all our valuations or give us strict limits on what we can or cannot or ought to value, but does lead us to expect that we are right to value certain things. We are still an animal with a whole series of value-facts, which in our case includes the care of utterly dependent offspring, social collaboration, pair-bonding and allo-parenting, instruction of the young, training into adult roles (which, subject to human learning, are particular and capable of improvement), political participation or obedience or both, and transmission of a variety of cultural practices, artifacts, and narratives. Morality is the way of doing those things together *well*.

At this point in our study we have only a set of *prima facie* "duties" or moral taste buds, which play a role in the norms by which humans socially interact. Certainly communities and cultures can combine these colors of the human moral palette into many different paintings. But which of these would be better or worse, morally? Which values should trump others, or even be the chief value? What to do when the moral values conflict, as they must? An ethics requires more than a set of moral goods; it requires an understanding of the meaning of basic ethical terms, or "meta-ethics," a comparison of major ethical perspectives, and the justification of some rational way of adjudicating the conflicts that inevitable arise in moral life. That will be our job in chapter 12. But first we must clarify a different norm, which will play a role in all our subsequent chapters. That is the norm of truth.

Chapter Eleven

Truth and Logical Validity

> In order to give an account of logic, we must presuppose and employ logic.
>
> —Henry M. Sheffer, "Review of *Principia Mathematica*"[1]

Whatever else it is, truth is the norm of assertive judgment. That is the claim made by the theory of judgment employed in this book. Philosophers have tried to analyze truth, to form a theory of it. Historically the most prominent account of truth is the *correspondence* theory, which holds that an assertion or proposition is true if it corresponds to or is adequate to or reflects or matches its object. In the nineteenth century, two other now canonical notions of truth were created: the *coherence* theory, according to which the truth of a claim is its coherence with other knowledge or claims; and *pragmatism*, developed by the American philosophers, which claimed that the truth of a claim is its adequacy for the guidance of conduct. A fourth developed in the twentieth century, deriving from Frank Ramsey on one hand and Alfred Tarski on the other: the *deflationary* account of truth, for which to claim a belief or statement true is merely to assert the statement, and nothing more can be said. Cheryl Misak has suggested that in some ways this deflationary notion is congenial to American pragmatism (Misak 2015).

The issue of truth has been naturally affected by theories of knowledge, as we have seen. But the other recent influence is the development of modern logic. Logic has meant several things in the history of Western thought. Two are very old: the study of forms of valid argument, versus invalid arguments or fallacies; and the identification of the most fundamental concepts to be used in inquiry. Then, in the second half of the nineteenth-century, mathematics underwent a revolution, and logic followed suit. Charles Peirce and Gottlob Frege each suggested the quantifier and a logic of relations. The result was an attempt, particularly by Frege, to formulate the basis for all mathematics through a new logic. The Logicists, including Frege and Russell, believed all mathematics could be derived from such a revolutionized logic. At the same time David Hilbert argued that mathematics was purely formal, in effect a grammar or a set of rules for manipulating symbols, like the rules of chess, while L. E. J. Brouwer's intuitionism argued that mathematics rests on mental constructions, so that discussion about mathematical objects whose construction cannot be given is illegitimate. Eventually the logical positivists viewed logic as a syntax, like the formalists, produced by convention. For most contemporary thinkers a logic is a syntax of constants, logical operators, and rules of formation and derivation by which one formula implies another, which then requires a "semantic model" to assign meanings to the nonlogical terms of the language in order to generate statements that are true or false.

Our question will be, can naturalism, if understood ordinally, contribute to an adequate context for a realist conception of logical validity and truth? We will explore this by following an historical discussion of logic in the positivist and American pragmatist traditions focusing on the Columbia Naturalist school. From the time of Peirce, through Morris Cohen, the positivists, the Columbia Naturalists, and the work of Hilary Putnam, the naturalism and pragmatism of the American tradition have offered resources to the discussion of truth and logic. Following recent commentators like Penelope Maddy, we will see if ordinal naturalism can support a realist conception of the norms of each.

Logic among the Columbians

After Russell and Whitehead produced the Logicist *Principia Mathematica* in 1913, some pragmatists became consumers of or contributors to the new formal logic. C. I. Lewis was the prime example. But once Wittgenstein and the new positivists adopted an antirealist view of logic, a serious confluence of positivism and pragmatism occurred. In the early 1930s the young Americans who popularized Viennese positivism and Polish Logic in America—Ernest Nagel, Charles Morris, W. V. O. Quine, and Morton White—were all influenced by pragmatism. Dewey's *Theory of Valuation* was published in 1939 in the positivist series, *International Encyclopedia of*

Unified Science. The relationship continued to the early 1950s, when Carnap and Quine amended positivism to accept that in the final analysis the choice among languages for describing facts must be "pragmatic"(Carnap 1950; Quine 1951).

In all this, logical realism seemed unnecessarily tied to classical Platonist or Aristotelian metaphysics, putting positivism and pragmatism arm-in-arm in opposition. This set the context for Columbia Naturalism. It was led by Dewey, who taught at Columbia from 1904 to 1930, and included John Herman Randall, Ernest Nagel, and Justus Buchler, among others. The school's manifesto was the volume *Naturalism and the Human Spirit* (Krikorian 1944). Oddly, it was dedicated to someone who was not a Columbian at all: the largely forgotten Morris Cohen.

COHEN'S LOGICAL REALISM

Cohen, as we saw earlier, regarded himself above all as a logician, inspired by *Principia Mathematica*, and was one of the few philosophers who knew Peirce's logic just as well. For Cohen, logic is the rules of the possible relations of all possible objects. They are not "laws of thought," for Cohen an utterly subjectivist claim. Cohen would expand on his view in his 1944 *A Preface to Logic.* The relation of logical incompatibility, he wrote, is "as hard an objective fact as the relations of gravitation, digestion, or warfare." Cohen rejected Russell's use of the term "subsistence." Abstractions, or universals, exist for Cohen. The fact that redness does not occur by itself but only along with other things—for example, a tomato or a stop sign—is no stranger than the fact that Jack being a brother cannot occur without Jack also being an animal or male. He concluded:

> Logic is the most general of all the sciences; it deals with the elements or operations common to all of them. That is, rules of logic are the rules of operation or transformation according to which all possible objects, physical, psychical, neutral, or complex can be combined. Thus, logic is an exploration of the field of the most general abstract possibility . . . Not only does it rule out impossibilities but it reveals the possibilities of hypotheses other than those usually taken for granted . . .[2]

This means possibilities must be real or "existent." If the physical principle $F = ma$ is valid, of what is it valid? Not merely any actual or past accelerating ponderable bodies, but all possible such bodies, and the relations among the universals mass, force, and acceleration in the future. Scientific procedure presupposes that "the logically necessary relations which hold between mathematical expressions hold of natural phenomena themselves."[3] But while physical entities obey invariances, not all their characters are expressed by such rules; there is always variation of other properties. Cohen accepted Peirce's point that no measurement or depiction of any quantity is absolutely determinate or precise. Like his teacher Royce, Cohen is rejecting nominalism, the doctrine that whatever is real is a determinate particular, commonly allied with physicalism (only physical particulars exist) or phenomenalism (only particular phenomena exist).

As we saw earlier, Cohen and Lovejoy had a controversy on the status of secondary qualities. Lovejoy argued that the relativity of secondary qualities indicated that they are subjective. Cohen refused this:

> [I]s [there] a contradiction in the assertion that the same object can be really red and blue? . . . it would be peculiar if the principle of contradiction, obviously a formal one, could tell us that certain empirical qualities like red and blue are contradictory, but that others like red and soft are not . . . Red and blue are certainly no more contradictory than kindness and cruelty, yet the same man may in one transaction display kindness to A and cruelty to B. . . . The principle of contradiction . . . can have no application to a single assertion which predicates different qualities of the same object in different relations.[4]

This notion Cohen called his "metaphysical babe," that each thing should be understood as a "complex-in-relations." As we saw earlier, Cohen recognized his view's similarity to neutral monism, noting that it "may as well be called [neutral] pluralism."[5] This was arguably the beginning of objective relativism. But Cohen's "babe" did not grow up, at least in his lifetime. Fortunately, cultural objects, like seeds but unlike people, can survive in stasis.

Nagel's Pragmatic Positivism

Among the most successful of Cohen's students was Ernest Nagel, who studied under Cohen at CCNY, and then under Dewey at Columbia, receiving his PhD in 1930, the year Dewey retired. Nagel was immediately appointed a Columbia professor. For some time, he remained close to Cohen; in 1934, they published a logic textbook together. As a new professor, Nagel traveled to Vienna and Poland, bringing back the logic of Tarski and Carnap (and he met Wittgenstein as well), as Quine had done in 1932–1933. Much later, Nagel would publish the first systematic study of the philosophy of science in English, his 1961 *The Structure of Science: Problems in the Logic of Scientific Explanation.*

In their textbook, Nagel and Cohen agreed that logic is concerned with "certain *general or generic traits of all things whatsoever.*"[6] But by the late 1930s, Nagel's view of logic had become the logical positivist view, essentially a syntactic system which must be interpreted through a semantics or model to yield true or false statements. Logic as such is not "about" anything, and is not even true in itself. The reason we employ logic is pragmatic: it enhances our explanatory and predictive powers, by allowing us, in Wittgenstein's early view, to "show" but not "say" the underlying structures of our meaningful statements. Nagel's mature thought is in a significant sense the meeting place of Carnap and Dewey, positivism and pragmatism. He was one of the few who thought Dewey's *Logic: The Theory of Inquiry* (1938) was what its title implies, a theory of experimental epistemology, and hence compatible with the new formal logic (Suppes 1969). At the same time, as we saw earlier, Nagel allowed to being an objective relativist. For him, this unique American invention held that: existence is plural, incomplete, and discontinuities and loose conjunctions are "ultimate"; there is no distinction between reality and appearance because every property or event is a genuine occurrence in some context or process; there is no absolutely privileged context; and qualitatively distinct features of human experience are themselves as ultimate as any part of nature.

Nagel's positivist notion of logic eventually forced a break with his undergraduate teacher. David Hollinger, citing a letter from Lewis Feuer, recounts that at a conference in the late 1930s, "Nagel turned on Cohen with great vehemence for believing that the 'external world' had a logical structure; such beliefs, asserted Nagel, were 'meaningless.' Cohen replied soberly that he did, indeed, hold such beliefs. Cohen 'became very pale' . . . while 'the audience sat tense,' watching Cohen's repudiation by one of his most brilliant students."[7] The two reportedly remained friends, but the break was real. Nagel later published a famous paper, "Logic without Ontology," attacking Cohen's words without using his name (Nagel 1944). The paper became the titular essay of Nagel's 1956 book, *Logic without Metaphysics*, where, after Cohen's death, Nagel waxed on the views of his own generation of "naturalists" who became acutely aware of the incongruity between our professed empiricism in regard to knowledge of matters of fact, and certain phases of the Aristotelian realism of men like Cohen.... For ... all statements about any traits of existing things are at best contingent truths ... if the propositions of logic and mathematics are a priori and necessary, as I believe they are, they cannot be construed as expressing factual relations in which things, events, or their properties stand to one another ...[8]

What were Nagel's arguments against the logical realism of Cohen and, implicitly, Russell and Frege? First was his positive conception of logic as syntax, a set of rules for combining symbols, which we prescribe to our use of language in inquiry. The Law of Non-Contradiction, ~ (p & ~ p), hereafter LNC, is a rule of sentence formation. Logical operators and variables refer to nothing; logical formulae cannot be true propositions because they are not propositions, only rules for acceptable combinations of signs. Once interpreted in English, the LNC can function as a prescription, like a rule in chess. But it is still not a description of anything, so it does not *mean at all.*

Second, the LNC has no noncircular justification. Let us interpret the LNC as applied to objects (of any kind) as: for any X, X cannot be p and $\sim p$ in the same respect at the same time. Now we can employ it as Cohen did and ask: can Fred be a brother and not a brother at the "same" time? Yes, if taken in two different respects, meaning in two different relations, a brother to Mary and not a brother to George. So Cohen held that the LNC restricts what can be true of Fred. But Nagel's question is, how are we to define the "same" respect or "same" time? *Only by using the LNC as the criterion of sameness.* Its prohibition is linguistic. Nagel employed an example that he and Cohen had used in their 1934 textbook, that a penny may seem circular or elliptical depending on your angle of vision, but the penny cannot be both at the same time from the same angle. The prohibition against being circular and elliptical at the same time in the same relation is dictated by the LNC, not by things themselves. So any argument that relations among possibilities themselves justify the LNC will be circular.

Third and related, logic is purely formal, and only what is formal can be necessary. Facts cannot be necessary, they are contingent, they could be another way; inconsistency can only be "located in discourse." Nagel writes: "Logical principles are compatible with any order which the flux of events may exhibit; they could not be in disagreement with anything which inquiry might discover ..." He continues:

> [T]he view that logical principles express the limiting and necessary structures of things . . . cannot be construed literally. For it is not things and their actual relations which are said to be logically consistent or inconsistent with one another, but propositions or statements about them . . . No one will hesitate to acknowledge that "The table on which I am now writing is brown" and "The table . . . is white" are mutually inconsistent. But this inconsistency cannot . . . be predicated of two "facts" . . . or "objects" for if there were such facts the view would be self-refuting.[9]

Nagel is claiming that while we do know and can identify cases of contradictory statements, hence prohibit one or both, we never identify *cases of contradictory facts*.

Last, is the interesting point that Nagel believes only this view of logic can defend its irreducibility. He believes a realist view of logic threatens to reduce it to something about the natural world, threatening psychologism, which would violate the naturalistic fallacy. Nagel concludes, "it is precisely because I believe logical principles should not be 'reduced to anything else' that I have espoused a conception of logic without ontology."[10] The only way to do so, he believes, is to regard them as a prescriptive syntax. In this, one can hear the echo, once again, of G. E. Moore's rejection of naturalism.

Buchler's Natural Complexes

A young Justus Buchler studied with Cohen as an undergraduate at CCNY, and then, doubtless on Cohen's advice, with Nagel at Columbia, writing a dissertation on Peirce in just the period when Nagel was breaking with Cohen. In the late 1930s, as a doctoral student, Buchler was enamored of Nagel's positivist views, and went on to become Nagel's Columbia colleague. In the 1950s, he clearly adopted objective relativism.[11] But in most other respects the rest of his career was a long road away from Nagel. In 1966, Buchler published *Metaphysics of Natural Complexes*, objective relativism's most complete formulation. We will not review it here, its key notions being familiar from chapter 2. But one aspect is specifically relevant to the argument over logic.

Buchler was at least passingly familiar with Carnap and Tarski from his work with Nagel (Buchler 1939). In 1951, as he was developing his own theory of human judgment, he wrote that, "Logical compulsion—the compulsion imposed by the laws of logic—is an elemental framework within which proception [i.e., experience] and communication occur. Consistency is a condition of survival in utterance. . . . there can be nothing in any judgment that actually refutes the law of contradiction. . . . The laws of logic exercise a conspicuous compulsion: we cannot reject them and still retain intelligibility . . ."[12] Buchler is trying to be a nonreductive Columbia naturalist here, but he has already moved away from strict adherence to Nagel. That the laws of logic might "exercise a conspicuous compulsion" is a positivistic impossibility. But Buchler is applying such laws only in the realm of judgment. He is struggling between his undergraduate teacher and his graduate mentor.

Buchler's most important dictum on the laws of logic is the following from *The Metaphysics of Natural Complexes*:

> The trait of "not entailing contradiction" is a trait that belongs to all possibilities in so far as they are prospectively actualized . . . it makes no difference whether we say that what is possible is possible "because" it does not entail contradiction, or that what does not entail contradiction does not "because" it is possible. . . . To hold that it is "logical principles" such as the principle of non-contradiction which ultimately determine "what is possible" is like holding that one side of a coin is more truly a side than the other . . . It could equally well be said that it is because of what is and is not possible that logical principles obtain.[13]

What is Buchler claiming? First, the laws of logic are rules of the necessary relations of possibilities, hence which possibilities are or are not actualizable in an order; "necessary" meaning the exclusion of certain possible combinations. As we have seen, for Buchler and Cohen, possibilities obtain, hence are natural complexes, like pasts, fictional characters, et cetera. Any actuality must have associated possibilities, any possibility must have associated actualities. Second, the diagnosis of contradiction or its absence requires the analysis of the order in question. Contradiction is the most general, and minimal, limit on what may or may not be actual in an order. Third, that any order has limits—without which it would not prevail at all—and that the rules governing symbols applied to statements about that order are *two aspects of one condition*. Buchler is unsure whether to claim the LNC applies to all orders, or to an order that overlaps with all other orders (either one would violate his objective relativism). He is claiming that there is no nonordinal answer to the question as to whether a logical rule determines what is possible or what is possible determines a logical rule. He is splitting the difference between Cohen's logical realism and Nagel's syntactic positivism. Each is a side of the coin.

Who was right, Cohen, Nagel, or Buchler? It will take us a while to determine this.

Truth and Such

As we saw earlier, the dominant account of truth in Western philosophy was always the correspondence theory, canonically formulated by Aristotle as, "To say of what is that it is not, or what is not that it is, is false, while to say of what is that it is, and what is not that it is not, is true."[14] The coherence and pragmatist theories of truth were then invented by idealism and American pragmatism, respectively. They remain competitors.

But a fourth was added, based in the new logic. It dates on the one hand to Frank Ramsey's notion of "equivalence," or as some call it "redundancy." Ramsey, colleague of Wittgenstein but also an admirer of Peirce, suggested that to call p "true" is merely to assert "p" (Ramsey 1991). Our assertion of a proposition is to assert its truth, and identity works both ways. So "true" is in effect equivalent to "asserted" or "assertible" and otherwise redundant.

The other root is Alfred Tarski. In his "The Concept of Truth in Formalized Languages" (1933), Tarski clarified an account of truth for a logical language that did not generate Russell's famous paradox, that is, "the set of all sets which are not members of themselves," which must both be and not be a member of itself (Tarski 1983). Tarski distinguished any language that we use to describe things, L, from its "metalanguage" ML, the language which specifies the syntax of L. The account of what "true-in-L" means belongs to ML, *not* L. He then proposed a criterion for any "extensional" theory of truth—one that allowed individual true sentences to be identified—namely, that such a theory must hold that any L-sentence "p" is true *if and only if* p. That is, "snow is white" is true if and only if snow is white. This would later be called "disquotation," or removing the quotation marks. The point is, every sentence of L can have an interpretation of its truth in ML, which stipulates that disquotation condition ("Convention T"). Keeping truth in ML, separate from L, prevents Russell's paradox. Tarski called this the "semantic" theory of truth, meaning that truth is restricted to the metalanguage of L, where L-sentences are interpreted and assigned truth-values.

Tarski cited Aristotle's definition of truth because he thought his own view had captured the core of Aristotle's correspondence theory. His analysis of the meaning of his Convention T showed that truth is dependent on, or tied up with, two conditions: *reference* and *satisfaction*. Simply, "F is G" is true if and only if what "F" refers to satisfies the predicate or function G.

Putnam once remarked that "[a]s a philosophical account of truth, Tarski's theory fails as badly as it is possible for an account to fail."[15] This sounds worse than it is; Putnam thought Tarski, and Davidson's later use of Tarski, revealed something about truth, but that it did not eliminate the need for a more substantive account. He concluded that Tarski's analysis does indeed show that assertability, truth, and reference are inseparable, that we cannot say what truth is without using reference and/or logical satisfaction. For Putnam, the core of Tarski's analysis is correct, but this does not endorse deflationism.

We saw earlier that Cheryl Misak considered deflationism compatible with pragmatism, largely because it is so minimal. In her excellent book on *The American Pragmatists*, Misak discusses the attempts of Sellars, McDowell, and Putnam to produce a "non-metaphysical" concept of truth, often influenced by deflationary ideas. Misak writes:

> Truth is out of our reach in that it marks the indefinite betterment of our beliefs and our practices of justification. . . . all pragmatists . . . reject the myth of the given and the representationalist idea that our epistemology should start with the thought that our beliefs . . . aim at mirroring the world . . . All pragmatists reject the picture that has experience giving us objective access to the inquirer-independent world. Some pragmatists [e.g., Peirce] argue that . . . we have no choice but to think that there is a world not of our making—a world we are trying to get right . . . Other pragmatists [e.g., Rorty] disagree and argue that when we start with our practices, we leave the world behind.[16]

Ordinal naturalism can allow us to avoid this conclusion while accepting parts of the pragmatic analysis. The judicious use of the objective relativism and emergence that Charles Morris thought were the proper metaphysics for pragmatism, comes to the rescue.

"Truth" is a property of certain assertive judgments, the ones that are true of what they are about. Their meaning can be complex, determined both by rules of use, their *Sinn* or intentional meaning (e.g., "the morning star"), and those objects thereby picked out, their reference or *Bedeutung* (Venus). One can say that what P is about makes P true or false. "True of" is analytically inseparable from the notion of "representation," as Tarski showed, and as Putnam agreed, thereby also inseparable from the notion of the *sign*, as that which stands for something else. The assertions we are mostly concerned with are sentences constituted by conventional symbols (in Peirce's sense) arranged according to a grammar or syntax. They have truth-conditions, into which the possibility of their truth can be decomposed. Whatever other interpretants they possess or stimulate, in inquiry we are concerned with their logical interpretants, namely meanings or concepts.

We can call this relation of the true sentence to what it is about "correspondence." It cannot be understood as "resemblance," which might hold, using Peircean language, for icons and diagrams. Correspondence cannot be analyzed or understood independent of representation (meaning) of a certain kind, which is something like literality or satisfaction. The way the true statement represents what it is about is not the same as the way the thermometer represents your temperature or the *Pietà* represents Jesus and Mary. The kind of standing-for relation which linguistic assertions bear to what they are about is an *emergent property* which arises in the semiotic functioning of humans alone. It cannot be reduced to or composed of concepts referring only to the entities, relations, and processes that obtain in either the nonliving world, or the pre-linguistic world. It ought not be surprising that we cannot eliminate or reduce "truth" or "true of," representation or satisfaction, to something more primitive not already implicated with it, just as we cannot reduce meaning or intentionality to something more primitive.

As to justification of sentences as true, the "mind-independent" claim about realism and correspondence was always too strong and too weak at the same time. The notion that something real is an objective, independent reality is utterly unclear: independent of what? Is anything independent *simpliciter*? Lots of things are the way they are independent of what we think or even whether we exist, but not independent of everything! Objective relativism puts it this way: *our propositions say or represent that* something is some way in its relations to some other things, of which I and you and we are cases. We are complexes-in-relation judging complexes-in-relation. The object's relation to my assertive judgment is strongly relevant to it—relevant to what the judgment is—while the judgment's relation to its object does not have to be, and usually is only weakly or "externally" relevant to it. This characterization of truth is independent of verification, of the process by which a sentence comes to be recognized as possessing it. The coherentist and pragmatic notions of truth rightly specify important ways that we know and justify the best practices of inquiry. But there is no reason to use them to define the norm or aim by which assertive inquiry governs itself.

Logic in Nature

Modern logic evolved in part as an attempt to produce a precise derivation of mathematics. Frege, the author of modern Logicism and a Platonic realist about mathematics, proposed that numbers could be analyzed as properties of sets. This did indeed work, and first-order logic seemed the basis on which all of mathematics could be derived. However, Logicism and with it realism seemed to crash on the shores of the paradoxes of set theory, encouraging formalists and positivists to claim that mathematical truths do not refer to anything. Nevertheless, to this day first-order predicate logic, employing functions and quantifiers on individual objects (rather than more functions and quantifiers), remains the great achievement of twentieth-century logic, generally believed to be adequate to formulating set theory with certain additions such as Zermelo-Frankel axioms with the Axiom of Choice (ZFC).[17] The question of realism in mathematics is far too complex to be adjudicated here, but it has generated comments directly relevant to what we have said about logical realism.

In her *Second Philosophy: A Naturalistic Method* (2007) Penelope Maddy argues that mathematical realism can be housed in naturalism. Her approach is opposed to "first" or foundational philosophy. She means simply that philosophy cannot operate logically prior to our best current empirical theories. This is a Quinean approach, which puts her in Otto Neurath's figurative boat, a vessel that must be rebuilt while sailing it. It establishes a continuity between the level of inquiry into everyday and scientific truth, and the account of logical and mathematical validity. The difference is a matter of degree. For Maddy, logical and mathematical validity hold by virtue both of certain features of the world and the basic human cognitive approach to the world, the latter being dependent on the former because of evolution. Our "most primitive cognitive mechanisms allow us to detect and represent the aforementioned features ... human beings are so configured cognitively because they live in a world that is so structured physically."[18]

Modern logic, Maddy claims, tracks the "K-F structure" of things, after the basic categories of Kant and Frege, that is, objects or individuals with functional properties in relation to other objects and properties, exhibiting various connectives (conjunctions, disjunctions, and negations), some of these relations bearing "ground-consequent" dependency. The property *p*, hence a function, divides up the world into what has *p*, what does not, and whatever we can't tell does or doesn't. She argues that in any such world a "rudimentary logic" holds partly *a priori* and partly *a posteriori*. Rudimentary logic is therefore contingent to our world, not necessary. As to whether the higher reaches of set theory are true *of* something, Maddy avoids a direct answer, arguing that "thin realism" and "Arealism" are two alternate, equivalent views, in somewhat Carnapian, pragmatic fashion.

Ordinal naturalism can augment this picture. First of all, contingency and necessity are ordinal. There is no nonordinal necessity. To say that the K-F logic holds contingently is entirely legitimate and compatible with the claim that it is necessary for the orders of nature that we know in relation to ourselves. Second, regarding what logic is "about," we can offer a direct answer: possible relations among actual complexes. This idea is not unique to objective relativists like Cohen and Buchler. Russell claimed in 1907 that "mathematics takes us . . . into the region of absolute necessity, to which not only the actual world, but every possible world, must conform . . . we now know that pure mathematics can never pronounce on questions of actual existence."[19] His student Wittgenstein remarked in the *Tractatus* that "[l]ogic treats of every possibility, and all possibilities are its facts . . . we cannot think of any object apart from the possibility of its connexion with other things."[20] The field we call "logic" is the study of the possible relations among complexes. There may not be "logical entities," but there are logical relations of complexes. And they too are complexes.

Possibilities have been a crucial topic in logic since the early modal logic of C. I. Lewis, which introduced the necessity ($\Box$) and the possibility ($\Diamond$) operators. Modal logic can concern: temporal modalities ("It was the case that," "It will be the case that"), epistemic modalities ("I know that" vs. "I believe that"), deontic modalities ("what ought/ought not be done is"), or alethic modalities, those relevant to truth, particularly "it is necessary that" and "it is possible that." As an extentionalist, rejecting the existence of meanings and universals, Quine refused to populate his world with possibilities, but Saul Kripke and David Lewis each rebelled against his view in making modal logic essential. Lewis took Leibniz's original notion of a "possible world," a non-actual world system, as a crucial contribution to the logical analysis of the actual world. The notion of possibilities as denizens of possible worlds became, starting in the 1980s, the dominant way of conceiving possibility in logic.

Recently, under the names of *modal actualism* and *dispositionalism*, some logicians have made a different analysis of possibilities. For the latter, a possibility is a "disposition to activity in some circumstances," as opposed to "categorical properties" which manifest at all times. For Andrea Borghini, "that which is, is what it is in virtue of what it could be. In other words, actual and possible existence are strictly and indivisibly connected."[21] Like these views, objective relativism understands possibilities as possessions or properties of some complex-in-relations, rather than a self-contained "world." Possibilities are as real, as experience-able, as capable of making a difference to other complexes as are actualities—which does not mean they are *efficiently* causal.

Maddy's naturalism is promising but can be amended. It may or may not be true that our logic essentially reflects the K-F language. That language is a very broad syntax which incorporates features that are widely distributed in the natural world with which we transact. They do not have to be *all* the features, but they are real features. Perhaps we focus on them because they are predictive and useful. But we are not limited by current, contemporary usefulness, which is why our cognition can advance. As Maddy suggests, our cognitive ability must have evolved, probably because it was useful or conferred increased advantage. But the use and application of much that was thereby conferred always had the potential for cognizing what was not originally useful, and it is precisely such accumulation of the formerly un-useful which eventually serves human cultural evolution.

Lastly, we can agree with certain nominalists and antirealists that logical formulae, the expressions of logical truths, are not descriptions or assertions of possibilities. The deep reason is that they are arguably the basic rules that establish the possibility of logical assertion, and as such, cannot be logical assertions. This was one of Wittgenstein's central claims. The mundane reason is that we no longer know what "true of" means *without a semantics*. Mathematical symbolisms are often of numbers (sets), or spaces, or other somethings—whatever is specified by the universe of discourse. But devoid of any interpretation or model, it is no longer possible to say they are true *of* something. So do they mean at all? We shall see.

Who Won the Columbia Family Squabble?

In historical terms, Nagel. Logic since the 1930s has indeed been widely regarded as prescriptive in the sense that it is ordered by uninterpreted syntactical rules laid down, requiring a semantic model to assign meanings which could then be judged true or false. Yet some theorists have continued to support logical realism. As in the indispensability argument of Eugen Wigner, how are we to explain why a meaningless but rule-governed syntax ought to be able, once interpreted, to be useful in questions of what is true of our world and predictions thereof? (Wigner 1960) Does the dialectic among the Columbia Naturalists provide any novel resources to this discussion? We begin by returning to Nagel.

Nagel was entirely right that there is and can be no noncircular justification of logic. But this is no different from Henry Sheffer's identification of the "logocentric predicament."[22] In general, the human cognitive system cannot possibly be shown to be true of objects in a noncircular manner *by us*, for any such proof would be part of itself. On the other hand, there is no good reason to doubt the general validity of our cognitive abilities *in toto*, or to doubt that some are at least partly, fallibly valid of what they judge. And we have already seen a plausible explanation of how they came to be largely valid: evolution. The same is true of the most abstract or general features of that cognitive system, namely logic.

But Nagel's claim that facts cannot contradict or be inconsistent is another matter. His justification is odd: since we cannot find a case of facts that contradict, we may not ascribe to facts the ground of that failure. With this, he wants to follow the other positivists, themselves echoing Hume in holding that necessity occurs only among the "relations of ideas," or more in our modern idiom, propositions. Even the logician Alonzo Church criticized Nagel on this, pointing out that the line between the necessary and contingent is fuzzy; if theory holism is accepted, then no strict line can be drawn between necessity and contingency, hence the former as well as the latter are subject to revision in light of recalcitrant experience (Church 1945). More relevant here, the claim that "facts cannot contradict" or "be inconsistent" presumes *nominalism*, that facts are particular and have no nonparticular features, including possibilities.

What Nagel ought to have written is that *actualities* do not and cannot contradict or be inconsistent, only possibilities can. Possible facts certainly can be inconsistent. But, if actualities possess, are rightly predicated with, possible relations to other complexes—which is to say, if we drop nominalism, and don't presume actualities to be utterly particular—and if their possibilities are constrained, we can then represent those constraints with logic, for example the LNC. Once one accepts that relations and possibilities are as real as anything, so each complex is dependent upon at least some relations or order, then relational constraints hold over the possibilities of complexes.

Nagel's defense of logic's irreducibility was in effect his positivist generation's defense against psychologism, the reduction of logic to human habits of thought. Given the abandonment of classical realism, whether in the form of Platonism, which was Frege's view, or the Aristotelianism of Cohen, how could a modern scientific naturalism be maintained without reducing logical rules to human psychology? For it is logic on which, at least retrospectively, we base rationality and science. Nagel made a revealing point in his 1949 defense of his view. He opposes the

> common error of attributing to things as inherent possessions attributes which they possess only under certain conditions . . . Doubtless it is true that the world is such that logical distinctions and relations appear in it in contexts of reflection and inquiry . . . I fail to see what . . . advantages are gained by supposing that a property known to be displayed only under specified conditions *must* be founded upon a *duplicate* property pervasive throughout nature.[23]

But does saying that actualities we encounter in inquiry are characterized and constrained by ordinal possibilities, the most minimal of which we express in logic, thereby create a "duplicate property"? Any more so than saying both "I am eating the bread" and "the bread is edible" violates Occam's razor? Are the discoveries and claims of mathematicians, and the most general rules of any logic, representative of anything? Indeed, are they *meaningful at all*? I believe ordinal naturalism allows us to answer in the affirmative.

Like all laws, logical formulae represent the possibilities of complexes. As rules for assertions they cannot be assertions. But are meaningful signs limited to assertions? As a Peirce scholar, Nagel should have said *no*. Logical terms and operators are symbols, conventionally chosen code, for somethings—possible objects, of any kind, entities, processes, relations, properties, or activities. However, the formulae made out of such signs are not "symbols"—that is, not conventional—but nor are they meaningless. In Peirce's language, they are *hypothetic icons* that exhibit or show or express the rules of relations among possible "objects." They are like diagrams but composed of abstract, conventional symbols. In this sense, the Wittgenstein of the *Tractatus* was mostly right about logic (though not of language in general). The rules that characterize how any sayings can be true cannot be "true sayings." However, this only means we are making judgments and formulating signs that mean about the limits of assertability; and these hypothetically *show*, rather than *say*. Frank Ramsey famously quipped in disagreement with Wittgenstein, "If you can't say it you can't say it, and you can't whistle it either." He was right about "saying."[24] But "showing" means iconically or indexically, rather than symbolically. Neither do we need to say logical rules "ground" or make legitimate all other truth claims—which, once foundationalism had been abandoned and ordinalism accepted, we neither expect nor need. Nor are they prescriptions, but they can *be* prescribed. They are attempts to make explicit, to cognize, the most general characters of what is knowable via propositional language.

Thus Buchler's claim is true but incomplete. The "sides of a coin" metaphor rightly reflects that the discrimination of complexes is always an identification of something in relation to other somethings. One could say that in splitting the difference between Cohen and Nagel, Buchler is refusing the choice between realism and antirealism, as others like Richard Rorty have claimed to do. However, Buchler's metaphysics is clearly not agnostic between those options. The two sides of the coin are distinguishable but metaphysically equivalent sets of natural complexes. The laws of logic represent the broadest conditions of the relations among possibilities of somethings that our species is uniquely able to handle as objects. As noted, *truth is an emergent property* of the relation of our intentional and linguistic species to nature and its manifold possibilities. There is no reason to believe that if we are unable to characterize the totality of our cognitive capacities, of which logical consistency must be a part, that the work done by these capacities is somehow unstable, just as there is no reason to believe that we will not continue to refine our notion of those capacities, and logic, in the future.

Chapter Twelve

Ethics of the Truly Social Animal

> In truth, almost all worthwhile human life lies between the extremes that morality puts before us.
>
> —Bernard Williams, *Ethics and the Limits of Philosophy*[1]

We have already suggested a set of *prima facie* moral values that go with human communities. But this is of course not an adequate ethics. Ethics is the study of morality in the broad sense. Part of it is called "meta-ethics," or the study of the meaning of moral terms and judgments and whether they can be rationally justified. "Normative ethics" concerns which substantive theory of morality is best, which is required rationally to adjudicate moral disputes, including decisions among and about the six moral values. Even if human societies generally are characterized by the moral taste buds described in chapter 10, that does not tell us how to adjudicate conflicts among them. So we must start again.

Most moral philosophers have a set of intuitions about, and arguments for, some normative ethics, usually one of the big four: a deontological ethics of duty like Kant's, for which rationality dictates the conformity of our will to universal rules of duty; some kind of consequentialism like John Stuart Mill's utilitarianism, for which an act is right if it maximizes a social good, like happiness or preference satisfaction; a virtue ethics like Aristotle's, for whom the moral question is what are the character traits of the best kind of person, who habitually makes the right moral choice in particular circumstances; and, the most recent addition, a contractualist ethics, originally derived from John Rawls's version of Kant, for which whatever moral rules would be agreed to by rational, equal individuals are valid. Normative ethics revolves around the issue of whether any of these can be justified.

Our approach in this chapter presumes a critical attitude toward much recent ethical theory. This criticism sets the stage for understanding what an evolutionary naturalist basis for ethics can do. The criticism is not new; it was made by three twentieth-century philosophers who all had their start in Oxford in the 1950s.

In 1958, Elizabeth Anscombe, most famous as Wittgenstein's translator, published a remarkable essay, "Modern Moral Philosophy." An early member of the Aristotelian revival in ethics, Anscombe argued that modern moral philosophy confuses morality with law. Modern thinkers regard philosophical ethics as a search for an ultimate rule. This search is, she argued, the product of the Judeo-Christian tradition that regards God as the supreme lawmaker. The trouble is, philosophers are now searching for an ultimate law in the absence of any reference to such a lawmaker. In her Aristotelian response, she argues that typically when we ask if act x is right or wrong, we ask whether it is a case of some act which is by its very meaning right or wrong, such as is a killing a case of "murder"? To decide x is murder *is* to decide it is immoral. She opposes the modern attempt to find an ultimate rule to justify that the kind of act (murder) is wrong, whether what makes murder wrong is its consequences (utilitarianism), or rational agreement (contractualism), or a universal self-legislation of a maxim (Kant).[2]

In 1981, Alasdair MacIntyre, who was part of the rationality debate of the 1950s and had been influenced by Anscombe, published *After Virtue: A Study in Moral Theory*. MacIntyre insisted that rational discussion of moral values cannot take place outside a cultural tradition with canonical practices, a common narrative, and a projected ultimate Good. He explained that such traditions were neither monistic nor hermetic; they are historical debates over the interpretation of its Good, texts and practices, and could translate and even judge the notions of another tradition superior to itself by its *own* criteria (he did this using a version of "critical rationalism," noted earlier). But without cultural practices, narrative, and a final good, there is nowhere for rational argument to go except to revolve in relativistic circles, ultimately equating "right" with "power." This he claims is our modern situation.

Another Oxford product Bernard Williams in *Ethics and the Limits of Philosophy* (1985) argued that the project that one could, or should, logically derive all moral "oughts" for action from one or two general principles that are differentiated from all considerations of success (i.e., moral luck), religion, culture, and historical particularity, thereby enabling the normative regulation of virtually all human behavior, is a fool's errand. Modernity has led philosophers to conceive of morality as something that, given an absence of religion, is meant to guide the lives of all citizens in a cosmopolitan, modern state by a single rule. That, it cannot do.

I would echo these thinkers in holding that much modern moral theorizing exhibits three problems. Contemporary moral philosophy often seeks a set of moral rules that (a) are fully disconnected from practical efficacy or success, aesthetic considerations, and religion; (b) are supposed to be universal, holding for all human beings, or at least all rational adults, unaffected either by differences between societies and cultures or social roles; and (c) hold for all historical periods, regardless of how vastly different human societies have been. By these criteria, a claim or prescription or their justification is morally adequate only if all "extraneous" social, practical, agent-relative, historically relative, cultural or aesthetic factors are excluded as irrelevant. My point is not that these predilections are intrinsically wrong but that they are a poor way to begin philosophizing about morality. "What moral rules ought we, as members of modern liberal societies in the industrial or postindustrial world, obey?" is an excellent question. Likewise, the even broader, "What moral rules ought any human in any period of history anywhere on Earth obey?" But we cannot presume a good answer to the first automatically answering the second provides necessary criteria for answering the first. If anything that appears to be a moral act or consideration is declared not to be moral at all because it fails to be universal and ahistorical, then we will have very few examples of morality to deal with.

The aim of what follows is to see whether obstacles lying in the path of an ethics that respects the naturalistic, moral realism of the basic moral norms of chapter 10 can be removed. We will be guided by one of the most interesting of the ethicists of the second half of the twentieth century, R. M. Hare, whose thought integrates parts of the most prominent normative ethical theories. This will seem odd in that he opposed naturalism, and as a noncognitivist, has often been regarded as an antirealist. But ordinal naturalism allows us to see that his approach is compatible with both naturalism and realism.

Some Meta-Ethical Issues

Meta-ethics is the investigation of the meaning of the terms used in normative ethics, but it can equally be thought of as the analysis of the nature of the subject matter of ethics. To begin, we can list the moral norms as *good*, *right*, and *virtuous*, all of which lead to an *ought*. Good is the broadest value term, and as I suggested earlier, is not intrinsically moral. For the great majority of human actions, goodness is supplied by success. Likewise, aesthetic value is good. Much the same might be true for "right," but good is broader. Virtue, as we use it today, is largely but not exclusively moral. For the time being, we can say goodness, rightness, and virtue are jointly terms for the moral obligations that ought to govern social interaction.

Analytic philosophers in the 1930s began to raise the question: what do moral claims mean? As we saw, the emotivists decided that since such claims could not be either analytic or synthetic truth claims, they must be emotive expressions, "yeas" and "boos," or more graciously, "I like this, I don't like that." But by the late 1940s and early 1950s, partly under the influence of Wittgenstein's circulated views, the pursuit of ordinary language philosophy led the Oxford thinkers to an obvious conclusion: nobody thinks "murder is wrong" means "murder is yucky." But what might be true is that moral claims are prescriptive rules, commands, "Don't murder," rather than descriptive truth claims. This came to be called "noncognitivism," whereas the view that moral statements are truth claims came to be "cognitivism" or "descriptivism."

Three big questions need to be answered in debating cognitivism versus prescriptivism. One is whether descriptive moral claims, such as "murder is wrong," can be shown to be rationally valid. After all, the problem with emotivism is that "I don't like murder" can't be shown to be more valid than "I like it." Second, and related to this, is the question of realism: do morally right acts have rightness as a property independent of our judgment that they are right? Noncognitivism would seem to answer with a nonrealist "no." Third is a kind of *internalism* versus *externalism* question (we have seen these terms in other subjects). Moral externalism holds that you can acknowledge a moral rule or judgment as valid but still not have a reason to obey it, just as, it is held, factual descriptions don't provide a reason for action. So you rationally could say, "*x* is right, but I am not going to do it." Internalism holds that the motive or reason to obey is internal to the validity of a moral judgment, so saying "it's right but I won't do it" would be irrational. Cognitivism or descriptivism seems inevitably externalist.

As we saw, morality fundamentally has to do with interpersonal action. That is, its primary role is to guide or govern the active judgments of social members in relation to each other. That is how it must have evolved, and it remains the core concern of morality. Not the sole concern—morality can govern behavior in private, how one thinks or feels, and can be applied to politics, to intersocial relations, et cetera. But as I have insisted, the first job of ethics is how people whose actions can affect each other treat each other. Whatever else morality must do, the first thing an adequate ethical theory must account for is normative interpersonal action, the moral rules of the most collaborative, joint intentional animal.

One other distinction is easy to forget in linguistic philosophy. The primary job of morality is to regulate active judgments, actions, not *assertive judgments about* actions. Certainly, moral assertions can sometimes themselves be regarded as an action, or a statement whose function is active, for example, if they are prescriptions or commands. But if the uttering of a sentence is considered an act, it has to be validated as an act, not as a truth claim. And of course in all walks of life, including philosophy, humans use truth claims to discuss and adjudicate actions. Right now, you and I are engaged in an inquiry in which we debate truth claims about the rightness of acts. We are talking about what action should be like; in inquiry, all we can hope for is to say true things about that. Succeeding in that task is not *being* moral or virtuous. The point of all this inquiry is to discover morally valid action regulations, not true statements. The point of ethics is to figure out which acts are more right.

The Ethics of Hare

In the early 1950s, Oxford ordinary language philosophy was booming, based in the new work of Wittgenstein, which was available to the *cognoscenti* even before its posthumous publication in 1953 as the groundbreaking *Philosophical Investigations*. The most prominent practitioners were A. J. Ayer, Gilbert Ryle, and J. L. Austin but also P. F. Strawson, Gertrude Anscombe, Mary Midgley, Philippa Foot, and Iris Murdoch, as well as Bernard Williams and R. M. Hare. (Note the sudden appearance of multiple female philosophers at the head of a major movement.) A kind of "new Aristotelianism" emerged in which analytic, linguistic techniques were used to discern the rationality of virtually any topic, including aesthetics and morals, in contrast to the earlier positivist declaration of those areas as irrational—yet still without an attempt to "ground" the results in any universal foundation. This was seeking the rules of "ordinary language" versus "ideal language" philosophy. As noted, their work fed into the rationality debate, including Peter Winch, Alasdair MacIntyre, and Ernest Gellner, forming the moment when cultural relativism emerged as a serious philosophical question, as we will see.

Foot and Anscombe regarded Hare's approach as an extension of the work of Stevenson and Ryle, analyzing moral statements as expressions of emotion or nonsense altogether (MacCumhaill and Wiseman 2022). But Hare's work was special. Most important was *The Language of Morals* (1952), which presented Hare's *rational prescriptivism*, meaning that moral statements are commands or prescriptions but have a logic of their own and thus can be the subject of rational argument. Hare remarkably thought Aristotle, Kant, and Mill intersect, that properly understood and applied their perspectives are not incompatible. While peerless in his meta-ethical, logical analysis, Hare was also a man of the world, with broad experience, including time in a Japanese prison camp (Hare 1979). Hare always recognized that the normative regulation of human action was the point of ethics, so any meta-ethics had to make possible a workable normative morality open to rational criticism.

Universality and Prescription

Hare's first prominent essay, "Universalizability," was a response to a paper of Gellner's (Hare 1955; Gellner 1955). Gellner had argued against Kantian morality as inadequate to particularist judgments, which he interpreted in terms of "existentialism." Kant's categorical imperative ruled that a decision to act in a certain way was only moral if the agent could wish it were universal law. Gellner distinguished such "U" claims (universalizable) from "E" claims (existentialist), in which an individual declares fealty to a particular person, family, or country, which is binding but *not* universalizable. Gellner's claim was that U reasons are the type one gives before a judge where there is equality before the law, whereas E reasons pop up in unique social ties, like romantic love or patriotism or family loyalty. His point is that the E relationships cannot be analyzed in U terms. One can't say, "I love you and thus will also love anyone who shares your relevant properties." Gellner associated this with Kierkegaardian existentialism, but what was actually in the back of his mind was traditional social commitments to kin and locale.

Hare thought this was a mistake. What makes the E type seem different can be overcome by including any clause of historical reference, for example, "the person with whom the agent has fallen in love," in a U statement. This is no different from the fact that you have to keep a promise to the person you made it to, and not others. More broadly, Hare pointed out the difference between the "universal" and the "general." The opposite of the general is any set or subset that falls under it: under the general term "apple," there are Macintosh apples, Empire apples, and also "this particular apple." Whereas the opposite of the universal is only the last of these, a singular designated by an ineliminable proper noun or indexical indication. Human moral claims are universal *but not necessarily general*. The point is that a universal can apply to any collection, however narrow, including one with historical reference, as long as the application is not *named*. That a lover should be loyal to their lover, or a citizen to their country, or a parent to their children is universalizable; it would only be singular therefore not universalizable if I said, "Fred must be loyal to his father John, but no other son needs to be loyal." Note that this means social roles and sociocultural differences can figure in moral claims: it is wrong for anyone that fits description *y* (including a relation or function) to do *x* in similar circumstances.

This analysis pushed Hare to reinterpret the difference between Kant and Mill. Kant formulated his moral principle, the categorical imperative, in several ways, the most famous being that one's will must be universalizable. Mill's Greatest Happiness Principle (or principle of utility) claimed that one ought to act so as to maximize social benefit, understood as pleasure or (in later versions) preference satisfaction. So, unlike Kant, Mill gives moral weight to indefinitely many consequences of the act; while lying is usually immoral, if a lie would in some special situation produce greater human benefit, one *ought* to lie. Not unreasonable if you are hiding Anne Frank in your attic. But this raises problems too. Hare's analysis lets him say of the consequentialist statement, "One ought not to tell lies unless this is necessary in order to save innocent lives," that it is "just as much a U-type maxim as 'One ought not to tell lies.'"[3] If Kant's universalizability is rightly understood, it can bend toward utilitarian conclusions.

Hare endorsed prescriptivism. He argued that "good"—referring not only to moral but practical or prudential and aesthetic phenomena—is a term of "commendation." To call something good is to commend it. Humans commonly give reasons for their commendations. In the case of *moral* expressions, the commendation becomes an actual prescription, what "ought" or "ought not" to be done. Descriptions are made true by a combination of syntax and truth conditions, hence facts. Moral statements include both a factual claim and an evaluation or commendation not reducible to factual claims, the former serving as the *reasons for* commending the act. And prescriptivism is clearly internalist; commendations, evaluations, and prescriptions are inherently motivating. It's irrational to say I morally should do it but I won't.

The logical structure of moral statements is thus to say: (1) some property justifies commendation; (2) x has that property; and (3) therefore x is commended. Rational arguments about the validity of such prescriptions are mostly arguments about the descriptive applicability of the second condition—in effect, "facts" based in truth conditions. When I say "John is a good person," and you disagree, we argue. I keep offering different reasons (descriptions) that show he is good, but my moral claim remains the same throughout. The evaluative conclusion (3), "John is a good person," can remain the same, while the truth conditions, hence standards for making it (1 and 2), can change. This is crucial for Hare. Purely descriptive or cognitivist approaches to ethical statements—of which "naturalism" is one kind—must regard every description as making a different moral claim, for example, "John is bad" and "John is good" are different proposed facts. Further, cognitivist descriptions lose motivational force, as noted. He thus remarkably claims that naturalism leads to relativism, since rational disagreements about the applicability of a descriptive predicate—which have to treat "x is commendable" as similar to the statements "x is blue" or "x is large"—inevitably turn into disagreements about social language use and are therefore culturally relative. So it is a good thing, he argues, that moral claims have a different logic. We will return to this.

A Multilevel Ethics

Hare strikingly claims that Kant's deontology and Mill's utilitarianism, when rightly understood, converge (Hare 1997). He is thus able to endorse a "rule utilitarianism," albeit one with more than a single level of analysis. Here we need some background.

When John Stuart Mill formulated the most famous version of utilitarianism, he included an ambiguity only noticed later. The Greatest Happiness Principle seemed clear and simple: maximize general happiness. But *to what* is that rule to be applied? Obviously, it seemed, to particular actions, like whether I may lie to Jody today in order to get her to loan me money. But one of the objections to utilitarianism was that it required the agent to perform a potentially very complicated calculation before every act. Perhaps my use of Jody's money will help a lot of people. How could I calculate all the results of choosing to be a professor rather than a lawyer? Mill answered that, in actual everyday life, the homely moral rules our culture taught us—"don't lie," "don't cheat," "don't steal"—are perfectly good utilitarian rules that, if followed, will produce general happiness in aggregate most of the time.

Reasonable, but this opens a new and worse problem. For it makes a major difference whether you apply Mill's principle to particular acts, like "should I lie to my friend *Jody today*?" or to general rules, like "should I ever lie?" The most famous objection to utilitarianism is that, according to it, in special circumstances we might have to do apparently immoral, even awful things, such as torture a suspect to save others, throw a homeless man onto the trolley tracks to avoid killing a doctor, or enslave a minority to benefit a majority, because these actions will generate less unhappiness in total. That is, *act utilitarianism*, meaning, the utilitarian principle applied to the particular act in this particular situation and its particular consequences, can generate nasty results. As J. J. C. Smart asked, should I turn over the innocent man to the angry mob in order to prevent twenty people from dying in a riot?[4] Like it or not, Smart concluded, the act-utilitarian probably has to accept that utility requires us to kill the innocent man. On the other hand, *rule utilitarianism* avoids such nasty cases. For it is likely that "Do not kill the innocent" will in fact maximize social happiness in the long run—even if the twenty people die today. The same for "don't ever lie." Fine.

But this solution comes with its own price. For we have reached the same conclusion as Kant! Rule utility seeks the rules we are willing to universalize, overlooking the difficult cases. Rule utility saves utilitarianism from its biggest problem by wiping away the extremes, but at the cost of turning itself into a consequentialist version of Kant's ethics. It appears to collapse into deontology.

Hare claims that all this presupposes a misreading of both Kant and Mill. He argues that the claim that Kant's moral philosophy must reject any consideration of consequences is false, or at least misleading. Kant does, he claims, dictate that any rational will includes its object as part of itself. No one can even define an act or a maxim without reference to its intended modification of the world. What must be excluded, for Kant, is the claim that *further* consequences outside the definition of the act can make an immoral act moral.

> To act is to make a difference to the course of events, and what the act is, is determined by that difference . . . if I am wondering whether to pull the trigger, the main morally relevant consideration is that if I did, the man that my gun is pointing as would

die. Killing . . . is causing death. . . . The intended consequence is what makes it wrong . . . So what the anti-consequentialists ought to be saying is something that consequentialists . . . can also say . . . that there are some consequences which are morally relevant, and that we ought to bring about . . . regardless of the other consequences which are morally irrelevant.[5]

In his *Moral Thinking: Its Levels, Method and Point*, Hare argues that moral conflict reveals the inevitable divergence of two levels of moral judgment (there is a third meta-ethical level, at which this very discussion takes place). At the first level are intuitions that express rules of thumb or the *prima facie* duties of David Ross, which "are just universal prescriptions," in the Kantian sense *or* the rule-utilitarian sense of Mill, for example, "Lying is wrong," "Benevolence is good." Hare is here fusing Ross's duties with Millian rules that are indistinguishable from Kantian duties, much like the values of Haidt. It is only when there is a conflict of such duties, a need to justify following one rule over another, that the second level is invoked.

That level, "critical thinking," is a decision under constraints imposed by the moral concepts of the first level and the factual situation, which may well be a matter of disagreement. Kant's universality thesis imposes a constraint on this level too, that the decision be both *act consequentialist and universalizable*: "critical moral thinking, which selects these principles and adjudicates between them in cases of conflict is act-utilitarian" yet must still "take no cognizance of individual identities," like all moral judgment.[6] That is, adjudication of conflicts between legitimate, rationally valid universal, first-level rules common to Kant's deontology and Mill's rule utilitarianism must invoke act consequentialist concerns at the critical level, deciding which rule yields more good over all. Everyday morality is rule utilitarian or deontological, as you like; only the hard cases require invoking act utility, meaning what is consequentially better for those affected. Of these levels, Hare remarks that "it is hardly an exaggeration to say that more confusion is caused, both in theoretical ethics and in practical moral issues, by the neglect of this distinction than by any other factor" (Hare 1981, 25).

Hare recognizes that the decision at the critical level is a "decision of principle" and so *not deducible* from a principle. Such a decision is inevitable if arguments over moral statements are pushed far enough, but for him this does not remove the rationality of the discussion. To make a value judgment at the critical level, he writes, is the real burden of adult ethical life, to rationally decide which rule applies or trumps other rules, meaning, which yields the most or more crucial good. It is a learned, acquired ability. In discussing those who would argue that, lacking a principle to make the decision leaves us with simple subjectivism, Hare responds with a wisdom rare in philosophical literature.

> Many of the dark places of ethics become clearer when we consider this dilemma in what parents are liable to find themselves . . . although principles have in the end to rest upon decisions of principle, decisions as such cannot be taught; only principle can be taught. . . . [The] plea of the subjectivist is quite justified. It is the plea of the adolescent . . . To become morally adult is to reconcile these two apparently conflicting positions by learning to make decisions of principle.[7]

RULES, CONSEQUENCES, AND VIRTUES

Hare also found that Aristotle's virtue ethics was to some extent compatible with Kant's deontological ethics and Mill's utilitarianism. He writes of Aristotle: "The will is a prescriptive, not a descriptive faculty. In this it is like Aristotle's *phronesis*. Aristotle himself is half a prescriptivist . . . like Kant and Mill."[8] This is because Hare regards what appear to be the most distinctive features of their approaches—rule-conforming duties, concern for consequences, and virtuous character—as compatible. It is striking that John Dewey, a naturalist whose ethics is not taken very seriously today, made the same point (Dewey 1932).

The six moral values of chapter 10 must in application generate *rules*. Human morality must be rule governed. This is rooted in joint intentionality. There is a reason for this: the most basic human social units are largely egalitarian. I do not mean they lack gender or age discrimination. But the band is a collaborative unit, and members will not collaborate or obey unless treated approximately equally in some intramural context. Among the collaborating foragers, the moral duty must be, "All of us must do x," "None may do y." They are still "universal" rules if ascribed to a role or set of characteristics—"No father/mother/friend/cousin may do that"—or to one class or stratum of a hierarchical society in which there is intramural equality—"No commoner may do that." Nothing about this displaces the role of empathy, sentiments, or moral psychology. But when social members understand these things as morally obligatory, they are understood as applying universally, and that entails rule governance.

That does not mean the end of all moral behavior is rule governedness. The end, not necessarily the "end in view" or intended aim of the act, must be *a* good. For otherwise there is no answer to the question, why is rule-governed behavior valuable? It is valuable in terms of contributing to some state or condition or purpose. Is there a single general rule that ought to guide second-level adjudication among the basic moral values? *It can only be teleological or consequentialist.* For we are now asking what justifies the commitment to rule conformity? The justification may well be: because duty preserves the society we belong to. If a normative theory is employed to adjudicate, it must invoke a purpose or end, some form of act consequentialism.

Lastly, as philosopher Jorge Garcia argues, we cannot call a normative system of action "moral" if it does not imply moral character traits on the part of the agent, that is, virtues and vices (Garcia 1990). Without reference to or implications for the moral status of the agent, and not merely the act, it is difficult to describe such acts and consequences as "moral." After all, some of the acts demanded by morality, or acts indistinguishable from them, can be performed accidentally, or in a state of automatism, or even by nonhuman agents. Moral significance requires that there has to be something about the agent's ongoing self revealed by and connected to performance. Without "virtue" the act cannot imply the moral credit of the agent. As we've seen, excellence is a term that spans the efficacious, moral, and aesthetic, but its specifically moral use is "moral virtue."

There is no reason these three approaches of rules, consequences and virtues must exclude each other (see figure 12.1). Morality as a set of

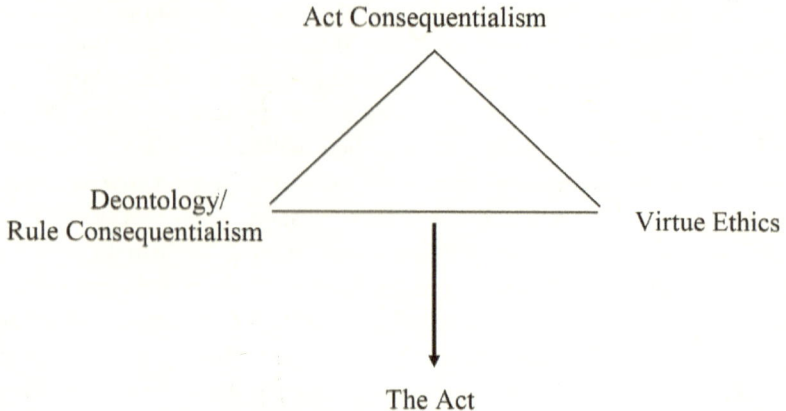

Figure 12.1. Contexts of the act. (Author created)

concerns about interpersonal action can typically involve (a) the rules that people ought to follow; (b) the consequences of following those rules for all affected; and (c) the character of the agent who does obey these rules or not.

One might even connect them to the joint intentionality diagram in figure 6.1: the act (home plate), I (1st base, character of the agent), You (3rd base, rules governing relations to concrete others), and We (2nd base, the decision as to what rule-governed act is best). You cannot have a human morality without rules that people in the relevant positions with the relevant traits are obliged to obey with respect to others; you cannot reason about and adjudicate inevitable conflicts among those rules without referring to the likely consequences of obeying them; and to call persons moral or immoral is to ascribe virtues and vices to the agents.

Naturalizing Hare

Hare clearly rejected naturalism. But *what* naturalism? For Hare, naturalism is a type of descriptivism or cognitivism that holds that the validity, hence truth, of a moral statement lies wholly in its truth conditions. Moral statements are supposed to be statements of facts; that "x is good" has a grammar like "x is blue" or "x is a mammal." The cognitivists in Hare's day were either "objective," claiming that some natural observable property is identical to the good, which was the direct target of Moore's naturalistic fallacy arguments, or "subjective," as with the emotivists, where a moral statement expresses the actual experience of the agent who is judging. And each of these fails very badly in the moral domain.

As noted, Hare believed not only such a perspective could not support normative prescriptions or rational validations, he argued that it led to relativism. Naturalism seeks to reduce moral judgments to statements whose meaning is solely determined by syntax and by truth conditions. Disagreements about truth conditions, he claims, become disagreements about language, for example, if two people see a wall, one says "the wall is white" and the other "the wall is red," this turns into a debate about the meanings of color terms. The relativism he refers to is social relativity in application of a natural predicate, as opposed to, an attitude of universal prescription toward what the predicate is applied to. Hare writes: "This very clearly shows what is wrong with naturalism . . . it pretends that what are in fact substantial moral principles are nothing more than linguistic rules. Naturalism confuses learning morals with learning a language" (1997, 68).

Indeed, this is related to the rationality debate common at Oxford in Hare's early years. He writes, "the truth conditions of a moral statement are inevitably relative to a culture and its mores and language" (129). Descriptivism, by identifying the "good" with those conditions, makes rational criticism of a culture's moral principles impossible. Whereas with prescriptivism, the evaluative ingredient "can be a culturally invariant element in them . . . [and] enables them to be used in rational discussion *between* cultures." What he means is, the commendatory element can be willfully, universally prescribed. Only a nondescriptive theory can keep the commendatory element semantically distinct from the factual conditions, allowing moral claims "such as any thinker in possession of the nonmoral facts must agree to" (134).

Some kinds of naturalism were, however, not out of court for Hare. Aristotle's ethics is rooted in a naturalistic view of humans as highly developed animals requiring habitual, social training. Hare's *prima facie* principles, understood as "rules of thumb," inevitably have a prudential element, like virtues "required as much for success" as strictly moral considerations. Hare's focus is not only on finding a rule but also, as in Aristotle, on the long-term development of the ability to follow those rules and make decisions in the hard cases, hence character. The task is "to make a success of practicing the more intrinsic virtues such as beneficence or justice."[9] Finally, Hare also recognizes functional statements, like "that is a good auger."[10] Functional statements always require a commendatory element, to wit "ought to be chosen," which supervenes on descriptive properties. But precisely for this reason, containing a commendation or "ought," Hare denies that such statements are "naturalistic" meaning purely descriptive.

My claim is that Hare's view is anti-naturalistic only if one accepts the positivist view of nature common in his day. But it is entirely compatible with an ordinal naturalism.

First, naturalism is not tied solely to "cognitivist" or "descriptivist" ethics, hence exclusive of evaluation and prescription. As we saw, all judgments, including assertions and actions, are both cognitive and evaluative, regardless of whether they function to assert or to modify the environment. We can thereby endorse *both* prescriptivism and descriptivism, albeit in different cases. An action, or active judgment, can be morally valid, the right thing to do, like donating to the poor. Likewise a prescription or command is another kind of action that can be morally valid, like saying, "You ought to donate to the poor." But we commonly make assertive judgments about what is right and wrong, "It is morally good to donate to the poor." The function of moral statements is indeed prescriptive, as Hare argues, namely to regulate human action. However, an assertion about which prescription is best can be assertively valid, true, if natural and social life include objective values.

And as we have argued, *they do*. Our ordinal naturalism has recognized that teleonomic purpose and value suffuse the biological order; the bird ought to have two wings. Once we get to organisms capable of minded purpose, we can say the dog ought to have gone around the right side of the tree instead of the left to find the rabbit. None of this is moral, of course. But it applies as well to the human world, to the various functional goods that are inseparable from staying alive, raising children, and all forms of human collaboration, especially social roles. Whenever the activity in question is functional, when engaging in the role or activity intrinsically invokes purpose, its function is contributing to inquiry; if it functions in the management of a set of activities, it is contributing to what is done, what actions result. It becomes a truth-conditional statement of fact, a "value fact" as we have argued before.

What for Hare is the relation between the evaluative and descriptive parts of a commendation that serve as reasons? He argues the evaluative moral properties *supervene* on nonmoral "naturalistic" or factual statements.[11] The prescriptive aspect or commendation of a moral statement is dependent on but nonreducible to the descriptive or factual aspects of the statement. If they were "reducible to" or "derivable from" the later, they would be natural, cognitivist, externalist, and relativist. Hare believes the evaluative or prescriptive meaning/function of the statement can remain the same while the descriptive meaning changes, because the former "supervenes" on the later (Hare 1997, 21). Indeed,

> [s]o the objectivist naturalists' project is the right one, though he executes it badly . . . He has grasped that moral statements are made about actions for reasons, namely that they have certain non-moral properties. An act was wrong, for example, because it was an act of hurting somebody for fun. This property of moral statements, their supervenience on non-moral statements, is crucial . . . But the objective naturalist . . . mistakes supervenience for entailment, and thus makes into analytically true statements what are really substantial moral principles . . . (126–27)

As you might expect, Hare's supervenience is simply what we have called *emergence*. It actually resembles Mead's earlier claim that the "mechanist" tries to reduce the emergent property to its physical base, while the teleologist treats the emergent property as if it were independent. The point is to do neither. The moral status of a human judgment—a nonlinguistic act, a linguistic prescription, or an assertion about what is morally right—is an emergent property of a joint intentional, social-self-conscious commendation with respect to some human activity or process which it promotes (or inhibits). That moral status is itself a feature of the act for objective relativism, hence ordinal naturalism, albeit an objectively relative one. If that commendation is a universal prescription for action, it is moral.

There is one final benefit of our naturalistic account for Hare. Our discussions of joint intentionality allow us to address what for some is a fatal problem with Hare's position. Many philosophers today believe that rule consequentialism is unsupportable. The reason is that any attempt to apply it while nevertheless retaining its fundamental consequentialism will reduce it to act consequentialism. Consequentialism, they hold, must inevitably be cashed out in acts in particular situations, with act utility's attendant problems, for example, murdering the innocent man to save twenty. We can suppose the social consequences of following the rule "do not lie," or "lying is wrong," are beneficial. But also suppose that in some particular case it seems that lying is more beneficial, for example, telling an anxious person on Monday before a speaking engagement that they look well when they don't. At that point, the rule consequentialist must modify her "don't lie" rule, for example, "don't lie, unless you are speaking to an anxious person on Monday and the lie might make them perform better," or "don't lie unless lying maximizing good consequences," or "don't lie, *ceteris paribus*" (all other things being equal). Rule utility either leads to endless exception clauses or falls back into act utility. The point is that rule consequentialism seems to collapse into act consequentialism (Hooker 1999).

But as noted our earlier analysis in chapter 6 helps us here: human morality *must* be governed by first-order universalizable rules. I am not claiming that no moral act can under any circumstances fail to conform to a rule, nor that rules are prior to consequences or virtues. I am claiming that joint intentional, socially self-conscious language users cannot morally constrain their social action without occupying perspectives and positions that are rule governed, meaning the action is what any other agent of the relevant kind in the relevant situation ought to do, and the reasons for the act could be explained. Rules governing permissible and impermissible acts in socially common situations are unavoidable. Act consequentialism *cannot* account for the moral behavior of everyday social agents and cannot guide it; humans in a social group cannot regulate their behavior by each guessing all or most relevant consequences of an act while regarding each other's guesses as normative. The sole everyday principle cannot be, "Do whatever you think is best for everybody in the long run." It would leave them unable to function without clear expectations of others' behavior. The moral action must be guided by first-order rules to which each agent of the relevant type of function is equally obliged. Joint intentional creatures, who guide their acts by alternating between the perspectives of self, others, and potentially of all social members, can only formulate shareable linguistic prescriptions as rules for which each of some relevant description is equally one. Humans require a set of rules governing collaboration, such as "do not kill other social members," "do not cheat," "do not break promises," "care for children," "do your duty," "treat others with the proper respect," and "do not steal."

The way to handle the problem of applying rules that are generally morally obligatory to unusual, exceptional cases is not to reject the rule or even redefine the rule, but to recognize that *prima facie*, first-order rules can require critical adjudication in terms of circumstantial consequences. *Their general, continuing validity is not thereby undermined.* Moral rules are molar, not molecular. They are social rules for agents in interpersonal interaction. They formulate the normal rules of living well together. Critical adjudication in cases of moral conflict need not happen every day to every social member. Most people do not regularly cheat or steal or ignore their suffering children or break promises. All do sometimes; a few do consistently. In extreme or crisis situations, or under pressure of social change, the frequency goes up. Wherever we find social stability, we find that most members possess that same "social trust" in the commonality of moral behavior. Critical adjudication does not negate the first-order obligations. It is a matter of regret that I must break my promise to a friend when I decide at the critical act consequentialist level to contravene my first-order obligation because of some greater crisis to be dealt with. My critical decision is, I believe, universalizable. Which I hope she will eventually understand.

Conclusion

But something seems missing. If we endorse consequentialism, what *telos* is the end or goal or good employed in this critical adjudication of consequences? What is The Good, or the highest good, the chief good? Mill recommended happiness, later utilitarians preference-satisfaction. What is the standard or telos for a naturalistically revised consequentialism? Rule consequentialism claims that the moral universalizable obligations (the everyday moral rules) are right when they lead to greater goods for those affected. But goods by what standard?

There is one minimal good that human social members must presuppose and cannot contradict, and which the interaction rules of members must serve: *the maintenance and reproduction* of *human social life*. Morality is primarily the set of norms for interpersonal action serving the maintenance of the social group in which the agent is located, with whatever goods are regarded as attendant on that aim. Its value is the maintenance of social life as normatively good, with normative moral goods. Morality constitutes the *bottom-up* rules of social life, we may say, starting with interpersonal interaction, which serve to make possible the reproduction of society (we will see the top-down rules later). To preserve something means not only, but implicitly, to preserve its components, hence individual members. Whatever is regarded by social members as the goods of that society—of which there can be many in conflict, and on which the members can disagree—cannot be separated from what the society is, from its identity, and hence what "preserving it" across generations would be. Morality is the human way of living together; it is human *eu-sociality*, the way of living together *well*.

The apparently collectivist nature of this necessary minimal good raises for some the moral conflict between what is best for the individual and best for the group. But this is often miscast. Local society is dependent on its members. Especially in foraging or subsistence agricultural locales, premature death of any member is the thin end of the wedge of the destruction of the group. Bands were only one bad disease or bad season of hunting or weather from being destroyed. Unexpected loss of individuals is a threat to society. At the same time, it is true that if indeed each human life has value, if each individual has rights, then the death or violation of rights of many individuals is even worse. Deontological ethics, which claims that the violation of a moral duty to a person cannot be justified by beneficial consequences for many, does not deny that the death of five people is a greater evil than the death of one. *Kant could count.* The loss of the innocent individual is evil; if so, the loss of many innocents is more evil still. By all means, a rule consequentialism in any society may well enforce the good of the group over the good of a few individuals. It will always do so. At the same time, a society based in equality and individuality can rightly enforce the good of the individual against the whims of community. There are multiple possible goods, and concern for the individual can maximize some of them.

But is social reproduction The Good, the highest good, the chief norm, by which all moral values and rules should be judged? No. Nor is happiness nor preference satisfaction, which, if they were to be adequate, have to be defined so broadly to have little concrete significance. People may of course decide that happiness or preference satisfaction is the standard. But they are not required to. For the current rule consequentialism, modeled on Hare's multiple levels, critical level decision in conflicts of the *prima facie* moral norms is whatever produces the most goods, quantitatively or qualitatively, for those social members affected. That is, I claim, the moral conclusion. But is there no The Good or the Highest Good for human action? *If there is such a thing, it is not the business of ethics.*

Part of the reason is that societies can differ legitimately in what the good or goods are that will be used to adjudicate and justify second level disagreements over the first-order level *prima facie* obligations or values. If we say that some particular form of society, based in a political and economic or cultural description, real or imagined, constitutes The Good, then we are saying all other social, economic, and cultural forms are ethically wrong. For example, we may believe that a modern, secular, liberal, republican society is best politically. Does that mean all other human communities failed *ethically*? To ask whether human morality dictates that a modern liberal republican society is best is like asking, "in which period of human history ought we live?" Is the job of ethics to decide in which period of history one ought to have lived?

Any attempt to decide the highest good, the chief purpose, the final norm or criterion for social human beings, would in effect be an attempt to answer the question, "How then shall we live?" Even Bernard Williams began his *Ethics and the Limits of Philosophy* by writing, "It is not a trivial question, Socrates said: what we are talking about is how one should live."[12] This is a fine question. But is it an *ethical* question? How I should live involves a host of decisions that are either personal to me, or historical. Ought I be a butcher, a baker or a candlestick maker? How about a milkman—a job my father had which no longer exists? Should I marry and, if so, whom should I wed? Should I have children? Should we be hunter-gatherers, or farmers, or herders, or capitalists? Which language should we speak? Any "answers" to such questions, any "right" answer, would imply that we all ought to live the same form of life.

"How then shall we live?" is not an ethical question. It is an *existential or spiritual* question. Whatever "The Good" is, it must at the least include or govern all values humans should honor, including truth, justice, beauty, as well as ethical rightness. So the decision as to the highest good is not ethical. If you try to get morality to answer that question, it becomes an inquiry about the sense and significance of human existence in general. This question is entirely legitimate but also maximally omnivalent. To press ethics to decide the point of human existence is to render ethical discourse of normative human relations utterly indeterminate, making the most global of all questions determinative for the field that must decide whether I may lie to my neighbor. That was always too great a burden for ethics to bear.

Chapter Thirteen

Political Rights, Political Wrongs

> When someone is honestly 55% right, that's very good and there's no use wrangling. And if someone is 60% right, it's wonderful, it's great luck, and let him thank God. But what's to be said about 75% right? Wise people say this is suspicious. Well, and what about 100% right? Whoever says he's 100% right is a fanatic, a thug, and the worst kind of rascal.
>
> —Czeslaw Milocz, *The Captive Mind*[1]

The word "politics" comes from the Greek word for a self-ruling city, the *polis*. What is a good *polis*? And what is the relation between ethical and political norms? Ethics first of all concerns interpersonal interaction, and is socially transmitted. There doubtless have been societies in which the moral largely coincided with the political, and both with the religious or cultural. But ours cannot be one of them. Once the political leaves behind the band, tribe, and chiefdom, and becomes focused on states including many millions of strangers from different ethnicities over distances most will never travel, it cannot be. Empires made no bones about this, since one cultural group ruled everyone else. But the mere fact that today we live in a republican nation state tempts us to apply our own local, moral norms widely. This is not wrong. But it has its limits.

Distinguishing the ethical and the political will sound like a version of what is called "political realism." Here we have an odd linguistic situation, one word with two very different uses that are close enough to cause confusion. I will defend a "realist" view of political values on the basis of the ordinal naturalism of this book. In this case, my realism happens also to invoke something called "political realism," which is different. Political realism holds that political, especially international, affairs should not be expected to be moral, or at least not moral in its usual sense, because it is inevitably motivated by interests and power. I will not defend that view. Some political acts, policies, and systems are normatively good or bad, right or wrong; those terms are as applicable in politics as in ethics. But the application doesn't have to be the *same* as in the ethics of members with respect to each other. Political realism can be "prescriptive," holding that politics has norms other than mere success, even though civic morality, the morality of everyday domestic affairs, cannot constitute all of them. Morality and politics interact but are not the same. Politics has a different job to do.

Since my account remains naturalistic, a word should be said about the most famous application of "nature" to politics. Politics by "natural law" or "natural right" implies that human nature requires certain kinds of political arrangements, or that humans naturally are endowed with rights or norms. In the seventeenth and eighteenth centuries, political thinkers trying to give a nonreligious justification of modern republicanism claimed whatever humans in the "state of nature" would have rationally chosen for their political system must be politically right. In reality there never was a pre-political state of human nature. As we have seen, humans are indeed naturally social and moral, naturally engaged in collaborative agreement, hence naturally political. The rooting of politics in the objective, natural morality of human communities is valid. But that does not mean that one political system is more "natural" than others. Human nature has obviously been compatible with monarchy, aristocracy, feudalism, syndicalism, communism, rule by tribal elders, or males over females or one nationality or ethnicity or race over another, including all manner of serfdom and slavery. It cannot be plausibly claimed that modern liberal democracy is more "natural" than a hundred thousand or more years of human politics. If a modern liberal republic of equality, rights, and self-rule is "right" or "just," it cannot be because it is more in line with nature as such. It may, however, be more in line with certain aspects of human nature that we moderns chose to reaffirm.

Likewise, unlike natural law, political right cannot be independent of culture and history. Because politics is emergent from and dependent on societies, and societies not only differ but have changed radically over time. Most norms by which we judge our politics today cannot possibly be applied to other historical periods, nor vice versa. For five decades, the American political theorist who has most consistently pursued an historical and cultural approach to political norms is Michael Walzer. He will be a frequent companion in what follows.

Political Norms

There have been many forms of political order, inevitably, since there have been many forms of human societies. If our definitions of political terms and norms are to be valid, they need to be defined in such a way that they can apply anywhere and anytime.

Here Aristotle is helpful. Aristotle gave politics a special importance, even defining humans as the "political animal," akin to his more famous definition of us as "rational animals." In the *Politics*, the political community or partnership (*koinônia he politikê*) is the "most authoritative of all and embraces all others" (Aristotle 2013). Collections of households make up a village; the *polis* or city arises from the partnership of several villages. The *polis* is the smallest partnership that is fully self-sufficient. It exists by nature, but by nature it is concerned with living "well" or virtuously, not just surviving. In his *Nicomachean Ethics* Aristotle makes clear that the science of politics must be the "most authoritative of the sciences" (Aristotle 2012). Now, the political cannot be temporally prior to the ethical; wherever there are humans living together, there is morality. But Aristotle is right that the social unit cannot even be identified without reference to the political. Politics is a trait of societies taken as relatively independent wholes. Our previous chapters have presumed highly social human individuals, but only now do we treat a subject, politics, which is a feature of humanity as collectives, *as societies*.

By "society" I mean a relatively autonomous, largely endogamous, cooperative human group who live their lives in proximity (whether sedentary or nomadic). Of necessity they cooperate in some horizon of intelligibility and propriety. Among all associational activity and institutions, we can then distinguish, as Gellner does, their economic or productive dimension, their culture, and their political dimension. We have to say that politics was always present, before modern states, before empires, before any "states" at all, so we cannot define the political in terms of state, nation, law, or even territory.

The political dimension of social life is best defined as *the decision-making and decision-enacting process for society as an autonomous whole*. Whether this is accomplished by a chief, elders, or any group advising leaders, or all citizens "under the oak tree" as Rousseau imagined, makes no difference. The phrase "decision enacting" emphasizes that decisions must be capable of being put into practice, must be potentially enforced, or they are not political. The qualifier "autonomous" means sovereign.

I do not mean there is no political dimension to a nonautonomous, nonsovereign society, but the degree to which the social unit is sovereign is proportional to the degree to which the phenomena in question are political. Less autonomy, less real politics. The political dimension of a society then involves three areas or functions: *governance, law,* and *political activity per se.*

Government is the social agency in which the power to enact decisions, and perhaps to make them, is invested. It is composed by persons in offices; we do not have to distinguish here between societies in which authority is invested in the person versus the office. As we know there is ambiguity here; some traditions use "governing" for the executive function only (e.g., the executive branch), whereas others use it for legislation and/or the judiciary as well, and within the executive power, between Head of State and Head of Government (e.g., prime minister). I am using it in the broadest sense including execution, legislation, judiciary, and responsibility for external or foreign relations as well as internal governance.

Max Weber defined politics in terms of "the state" and gave the latter its most famous definition as "a human community that (successfully) claims the monopoly of the legitimate use of physical force within a territory. . . . Hence, 'politics' . . . means striving to share power or striving to influence the distribution of power, either among states or among groups within a state."[2] Weber connected this to his analysis of modern bureaucratization, modernity involving the transition from patrimonial or descent based governance, and traditional and charismatic authority, to legal, impersonal authority.

Francis Fukuyama has recently made great use of this definition, emphasizing that a state requires: (a) centralized power, including all instruments of force under one command (so for example no rival militias); (b) with a nonpatrimonial, meritocratic, administrative bureaucracy (not clan or tribe based); (c) ruling over a fixed territory (and not just a people or tribe).[3] Bands require governance, hence politics, although the members doing the governance may be all adult social members. Tribes are usually extended clans, or sets of intermarrying clans, with various kinds of leaders. All were segmentary, so at each level of scale there is an autonomous layer of nested social membership, expressed in the famous Arab saying, "Me against my brother; my brother and I against my cousin; my cousin, brother, and I against the stranger." Chiefdoms are thought to require agricultural/pastoral surplus that can be doled out as favors, an otherwise tribal/clan federation with a Big Man as head. States arose first in Bronze Age Mesopotamia with writing, metallurgy, and cities based on massively centralized power and systematic taxation, then appeared in other rich riverine valleys. The political history of regions and subcontinents ever since is then largely an oscillation between (a) sets of competitive independent states, some abutting and defending themselves against tribes and chiefdoms; (b) empiric conquest by one state over the others, with varying degrees of local autonomy nevertheless controlled by and sending taxes to the center; and (c) decentralization into feudal, usually more patrimonial states where the king is merely *primus inter pares* (first among equals) and local nobles retain their own militias. At any rate, all are to some degree centralized political agencies exercising a power that has to be called political over vast numbers of persons, and often territories, deserving to be considered states.

And they have law. Wherever there are humans there are customary rules and the dicta of leaders, but "law" is the recorded rules for society dictated and/or enforced by state authority. Recorded law seems to have begun at least in the early second millennium BCE in Mesopotamia and Egypt. The laws of a polity can directly reflect traditional norms, but they have to be promulgated, announced. Any large society of strangers with literate urban elites that exists for multiple generations must have law. In a modern society it is understood by its participants as distinct from economics, culture, and ethics, but of course influenced by them. There is always "positive" law, meaning the law actually promulgated and enforced by governance, which arises out of a literate, urban, centralized codification of preexisting customary law. But in some societies there is also belief in divine or natural law which limits and justifies positive law. This has been crucial to political development, especially in Abrahamic societies (Jewish, Christian, Islamic), depending on the institutions administering the law (Fukuyama 2011).

Political activity can be far broader. It is above all activity of citizens or office holders meant to influence or participate in the decision-making process of society. Private conversations of rulers, court intrigues, legislators' deal making, interest group lobbying, party meetings, mass rallies, voting, running for office—all are political activity. The creation and enforcement of law, and the workings of government involve political activity, but the latter can extend far beyond both. It potentially applies to all citizens, part of the time. For our purposes, we can say that social members are, with respect to the political, *subjects and/or citizens*. All those who must obey the law and governance are subjects. In some societies, those subjects are also citizens, meaning the political process is responsible to their agency. The terms "civility," "citizen," and "civil society" have a long history (Cahoone 2002, 211ff). When we refer to members as citizens we are saying more than that they are subjects; we are saying they are possible participants.

Now, what are the norms of the political in the broad sense? We can and do use "good" and "right" and "ought" for them, just like morality, but some other terms are particularly associated with the political.

Legitimacy is uniquely political. It applies not to the political society as a whole but to what must be the qualification of the political process and any agency carrying it out, like government. The right people at the right time in the right way produce a decision and act on it. It is indeed derivative of the moral norm of *authority*, one of the values we discussed in chapter 10. Its justification is usually historical; the rightful leader today is she who was the rightful leader yesterday, reaching that position by the rightful process. Of course there are many kinds of nonpolitical authorities in various social institutions. What is authoritative in political terms is not only persons but also offices and procedures. As codified by law, this may be relatively modern, but we cannot doubt that in hunter-gatherer societies the new elder or chief or warlord had a typical process of gaining and exercising authority, the continuation of which was important for maintaining legitimacy. One might say the moral norm of loyalty is also relevant here, and it may be.

What about *justice*? In the Western tradition, justice has sometimes been called the "first virtue" of political societies. The classical notion of justice, which appeared in Plato but was put in its famous form by Cicero and codified by the emperor Justinian, was *justitio suum cuique distribuit*, or "justice renders to each his due." This obviously has roots in relations among citizens in the honoring of promises and contracts; it was in fact one of the four cardinal virtues for the ancient Greeks, accompanying courage, temperance, and wisdom.

Justice famously applies in two contexts: *retributive* (or reparative or restorative, if one prefers), where someone has committed an unjust act, and punishment and/or reparation for the victim is required; and *distributive*, when some distribution of some good across social members is just or unjust. Some things are just only when equal, but others are not: equality itself can be unjust, such as to treat a "superior" as an inferior. But justice is also a preeminent process norm for governmental actors. One of the prominent functions of leadership or government is adjudication of conflicts between citizens. If anything is supposed to be just, adjudication must be! Justice in a given society applies *suum cuique* to a wide variety of social goods according to their cultural meaning, as we will see below. But the relevant point here is that the decision-making and -enforcing process is supposed to be just with respect to members, that is, citizens.

Clearly, law is central to domestic justice in treatment of citizens. While we have little room here for philosophy of law, it is striking how the major competing theories differ mainly over the relation of law and judicial decision to extra-legal norms. If positive law is binding, and not merely social custom nor religious dictate, what is the basis of its unique normative obligation and legitimate enforcement? The *natural law* tradition holds that the law must be based in universal, rational, moral-political rules embedded in human nature (e.g., John Finnis 2021). Its antithesis is *legal positivism*, originally formulated in 1832 by John Austin, for which law is not descriptive or anchored in anything but the promulgations of legislatures and judicial decision (from Austin 1995 to H. L. A. Hart 1976). *Legal formalism* holds that the legal statues and principles are informationally autonomous and complete (Antonin Scalia 2018 but also Ronald Dworkin 1986). Its antithesis *legal realism* (from Justice Holmes 1897 to Roberto Mangabeiro Unger 2015) holds that judicial interpretation legitimately requires social and political judgment to make decisions.

Lastly, there is an undeniable and indeed natural end or purpose of politics: *social reproduction*. The ultimate intrinsic goal of politics is social continuation into future generations. As Oakeshott famously put it, "In political activity, then, men sail a boundless and bottomless sea: there is neither harbour for shelter nor floor for anchorage, neither starting-place nor appointed destination. The enterprise is to keep afloat on an even keel . . ." (Oakeshott 1991, 127). As I have argued before, this is inevitable because politics is the activity of a society *as* a society (Cahoone 2002). One might say this conflates politics with morality. But the home of morality is the regulation of interpersonal relations from the *bottom up*. Politics is social reproduction from the *top down*—or, in a nonhierarchical society, from *whole to part*, the regulation of the acts of social members by the collective. Whatever else it also aims for, politics must aim at social continuation.

This means that more than in ethics, in politics success matters normatively. The relation of success to normativity in politics greater than in the moral domain. When the child is drowning, and one observer dives in to save her and flounders, while another saves her, we may accord both the same "moral" credit while valuing the successful hero with greater respect. In the sphere of politics the failed leader is blameworthy. The leader is acting for society; all may suffer, perhaps horribly, from the leader's political failure. Political decisions are inherently collective and consequentialist. The government that, with the best of intentions, leads society to destruction, or starvation, or great loss, is wrong, not right. This does not mean deontic rules of duty do not apply, or cannot be invoked in political decision making. They can and are. The point is the consequences are never normatively irrelevant in politics. Politics requires what Weber called an "ethic of responsibility" where agents weigh and calculate the manifold possible results of any policy; an ethics of "conviction" or commitment to ultimate ends is not ruled out but cannot be sufficient.[4] The normative credit we give to a failed idealistic politician is moral, not political.

So, we can now qualify our notion of politics normatively: whatever else it serves, politics is supposed to be the process of *legitimate social decision making and enacting aimed at the just preservation of society*. Justice is indeed an intrinsic political norm, but it is an adverbial norm on how the goal of preservation is to be accomplished. To be just, a society must first exist and be in the position to exert some control over itself. Whatever puts in question the ability of the society to continue the processes of social life is a threat. The point of this discussion is not to agree with political realism, or Hobbes, or any one of a variety of anti-liberal theories of politics. Not at all. It is to say that the three norms above are intrinsic to any politics. What kind of law, government, and political activity we ought to have today is another question.

Modern Liberal Republicanism

We have already discussed the vast changes of the modern world. These changes, beginning in the sixteenth century, remade Europe and North America by the eighteenth to nineteenth centuries, and the rest of the world in the twentieth. All we need here is to recognize that certain changes in the political domain have been more or less universal. That is, there are certain traits a state has to have since the twentieth century—when modernity spread virtually everywhere—that it did not have to have before, often because it was impossible. This holds not only for liberal republican societies but for all modern states, and while liberal republicanism helped to instigate them, it can no longer define itself by them. They apply even to illiberal, autocratic regimes.

(1) A modern state must indeed have a monopoly on the legitimate use of force in a society, but now more precisely, in a territory. Further, it has to have an administrative bureaucracy, and promulgate and (more or less) rule by law. This power must reach every corner of the territory over which the state is sovereign.

(2) Governance has to accept the universal equality of its adult citizens as equal individuals with rights, protected by law. The rights are highly variable, for example, in religion, speech, or sexual behavior, and do not have to be political; but there must be rights, and they must be equal. With this, legitimacy requires some form of cultural unity subtending the reach of the state, in service of "the people" understood by whatever criteria. (This does not mean a functional nation state has been achieved.)

(3) A modern state is effectively responsible for progress, or rather, economic and material welfare and growth. Because we are no longer in a Malthusian world, governance cannot just provide security and order. Of course, states have always managed themselves economically. But only today does their legitimacy explicitly depend on it, both externally and internally. Certainly autocracy or oligarchy can avoid the consequence of negative judgment longer, especially with extensive natural resources.

Among such modern states, some are "democracies" or "liberal democracies" or simply "liberal." By these, I mean the liberal form of the modern republican tradition from its seventeenth-and eighteenth-century Dutch, English, American, and French sources, which has spread to many countries around the world. What does this modern liberalism require? Liberalism is a set of principles operationalized in structures and processes, primarily: (a) executive power controlled by rule of law, including a constitution, with an independent judiciary (there are different ways of ensuring this), governing both public and private offices; (b) open democratic election of at least legislative and executive powers, a suffrage approaching that of all adult citizens, including nonpolitical institutions like public education and a free press; (c) guaranteed individual liberties, including political liberties, religious and cultural expression, alienable property rights in an significantly free market economy, and opportunities for the development of and participation in plural institutions of civil society. The rights Enlightenment liberalism asserted originally applied only to a selective franchise—albeit one a thousand times the size of earlier enfranchisement in any of the urbanized and commercial civilizations of Earth's history—but approached universal adult suffrage virtually everywhere only in the twentieth century.

Political liberalism arose in the West along with a set of other aspects of modernity, like science, technology, and rational techniques of bureaucratic administration. But three features directly relevant to liberal politics yet particularly controversial are the market economy, nationalism, and finally culture and cultural identity.

The Market

Liberalism has been linked to market economies since the late eighteenth century. It had to be. As Arendt claimed, you cannot have a free or republican society without private property because the alternative is that either clans or executive power control all property (Arendt 1998). A liberal society is different still because it supports alienable property rights in a market of exchange. Not only is this a great engine of prosperity, it is pragmatically crucial to the existence of a *civil society*, "that set of diverse non-government institutions which is strong enough to counterbalance the state"(Gellner 1994, 5). Economics is the production and distribution of human material needs, where need is elastic and can change. It is too important to belong to the state. As Gellner argued, "The autonomy of the economy is needed, not merely in the name of efficiency . . . but so as to provide pluralism with a social base which it cannot any longer find anywhere else" (212). For liberalism the sphere of the production of needs can and should be regulated, but never owned or controlled, by the state.

At the same time there are no pure, meaning unregulated, free markets. In the first half of the twentieth century socialism moved to the right and capitalism to the left, meaning new forms of each were invented. European social democracy, English "new liberalism," and American Progressivism developed out of revolutionary Marxism and the theory of state socialism, and capitalism adopted policies of economic management and social insurance leading to the New Deal. Today all major capitalist economies are "mixed," from the United States to Sweden to Botswana to Japan. What position on this continuum of more or less governmental regulation any given country occupies, or ought to strive to occupy, is a substantially pragmatic, political, economic matter involving what works best in its particular conditions. And since the abandonment of international *state* socialism by virtually all countries since the 1980s, world poverty has decreased enormously.

Capitalism is often criticized for creating economic inequality. The criticism is true, but liberal inequality is less burdensome than traditional legal inequality. Further, as Walzer has argued, the question is less whether wealth is unequal than what social goods can be bought with that inequality (Walzer 1984). Class differences in ownership of commodities is one thing, but when wealth determines access to health care, education, justice, and basic life chances, it threatens the basis for social membership. In general, the greatest danger of capitalism remains the "creative destruction" of the free market system, as Schumpeter put it (Schumpeter 2011). Left to itself, capitalism will erode the sociocultural context on which it depends (Muller 2003). The rationalization of economic production produces massive historical gains, but as Edward Shils remarked, "Rationalization has thus far been successful because it has not been completely successful."[5] Capitalism is an economic, not a social, political, or cultural, process; its results are salutary only when embedded in a society strong enough to manage it. The same is true of modern science, modern technology, the modern state, and even democracy itself. Modernity is dangerous.

Many liberals think of liberalism as *cosmopolitan*. This is partly right. To be a cosmopolitan is to be a "citizen of the world" (*kosmopolitês*). As some would have it, the eighteenth-century Enlightenment turned modern society strongly in the direction of cosmopolitanism. The social contract theory of Hobbes, Locke, and Rousseau, the "Rights of Man" [*sic*] promoted by both American and French revolutions, Kant's deontological ethics, and Bentham's and Mill's utilitarianism—the Enlightenment is shot through with a new universalism and naturalism. Modern cosmopolitanism arose along with capitalism. Voltaire's wit is worth repeating:

> Enter into the Royal Exchange of London . . . in which deputies from all nations assemble for the advantage of mankind. There the Jew, the Mahometan, and the Christian bargain with one another as if they were of the same religion, and bestow the name of infidel on bankrupts only . . . On the separation of these free and pacific assemblies, some visit the synagogue, others repair to the tavern . . . a third kind hasten to the chapels to wait for the inspiration of the Lord with their hats on; and all are content.[6]

This was in direct opposition to the Greco-Roman tradition of civic republicanism, which made the "public-spiritedness" of the citizen crucial to political freedom. For this had often had a martial component: the citizen is a landholder who can fight for his *polis* or republic. Liberalism turned the interest of the ambitious from military to economic conquest.

николаизм

NATIONALISM

But as we saw, modern liberalism and the market economy arose along with nationalism. Nationalism means nothing more than correlation of a state with a people. It was the basis for the breakdown of aristocracy and the establishment of equality among millions of strangers over a region, and was crucial to the possibility of market economies and mass education. Nationalism was "the form in which democracy appeared in the world, contained in the idea of the nation as a butterfly in a cocoon."[7] Whenever someone argues that a people have a right to self-determination—be they South Africans, Palestinians, Native Americans, or others—they are employing nationalism. The anti-imperialism of the twentieth century was unthinkable without it. Some people fear the implications of "blood and soil," but as I have argued, blood is descent, not race, and all peoples live on some soil (Cahoone 2005). There are multiple forms of nationalism, some good, some very bad.

What kind of nationalism is compatible with liberalism? Any that is consistent with the rule of law that grants equal rights to all citizens—and as of the twentieth century, that must be extended to all adult permanent residents. Nationalism need not mean intolerance. Walzer argued in his 1997 *On Toleration* that there are five historical "regimes of toleration" or political structures that permitted cultural and ethno-racial toleration under sovereignty: (1) international society itself, whenever it is peaceful; (2) multinational empires (e.g., the millet system of the Ottoman empire); (3) consocations of two or three linguistic, cultural groups (e.g., Switzerland, Singapore, Lebanon in better times); (4) nation-states in which there is a dominant representation of a culture but legal toleration and full citizenship for others (e.g., France); and (5) immigrant societies like the United States. In the American case, twentieth-century American nationalism is "civic," not ethnic (Walzer 1996). A civic nationalism is sufficiently "thin" that it is not violated by multiple cultural memberships or identities; this is so even if the latter are inherited, fixed or unchangeable.

This touches on the question of immigration. Anything called a political society must have an inside and an outside, and must be ruled from within. Walzer wrote: "Neighborhoods can be open only if countries are at least potentially closed. . . . To tear down the walls of the state is not . . . to create a world without walls, but rather to create a thousand petty fortresses."[8] But the degree of border and immigration control is rightly a matter of a negotiation between democratic decision and moral or political obligations that transcend national borders. Unlike modern economics or science, a republican politics requires social self-rule, which is always in tension with cosmopolitanism.

In fact, nationalism and cosmopolitanism were always two sides of the modern republican coin. Cosmopolitanism without nationalism is *de jure* (in principle) a violation of the social self-governance; a nationalism without cosmopolitanism is *de facto* (given modern realities), doomed to fail. An internationalism without significant national sovereignty would be like the Marxist vision of the socialist utopia: a world with mere "administration," hence no republican politics at all. Nationalism without a cosmopolitan spirit would be isolationist and authoritarian in its economic, cultural, and scientific life, and cease to be "liberal" at all.

Culture

Classical liberalism often argued for the apparently cosmopolitan view that governance, law, and perhaps even politics ought to be largely neutral with respect to the particular customs and cultures of its citizens (analogous to religious neutrality). The 1970s saw the extreme version of this in the "deontological liberalism" of Robert Nozick and John Rawls, which insisted that political norms are to dictate "the Right" or procedural rules of association, and be neutral regarding citizens' notions of "the Good," or the values and purposes in life (Rawls 1971; Nozick 1974). But starting in the 1980s, "multiculturalism" found this inadequate, arguing that race-, ethnicity-, and culture-neutrality (and also gender-neutrality) merely allowed nonpolitical American society to remain frozen in its majoritarian, patriarchal form. Many argued for embracing a conception of citizenship that did not abstract from cultural group identity, even endorsing a "right to culture." That would recognize that members of minority ethnic groups are culturally disadvantaged, rather than pretending to ignore their cultural identity. This is to say, the rules of civil status, or "civility," are not fully independent of cultural membership and practice.

As I have argued elsewhere, the multiculturalists were right, but their rightness has consequences that were, for them, unwanted (Cahoone 2005). If the political domain cannot be just while ignoring cultural views and cultural membership—and I agree it cannot—that means the legal-political-governmental system will not be culturally neutral; it will express some cultures and not others. It can permit and tolerate more than it can endorse or express. We must accept that liberal society, its rules of relations among citizens or civility, obtains only in and through cultural histories. Political norms cannot be wholly independent of other sociocultural norms and values, thus liberal politics must be undergirded and interpreted by extra-political commitments. This means accepting that liberal or civil society, in its politics, law, and government, can never be neutral with respect to cultures. It cannot treat all cultures equally.

Indeed, liberal civility must restrain and sometimes oppose culture, including the majority culture. As Shils argued, "civility requires respect for tradition because the sense of affinity on which it rests is not momentary only but reaches into the past and the future." [9] Liberal civility is, after all, all about limitation; as Shils claimed, it "permits neither the single individual nor the total community the complete realization of their essential potentialities."[10] Civility inhibits tendencies within a culture toward what he called ideology, and we might call the complete fulfillment of any group's cultural hopes. At the same time, civility, the rules of citizenship in a liberal society, *needs* cultural tradition. For civility must be interpreted, and the transmission across generations of the store of interpretive resources *is* culture. So arguably liberal societies require, to stretch a notion from Rawls, an *overlapping cultural consensus*, the joint endorsement of an account of human goods promoted by key liberal institutions and processes (Cahoone 2005). Indeed, this is presumed by distributive justice, which cannot be independent of the meanings of the goods being redistributed. Walzer writes, "Every substantive account of distributive justice is a local account."[11]

Thus the relation of liberal republican political/legal institutions and culture is a *dialectical* one. Civil life cannot mean and be valued in itself without culture, and culture cannot be the culture of free equal citizens unless it restrains itself from treading on civility, itself part of the complex of cultural values that inform life in the *civitas*. Neither side can win; each must support the other while struggling against it—each must limit its prevalence in order to survive.

We must remember just how diverse modern Enlightenment liberalism is, and was. Its eighteenth-century roots may have been racially and culturally monochromatic, but between 1776 and 1798 the ideas of capitalism (Smith) and socialism (Godwin), conservatism (Burke) and feminism (Wollstonecraft), and cultural nationalism (Herder) and cosmopolitanism (Kant) all received their classic formulations. Liberal thought has since endorsed individualism and communitarianism, promoted natural rights (Jefferson) and declared natural rights "nonsense on stilts" (Bentham), has been republican and monarchist, presidential and parliamentary, *laissez-faire*, neoliberal, progressive, and social democratic. Liberal countries today include states on every continent with every color and religion of members: not just the United States, not just Anglophone countries or Scandinavian countries, nor West European and North American, but Japan, Taiwan, South Korea, Bulgaria, Mongolia, India, Peru, Argentina, Botswana, and a host of others. Different populations with different cultures, different histories, different geographies, different natural resources. There is no one model, one ideal—nor could there be.

Politics and Ethics

Modern egalitarian societies changed the relation of politics and ethics. This was inevitable. Modern society in general, and liberal societies in particular, tore down the aristocratic structure of virtually all Axial, hierarchical, agro-literate societies. In those premodern states governance was in principle separate from the civic morality of citizens and subjects; it was the unique purview of separate castes, to which the moral rules by which subjects adjudicated their local interactions rarely trickled *up*. Political realism is the traditional, one is tempted to say "natural," Axial Age theory of international relations. The modern age destroyed that separation, made all equal members of one society, and in the liberal case, limited power and made it dependent on its service to, and approval by, citizens. Indeed, the earliest republican theories in the West are precisely attempts to root the normative rules of law and government in a non- or pre-political moral character, for example, the state of nature. Political thought has ever sense regarded political norms as derivative from and subject to moral norms. The horrors of twentieth-century warfare might seem to disprove this point. But in the twentieth century this change coincided with the creation of the most dangerous entity in human history, the technologically advanced, fully mobilized nation state. My point is not the modern republican societies are "more ethical," although they surely are in some ways. It is only that political actors and government cannot ignore the relation to civic ethics. But that raises its own problems.

Politics is an activity, a process, engaged in by persons, including not just citizens, but officials and leaders. They often vie for power or policy or both, that is, compete to fill powerful offices or form domestic parties or alliances that will influence political decision making and enacting. They are people whose life has a lot more politics in it than the lives of most citizens. They are social members with the same moral endowment and obligations of others, but who have a specific duty to serve the just reproduction of society. This can involve domestic actions, where justice is famously the highest norm—for example, just treatment of citizens, just decisions among them, service to society rather than to the self—but also external actions, where leaders serve to represent society in relation to other states. In either case their duties raise the question: *Can it be politically right to do what is morally wrong?*

This is the problem of "dirty hands." The classical Pauline dictum held that "one can never do evil that good may come of it." But politics, and warfare above all, seems to violate this dictum. As Arthur Schlesinger Jr. put it, "Saints can be pure, but statesmen must be responsible."[12] Hans Morgenthau was more blunt, writing, "Political ethics is the ethics of doing evil," although he adds that "[t]he perfectionist thus becomes finally a source of greater evil."[13] How can it be right to do wrong? The very ability to do good in the political domain requires successful competition over power. The domain of politicians, of those whose main business is politics, is inherently agonistic. Politics is, as Max Weber noted, the "slow boring of hard boards."[14] Especially in democracy, where the number of parties whose consent and interests matter increases.

Walzer gave a famous analysis in a 1973 essay in which he accepts that politics is a devil's bargain. Political actors must, as Machiavelli said, "learn how not to be good." The "good man" in politics sometimes "must do terrible things to reach his goal."[15] When the welfare of the people is at stake, when following civic moral rules would lead to crisis or disaster, the politician may have to violate those rules. To the question, Can one govern innocently? Walzer responds negatively: "a particular act of government . . . may be exactly the right thing to do in utilitarian terms and yet leave the man who does it guilty of a moral wrong. . . . We would not want to be governed by men who consistently adopted [the absolutist] position. The notion of dirty hands derives from an effort to refuse 'absolutism' without denying the reality of the moral dilemma."[16]

We should note that Walzer presumed a deontological ethics. Thus, in his words, we sometimes politically ought to violate a moral duty because of the act's consequences. But for consequentialists, particularly act-utilitarians, that is not a violation: the duty is determined by the good consequences! "The ends justify the means" can be perfectly moral for consequentialism. So we will put his point differently. Dirty hands signifies a conflict between two *kinds* of moral standards such that an act evil by one kind of standard is permissible or obligatory by another. First, the act contemplated must violate basic moral rules, unfairly distributing serious and irredeemable harms to some people while helping others. Second, the act must nevertheless be obligatory because of the greater evil of *not* committing it. Walzer tries to balance the moral scales by saying that it leaves the leader who commits such acts responsible but not blameworthy. For "blameworthy" would mean that the agent ought to be punished and that the act should not have been performed. The case of dirty hands means bearing the burden of an evil that it was right to do.

The most extreme examples often involve war. In Walzer's rightly famous *Just and Unjust Wars: A Moral Argument with Historical Illustrations* he defended just war theory—the view that going to war is sometimes just, and some acts of war are just (Walzer 2015). Just war theory opposes political realism, which Walzer took to be the view that war is amoral so there is no morally better or worse form of warfare, and pacificism which holds that all wars and acts of war including violent self-defense are unjust. Walzer mobilized and updated the historical Just War theory, from Augustine and Aquinas among others, and its dicta about *jus ad bellum*, or when it is just to go to war in the first place (i.e., decided by a right authority, for a legitimate cause, with a rational expectation that more good than evil will come from going to war), and *jus in bello*, or which actions in war are just (i.e., those from which more good than evil can be expected, proportionality of response, and discrimination or refusing to target civilians).

Walzer supports the notion that where there is a just war rule, no violation can be morally right. Thus, tit-for-tat reprisals to prior violations by the enemy are not justified. Walzer claims that "[t]he rule is absolute: self-preservation in the face of the enemy is not an excuse for violation of rules of war."[17] There is also no "sliding scale" by which the better one's cause in going to war, or the more evil one's opponent, the more violations of *in bello* rules can be justified. The lives of one's own countrymen do not count more than enemy lives. He uses the example of a Chinese feudal lord, the Duke of Sung, who in 638 BCE repeatedly refused to attack a larger force still in defile because it violated traditional ethical rules. Mao had famously declared, "We are not the Duke of Sung." Walzer's retort is "*we are all the Duke of Sung.*"[18] But to be fair, his complete quotation is "until the very last minute we are all the Duke of Sung."

That is because Walzer allowed a famous exception: *supreme emergency*. One must be the Duke of Sung up until the point of supreme emergency. A nation is in supreme emergency when it faces, not merely defeat, but its imminent death as a political community, meaning massacre, enslavement, or the prospect of living under a brutal regime. He later called this doctrine the "utilitarianism of extremity." This category allows military necessity under special conditions to justify all sorts of acts that the rest of his theory would condemn. His primary example is the war against Hitler. But he uses the same criterion to *deny* the legitimacy of British and American continuation of city bombing of Germany in late 1944 and 1945 because by that time supreme emergency had ceased to exist. Likewise the atomic bombing of Japan fails because the United States was never in the position of supreme emergency, hence did not have to demand unconditional surrender from Japan.

Walzer's account, to which he has added in recent years, is among our finest attempts to distinguish the moral and immoral in war. But it remains problematic. It is not clear how, *in bello*, any leader or commander can fail to hold the lives of his or her citizens or troops more dear than those of the enemy, since it is to them that the leader is responsible. Likewise the temporally prior act of aggression will and must justify an identical act of the patient in response, if there is just war. The adherence to the traditional aristocratic war rules, such as attacking only at the agreed-upon time, could never be justified to a modern democracy as explanation to citizens for the loss of their sons or daughters in a fight with an aggressor, even far from supreme emergency. So a modern democracy is *least* able to emulate the noble Duke of Sung. There may not be a sliding scale of moral right, but there *is a sliding scale of political right*. Even if it is the leader's moral duty to try not to take the next step down the slope, it may be his political duty to take it.

Political acts can be right or wrong, like all active judgments. But because they concern decisions for entire societies and are responsible to their continued existence, what is valid or right politically, while impacted by morality, is not reducible to it. Politics must take into account the moral rules of interpersonal relations, and imagine a social future in which they hold, or perhaps are even enhanced or more fully applied. But its own circumstantial decisions cannot always be bound by them. For while morality is based in universalizable moral rules, the adjudication among them at the second-order or critical level is act consequentialist, often in terms of what favors social reproduction. *And politics lives at that second-order level.* A threat to the social group is a threat to everyone, including all family members and loved ones of the person sacrificed. The notion of *Fiat justitia ruat cælum* (let justice be done though the heavens fall) cannot be politically right. For if the heavens fall, all my fellow citizens, to whom I am obligated, will die.

If the leader's morally right decision—not to lie, betray, sacrifice innocents, or commit a heinous act—predictably leads to social catastrophe, if it does massive harm to the society to which the leader is responsible, it must be politically wrong. Political right does not always conform to moral right. As a process of decision for society as a single agent, politics and morality operate on different scales, just as do biology and psychology.

Political norms are emergent from collective life and its inherent interpersonal morality, the interests of social members, and their local social processes. A normative or prescriptive realism does not accept a society's interests as amoral facts; it regards them as *prima facie* normative goods. The point is that moral reasoning and self-interest are not external constraints on each other, but intertwined. For anyone attempting to make decisions for the polity—citizens in an election, leaders in a crisis, officers in a battle—must take into account the collective self-interest of citizens. For the "self" of self-interest is now a community of real persons to which the official is obligated. The political right, as responsible to the collective reproduction of society, does not always conform to moral right of normative interpersonal relations. The leaders in question can be *morally wrong but politically right*. The political norm is not thereby violated, even if it is right to desire a politics that rarely allows itself to be faced with that divergence.

Conclusion

Is there a rational political justification for modern liberal republicanism, or what most people simply call "liberalism"? Is it the right or best *polis*? Of course the vast majority of thinkers in liberal republican societies believe so, but most now acknowledge that the arguments are not conclusive. They usually come in two forms: first, a deontological claim that the individual equal rights recognized by liberal republican societies—and these do differ around the margins—are universally, perhaps naturally, valid and hence so is liberal republicanism; and second, that liberal republican societies generate the most goods in education, economic opportunity, standard of living, and personal satisfactions.

It has long been recognized that both of these presuppose the cultural prioritizations of certain values. That is, someone for whom life in a religiously observant society or a more ethnically and culturally homogeneous society is the highest priority may disagree with both liberal justifications. One can say those in liberal societies tend to share high valuations for individual liberty or free expression. So rather than being independent of culture, liberalism has its own validating culture or set of validating cultures. Regarding standard of living and opportunity for material success, those values, while not prioritized by someone who most prizes raising their children in a particular religious or ethno-national community, probably have wider appeal to people of many different cultural groups.

In terms of the basic norms of all political societies that we developed earlier, we can say the following. *Governmental legitimacy* surely does come directly from liberal democratic electoral processes, but it does not have to. Those favoring an illiberal government because it provides cultural or religious homogeneity, or represents traditional forms of authority, find their governments just as legitimate. While the notion of what counts as *justice* will vary from culture to culture, however, one can reasonably argue that liberal democratic societies, which make a certain kind of rule of law one of their primary aims, are likely to achieved a degree of justice greater than others. Third is *social reproduction*. Any society with a sufficiently strong centralized authority (as opposed to a failed state) that is stable for multiple generations is, for now, supporting social reproduction. But do we have good reason to believe that it will last?

The justification of Enlightenment liberalism can be attempted in many ways, but the most decisive is *consequentialist*: whether human societies under modern conditions are better off with it or without it. Political and civic concerns are not only things that matter—security and order, economic growth and opportunity, the pursuit of rational inquiry including science, and cultural creativity all matter as well. Liberalism has until now indeed been a massive success: it does permit and promote an unprecedented degree of several kinds of equality, self-rule, and individual liberty; the degree of material progress has been unprecedented; and, the ability to inquire and discover truth as well as create art in a broad spectrum of ways unique. One of liberalism's strongest suits is that it has proven to accept major reforms as well as tinkering around the edges of institutional pluralism and individual liberty under legal equality. It has reduced many kinds of injustice and supported an institutional pluralism that is crucial to limiting the massive technological, corporate, and governmental power modernity unleashed. Even if its progress threatens local community and traditional religious identity, it permits them; whereas autocratic and fundamentalist regimes outlaw recalcitrance. Modernity is change, and to this point it appears that liberalism is the best way to promote yet control such change. That is, liberal republican capitalism is arguably that political form that has made most pervasively available the widest variety of social and personal goods under modern social conditions.

Might this cease to be true? Yes. In the mid–twentieth century, both fascism and communism offered themselves as modern, egalitarian, materially progressive alternatives, but they failed (as well as slaughtering millions of people). As long as the most transparently democratic, the most individually free societies, with functioning legal systems and comparatively low levels of corruption, are also the societies that are most materially abundant with higher livings standards, life expectancy, and greater educational and economic opportunity, with relatively safe food and water and comparatively lower levels of crime—there is no problem justifying modern liberal republicanism. But if that combination ceased to be true, if the Enlightenment gamble that science or free inquiry, popular sovereignty, individual liberty, and social progress go together, were to fracture, then history would impose a nasty choice.

At the moment, some people in developing countries seem to envy the Chinese economic miracle, and nationalist authoritarianism has revived in response to three decades of globalization. As of now, few outsiders want to be controlled by those ruling authorities. But that could change. For the perceived legitimacy of liberal democracy is, Fukuyama rightly claimed, "conditioned on performance."[19] And uniquely so. The poorly functioning liberal government cannot say to its citizens: "Our government represents God's will for you, or the survival of your ethno-racial group, or a utopian future no one has seen yet! So you must continue to support us despite how much of a mess we have made!"

Which highlights a final point, in liberalism's favor or disfavor, as you prefer. In different senses, Karl Marx and Carl Schmitt were right about liberalism: liberalism reveals nakedly what political power in itself is about and for, and it is not about either utopian achievement of humanity nor the existential assertion of a people. In Shils's terms, liberalism has neither a transcendental (Marx) nor primordial (Schmitt) justification. The intellectual achievement of the Enlightened liberal tradition is to *deny that The Good is political*. The Good is achieved in private life, not in the sense of personal or even domestic life, but in the sense of nonpolitical social, economic, and cultural spheres of activity. The political order serves to provide a framework for the pursuit of The Good by free members, their families, and associations in the context of civil society. Each liberal society must respond to novel problems in each generation because modernity *means* the endless production of novel problems. As liberal societies evolve, their social pendulums will forever swing between desire for greater individual liberty and need for greater social order, between desire for economic growth and need for economic redistribution. It makes no sense to reject liberal institutions, the pivot of our pendulum, for the fact that the bob, having recently swung in one direction, now wants to swing back. As long as the pivot continues to move in the best direction.

Chapter Fourteen

Art Works

> We emerge as a species that continually makes into art whatever is in its power to change, and in that sense is, biologically, condemned to art.
>
> —Valerius Geist, "Big Game in the City"[1]

Aesthetic values might seem to be those least amenable to a naturalistic account. Some philosophers considered art to be objects of disinterested contemplation. Art explores the heights of religious rapture, heroic nobility, and purely conceptual innovation. Whatever else art is, it is "artificial," not natural. Perhaps depicting natural or social images, either real or imagined, like battle scenes, famous leaders, or human activities, might seem "naturalistic," hence something naturalism could understand. But the revolutions of art in the twentieth century were so radical as to seem to deny that art is about anything, certainly not religion or history or even reality at all. Indeed, it is hard to see how any theory can account for art, much less a naturalistic one.

Classically, from the ancient Greeks through the seventeenth century, artworks were thought to represent objects or events, either from the actual world or from mythology, by *mimesis* or imitation. The art work presents a semblance of something, looks or sounds or acts like something. Plato's notion from the *Symposium* of the best art as a visible image of order which attunes the soul, and Aristotle's conception of tragedy in *The Poetics* as a heroic narrative which purges the emotions, remained powerful for almost two millennia. So art was an imitation which, in the best cases, ennobled the soul. Then the eighteenth century saw an explosion of interest in art under the new term "aesthetics," from the Greek *aesthesis* for perception. This led to Romanticism in Germany and England which argued, among other things, that the essential work of art is the *expression* of human emotions or feelings. The artist alone is able to externalize what lies within the human heart.

Then the years 1850 to 1950 brought epochal revolutions in many of the arts associated with the term "modernism." The notion of art as a critical commentary on social reality by an artistic "advanced guard" became common. Art was to explore new territory, sometimes to shock, and sometimes to put in question the very boundaries of art. *Mimesis* was replaced by "abstraction," and "significant form," a formal organization of lines, colors, tones, sounds, characters, facades, etc., which need not refer to or resemble an external reality, nor express some psychological reality. Some radicals, and "postmodern" forms of art after 1950, broke down the very distinction between art and everyday objects.

In the post–World War II period, the philosophy of art reacted to these changes while being influenced by the new ordinary language movement in analytic philosophy. The question as to the definition of art was paramount, but there were others. Was art made art by something intrinsic to the artwork, or by its relation to the audience? Is there a special kind of aesthetic experience or attitude required for appreciating art, or is that idea defunct? How metaphysically to understand something that is on the one hand a particular event of sounds or bodily movements (music, dance) or words and sentences spoken or printed on paper (poetry, drama), yet somehow remains one identical artwork across every performance and reprint?

We will trace the analysis of art and the aesthetic through a few key figures, focusing on the American philosophical tradition. Oddly enough, Columbia Naturalism played a prominent role in the development of the philosophy of art in this period. John Dewey, Susanne Langer, Justus Buchler, Mary Mothersill, Arthur Danto, and Joseph Margolis, all Columbians in one way or another, were key. Not that this family was superior to others, but its adoption of pragmatist and quasi-pragmatist notions seems to have been very influential. My claim will be that the combination of objective relativism and emergence form a useful background for conceptualizing aesthetic experience and modern art in its multiple forms. But first we must begin with the foundation of modern aesthetics in Kant and Romanticism. For as we will see, their concepts keep coming back.

The Germanic Background

"Aesthetics" began with the Earl of Shaftsbury, Alexander Baumgarten and Edmund Burke in the eighteenth century. They brought it into being as a study of a special kind of intrinsically judgmental human experience, called "taste," whose object was beauty. Kant lies on the border of this approach and the later German-English Romanticism which he partly inspired. Twentieth-century philosophy of art has been regarded by many as a rejection of Kant. But rumors of the death of Kant's aesthetics are greatly exaggerated.

The 1790 *Critique of Judgment* was part of a systematic philosophy in which Kant was trying to place aesthetics in the context of natural teleology or purposiveness. "Judgment" (*Urteilskraft*) for Kant is a distinctive cognitive power, different from the understanding (*Verstand*) of experience through concepts in science, and from reason (*Vernunft*), the faculty of imposing laws in morality. Unlike understanding and reason, judgment "thinks the particular under the universal." There are two kinds of judgment: "reflective" judgment which moves from the particular to the universal, and "determinant" judgment that applies the universal to the particular. Judgment of the first kind is the faculty of taste.

Kant famously used the notion of *form*, making him a precursor of the modernist notion of significant form. But he used it as an embodiment of purposiveness. Kant wrote,

> There can be, then, purposiveness without purpose [*Zweckmassigkei ohne Zweck*], so far as we do not posit the causes of this form in a will, but yet can only make the explanation of its possibility intelligible to ourselves by deriving it from a will. . . . Thus we can at least observe a purposiveness according to form, without basing it on a purpose (as the material of the *nexus finalis*), and remark it in objects, although only by reflection.[2]

Aesthetic judgment finds a kind purposiveness in the form of the natural object or appearance. The aesthetic value of the experience of something lies in the orderliness of the whole, in its "designedness." Aesthetic judgment involves feelings of pleasure stimulated, not directly by an object, but by the free play of the imagination (the faculty which unites the manifold of experience), where imagination plays with concepts of the understanding (in the case of beauty) or ideas of reason (in the case of the sublime), but is not constrained by them. The result is a harmony in our representation of the object that yields "disinterested pleasure" generated by the satisfaction of the cognitive faculty.

This describes all aesthetic judgment for Kant. But in the case of aesthetic judgment of art, as opposed to nature, the judgment must include the expression of an aesthetic concept or ideal, meaning a concept of the understanding.³ This concept is "indeterminate," not determinate like the concepts applied by the understanding in judgments of science. The content of the art work can therefore signify something that is, for Kant, non-natural. Kant is skating a difficult edge here: the artwork must be free and indeterminate, unlike the scientific use of concepts, but at the same time have its own necessity and universal validity, so all rational agents "ought" to share the same judgment of the work. He writes, the artwork seems to us "as free from all constraint of arbitrary rules as if it were a product of mere nature"—hence a kind of internal necessity.

Beauty is then the "form of the purposiveness of an object, so far as this is perceived in it without any representation of a purpose."⁴ Beauty is an ideal, a trait of representation of the object in our imagination. So our judgments of the beautiful are objective and rational. This applies as well to the *sublime*, the other chief aesthetic value, the character of an object that is boundless, where a kind of "negative pleasure" results from the overwhelming of sensory powers. Whereas beauty is classically proportional and harmonious, the sublime is awesome, so overwhelming that it generates a cognition that goes beyond our representational ability. Here we have a spiritual experience whereby the sensible relates somehow to the "supersensible."

As noted Kant introduces the notion of play (*spiel*) into the discussion to describe the activity of our representational powers. He wrote, "The subjective universal communicability of the mode of representation in a judgment of taste . . . can refer to nothing else than the state of mind in the free play of the imagination and the understanding . . . ."⁵ But this internal, imaginative free play is also connected with play in general; free art, versus "mercenary" craft, must be "purposive as play," that is, pleasant in itself rather than serving an external purpose. This idea was influential for the Romanticists who followed Kant, and promoted both the unique spiritual role of art and its expressivist interpretation. Friedrich Schiller declared that, "Man shall *only play* with Beauty. And he shall play *only with Beauty*. For . . . he is only wholly Man when he is playing*.*"⁶ This conception of play would return to philosophical discussion in the twentieth century, in the work of Johann Huizinga (1955) and Roger Callois (2001). In fact, Huizinga employs a phrase reminiscent of Kant, namely that play is "pointless but meaningful."⁷ While Callois and Huizinga differed in their analyses, they agreed at least that play is (a) "non-serious" meaning noneconomic and voluntary in the broad sense; (b) noncumulative or nonhistorical, meaning each game *starts again at zero*; and lastly, (c) must therefore be framed, bounded to keep out the forces of practical necessity and the real-world inequalities between competitors.

Kant's core notions have been harshly criticized, some would say abandoned in the past century. But we should not be too quick to bury him. For example, his today unpopular notion of disinterested pleasure meant merely absence of self-interest, charm, or practical fulfillment of goals, which not a few contemporaries would likewise allow. As with play, the issue here is whether there is a particular impractical, noninstrumental attitude or point of view which the audience, and in anticipation the artist, must adopt that separates art and play from other human interests. This was compatible with special valuation—the object or event must be encountered as having value through an appreciation that takes it seriously in its *own terms*, a willingness to allow one's imagination to be led by the work. In the case of drama and fiction, the Romanticist Coleridge gave the modern form to an idea as old as Cicero, which is that literary art demands "the willing suspension of disbelief," on the part of the audience. This is all part of a recurring theme, as we will see; the aesthetic and play attitudes, while fallen into disrepute in the aesthetics of the past half century, remain significant. Kant's attempt to give a transcendental, that is, a universal and necessary ground for aesthetic reflective judgments—hence the claim that the judgment should be agreed to by all rational others, independent of history and culture—is one thing. But his explanation of what is involved in such judgment—form, purposiveness, pleasure, free play of the imagination, concepts of the understanding but employed indeterminately, aspiring to an "inter-subjective" validity unlike that of science or morality—have all come back in one way or another (Guyer 2008).

Columbians and Other Aesthetes

The nonreductive naturalism of the Columbia school played an unexpected role in American aesthetics. Dewey, Columbia naturalism's patron saint, published the most extensive treatment of art as rooted in experience, *Art as Experience*, in 1934. Soon after two German émigrés arrived: Paul Otto Kristeller, the Renaissance historian, taught at Columbia starting in 1939; then Ernst Cassirer, the great German philosopher of culture—which is to say art, myth, language, and science—came to Columbia in Fall 1944 but died the next April. Susanne Langer, a student of Whitehead and scholar of Cassirer whose 1942 *Philosophy in a New Key* would spark her career in philosophy of art, lectured at Columbia from 1945 to 1950. Mary Mothersill, who had taught at Columbia from 1951 to 1953, returned in 1964 to teach at Barnard and the Columbia Graduate School for decades, publishing the major work *Beauty Restored* in 1984. Meanwhile two men who would become dueling philosophers of art received their Columbia PhDs: Arthur Danto in 1952 and Joseph Margolis in 1953. Danto was later hired by Columbia. He remained a colleague of Justus Buchler for more than twenty years, replacing Buchler as the Johnsonian Professor of Philosophy in 1974, the same year that Buchler's own book on poetry was published. A major non-Columbian, Nelson Goodman, himself influenced by the pragmatism of C. I. Lewis and Columbia's Sidney Morgenbesser, in some respects followed the approach of Cassirer and Langer. The point is that Columbia's naturalism and pragmatism helped to produce a number of the chief philosophers of art of the second half of the century.

Dewey's Experience

In *Art as Experience*, Dewey sought to show that his pragmatic or "instrumentalist" form of naturalism was up to the task of understanding aesthetic experience and art. He aimed to demolish the opposition of fine art versus decorative art, high versus low culture, and art versus nature. This was the application to aesthetic experience of his lifelong attack on the dualism of facts and values, and of contemplation and practice. And as a social critic, he sought the reinvestment of practical life with aesthetic value as a persistent source of meaning.

In Dewey's analysis, experiencing is a process of organism-environment transaction. It is divided into overlapping processes or histories. A life, a year, a season, a march, a migration, a day, a hunt, a storm, a meal: each has a beginning, middle and end. Humans recognize two ways of appreciating and handling such processes: as a series of steps or events that lead to an end, and as the character or quality of the end itself. This holds, he remarks in his most famous analysis, for anything that can be called *an* experience: the delineation of "an" event within the unending process of an organism's experiencing is possible because of ends which culminate some local process, marking it off. The steps or means of the process are analyzed relationally by cognition to fund our manipulation of nature, while the end exhibits unique "consummatory qualities," finalities of enjoyment which provide the ends of future behavior. These consummatory fulfillments are literally "art in germ," and guide humans when engaged in a process of making. Dewey wrote, "The doing or making is artistic when the perceived result is of such a nature that its qualities as perceived have controlled the question of production. The act of producing that is directed by the intent to produce something that is enjoyed in the immediate experience of perceiving has qualities that a spontaneous or uncontrolled activity does not have. The artist embodies in himself the attitude of the perceiver while he works."[8] While Dewey does not reject *mimesis*, art for him is fundamentally expressive. There is a subject matter to the artwork—without which, Dewey says, we have only an "esoteric" sort of art—but it is a subject matter digested and transformed in order to express qualities of experience available to artist and audience. Even abstract art does not abandon reference to the real world or content of experience. There is form, but form is characteristic of an experience.

We will see that the aesthetic-experiential approach of Dewey's is certainly justified as a necessary condition of art, in contrast to the anti-aesthetic or "anaesthetic" approach of some recent art theory (Shusterman 1997). Nevertheless, Dewey's view under-determines the phenomenon of art; art may be a product of human experience, and be intended to affect human experience, but it is not an experience.[9] Likewise his term "consummatory" is unfortunate: in anthropological and experiential terms "consummation" is just what it sounds like—the satisfaction of hunger or sex. It is the nature of most artworks that they must not be eliminated in the act of enjoyment. Lastly, Dewey shared a Romantic view that tends to turn the aesthetic into the highest of values, the location of the "meaning" or purpose of human life, a kind of atheistic replacement for the spiritual. The artwork almost mystically integrates self and object, he wrote, "no such distinction of self and object exists in it, since it is esthetic in the degree in which the organism and environment . . . are so fully integrated that each disappears."[10] In the penultimate chapter of his 1929 *Experience and Nature* Dewey concluded: "But if modern tendencies are justified in putting art and creation first [before contemplation] then the implications of this position should be avowed and carried through. It would then be seen that science is an art, that art is practice . . . When this perception dawns, it will be a commonplace that art . . . is the complete culmination of nature, and that science is properly a handmaiden that conducts natural events to this happy issue."[11]

As we have seen, Dewey was viewed as an objective relativist in his value theory. The most prominent proponent of that view was C. I. Lewis, the first thinker responsible for the interweaving of pragmatism and positivism. He produced an influential value theory in his *An Analysis of Knowledge and Valuation* (1946). For Lewis evaluation is a kind of empirical judgment and knowledge. He analyzed the aesthetic value of an object as the potentiality to result in experience of a kind, a potentiality that can be judged empirically. The artwork is "a continuing source of . . . enjoyments" of a certain kind. That is an objective claim, just like "bread is nutritious." His view was supported by some (Lafferty 1949). But the notion of potentiality seemed an attempted end-run around the basic problem of whether the aesthetic properties of the artwork are possessed independently or rather are entirely "response-dependent." Jerome Stolnitz countered with what came to be called an "internalist" view, holding aesthetic properties are internal to the experience of the artwork, which requires an attitude of Kantian disinterested sympathy similar to Monroe Beardsley's "Aesthetic Point of View" (Stolnitz 1960; Beardsley 1958). At any rate we can say the Lewis position is not an inevitable version of objective relativism. The value of an object or an event is not a potentiality for experience, although it can have that potentiality. To this we shall return.

Langer's Clothesline

Susanne Langer was unique: a student of Henry Sheffer and Alfred North Whitehead who published a textbook on logic; famous as an aesthetician; and a naturalist philosopher of mind. She was heavily influenced by two of the great neglected and systematic philosophers of the twentieth century, Whitehead and Cassirer. As a philosopher of art Langer is normally grouped with those who understood artworks as expressions of human emotion or feeling. This is true, but misleading. Langer defines artworks as symbols, understands expression in a very broad sense, and explicitly incorporates the significant form concept of modernists like Clive Bell and Roger Fry. Her most basic point is that art is a *presentational* symbol, versus the *discursive* symbols of language and mathematics.

Discursive symbols mean via convention, belong to a code, with a vocabulary and a grammar or syntax, the combinatorial rules of which are captured by logic. The artwork creates and presents a "semblance" or appearance to be experienced. It thereby expresses a pattern of human sentience or feeling. What is shared between the artwork and the sentience is a "functional form," just as the river bed expresses the flow of the river. The artwork does not denote, it connotes. Hence its meaning is best conceived as an "import." Art exhibits "what it is like to be" conscious, experiencing, sentient. Arts do this in different ways: the visible, plastic arts employ forms of *space*; music forms of *time*; drama and poetry forms of *events*; and dance the forms of *forces*. Sentient life, for example, is characterized by rhythmic series, and only music can have this import. The artwork is holistic, not linear. In her lovely metaphor, the artwork is a presentation, like wearing an outfit, whereas a verbal paraphrase of the work is like stringing its pieces on a clothesline.[12]

It is a major point for Langer that the arts are cognitive, even logical, because they provide a way of understanding patterns of sentience. All art "abstracts," which is to say selects and formalizes. Still, the core aim of art is the realization of *forms of feeling*, which we humans cannot communicate about adequately in any other way. This view, as everyone recognizes, cannot make much sense of a host of twentieth-century developments, including the work of Michel Duchamp, Andy Warhol, Robert Rauschenburg, and others. However, her notion of art as symbolic would later be taken up by Nelson Goodman and pressed in a different direction. So what we have in Langer is a combination of a mimetic (semblance), expressive (sentience) and formal (significant form) theory of art.

A number of American thinkers have questioned her categorization of symbols. Her basic distinction between "signals," meaning natural signs and symptoms, and symbols, was taken from Mead's student Charles Morris. The symbol was then broken into presentational and discursive, as noted. American philosophers inspired by Peirce's theory of signs—for example, Colapietro (1997), Dryden (1997), Glazer (2017), Innis (2009), and Kruse (2005)—find that she ignores Peirce's basic usage that "sign" covers anything that stands for anything to someone, whereas "symbols" are a narrower term for conventional (e.g., linguistic and mathematical) signs.

Given my earlier claims about Mead and Peirce, I believe Langer's usage can be altered, while maintaining its insights. As I argued in chapter 6, with no prejudice regarding attempts to apply the concept of "sign" more broadly, the kind of signs extensively used by humans are *learned, artificial, communicative (hence public) vehicles of meaning*. Human signs are learned communicative creations.[13] Langer would agree that artworks are such signs. But what kind? They cannot be what Peirce called "symbols," for exactly the reasons Langer stated: they are not conventionally chosen, arbitrary marks, with an alphabet, vocabulary, and syntax.

It might seem obvious that some artworks, especially visual or plastic, resemble something and mean thereby. An icon, or more precisely what Peirce called a *hypoicon*, can be an image, a diagram (in which the relations of parts resemble relations of the object's parts), or a metaphor (where a relation signifies a relation characteristic of the object). Anything that functions diagrammatically or metaphorically is an icon. Second, any sign can be a "degenerate" member of its category, meaning that an icon may have a secondary indexical function, or vice versa. A picture or painting of a smiling figure is an icon *of* a causally related index of the facial arrangement that represents emotion. This greatly widens the scope of iconic-indexical signage. For the agent's physical expression of emotion is directly linked to that emotion—indeed, it *is* emotion for many psychologists. Lastly, it is clear from Peirce's examples that "index" includes not only signs which refer to something causally affecting it, like the weathervane moved by the wind, but also signs that causally impose an interpretant on the interpreter, for example, a rap on a door. As Kruse suggests, referring to Peirce's distinction of emotional, energetic, and logical interpretants, in some works of art "a feeling becomes . . . interpretive." She writes, "any framed perceptual-imaginative array may be designed to, and actually cause, an emotional interpretant. Likewise, any concept, or meaning in the linguistic sense, can be a logical interpretant. There could be cases of energetic or dynamic interpretants—one thinks especially of music—but it is interesting that the experience of some artworks involves deliberately suppressing action."[14]

Indeed, the hardest case for signs is that of "pure music," appropriate since Langer was particularly concerned with music and dance. Stephen Davies argues pure music, without voice or literary and narrative references, is still the appearance of emotion (Davies 1994). The dynamics of a musical piece "resembles" something about either the phenomenology of an emotion (e.g., the feeling of quickening of pace, excitation, movement) or the physiognomic expression of the emotion (e.g., the smile looks happy, the frown looks sad). He claims they do so, as Langer suggested, by dynamic, temporal rhythms of human emotional behavior, in effect, what Peirce considers an "energetic" or causal interpretant. None of this would be strange when applied to a joint intentional sign user, capable of reading and sharing others' mental states.

My point is that we can read Langer through Peirce's notions of indexical as well as iconic signs as standing for two cases that intertwine and merge in some art forms. And we may remember that intentional "standing for" is "of," not solely "about" something ("aboutness" being commentary, predication, subsumption under a category). Is John Cage's *4'33"* about anything? Not necessarily, but it is certainly "of" something: it is a communicative, designed sign of silence or ambient sound. It may also be "about," a commentary on something, like what constitutes music, which leads to various logical interpretants (and is supposed to).

Buchler's Exhibitions

Buchler, formulator of our tripartite theory of judgment, is relevant here. The art that informed his aesthetic work was poetry, leading to his 1974 *The Main of Light*. It is the most complete development of his notion of exhibitive judgment. Buchler spends much of the book rejecting the metaphysical dualisms that dominate the philosophy of art—the actual versus the possible, particular versus universal, imaginary versus real, cognitive versus emotional, and so on. As we already know, art for Buchler is a selective arrangement of materials to be experienced or "proceived." The art work judges from a point of view; it is cognitive, but not assertive, it makes an addition to the world but is not active or consequential. Buchler wrote, "Exhibitive judgment, exemplified on the methodic level by art, but in no way restricted to the commonly recognized arts, is the process whereby men shape natural complexes and communicate them for assimilation as thus shaped . . . distinguished from their bearing on action and belief."[15]

All methodic judgment or query is exploratory, but poetry uniquely so. A "poetic finding opposes no others," Buchler announces, it lives in the world of ontological parity because its task is to expose the prevalence of some complex. Poetic speech is not, like ordinary speech, enslaved to the ontological priority of the real vs. the apparent. Its query is peculiarly uninhibited hence unlike either science or morality. Coleridge's "suspension of disbelief," Buchler argues, "can be salvaged as the sense of the parity of all complexes as complexes." Whatever complex is explored gets its "sovereignty" recognized by poetry. He concludes, "The kind of exhibitive judgment that can be called poetry, then, is the product of query that defines a complex as prevalent, thereby contriving to convey a sense of the complex as ineluctably what it is."[16] However, it remains communicative, "the recognition of prevalence communicating itself." Because his major concern is with poetry Buchler is not tempted by discussion of perception or "acquaintance." The artwork is a something which exhibits its prevalence to be "assimilated as such"—this is Buchler's way of rendering the notions of disinterested sympathy or the aesthetic point of view of the work in and of itself.

Mothersill's Cactus

There is no evidence that Mary Mothersill was influenced by the naturalists at Columbia, but she had been a student of C. I. Lewis, and her account of aesthetics clearly rejected the attempt to separate the aesthetic from the empirical and causal. Mothersill's aim in her *Beauty Restored* was to find a midpoint in understanding the validity of aesthetic judgments between those (like Santayana) who believed they can have no general or objective validity and others who (like Kant) believe they can make a universal claim that commands others to agree. She argues that while it is true that there are no laws or principles of aesthetic value, nevertheless there are "genuine" aesthetic judgments which can be true or false. This has been, she thought, obscured by recent "anti-theorists" who abandon any account of the validity of critical judgments. The key to the problem is to restore the sense of our "standing" concept of beauty.

For Mothersill any aesthetic judgment claims that a particular object is the cause of pleasure in virtue of having an aesthetic property. And to say it has an aesthetic property is to make the contingent claim that it is beautiful. The aesthetic properties of objects are complex, "gestalt" properties, properties of the relations among properties of the object (e.g., among brush strokes, colors, rhythms, characters, etc.). Aesthetic statements are avowals of personal experience or acquaintance, but they also make a claim, a "verdict," which normatively commends the object to others (Mothersill 217). Kant was wrong to demand that aesthetic judgments "command" assent and Santayana to deny that they claimed validity at all.

One of Mothersill's key points is that aesthetic judgments are particular or singular. Using a concept from Aquinas she argues that the aesthetic judgment reports an experiential recognition of the thing in itself, an *apprehensio ipsa*. The beautiful, pleasure-causing properties are recognized in experience or acquaintance. Beauty is "that of which the *apprehensio ipsa* pleases." This applies to any kind of object, not only art but natural phenomena, including her own "pride and joy," her cactus (Mothersill 1984, 352). The key is that the beauty belongs to the *particular* object of acquaintance alone. Thus while objective, aesthetic judgments cannot yield lawful criteria for which any object having them must be "beautiful."

This means that aesthetic criticism, the evaluation of the aesthetic properties of the object, is ostensive and pedagogical, and can only guide further acquaintance by the viewer, not serve as an assertive proof. In citing Arnold Isenberg's analysis of criticism of El Greco's *The Burial of Count Orgaz*, and its "steeply rising and falling curve," she writes, "The critic speaks as we do, but his words serve what one might call an 'ostensive' function . . . to redirect our attention . . . and so bring about what Isenberg calls 'communication at the level of the senses'" (Mothersill 1984, 338–39). As Guyer remarks of her view, "it's *that* line outlining *those* figures with *those* colors creating *that* mood" that pleases and hence is the aesthetic property (Guyer 1986, 249). The critic's assertions lead the reader to perceive that the verdict is true.

Now, we would say that Mothersill is attempting to defend the rational validity of assertive judgments of or about aesthetic merit or value, not the exhibitive validity of the artwork *per se*. She makes the critical judgment a verdict or commendation, akin to Hare's analysis, although the aesthetic commendation is not universal and prescriptive. The truth claim of the aesthetic assertion is intersubjective for her, and objective and rational in that reasons are given for it. We could add, it is fallible. The object is endlessly interpretable, because always incomplete. The aesthetic claim functions outside any progressive ethical, practical, or cognitive advance; the criticism of an old work shows us something new about it we had not noted, but does not put away all earlier appreciation as obsolete and mistaken. What is most striking is her restriction of claims of beauty to the particular. The kind of assertive judgment that is aesthetic, which is genuine and potentially valid (true), is the assertive judgment about a particular with which one is acquainted. The *ipsa* possesses its aesthetic properties intrinsically, but as we have seen "intrinsic" cannot mean non-relational. We will return to this.

Goodman's Forgeries

Nelson Goodman's *Languages of Art: An Approach to a Theory of Symbols* (1976) was first published in 1968, six years before Buchler's book and fourteen before Motherill's. But it belongs to a later era. Only now in our penny-history do we move into the period when American philosophers of art begin to deal with both the last gasp of aesthetic modernism (abstract expressionism) and the "postmodernism" of Pop and Conceptual Art, such as Warhol, Rauschenberg, and Cage, among others. These developments not only put *mimesis* and expressionism out of favor, but raised ontological questions about the boundaries of art and the identity of artworks.

Somewhat reminiscent of Langer, Goodman began with logic and philosophy of language. Like Quine, Goodman was a nominalist for whom our logic inevitably operates on particulars and underdetermines any objective view of the world, leaving us with a pragmatic choice of ontologies among predicates that are "projectible" or capable of adequate use. Unlike Quine he endorsed a symbolic "irrealism," or more alliteratively, a "radical relativism under rigorous restraints." Noting Cassirer's monumental *Philosophy of Symbolic Forms*, he agrees that human symbolic activity constructs "worlds," actual worlds in which science, art, and language operate, out of particulars that can only be known or handled symbolically. These *Ways of Worldmaking* are the warp and woof of human cognition (Goodman 1978).

Goodman points out the problems with traditional *mimesis* or resemblance. There is "no innocent eye," every perceptual representation is a "representation as." When a painter represents or denotes *y* as a "soandso," ostensibly through similarity, its resemblance is relative to a technique, a description, and a learned culture. There remain as many unsimilar properties to be ignored as similar to be cited (e.g., the painting is flat, framed, etc.). The properties of the picture can stand for or refer to something, hence *denote* it, but they can also *express* something. The tailor's swatch of cloth expresses, or "metaphorically exemplifies," in that it possesses the properties ascribed to the represented. Goodman reserves "the term 'expression' to distinguish the central case where the property belongs to the symbol itself . . . Properties expressed are . . . not only metaphorically possessed by also referred to, exhibited, typified, shown forth."[17] Artistic signs express.

Famously Goodman takes up the issue of authenticity in art, which directly connects to the problem of identifying works. His core idea is that, "There is no such thing as a forgery of Gray's *Elegy*," referring to Thomas Gray's 1751 poem "Elegy Written in a Country Churchyard." Literature, like music, dance, and theatre, is "allographic"—the creator's work is fully exemplified in any performance based on it or reprinted from it, even though each may be slightly different. Whereas most painting, sculpture and architecture are "autographic," completed only once, and carry their history with them, so any exact copy is a forgery. An allographic work of music is "a class of performances compatible with a score," so you have heard Beethoven's Fifth Symphony if you attended its performance anywhere. But seeing the *Guernica* means going to Madrid.

Metaphor is central to Goodman's notion of aesthetic expression. It is useful to compare it with another famous analysis. Donald Davidson argued that the "meaning" of a metaphor is entirely literal; the difference between a metaphorical and non-metaphorical expression is not a matter of "meaning" but rather of *point*, what the expression is "used to do." Like lying, metaphor is not saying at all; it is showing something you have "been led to see," not expressed by any proposition (Davidson 1978). Goodman rejects Davidson's account, saying metaphorical statements have a new meaning, and can be true *as* metaphors (Goodman 1979).

This disagreement is instructive. Metaphors mean by putting a symbolic, "literal" linguistic expression in a frame of use whereby it has an iconic or indexical meaning. This is "showing." Davidson is interpreting metaphor in terms of a literal assertive contribution to a statement that has an *exhibitive* function—metaphor is an exhibition contributing to what may be an otherwise assertive project. To the extent the project is assertive, it may be true. If so, there is a paraphrase that works. The "truth" of a metaphorical statement, like Goodman's "The lake is a sapphire," can be cashed out in paraphrase. To the extent that the paraphrase it not equivalent, the statement is aesthetically compelling. Which does *not* make it less of a valid judgment for us since assertion and exhibition are both judgmental. Goodman and Davidson both cite something, but as we will see, like Margolis and Danto, differ on where to put it.

Danto's Cleaning Products

Arthur Danto, student and later friend of Langer's, became the most prominent philosopher of art in America starting in the 1980s. In his pre-aesthetic work, Danto had been obsessed with an example from Wittgenstein's *Philosophical Investigations* (para. 621): is there a difference between the fact that you raise your arm and the fact that the arm goes up? (This is the same as Alicia Juarrero's question, "What is the difference between a wink and a blink?") Narrative sentences from everyday life or biography or literature, which imply that the event at t_0 cannot be understood without the event at t_1 or t_5, are compatible with the methodology of the natural sciences, but distinctive. Human agency cannot be reduced to the physicalist "arm goes up" description. As he later wrote, "The difference between a basic action [arm "raised"] and a mere bodily movement [arm goes up] is paralleled in many ways by the difference between an artwork and a mere thing."[18]

In an enormous output of art criticism and philosophy of art, Danto was most famous for two interventions. His 1964 "The Artworld," inspired by Warhol's *Brillo Box*—a box of Brillo soap pads—pointed out that not only Warhol, but Duchamp's "readymades"—the latter's 1915 *Bottlerack* and 1917 *Fountain*, which was a urinal—make it impossible to distinguish between an artwork and a perceptually indiscernible "mere real thing"(Danto 1964). A philistine who considers *Fountain* a mere urinal, hasn't "mastered" it. Even the postmodern artist cannot, in rejecting mimetic representation, say "My work is just a bed, another piece of reality." Because if so, she could not scold the security guard at the gallery for sleeping in Claes Oldenburg's *Bedroom Ensemble*! If the dozing guard made a mistake, what kind of mistake? Danto continued, "To see something as art requires something that the eye cannot decry—an atmosphere of artistic theory, a knowledge of the history of art, an artworld." As Danto said of the marginal Icarus figure in Brueghel's *Fall of Icarus*, to utter "That white dab is Icarus," is an example of a distinctive "is" of aesthetic identification. Only a theory of art held by the art community can fund that identification. This was the "institutional" theory originally of George Dickie.[19] It was more fully explored in Danto's 1981 *The Transfiguration of the Commonplace: A Philosophy of Art*.

Danto's 1985 "The Philosophical Disenfranchisement of Art" went further. Exploring a connection to Hegel, Danto argued that the entire history of at least visual art had been a progressive attempt for more "accurate" perceptual representation. But after the invention of photography and film, art had to explore new territory and thereby became "philosophical." The very concept of art became art's dominant topic. And by the time of 1964 and Warhol's *Brillo Box* it had in full self-consciousness exhausted its historical explorations, reaching its end. He would later write, "I was somewhat saddened by the idea of art having come to an end . . . it had been an immense privilege to live in history."[20] What was left afterward was "a kind of play."

But in other respects Danto held rather traditional notions. He admitted to being an "essentialist" regarding the definition of art, at the end of *Transfiguration* referring to his view as an expansion of Peirce's idea that human beings are themselves signs. Hence Warhol's *Brillo Box* is the presentation of a metaphor: "the brillo box-as-work-of-art . . . externalizing a way of viewing the world . . . offering itself as a mirror to catch the conscience of our kings." In 1992, he wrote that "The thesis which emerged from my book *Transfiguration of the Commonplace* is that works of art are symbolic expressions, in that they embody their meanings."[21] Notice that he is close both to Goodman and in another sense to Langer. Commenting on his own history from the perspective of 2007, Danto noted his relation with Kant's aesthetics: "I was fairly bearish about the importance of aesthetics for art . . . I emerged with what I thought of as two necessary conditions for a philosophical definition of art—that art is about something and hence possess meaning; and that an artwork embodied its meaning . . . I condensed this by calling works of art *embodied meanings* . . ."[22] Indeed, in his final attempt to define art, *What Art Is* (2013) Danto is motivated by Descartes's seventeenth-century question of how we can know we are not dreaming. Given that, Danto says, there is no internal way to distinguish dreaming and waking, art is "dreamlike." He declares, "I have decided to enrich my earlier definition of art—embodied meaning—with another condition that captures the skill of the artists . . . I will define art as wakeful dreams."[23]

Margolis's Stories

Unlike Goodman and Danto, soon after receiving his PhD Joseph Margolis turned right to aesthetics. Already in 1958 he began with a metaphysical analysis of the "intermittent existence" of works of art, by which he meant that if we identify the work as something other or more than its physical properties or not identical to a particular performance, we are committed to the view that the artwork does not "always" exist. The artwork is a vertical, "two-story" object, a physical object with physical properties *and* an aesthetic object with aesthetic properties, the latter related to and dependent on creator and/or audience (Margolis 1958; Pryba 2021).

His crucial idea came in the 1974 "Works of Art as Physically Embodied and Culturally Emergent Entities." He revisits Kant, arguing that "Kantian 'purposiveness without purpose (generously construed . . .) fixes the form of rationality that may be minimally assigned to anything construed as a work of art."[24] The embodiment of the work of art in a physical body grants "convenience of reference and identity" as in identification, without it being identical to that body. Similarly, we cannot apply to art a simple "token-type" or "particular-universal" distinction. Picasso's *Les Demoiselles d'Avignon* is both a particular thing, a particular painted canvas on the wall at (currently) MoMA in New York, and at the same time, something which can be reproduced and instantiated in copies (Margolis 1977). The artwork cannot be a universal *or* a particular. It has to be a both, a particular (token) which can itself be embodied in other tokens. So it must be a strange object, a "token-as-a-type."

Margolis explicitly called this phenomenon *emergence*. He modified it from Herbert Feigl and Mario Bunge, and more fully worked it out in his 1978 book, *Persons and Minds: The Prospects of a Nonreductive Materialism*. There he argued that cultural entities in general, including works of art, have a distinctive, ambiguous metaphysical status as "physically embodied and culturally emergent." The embodiment gives you the physical individuation, the emergence the "resistance" to reductionism: "A cultural system is a system of tokens-of-types."[25] This provides the basis for his later account of cultural entities in the 1999 *What, After All, is a Work of Art?*

> That cultural entities are histories, Intentional careers—whether artwork, words and sentences, actions, machines, or selves—embodied in physical, biological, electronic, or other artifactual objects or events. . . . Intentional and non-Intentional properties may jointly be ascribed to such entities . . . [which] are intrin-

sically interpretable as such . . . [an] interpretive objectivity is best served by a relativistic [non-bivalent] logic . . . [and] the natures of such entities are open, without paradox or loss of realist standing, to all the diversity, variability, transformation, incongruence, and historicized novelty that cultural history is known to generate.[26]

Here we also see Margolis's endorsement of what he termed "robust" relativism. In certain domains of inquiry bivalence, the notion that either proposition p or $\sim p$ must be true, can be weakened and replaced by non-bivalent truth-like values, like "apt." Wordsworth's *Lucy Poems* bear two equally valid but incompatible interpretations: both are "apt" or "reasonable" which bivalence would indict as a paradox (Margolis 1976). Thus the strict bivalence rightly expected of mathematics and natural science cannot apply to all inquiry. Likewise the degree of determinacy of the subject matter varies. Margolis points out that we cannot assume there must be a fact of the matter as to whether Sherlock Holmes has a mole on his back or not. This is a straightforward Peircean denial that reals are entirely and absolutely determinate; they need only be partly determinate.

Margolis applied his emergentist view to human beings (Margolis 2001). Humans are naturally evolving primates, *Homo sapiens*, who uniquely employ the medium of language and culture, in which "selves" occur. The things of art are special, intentional things, in a different way than minded animals are; the latter are characterized by intentional activities, whereas the former are intentional products, meaning they signify. This leads Margolis to the notion of "selves as texts." Human selves are cultural artifacts.

The Final Columbian Squabble

Margolis and Danto had their own aesthetic feud. They commented on each other's work at various times, but we will narrow our focus to Margolis's paper "Farewell to Danto and Goodman" published in 1998—the year Goodman died—to which Danto responded. Margolis criticized Goodman and Danto as reciprocally mistaken about the ontology of art. Goodman, an avowed nominalist, tried to reduce artworks to extensional particulars whose identity is established by perceptual properties which constitute them as expressive symbols. Margolis accuses Goodman of cleansing allegedly allographic artworks of their autographic features to make his point. There are, for example, musical and other performative works that are not scored or scripted, or scored or scripted differently by different artists/performers. For Margolis all art is autographic; the allographic depends on the autographic. To claim that "forgery" is in principle impossible for any work because individuation of an artwork is solely perceptible, is wrong.

At the opposite end of the spectrum, Margolis argues Danto attempts to individuate and identify an artwork entirely *independent* of its perceptual properties. Hence nothing is an artwork unless identified as such by the relevant historical/artistic community. He accuses Danto of assuming that reality is an entirely perceptual affair opposed to art, hence art is imperceptible *as* art. Danto is then forced to make recourse to the "imaginary," "rhetorical," "mythical," "dreaming," to make art. Margolis concludes that on Danto's theory, by denying any perceptual access to their intentional properties, artworks cannot be identified, bought or sold. That is, for Danto "artworks simply do not exist"![27]

Danto's response was telling. Danto does indeed say that the cultural, artistic object is not perceptible because the perceptible object can be imagined without meaning or aesthetic properties—the bottlerack in the store is perceptually indistinguishable from Duchamps' readymade *Bottlerack*. Danto suggests that philosophers like Margolis fail to recognize that artworks have "relational properties." He thinks Margolis is trying to build the aesthetic *into* the entity, the object or event, failing to see the importance of context and relations. Danto writes,

> Thus I may say I saw B's father in the audience, and I may be right. But being B's father, like being a work of art, carries references to a relation complex which, if it does not hold, falsifies my claim . . . I would restrict perception for such properties 'B's father' has whether the relationships I took for granted hold or not. *Relations do not penetrate their terms.* . . . Relational properties appear to have been uncommonly difficult for philosophers to grasp . . . The issue between Margolis and me has to do with the limits of perception . . . My interest is in truth-conditions, his in the richness of culturally enriched minds [my emphasis].[28]

The perceptual, physical "real" object is what it is regardless of relations, but interpretations "constitute" works of art: "Interpretation is in effect the lever with which an object is lifted out of the real world and into the artworld."[29]

In contrast, for Margolis the art object is a peculiar kind of entity, a metaphysically distinct kind, whose extensional, perceptual, physical, token features are paired with emergent intentional, typic features, and the two are not separable. In this they are similar to a human agent, hence selves are texts. His final pronouncement emphasizes that emergence is what Danto is missing, namely, that there is a relation of asymmetric dependence between the art work and the "mere real object" which it is, and which makes the artwork a different kind of entity (Margolis 2015).

What to make of this squabble? Neither Margolis nor Danto fail to acknowledge relations. The question is, *where do they put them*? For Danto, *Bottlerack* is constituted by relations, but the bottlerack is not. Here our objective relativism must intervene. Some relations do "penetrate" their terms: horizontally, between related systems, and vertically, between the sub- and super-venient. Margolis accepts the vertical or emergent relations, but in a restricted way.

Ordinal naturalism recognizes that emergence applies not only to intentional or cultural things. The dog's paw also can be raised: in relation to physics, the paw may just "go up," but for biology and animal psychology it is raised. X "raised an arm," x is "B's father," and x "is an artwork," are relational, *but so are* "x's arm went up," x is "a thing," x is a "a black square." Each of the former is "intentional," meaning either psychological or cultural or both; the latter are biological, sociological/biological, and material. If I am both a professor and a father, but have the same perceptual properties in each role, is there a mystery? If a student says, "Cahoone is not a father, he is a professor" what kind of mistake is made? Cahoone has an identity compatible with distinct ordinal integrities. Indeed, in some orders Cahoone is indistinguishable from a material object, for example, while falling from a window (as long as we ignore the screams).

Back to art. Duchamp acquired a bottlerack, x. He selected it, arranged it, and framed it—in effect putting it on stage in a particular spot—as *Bottlerack*, an artwork. Whether the artworld decides to consider it valid as an artwork is an open question for query. X has most of the same properties before and after, that is, in the variety of contexts in which it does or did function, its integrity in those remains pretty much the same. But in the exhibition x has acquired a new integrity, a new function, in a new context. It already was a cultural object, as was the urinal which became *Fountain*, but not an art object, art being a special, arguably "high" part of culture (a distinction Duchamp was in the process of shredding). Previously it was a tool, like a table or chair. Indeed, the interpretation of x as an artwork will likely dwell on precisely that acquisition; as Danto rightly said, art theory had elbowed its way to the front of the gallery.

Margolis rightly understands that the cultural entity or event is distinctive, is "made," is both physical/material and "intentional." But so are many things, like baby seals made by mommy-and-daddy seals. The creator of the artwork is not a "text," because "text" is not the only model of intentionality, mind being distributed among a host of neurally complex animals. That human selves are cultural does not replace or negate their utter biological dependence. Nor does the fact that the self is a process rather than an entity make it uniquely cultural or intentional; there are processes throughout nature. What needs to be added to Margolis is (a) "objects" can be processes or states, structures or relations, and properties, as well as entities or systems; and (b) there are two forms of dependence, horizontal and vertical that are relevant here, applying to all sorts of complexes, not just cultural ones. Since emergence is wider than culture, there is no need for Margolis's "constructivism" or the "symbiosis" of physically real and humanly made. The intentional, semiotic, cultural, and artistic are as at home in nature as their unusual creator species.

How, After All, Does an Artwork?

The artistic developments pushing the views of Goodman, Danto, and Margolis tended to undermine belief in the necessity of aesthetic experience and an aesthetic attitude. But not entirely successfully. Richard Shusterman revived and extended Dewey's approach with his notion of "somaesthetics" (Shusterman 2000). He argues that the views of Dickie, Goodman, and Danto misleadingly assume experience to be an immediate, un-interpreted given, and press the view that art is semiotic, interpretive and "anaesthetic" (Shusterman 1997) He is right, but from the viewpoint of ordinal naturalism, which is to say, objective relativism plus emergence, there is no great need to choose among these approaches.

Humans are uniquely capable of aesthetic experience. Many creatures delight in and are fascinated by sensual presentations, and some engage in play with them. But only humans are capable of not only finding value but *meaning* in such presentations. The terrifying storm or beautiful mountain scene, the sun, moon, and stars, the unique animal or tree or found object, entail not only the appreciation of or fascination with something uniquely valued, but something that means, something to be *interpreted*. This presumes the location of an image or auditory sequence or tactile experience in the joint intentionality of human self-consciousness. The aesthetic point of view or attitude, which aesthetic experience must take on and embody, is *emergent*. It is the experience of something with intrinsic value for a social and semiotic experiencer. The functioning of the natural sign or symptom, the special or sacred object or event, takes on a novel meaning in the domain of human experience that it cannot otherwise have.

Then there is a second distinctive human capability: we *exhibitively make*. Artwork is made, "ready" or not. The minimal sense of making is arrangement, hence at least selection and framing—so it has a beginning and end, distinguished from what is outside, from the consummatory, the needful, the utilitarian, the cumulative. Here Buchler's term is entirely apt: art is an exhibitive arrangement. That the work "exhibits," is not so far from the claim that it expresses or exemplifies (Goodman), or embodies (Danto and Margolis), or presents (Langer). It means *in the manner of* presenting or expressing or exhibiting. It must be a kind of communicative sign, designed to communicate to other humans. Artworks perform their function not as symbols employing arbitrary codes, but as perceptually and imaginatively experienced complexes that "stand for something" either iconically or indexically or both, something which generates an interpretant that might be emotional or dynamic or logical-intellectual. That there are some forms of later twentieth-century art whose function can only be a contemplation or revision of the boundaries of art itself is still a "meaning." And that is why they are offered up for interpretation, even if the artist resists any particular reduction to a "final" interpretant.

The art work and its aesthetic properties are emergent, like many, many things including its creator and audience. Which is to say the art work is a complex composed of materials, events, and signs, arranged and produced by a uniquely joint intentional creature, in its unique activity of exhibitive making, designed and framed for aesthetic experience. The, one might say, vertical dependence of the work and its aesthetic properties on its material and energetic properties does not undermine their prevalence. The artwork is a human arrangement or product which, in being assimilated as such, is a communicative sign valued in itself.

As to the artwork's identity, some philosophers make it independent of relations to other things, including the experience of an audience, while others allow it to be entirely constituted by a critical community or audience. Objective relativism makes a contribution here as well. The artwork is intended to be, and is experienced in "itself." That is the point of art and how it is experienced as a cultural product, like any game or sport. But nothing is devoid of relations; independence is relative and a matter of degree. The artwork is indeed designed to be experienced and evaluated independent of a host of contexts and considerations, but not all. The identity of x is not undermined or opposed by its dependence on other things, including its, we may say, horizontal dependence on relations to other cultural artifacts or a human audience. It is still the nature of exhibitive making to present something for direct appreciation in itself.

We can explicate this minimal analysis by employing a variety of common theoretical terms. The artwork is (1) *a formed content*, that is, something arranged in some manner or mode of presentation, at the very least selection and framing; (2) presented to be *experienced or enjoyed in itself as meaningful*, which is to say valued in its presentation *as* meaning by the human species or some subset of it (everyone, or a culture, or an educated social group); (3) that functions as *an iconic and/or indexical sign* (of or about something), thereby meaning via resemblance (*mimesis*) and/or a dynamic, causal relation (expression), yielding interpretants that can be emotional and/or energetic and/or logical. This can be summarized in a diagram reminiscent of our old joint intentional diagram (see figure 14.1).

My point is that there is no reason to deny that the representationalist, expressionist, formalist, and experientialist approaches to artworks all have a place. The artwork means, and this meaning can involve any kind of representation or *mimesis* in the sense of resembling or referring to anything whatsoever, and/or the expression and presentation of any attitude or

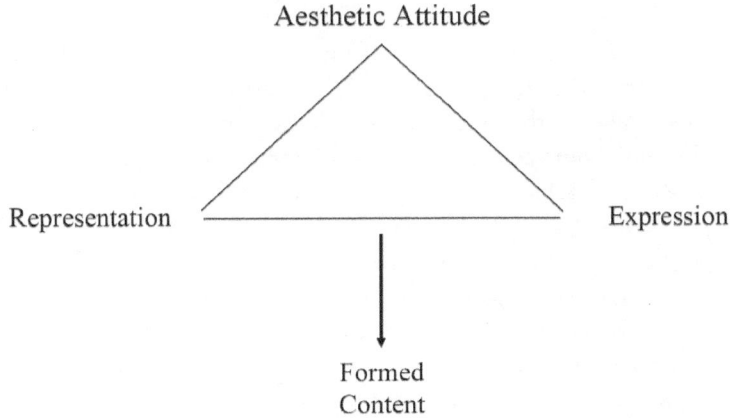

Figure 14.1. Contexts of the artwork. (Author created)

emotion. Both *mimesis* and expression are meanings of the communicative sign of the artwork. Aesthetic experience presumes an aesthetic attitude and must be characteristic not only of the individual experiencing the artwork, but the creator, and hence of some community or *we*, otherwise the artwork would not be created. The work is designed to be experienced as an artwork, rather than as something else. And it does this through selection and manipulation both of a something to be presented and how it is to be presented. Its creation is a mode of human judging, which cannot be reduced to either sensory experience itself, or assertion, or action. It is something special we humans do.

Finally, critical assertive claims of and about such works can indeed be true or false as Mothersill claimed, or more true or more false. But like all claims they are fallible and incomplete. Indeed their truth or falsity, unlike the domains of science and morality (or politics), are recognitions of the actual or prospective functions of the work and its properties in various orders of experience. The distinction is between the aims of assertion and action, and the aim of exhibitive making. The first two are inevitably historical and cumulative, the latter is not. Art's function is the meaning-in-presentation of a complex, new aspects of which in newly applied contexts can always be noted, with no requirement that prior interpretations be jettisoned as pointless or destructive or wrong.

The artwork, unlike the act or statement, is supposed to be considered distinct from its predecessor or consequent. It is a made exhibition, the occasion for experience, whose interpretation can be informed by all sorts of considerations—including assertive (truth of the work's "message" or what it "says" or the beliefs behind it) and active (its impact or intended impact on the audience, the politics of the creator or the times), but is not limited to them. The interpretation of the work in a variety of relations and contexts renders the meanings which can be expressed open-ended. But not infinite. Some claims about Wordsworth's Lucy Poems, even about their meaning and value will clearly be *false*. But there will be some range of interpretations about which we cannot come to that conclusion. There will be degrees and forms of attunement, layers of meanings available, some of which may go beyond what the creator intended. Here Buchler would say that the process of interpretive query into an artwork, unlike inquiry or active elaboration, is a potentially endless process of ramification of the meanings the work evokes in different contexts.

This might lead one to ask, what about the relation of art and truth? What of John Keats's famous line "Beauty is truth, truth beauty," or Nietzsche's claim that the world's is only "justified" as an aesthetic phenomenon, or Orson Welles's quip that drama is "an unreality that is true." If a made exhibition were "true" in the sense that inquiry tries to be, that would mean it "says" something logically equivalent to its translation or paraphrase. That would make the artwork a statement. But perhaps the connection of art and truth could mean that the artwork iconically or indexically *shows* a reality or something about reality that gives us an insight like any conventional symbol can (Welles), or that the value or purpose of reality can only be shown (Nietzsche), or that art creates a reality which has a special, permanent, value unlike anything else humans do (Keats). Aesthetic value and query can be preserved without being confused with science, or politics, or religion. The problem is not with truth as a norm or the requirement of bivalence, but with the complexity of the aesthetic object, its manner of signification, and the variety of meanings of which it can be the occasion. Which, aesthetically, is not a problem to be solved at all.

Chapter Fifteen

The Good

> ... as long as life is left to itself and is understood in its own terms, it knows only that the conflict between these gods is never-ending. Or, in nonfigurative language, life is about the incompatibility of ultimate *possible* attitudes and hence the inability ever to resolve the conflicts between them. Hence the necessity of *deciding* between them.
>
> —Max Weber, "Science as a Vocation"[1]

This part of the journey is coming to a close. Our supplies are long exhausted, the bedroll beckons. But one last hill awaits.

We began by noting Max Weber's remarkable 1917 lecture "Science as a Vocation." It is a work of philosophy in the language of history as a contribution to politics. Several essays for the price of one. It was one of the sources of Weber's notion of value-free social science. As noted, he argued that you shouldn't trust your professors when they tell you who to vote for. The task of the scientist is to determine facts. As a citizen you must judge facts but also values, and your professor has no greater insight into values than you do. But the ultimate aim of his paper was the more remarkable claim that the modern world is "polytheistic." That sounds bizarre. The modern world seems hard pressed to support belief in one God, much less several.

What Weber meant was a polytheism of *values*. He was referring to such values as truth, moral goodness, political right, and aesthetic value, but also more concrete things, like family versus work, individual creativity versus communal acceptance, financial success versus personal satisfaction. In traditional society there was God, an ultimate ideal that embodied all positive values simultaneously. The church—whichever one you belonged to—and often the state preached an integrated set of values. But without

God, or more generally, without a society in which religion influences the organization of all life and culture, the unity of values is gone, as least as far as public, social life is concerned. Rationalization promotes the separate pursuit of each value, devoid of traditional limits. Each value makes its own claim on us, so serving one makes us sin against other gods, or ends, in a zero-sum game. My devotion to work steals time from family, and family and work from public life. Devotion to scientific truth, the concern for interpersonal morality, political justice, economic improvement, or art can all block or corrupt devotion to the others. Any judgment that one value is more important must be made on the basis *of* that value, there being no neutral bar of judgment. Of course we can and do try to balance, but still each value potentially diminishes, sometimes violates, the others. Which is the right balance? That is just up to me (or us). I am left with an ultimate choice on which the validity of my whole life stands or falls, and no shared public authority can validate my decision. Weber's response?

> To anyone who is unable to endure the fate of the age like a man we must say that he should return to the welcoming and merciful embrace of the old churches . . . We shall not bear him a grudge if he can really do it. For such a sacrifice of the intellect in favor of an unconditional religious commitment is one thing . . . it is a very different thing if one shirks his straightforward duty to preserve his intellectual integrity . . . [and] instead resorts to feeble equivocation . . . that embracing of religion . . . ranks higher to my mind than the professorial prophecy that forgets that the only morality that exists in a lecture room is that of plain intellectual integrity.[2]

Modern rationalization, as Weber called it, differentiates all value spheres and thereby gives us tremendous returns of economic plenty, scientific knowledge, republican politics, and personal freedom. But it also made certain things impossible, namely the social recognition of a highest value. In modern society we gain freedom at the price of "alienation," or as sociologist Peter Berger put it, "homelessness" (Berger, Berger, and Kellner, 1974). Separating my individual self from my kin and social roles gives me freedom but also leaves me searching for an identity, a home, with a fixed center of value. Certainly we inherit and are taught values and a culture; we do not start from zero. But freedom means the self can choose among roles without death or ostracism. "How then shall we (I) live?" becomes a personal choice, with no public or objective justification, no conviction that we all ought to act following the one best course for a human being.

In what may seem like an odd source to cite in this context, we find a related claim in Isaiah Berlin's essay "Two Concepts of Liberty." Berlin argued, "the belief that some single formula can in principle be found whereby all the diverse ends of men can be harmoniously realized is demonstrably false. If . . . the ends of men are many, and not all of them are in principle compatible with each other, then the possibility of conflict—and of tragedy—can never wholly be eliminated from human life."[3] Berlin is denying "the unity of the Good." That is, the notion that all human goods, or all the most important human goods, are connected or at least commensurable and integrable. To say they are connected would mean intellectual wisdom, good character, aesthetic creativity, courage, being good at your job, and being a fine father or mother are linked, that having one makes it likely to have the others. Or at the very least, one might believe they are integrable, that they could go together without conflict, and do in the best persons, as Aristotle held.

The doctrine of the unity of the good is at least as old as Plato. He famously made The Good (*tou agathou*) the highest of all his Forms, that is, the most important of the universal, unchanging, nonphysical Reals that are the ultimate existences. The Hellenistic Greek Plotinus was able to give a theistic interpretation of The Good as the One, the ultimate reality. Philosophers to this day speak of the search for "The Good," usually meaning not a divine existence but the ultimate, chief, and unifying good for human existence. To search for The Good must at least imply that some good is primary, ultimate, and either determines or hierarchically integrates all other intrinsically good things.

Some have taken this value pluralism, this denial of the unity of the good, to mean that there are no objective values, and no rational way to adjudicate them. This, we have shown, is *false*. The bird is supposed to have two wings, water is savior to a thirsty man, infants ought to be cared for, social relations should obey moral rules, political decisions should be legitimate and just, artworks should be aesthetically compelling. Certainly there are differing views and judgments of each, but the central problem is the adjudication *among* these values. The point of Weber and Berlin is that in a modern society the value spheres are not reducible to a common currency, not decidable by a rational method of query we can all agree, not resolvable into valid hierarchy of values regarding which anyone who disagrees can be called "irrational." That leaves us with a pluralism of unifunctional approaches each of which yields fairly reliable results, as long as we remain unifunctional. But the polytheistic values are in conflict, and there is no rational way to discover their meeting point or ultimate source.

Now we see why it is indeed easier rationally to agree on what is true in inquiry than what is valuable or good overall: because inquiry is one process with one norm. That was why "facts," however hard to know and however much our knowledge of them changes, do not involve decisions among options devoid of a rational solution. Likewise, if we ask which production method yields the highest volume of a product at lowest cost, we have a rational solution; or if we ask what social policy yields the greatest aggregate happiness in a specific time frame. But once we ask the broader questions as to *what is good*, which can incorporate multiple values, we moderns engage problems our unifunctional institutions and Weberian manners of query cannot by themselves resolve.

Omnivalence and the Decline of Axial Reason

Pluralism of values is in fact not novel. What makes us human is in part our responsibility and sensitivity to a variety of norms. The norms have distinctive characters. All human societies debate and adjudicate these plural values, and make choices. But the judgments which adjudicate or order the norms of judgment must be *omnivalent*. Omnivalence, we saw, is the name for failing to recognize the independence of the norms of judgment and query, or what is the same thing, evaluating truth, success, ethical or political rightness or aesthetic validity indifferently as "good." One may say omnivalence is the common context for human judgment, that segregation of the functions of judgment is the exception. Inevitably we live omnivalently. We routinely shift between using the unifunctional and the multifunctional, between established institutional methods with separated modes of judgment and throwing everything together into the soup pot to see how it tastes. We must "reasonably" weight different norms and values for which there is no method of comparison other than thought and discussion. Reason is, I suggested, methodical meta-judgment, the way a society methodically adjudicates among conflicting judgments of any or all modes. "Rational" means consistent or coherent, and applies differently to each mode of judgment. In situations of omnivalence humans cannot restrict considerations to rational considerations of evidence for a claim, or comparing acts by their outcomes, or finding the most aesthetically compelling construction. That is, the method of inquiry, or the active methods of conforming action to prior rules or experimentation with moral limits, or the gradual construction of a work of art through multiple drawings or drafts, have to be combined, yielding a result that is called "good" or "best" but which may not the most true, most ethical, most efficient, or most beautiful.

We suggested in chapter 9 that the three great epochs of *Homo sapiens* existence on Earth—the hunter-gatherer, the agro-literate, and the modern-industrial—employ different versions of methodical meta-judgment, or reason. In Durkheimian reason, ordinary omnivalence was the norm, by which I mean that no hard and fast distinctions between the norms of query were made. The true, the good or right, the beautiful, and the successful were intertwined, and all deeply social. Durkheimian peoples were entirely competent to distinguish between the ritual to increase fertility and the actual results. But their basic mode of rationality operated by citing exemplars of the best and worst, by analogical thinking. They deployed a holistic set of considerations, without a logical hierarchy, ranging over plural saliences and narrative exemplars, which they could only do because it took place in a simplified and unified form of society. On the normative continuance of society, the facts, obeisance to authority, and aesthetic value of ritual had an equal claim.

Axial civilization created a new forms of methodical meta-judgment, like volcanic islands growing in the omnivalent sea. Certain zones of unifunctional judgment were carved out, at least for upland elites. Each of these gave a structured path of judgments leading to a goal and validated by one norm separate from the others. Durkheimian reasoning was not destroyed by hierarchical, transcendent logic in the Axial Age, but it was supplanted. The folk cultures of commoners remained largely Durkheimian, albeit bowing to the truth, rightness, and beauty dictated by the cultural and political center. Elites were particularly capable of violating omnivalence—of tactical reasoning about engineering and military projects, and a clarified written process of reasoning regarding the doctrines of religion and their interface with political and economic power. What we call foundationalism, logic, law, science, and engineering all involved such precisely stated, doctrinally formulated, written, standards for argument. The morally right, the true, the successful and powerful, the aesthetically compelling became distinguishable.

Yet integrated. For axial civilization possessed for personal, public, and even official purposes a transcendent Go(o)d or the Divine that integrated all values. Axial rationality affirmed the logical and rational transcendence of a norms that were merged in God. The Hebrew Prophets Isaiah and

Jeremiah, the Persian Zoroaster, the authors of the Hindu Upanishads, the Buddha, Confucius, Lao-Tzu, and the Hellenic Greek philosophers, followed later by Christians and Muslims, all affirmed a transcendent standard that was the Ideal fulcrum of Real. That ideal provided the source, justification, and fulfillment of the unity and hierarchy of values. The good, the true, the beautiful, and the powerful may not have been identical. But they lived at the same address.

This was destroyed by Weberian modernity and its unifunctionality. There is no longer any single, multifunctional source of social legitimation, which combines truth, ethical and political right, and aesthetic value that is publicly effective. Those are now separate pursuits. The sea has risen, isolating the upland norms of Axial civilization. This leaves us with a counter-intuitive conclusion: the end of the Axial Age has left us a modernity which oddly resembles the Durkheimian Age.

I do not mean we live like hunter-gatherers. I mean that as hunter-gatherers were pre-Axial, we are post-Axial, hence jointly *non-Axial*. The loss of the transcendent—which thinkers have been bemoaning or celebrating since the late nineteenth century, but came to be embodied in mass society and culture only after the Second World War—is simultaneously the loss of public multifunctional normativity. The rejection of philosophical foundationalism is part of this. What some calling themselves "postmodernists" claimed was the loss of "metanarrative," that is, the loss of a socially functional, rationally validatable world view which judges both reality and values, was in fact the loss of Axial Reason (Lyotard 1984). The rationality of each norm or value is decontextualized, meaning absence of communal certainties that could hierarchically relate and integrate the various goods. Individuals can of course seek The Good, and reaffirm the transcendent, but modern society cannot organize itself that way. Our Weberian reason is not a return to the undifferentiated Durkheimian reason of the hunter-gatherers, for each value now has its own unifunctional methods and norms. However, like the hunter-gatherers, our methodical meta-judgment cannot claim to order our values by a rational method which captures The Good or God or the Divine.

In his 1981 *After Virtue*, MacIntyre argued that the modern world has only fragments of earlier traditions, as if after a cultural collapse. It is the cultures of Axial civilizations that he saw were fragmented in modernity, demoted to options, modes of query, among which individuals and societies may sample. But this is the result of *progress, not collapse*. For progress is unifunctional, proceeding by the exclusion of extraneous values from each of our major institutions: economic, political, artistic, scientific, and so on. However much the individuals who move among these institutions take omnivalent decisions about their own lives, within each institution they must think and behave accordingly.

The Spiritual, the Existential

There is a final dimension of human valuing that we have only rarely touched on in this work because it is intrinsically and obviously omnivalent. It is populated by the questions: What is the chief or highest Good? What is the purpose of human living? What is the sense and significance of human existence? What ultimate source or existence can provide the anchor for such values, the perspective in terms of which the highest can be judged? Such questions seek one context applicable to all judgment in human and social life, in which to answer which good or norm is ultimate and determinative for all contexts. The question, "How then shall we live?" is not a moral one. Nor is it political. Nor is it aesthetic.

There is a common name for these questions: *spiritual*. "Spiritual" is a loaded term; it seems to imply the existence of spirits, and that we are them. It is sometimes a watered-down notion of "religious." Religion is the great traditional representative of omnivalence, as noted. Not because God is "transcendent" or the creator but because God is the repository, the beginning and end, of all ideals, of the highest values, hence of truth, goodness, justice, and beauty. Whether in the form of a philosophical Good or One, a personal Lawgiving Creator God, an impersonal pantheism of Brahma and its Dharma, a divine process from which all emerge under the Mandate of Heaven, in each case this is a transcendent conception of the sacred along with a need for salvation, calling the individual to confess fealty to or harmonize with the Ideal.

But the role of spiritual or religious judgments in deciding The Good, the highest purpose, the fulcrum of value judgment, could just as well be called *existential* after the work of twentieth-century Existentialist philosophers such as Heidegger, Sartre, Camus, and De Beauvoir. They respected the question but denied that it could be answered by rational inquiry, society, religion, or nature. Surely, the two terms differ in emphasis. "Spiritual" implies the agent is sensitive or attuned to something beyond itself and the human community; "existential" emphasizes the individual's choice or will. But they operate in the same omnivalent dimension of judgment. Each seeks a judgment in terms of which all others are to be understood. In spiritual or religious conversation, that judgment is faith, in existentialist parlance, it is decision. The difference is significant but not in terms of the present discussion. In either case it is an omnivalent judgment serving to orient the agent with respect to the one most relevant context for other judgments.

The spiritual or existential is not in itself moral, aesthetic, ethical, or political, although it may affirm the primacy of any of these. So any attempt at judging the unity of The Good, at an objective purpose or meaning of human life, cannot be a question of inquiry or of ethics or politics or art. It is spiritual or existential. The natural question for a philosopher to ask is, can there be objectively valid, that is, rational, answers to such questions? Can philosophy as inquiry come rationally to judge that one or a few answers to such questions are valid, while others are false?

Here we have a simple answer. To the extent that rational inquiry is understood unifunctionally, in the modern Weberian way, the answer is *No*. There are many goods, many purposes for a life to serve. There is surely no dearth of meanings for a human life. But to ask for "the" meaning, the right or true or best meaning, is either a choice or decision, in the existentialist language, or an attunement or acceptance, in the spiritual vocabulary. The function is the same. We cannot unlearn Weberian rationality, go back to Axial or even Durkheimian rationality, and still claim to accept the fruits of the former, to function in a unifunctional fashion in most of our lives.

So where does this leave us? We can as individuals affirm and exhibit an omnivalent normative reference with respect to which all social contexts gain their ordered relative priority—that is, existential decision and spiritual affirmation are always possible. It is just that we no longer have an objective, generally shared, rationally validatable way of doing this. This feels like a "problem," and in a sense it is. Paraphrasing William James, we are on a ledge in the mountains in the midst of blinding snow, with glimpses now and then of different paths ahead, and we must make a choice (James 2011). But if so, it is a problem that is the unique capacity of humans to confront. We must use all our wits, all our affective and cognitive sensitivity, and our will, to come to our conclusion. That there is no unifunctional method which reliably assures us of the best choice does not mean either that every choice is as good as every other, nor that the choice does not matter.

What then does ordinal naturalism, the approach of this book, contribute to this question, if anything? Surely not a "solution," whatever that might mean. But it does imply two things.

First, whatever values or norms are asserted in spiritual or existential judgment, whatever omnivalence is recognized or affirmed, they will presume *social reproduction of Homo sapiens on Earth*. The continuation of human societies, with the features of our planet on which we depend, is presumed. What we know to be valuable is life on Earth, and human social life, with its cultural creations. Social reproduction, the maintenance of human societies, is required—with that goes whatever is necessary to that maintenance. Nothing about this context means one cannot critique and reform society. Indeed, one could reject it, but that would mean rejecting virtually all that is good along with all that is bad, which cannot make sense. All the norms we have considered, and others we have not, presuppose the continuation of human societies. That continuation is a good on which most others depend.

Second, and less obvious: objective relativism dictates that, whatever the validity of the various forms of methodic query we engage in is *not* dependent on the Highest Good. The absence of an Axial justification does not undermine the validity of what is attained in the multiple spheres of query and method. It has been the thrust of the objective relativism and fallibilism of this book that the local is not de-legitimated by the absence of the deepest or widest context of justification. That is true here as well. The rationality and validity of judgments in the truth-functional, the moral, the efficacious, the political, and the aesthetic value spheres do not require an omnivalent justification and are not undermined by the absence of one. Judgments made in response to the omnivalent questions above—How then shall we live? What is the meaning or purpose of life? What is the highest good?—can augment the robust judgments of those spheres, add to them, can change the interpretation of them, but do not save them from invalidity.

The achievements of modernity are undeniable and overwhelming. Anyone who honors those achievements—and anybody who lives in modern institutions does so at least practically—must accept that the existential or spiritual do not and cannot replace the differentiation of the modes of judgment and their relevant institutional expressions. The existential-spiritual can only supplement, not override. The validity of a spiritual or existential judgment of the Highest Good or the main purpose in life, however it might be determined, does not occlude or cancel the validity of aesthetic judgment, assertive judgment, political judgment, or ethical judgment. It is additional. Perhaps it is emergent, meaning it depends on and extends, reintegrates them into a further dimension.

If so, then the spiritual (or the existential) need not be, as Weber thought, a "sacrifice of the intellect." Nor is the search for meaning and purpose thereby doomed; it is just incomplete and fallible. In virtually all societies in history, Durkheimian or Axial, the meaning or purpose of a human life was almost never in doubt. So while there is today no foundational answer, no noncircular justification of our particular versions of our four norms that can be presented by inquiry, and no omnivalent source we can rationally determine that embraces and justifies them all, we can however improve our application of each of these values, and seek goods that supplement but do not found or undermine them. We can maximize human goods while continuing the fallible search for The Good.

In this sense, MacIntyre was very close to being right when he declared that the good life for man is the life of seeking for the good life for man.[4] All that was needed is the clarification that this is not the moral or ethical good life but the *spiritual or existential good* life. The good life for human being is the life seeking for the best life for a human being, and that is more than ethical. MacIntyre's dictum captures, not the moral life, but the form of query that is, or supports, the spiritual life. The search for The Good or the highest of all goods is, as far as we can tell, never ending. The moral life, the aesthetic life, the search for truth, and the political life preserve and better human existence thereby permitting more individuals to search for The Good.

Alone among creatures, human generations do not start over at zero. We are historical. New forms of social institutions and human experience evolve over time. Inquiry, including philosophical inquiry, can only work with what has arisen thus far, apparent in this tiny corner of the universe. A mere three centuries ago, no one had any reliable inkling that humans arose from nonhumans, that we could defeat the Malthusian fate of all earlier peoples, that the universe itself evolved, that humans of all races were indifferently capable of high culture, that humans of all social classes could find a way to legal equality and cooperate in self-rule, that most newborns could reliably outlive their parents. Learning matters to value decisions. Since the conditions of human existence keep changing, it is not surprising that the search for the clarification and harmonizing of human norms remains, as our past is rolled into an unknown future.

We have arrived. Where? Not at an end, nor a final destination. Just a rise, a bench in the hills, from which the muddled traffic behind looks more manageable, from which other more passable routes can be seen. A place from which the next leg of the journey can start tomorrow.

Notes

Introduction

1. Donald Campbell, "Evolutionary Epistemology," 438–39.
2. One recent example is Crispin Sartwell's 2017.
3. Charles Sanders Peirce, *Collected Papers of Charles Sanders Peirce, Volumes One and Two: Principles of Philosophy and Elements of Logic*, Preface, 1.10.

Chapter One

1. Max Weber, "Science as a Vocation," 17.
2. Steven Weinberg, *The First Three Minutes: A Modern View of the Origin of the Universe*, 149.
3. Jean-Paul Sartre, *Nausea*, 127–28, 133–34, 156.
4. Bertrand Russell, "A Free Man's Worship," 46–47.
5. Friedrich Nietzsche, *Beyond Good and Evil: Prelude to a Philosophy of the Future*, Book I, sec. 9, 10.
6. John Stuart Mill, "Nature," 28–29.
7. David Hume, *Treatise on Human Nature*, 3.1.1.
8. G. E. Moore *Principia Ethica*, 7.
9. Moore, *Principia Ethica*, 8–9.
10. Moore, *Principia Ethica*, 10.
11. Michael Ruse, "Evolution and the Naturalistic Fallacy," 96–116.
12. Max Weber, "Objectivity in Social Science and Social Policy"; "The Meaning of Ethical Neutrality in Sociology and Economics"; "Science as a Vocation."
13. Lawrence Cahoone, *Cultural Revolutions: Reason versus Culture in Philosophy, Politics and Jihad*, ch. 7.

14. This concept was originally suggested by Philippa Foot (1958) and later taken up by Bernard Williams (1985).

15. Weber, "Science as a Vocation," 27.

Chapter Two

1. Morris Cohen, "The Distinction between the Mental and the Physical," 267.
2. Hilary Putnam, *Reason, Truth, and History*, 167–68.
3. John Passmore, *One Hundred Years of Philosophy*, 174.
4. Bertrand Russell, *The Analysis of Mind*, 5.
5. Passmore, *One Hundred Years of Philosophy*, 258.
6. Arthur O. Lovejoy, *The Revolt against Dualism*, 1; John Herman Randall, "Epilogue: The Nature of Naturalism," in Krikorian, *Naturalism and the Human Spirit*, 367.
7. Ernst Mach, *Contributions to the Analysis of Sensations*, 10–16.
8. Russell, "On the Nature of Acquaintance: II. Neutral Monism." See also John Ongley and Rosalind Carey, *Russell: A Guide for the Perplexed*, and Eric Banks, *The Realistic Empiricism of Mach, James, and Russell*.
9. E. B. Holt, *The New Realism*, 372. One other thinker taking a similar perspective was Evander McGilvary (1933, 1977). It is interesting to note that J. J. Gibson (1979) was a student of Holt's; see Heft, *Ecological Psychology in Context: James Gibson, Roger Barker, and the Legacy of William James*. Thanks to Elizabeth Baeten for this.
10. Lawrence Cahoone, "The Metaphysics of Morris. R. Cohen."
11. Morris Cohen, "Qualities, Relations, and Things," 620–22.
12. Morris Cohen, "The Distinction between the Mental and the Physical," 266–677; my emphasis.
13. Montague would later, and independently, name Holt's position "relativist objectivism." W. P. Montague, "The Story of American Realism," 151.
14. One other neglected figure who came to a similar view independently was Evander McGilvary, with his "perspective realism" (McGilvary 1933, 1977).
15. Arthur E. Murphy, "Objective Relativism in Whitehead and Dewey," 122.
16. Charles Morris, *Six Theories of Mind* and *The Pragmatic Movement in American Philosophy*.
17. Ernest Nagel, "Philosophy and the American Temper," 52ff.
18. Justus Buchler, *Metaphysics of Natural Complexes*.
19. William James, *A Pluralistic Universe*, 34; Morris Cohen, *Reason and Nature*, 152–53; Randall, *Nature and Historical Experience*, 130.
20. Thomas Nagel, *The View from Nowhere*, New York: Oxford, 1986.
21. Buchler, 1990, 32ff.

22. Ernest Nagel, "Philosophy and the American Temper," 53–56.

23. Thus it satisfies the "*tu quoque*" critique described by W. W. Bartley in his "comprehensively critical rationalism." W. W. Bartley, *The Retreat to Commitment*, 118ff.

24. Charles S. Peirce, "Some Consequences of Four Incapacities," in Buchler, *Philosophical Writings of Peirce*, 229.

25. Yuval Dolev, *Time and Realism: Metaphysical and Antimetaphysical Perspectives*.

26. Charles S. Peirce, *Collected Papers of Charles Sanders Peirce, Volumes One and Two*, 1.248.

27. Cohen, "Qualities, Relations, and Things," 617–27.

Chapter Three

1. Karl Popper, "Natural Selection and the Emergence of Mind," 142–43.

2. Beth Singer, *Ordinal Naturalism: An Introduction to the Philosophy of Justus Buchler* 1983. The only applications of Buchler's views to a physicalist or natural science context are Stanley Salthe (1985), John Ryder (1990), and Cahoone (2013a).

3. George Henry Lewes, *Problems of Life and Mind*, 412; Samuel Alexander, *Space, Time and Deity*; Conwy Lloyd Morgan, *Emergent Evolution*; and C. D. Broad, *The Mind and its Place in Nature*. Among the North Americans it was adopted by Mead, his colleague Morris, and Roy Wood Sellars. See also David Blitz, *Emergent Evolution: Qualitative Novelty and the Levels of Reality*.

4. See Mark Bedau and Paul Humphreys, *Emergence: Contemporary Readings in Philosophy and Science*; Ansgar Beckerman, Hans Flohr, and Jaegwon Kim, *Emergence or Reduction? Essays on the Prospects of Nonreductive Physicalism*; Cahoone, *The Orders of Nature*.

5. Wimsatt, *Re-Engineering Philosophy for Limited Beings: Piecewise Approximations to Reality*, 275–87.

6. Ibid., 218.

7. Ibid., 249.

8. Ibid., 203–4, his emphasis.

9. More precisely, the physical is the smallest components (quantum theory), widest environments (general relativity, cosmology), and most general processes (thermodynamics) of spacetime-energetic systems (Cahoone 2013b).

10. This was Buchler's most central metaphysical term, now understood differently.

11. Or *Homo sapiens sapiens*, our species of Homo which arose approximately 250,000 years ago.

12. Richard Feynman, *The Character of Physical Law*, 125–26.

Chapter Four

1. Lazlo Tisza, quoted by Abner Shimony, "Some Proposals Concerning Parts and Wholes," 224.
2. Willis Ellis. *Sourcebook in Gestalt Psychology*, 25.
3. Jacob Von Uexküll, *A Foray into the World of Animals and Man*.
4. Ibid., 48.
5. Jacob Von Uexküll, *A Theory of Meaning*, 151.
6. Maurice Merleau-Ponty, *The Structure of Behavior*, 125.
7. Ibid., 210.
8. Maurice Merleu-Ponty, *Nature: Course Notes from the College de France*, 116.
9. Ibid., 173.
10. Hans Jonas, *The Phenomenon of Life*, 79, 83.
11. Ibid., 4.
12. Ibid., 126.
13. John Dewey and Arthur F. Bentley, *John Dewey and Arthur F. Bentley: A Philosophical Correspondence, 1932–1951*, 403, 426–27.
14. David Blitz, *Emergent Evolution*, 114.
15. Conwy Lloyd Morgan, *Spencer's Philosophy of Science*, 28–29.
16. George Herbert Mead, *Mind, Self, and Society: Psychology from the Standpoint of a Social Behaviorist*, 239.
17. Ibid., 198.
18. Mead, *Philosophy of the Present*, 63–64.
19. Mead, *Philosophy of the Act*, 641. Mead and his student Morris are the only philosophers who combined objective relativism and emergence, unless one includes Joseph Margolis.
20. Asa Gray, "Scientific Worthies," 81.
21. Frances Darwin, *The Life and Letters of Charles Darwin*, volume II, 308.
22. Jacques Monod, *Chance and Necessity*, 80.
23. Monod, *Chance and Necessity*, 14ff.
24. Colin Pittendrigh, "Adaptation, Natural Selection, and Behavior."
25. Ernst Mayr, "Teleological and Teleonomic: A New Analysis."
26. Ernst Mayr, *The Growth of Biological Knowledge: Diversity, Evolution and Inheritance*, 633–76.
27. Wimsatt, 32 ff.
28. Ibid., 12.
29. Ibid., 66–67.
30. Rolston, "Are Values in Nature Subjective or Objective?" 141.
31. Ibid., 150.
32. There seems to be evidence that selection is, as Darwin thought, "multi-level," and that sometimes the phenotypic properties that are selected *for* are social

or group-relational properties and not solely individual properties, even if the unit thereby selected is an individual's genotype. But it may be rare.

Chapter Five

1. José Ortega y Gasset, *Meditations on Hunting*, 88.
2. Tyler Burge, *Origins of Objectivity*, 314.
3. Ibid., 311.
4. Antonio Damasio, *Looking for Spinoza*, 36.
5. See Sperry, "A Modified Concept of Consciousness" and "Mental Phenomena as Causal Determinants in Brain Function"; Wimsatt, "Reductionism, Levels of Organization, and the Mind–Body Problem"; and Bechtel et al., "Bill Wimsatt on Multiple Ways of Getting at the Complexity of Nature."
6. Nicholas Humphrey, *Seeing Red: A Study in Consciousness*.
7. In defending externalism, Putnam famously declared about human minds that "meanings just ain't in the head." To be sure, the "meaning" of a mental state isn't an entity that is "in" anything. But without heads, or brains, *there ain't no meanings neither*. See Hilary Putnam, "The Meaning of 'Meaning.'"
8. Damasio's view is not equivalent to Paul MacLean's division of the "reptilian," "paleomamalian," and "neomamalian" layers of the human brain; see Paul MacLean, *The Triune Brain in Evolution: Role in Paleocerebral Functions*.
9. Fred Dretske, *Explaining Behavior: Reasons in a World of Causes*, 44ff.
10. Jaak Panksepp, "Review of Antonio Damasio, *Looking for Spinoza*," 122.
11. J. J. Gibson, The ecological approach to visual perception, 1979. Note that Gibson was a student of E. B. Holt, the American "New Realist."
12. Valerius Geist, *Life Strategies, Human Evolution, Environmental Design: Toward a Biological Theory of Health*.

Chapter Six

1. James Stockdale, *A Vietnam Experience: Ten Years of Reflection*, 32.
2. "Hominin" refers to our ourselves and our bipedal ancestors; "hominid" refers to all great apes.
3. George Herbert Mead, *Mind, Self, and Society*, 44.
4. Frans de Waal, *Good Natured: The Origins of Right and Wrong in Humans and Other Animals*; Raimo Tuomela, *The Philosophy of Sociality: The Shared Point of View*; and Michael Tomasello, *A Natural History of Human Thinking*.
5. To be distinguished from the more specific feeling bad for another's distress (sympathy), emotional contagion, and other phenomena (Stueber 2019).

6. Ibid., 73.

7. Mary Warnock, *Imagination*, 171.

8. One issue here is the ability to attribute false beliefs to another—that is, to attribute to them a perspective that is contrary to what you know to be true—which human children develop only around four years of age.

9. This diagram is inspired by the diagram of Peter Hobson, *The Cradle of Thought: Exploring the Origins of Thinking*.

10. Just to remind: it is not required to be a "self" to be something of value. To think otherwise is a kind of narcissism. The *Guernica*, the Grand Tetons, and the biosphere must be preserved but not because they are "like me."

11. Thomas Suddendorf, *The Gap: The Science of What Separates Us from Other Animals*, 54.

12. Ibid., 85.

13. Mead, *Mind, Self, and Society*, 135.

14. Helen Keller, *The Story of My Life*, 36–37. This same passage was explored in 1964 by Heinz Werner and Bernard Kaplan, *Symbol Formation: An Organismic Developmental Approach to Language and the Development of Thought*, 110–11.

15. Ernest Gellner, *Plough, Sword, and Book: The Structure of Human History*, 37.

16. Benjamin Libet "Unconscious Cerebral Initiative and the Role of Conscious Will in Voluntary Action," 529–66.

17. John Locke, *An Essay Concerning Human Understanding*, Book 2, chap. 2, sec. 14.

18. Daniel Dennett, *Freedom Evolves*, 242. Dennett's point is really about time, or process, in the same way that Bergson's analysis of process rejects Zeno's "paradoxes." If time could occur as infinitesimally brief moments (like points on a geometrical line), no process could ever begin and end.

19. Benjamin Libet, "Do We Have Free Will?," 47–57.

20. Max Velmans, "Preconscious Free Will," 42–61.

21. Antonio Damasio, *Self Comes to Mind*, 269.

22. Mary Midgley, *The Ethical Primate: Humans, Freedom, Morality*, 168.

Chapter Seven

1. Marjorie Grene, *A Philosophical Testament*, 47.

2. Konrad Lorenz, "Kant's Doctrine of the A Priori in the Light of Contemporary Biology," 186–87.

3. Donald Campbell, "Pattern Matching as an Essential in Distant Knowing," 54.

4. Ibid., 170.

5. Ibid., 172.

6. Donald Campbell, "Neurological Embodiments of Beliefs and the Gaps in the Fit of Phenomena to Noumena," 183.

7. W. V. O. Quine, "Epistemology Naturalized," 126–27.

8. This figure is based on a figure from Robert Brandom's excellent "Study Guide," appended to the 1997 edition of Sellars's book *Empiricism and the Philosophy of Mind*, 126.

9. Hilary Putnam, *Reason, Truth, and History* 1981, chap. 3.

10. Hilary Putnam and Ruth Anna Putnam, "What the Spilled Beans Can Spell," 161.

11. Hilary Putnam, "Naturalism, Realism, and Normativity," 24.

12. Putnam, "Naturalism, Realism, and Normativity," 325.

Chapter Eight

1. Ernest Gellner, *Plough, Sword, and Book: The Structure of Human History*, 51.
2. Justus Buchler, *Nature and Judgment*, 32.
3. Justus Buchler, *Toward a General Theory of Human Judgment*, 141.
4. Justus Buchler, *The Main of Light: On the Concept of Poetry*, 101.
5. J. L. Austin, *How to Do Things with Words*.
6. Hanna Arendt, *The Human Condition*.
7. Buchler, *The Main of Light: On the Concept of Poetry*, 1974.

Chapter Nine

1. Edward Shils, *Tradition*, 316.

2. M. G. Smith, "On Segmentary Lineage Systems," 1956. See also Emile Durkheim, 1933, volume 1, chapter 6, 175ff.

3. Paul Shepard, *The Tender Carnivore and the Sacred Game*, 1973.

4. Ernest Gellner, *Plough, Sword, and Book: The Structure of Human History*, 51.

5. Cahoone, *Cultural Revolutions: Reason versus Culture in Philosophy, Modernity, and Jihad*, 38–55.

6. The coincidence of the fall of Constantinople to the Ottomans (1453), the Gutenberg Bible (1454), the Moscow Rus defeat of the Golden Horde (1480), final Reconquista of northern Spain from the Muslims (1492), the Portuguese/Spanish voyages of discovery (1419–1519), the high Italian Renaissance (1450–1520), and the looming Reformation (1516) makes 1500 CE a convenient place to start.

7. Jürgen Habermas, *Theory of Communicative Action*.

8. Habermas's objective certainly had another aim quite different from the current project; he wanted to show that the "mediatized" money and bureaucracy

system comes to dominate and exclude other aspects of the lifeworld, like constative discourse aimed at achieving understanding—the basis of democracy—from power. Doubtless this is partly true, although my analysis of it would be different (Cahoone 2006).

    9. Peter Berger, Brigitte Berger, and Hansfried Kellner, *The Homeless Mind: Modernization and Consciousness*.

    10. Max Weber, "Science as a Vocation," 13.

    11. Niklas Luhmann, *The Differentiation of Society*, 238.

Chapter Ten

    1. Erazim Kohák, *The Embers and the Stars: A Philosophical Inquiry into the Moral Sense of Nature*, 62.

    2. Charles Darwin, *The Descent of Man and Selection in Relation to Sex*, 88.

    3. Mary Midgley, *The Ethical Primate*, 178–79.

    4. Haidt adopts a multilevel selection theory, meaning he accepts "group" as one of the units natural selection can work on, not only the gene or the individual. This is a long controversy. The current consensus seems to be that group selection is possible but happens only in extraordinary circumstances, for example in highly homogeneous groups in some direct competition or clash, where the high-cooperation heredities of one group can make the low-cooperation heredities of the other group essentially disappear. There being other ways of explaining the intragroup success of cooperative individuals over time without group selection, we need not debate this here.

    5. David Ross, *The Right and the Good*.

    6. Mary Douglas, *Purity and Danger*, 36.

    7. Robert Wright, *The Moral Animal*, 160.

    8. John Rawls, *A Theory of Justice*, 96.

Chapter Eleven

    1. Henry Sheffer, "Review of *Prinicipia Mathematica*," 228.

    2. Morris R. Cohen, *A Preface to Logic*, 7.

    3. Morris R. Cohen, "The Subject Matter of Formal Logic," 682.

    4. Morris R. Cohen, "Qualities, Relations, and Things," 620–22.

    5. Morris R. Cohen, "The Distinction between the Mental and the Physical," 266.

    6. Morris R. Cohen and Ernest Nagel, *An Introduction to Logic and Scientific Method*, 185–86.

7. David Hollinger, *Morris Cohen and the Scientific Ideal*, 124.
8. Ernest Nagel, *Logic without Metaphysics*, xii–xiii.
9. Ernest Nagel, "Logic without Ontology," 217.
10. Ernest Nagel, "In Defense of Logic without Metaphysics," *The Philosophical Review*, 34.
11. Justus Buchler, *Nature and Judgment*, 128.
12. Justus Buchler, *Towards a General Theory of Human Judgment*, 69–70.
13. Justus Buchler, *Metaphysics of Natural Complexes*, 139.
14. Aristotle, *Metaphysics*, IV.7.1011b25.
15. Hilary Putnam, "A Comparison of Something with Something Else," 64. See also Putnam, "Does Disquotationalism Really Solve All Philosophical Problems?," 8.
16. Cheryl Misak, *The American Pragmatists*, 247–48.
17. Paraphrasing Russell, the Axiom of Choice allows us to treat sets like shoes and not socks: given an infinite number of pairs of shoes, we can form another infinite subset by choosing the left shoe from each pair.
18. Penelope Maddy, *Second Philosophy: A Naturalistic Method*, 226.
19. Russell, "The Study of Mathematics," 69.
20. Ludwig Wittgenstein, *Tractatus Logico-Philosophicus*, paragraph 2.0121.
21. Andrea Borghini, *An Introduction to the Metaphysics of Modality*, 172.
22. Henry Sheffer, "Review of A. N. Whitehead and B. Russell *Principia Mathematica*," 228.
23. Nagel, "In Defense of Logic without Metaphysics," 31.
24. F. P. Ramsey, "General Propositions and Causality," in *The Foundations of Mathematics and Other Essays*, 238.

Chapter Twelve

1. Bernard Williams, *Ethics and Limits of Philosophy*, 194.
2. I thank Daniel A. Kaufman for pointing out the Anscombe connection.
3. R. M. Hare, "Universalizability," 301.
4. J. J. C. Smart, "Defending Utilitarianism," 202–9. Actually borrowed from H. J. McCloskey, 599.
5. R. M. Hare, *Moral Thinking: Its Methods, Levels, and Point*, 164.
6. Ibid., 43.
7. R. M. Hare, *The Language of Morals*, 75–77.
8. Ibid., 129–30.
9. Hare, *Moral Thinking: Its Methods, Levels, and Point*, 192–93.
10. Ibid., 100ff.
11. R. M. Hare, "Could Kant Have Been a Utilitarian?," 127.
12. Bernard Williams, *Ethics and the Limits of Philosophy*, 1.

Chapter Thirteen

1. Czeslaw Milosz, *The Captive Mind*.
2. Max Weber, "Politics as a Vocation," 33.
3. Fukuyama's masterful *The Origins of Political Order* uses a Weberian notion of "state" that is rather modern—excluding patrimonialism, requiring cultural unity and complete territorial control. It seems to imply that ancient Egypt, Rome, the Mongolian Empire, and feudal polities can't be "states." Given the usual distinction of bands, tribes, chiefdoms, and states, I think they are states, just not "modern" (Fukuyama 2011).
4. Weber, "Politics as a Vocation," 83.
5. Edward Shils, *Tradition*, 316.
6. Voltaire, *Philosophical Dictionary*, vol. VI, part 4, "Presbyterian."
7. Liah Greenfeld, *Nationalism: Five Roads to Modernity*, 10.
8. Michael Walzer, *Spheres of Justice*, 37–39.
9. Edward Shils, *The Virtue of Civility: Selected Essays on Liberalism, Tradition, and Civil Society*, 51.
10. Shils, *The Virtue of Civility*, 49.
11. Michael Walzer, *Spheres of Justice*, 314.
12. Arthur Schlesinger, "National Interests and Moral Absolutes," 24.
13. Hans Morgenthau, *Scientific Man versus Power Politics*, 214.
14. Weber, "Politics as a Vocation," 93.
15. Michael Walzer, "The Problem of Dirty Hands," 175.
16. Walzer, 162–63.
17. Michael Walzer, *Just and Unjust Wars: A Moral Argument with Historical Illustrations*, 305.
18. Walzer, *Just and Unjust Wars*, ch. 14. The example is actually Duke Hsiang of Sung.
19. Fukuyama, *The Origins of Political Order*, 481.

Chapter Fourteen

1. Valerius Geist, "Big Game in the City: The Other Side of the Coin," 20.
2. Immanuel Kant, *Critique of Judgment*, sec. 10, 55–56.
3. Although Kant does at one point allow that such applies to judgment of nature too (Kant sec. 51), as Guyer points out (2008).
4. Ibid., sec. 18, 73.
5. Ibid., sec. 9, 52.
6. Friedrich Schiller, *Letters on the Aesthetic Education of Man*, 80.
7. Huizinga borrowed the phrase of Romano Guardini, that play is "*zwecklos aber doch sinnvoll.*" Huizinga, *Homo Ludens: A Study in the Play Element in Culture*, 33.

8. John Dewey, *Art as Experience*, 55.
9. Pryba points out that Dewey ought to have used the notion of "emergence," as we will see Margolis does. But as noted earlier, other factors prevented him.
10. Dewey, *Art as Experience*, 254.
11. John Dewey, *Experience and Nature*, 357–58.
12. Susanne Langer, *Philosophy in a New Key*, 81.
13. I would warn against the tendency to try to read sign activity into biology and further. Like panpsychism, this is an attempt to avoid the emergence of novelty by reading mind into life or even the physical. Evolution—physical, chemical, and biological—matters.
14. Felicia Kruse, "Emotion in Musical Meaning: A Peircean Solution to Langer's Dualism," 773.
15. Buchler, *The Main of Light*, 101ff.
16. Ibid., 137–41.
17. Nelson Goodman, *Languages of Art: An Approach to a Theory of Symbols*, 85–86.
18. Arthur Danto, *Transfiguration of the Commonplace*, 5.
19. Most people ascribe the first expression to George Dickie, "Defining Art," July 1969, but Daniel A. Kaufman points to the same idea almost simultaneously in T. J. Diffey, "The Republic of Art," 145–56.
20. Arthur Danto, "My Life as a Philosopher," 54.
21. Arthur Danto, "The Artworld Revisited: Comedies of Similarity," 41.
22. Arthur Danto, "Embodied Meanings, Isotopes, and Aesthetical Ideas," 125.
23. Arthur Danto, *What Art Is*, 48.
24. Joseph Margolis, "Works of Art as Physically Embodied and Culturally Emergent Entities," 188.
25. Joseph Margolis, *Persons and Minds: The Prospects of Nonreductive Materialism*, 235–37.
26. Joseph Margolis, *What, After All, is a Work of Art?*, 98.
27. Joseph Margolis, "Farewell to Danto and Goodman," 374.
28. Arthur Danto, "Indiscernibility and Perception: A Reply to Joseph Margolis," 325, 329.
29. Danto, *Philosophical Disenfranchisement of Art*, 39.

Chapter Fifteen

1. Max Weber. "Science as a Vocation," 27.
2. Weber, "Science as a Vocation," 30–31.
3. Isaiah Berlin, "The Two Concepts of Liberty," 169.
4. Alasdair MacIntyre, *After Virtue: A Study in Moral Theory*, 219.

Works Cited

Ahl, Valerie, and T. F. H. Allen. 1996. *Hierarchy Theory: A Vision, Vocabulary, and Epistemology*. New York: Columbia University Press.
Alexander, Samuel. 1914. *The Basis of Realism: Proceedings of the British Academy*. London: Oxford University Press.
———. 1920. *Space, Time, and Deity*. London: Macmillan.
Allan, George. 2008. "Objective Relativism." *American Philosophy: An Encyclopedia*, ed. John Lachs and Robert Talisse. New York: Routledge.
Anderson, Benedict. 2016. *Imagined Communities: Reflections on the Origin and Spread of Nationalism*. New York: Verso.
Andrews, Kristen. 2020. *How to Study Animal Minds*. Cambridge, UK: Cambridge University.
Anscombe, G. E. M. 1958. "Modern Moral Philosophy." *Philosophy* 33.124 (January): 1–16.
Arendt, Hanna. 1958. *The Human Condition*. Chicago: University of Chicago Press.
Aristotle. 2012. *Aristotle's Nicomachean Ethics*. Trans. Robert Bartlett and Susan Collins. Chicago: University of Chicago Press.
———. 2013. *Politics*. Trans Carnes Lord. Chicago: University of Chicago Press.
Austin, John. 1995. *The Province of Jurisprudence Determined*. Cambridge: Cambridge University Press.
Austin, John L. 1962. *How to Do Things with Words*. Oxford: Oxford University Press.
Banks, Eric. 2014. *The Realistic Empiricism of Mach, James, and Russell*. Cambridge: Cambridge University Press.
Baeten, Elizabeth. 2012. "Another Defense of Naturalized Ethics." *Metaphilosophy* 43.5: 533–50.
———. 2014. "Steps Toward a Zoology of Mind." *Journal of Speculative Philosophy* 28.2: 107–29.
Barrow, John. 2002. *The Constants of Nature: From Alpha to Omega—The Numbers that Encode the Deepest Secrets of the Universe*. New York: Vintage.
Barrow, John, and Frank Tipler. 1986. *The Anthropic Cosmological Principle*. Oxford: Oxford University Press.

Bartley, W. W., III. 1984. *The Retreat to Commitment*. Chicago: Open Court.
Beardsley, Monroe C. 1970. "The Aesthetic Point of View." *Metaphilosophy* 1.1 (January): 39–58.
Bechtel, William, Werner Callebaut, James R. Griesemer, and Jeffrey C. Schank. 2006. "Bill Wimsatt on Multiple Ways of Getting at the Complexity of Nature." *Biological Theory* 1.2: 213–19.
Beckermann, Ansgar, Hans Flohr, and Jaegwon Kim. 1992. *Emergence or Reduction? Essays on the Prospects of Nonreductive Physicalism*. New York: Walter de Gruyter.
Bedau, Mark, and Paul Humphreys. 2008. *Emergence: Contemporary Readings in Philosophy and Science*. Cambridge, MA: MIT Press.
Berger, Peter, Brigitte Berger, and Hansfried Kellner. 1974. *The Homeless Mind: Modernization and Consciousness*. New York: Vintage.
Bergson, Henri. 1903/1912. *An Introduction to Metaphysics*. Trans. T. E. Hulme. New York: G. E. Putnam and Sons.
———. 1998. *Creative Evolution*. Trans. Arthur Mitchell. New York: Dover.
Berlin, Isaiah. 1970. "Two Concepts of Liberty." *Four Essays on Liberty*. New York: Oxford University Press. 118–72.
Bernstein, Eduard. 2012. *The Preconditions of Socialism*. Cambridge: Cambridge University Press.
Blitz, David. 1992. *Emergent Evolution: Qualitative Novelty and the Levels of Reality*. Dordrecht: Kluwer.
Boehm, Christopher. 1999. *Hierarchy in the Forest: The Evolution of Egalitarian Behavior*. Cambridge, MA: Harvard University Press.
Borghini, Andrea. 2016. *An Introduction to the Metaphysics of Modality*. London: Bloomsbury.
Bradley, Francis Herbert. 1988. "My Station and Its Duties." *Ethical Studies*. Oxford: Oxford University Press.
Brentano, Franz. 1995. *Psychology from an Empirical Standpoint*. Trans. Antos Rancurello, D. B. Terrell, and Linda McAlister. New York: Routledge.
Broad, Charles Dutton. 1925. *The Mind and Its Place in Nature*. London: Routledge, Kegan, Paul.
Buchanan, Brett. 2009. *Onto-Theologies: The Animal Environments of Uexküll, Heidegger, Merleau-Ponty, and Deleuze*. Albany, NY: SUNY Press.
Buchler, Justus. 1939. "Peirce's Theory of Logic." *Journal of Philosophy* 36.8 (April): 197–215.
———. 1951. *Toward a General Theory of Human Judgment*. New York: Dover.
———. 1955a. *Philosophical Writings of Peirce*. New York: Dover.
———. 1955b. *Nature and Judgment*. New York: Grosset and Dunlap.
———. 1974. *The Main of Light: On the Concept of Poetry*. Oxford: Oxford University Press.
———. 1989. "A Conversation between Justus Buchler and Robert S. Corrington," ed. Robert S. Corrington and Buchler, *The Journal of Speculative Philosophy* 3.4: 261–74.

———. 1990. *Metaphysics of Natural Complexes*. Ed. Kathleen Wallace, Armen Marsoobian, and Robert Corrington. Albany, NY: SUNY Press.
Burge, Tyler. 2010. *Origins of Objectivity*. Oxford: Oxford University Press.
Cahoone, Lawrence. 1989. "Buchler on Habermas on Modernity." *Southern Journal of Philosophy* 27.4: 461–77.
———. 2002. *Civil Society: The Conservative Meaning of Liberal Politics*. Cambridge, MA: Blackwell Publishers.
———. 2005. *Cultural Revolutions: Reason versus Culture in Philosophy, Politics and Jihad*. University Park, PA: Penn State Press.
———. 2013a. *The Orders of Nature*. Albany, NY: SUNY Press.
———. 2013b. "Physicalism, the Natural Sciences, and Naturalism." *Philo* 16.2 (Fall–Winter).
———. 2018. "Emergence and Animal Mind: Shrinking the Explanatory Gap," in *Nature Alive: Essays on the Emergence and Evolution of Living Agents*, ed. Adam Scarfe. Newcastle, UK: Cambridge Scholars Publishing. 161–76.
———. 2017. "The Metaphysics of Morris R. Cohen: From Realism to Objective Relativism," *Journal of History of Ideas* 78.3: 449–71.
———. 2016. "Is Stellar Nucleosynthesis a Good Thing?" *Environmental Ethics*, 38.4 (Winter): 421–39.
Campbell, Donald. 1985. "Pattern Matching as an Essential in Distal Knowing," in *Naturalizing Epistemology*, ed. Hillary Kornblith. Cambridge, MA: MIT Press. 49–70.
———. 1987. "Neurological Embodiments of Beliefs and the Gaps in the Fit of Phenomena to Noumena," in *Natural Epistemology: A Symposium of Two Decades*, ed. Abner Shimony and Debra Nails. Dordrecht: Reidel. 165–92.
———. 1988a. "Evolutionary Epistemology," in *Methodology and Epistemology for Social Science: Selected Papers*, ed. E. Samuel Overman. Chicago: University of Chicago Press. 393–434.
———. 1988b. "Descriptive Epistemology: Psychological, Sociological, and Evolutionary," in *Methodology and Epistemology for Social Science: Selected Papers*. 435–85.
Caneles, Jimena. 2016. *The Physicist and the Philosopher: Einstein, Bergson, and the Debate That Changed Our Understanding of Time*. Princeton, NJ: Princeton University Press.
Čapek, Milič. 1971. *Bergson and Modern Physics: A Re-interpretation and Re-evaluation*. Dordrecht: Reidel.
Carnap, Rudolf. 1950. "Empiricism, Semantics, and Ontology." *Revue Internationale de Philosophie* 4: 20–40.
Carter, Brendon. 1974. "Large Number Coincidences and the Anthropic Principle in Cosmology," *IAU Symposium 63: Confrontation of Cosmological Theories with Observational Data*. Dordrecht: Reidel. 291–98.
Cassirer, Ernst. 1953. *Language and Myth*. New York: Dover.

Chase, Philip. 1999 "Symbolism as Reference and Symbolism as Culture," in *The Evolution of Culture: A Historical and Scientific Overview*, ed. Robin Dunbar, Chris Knight, and Camilla Power. New Brunswick, NJ: Rutgers University Press. 34–49.

Church, Alonzo. 1945. Review of *Logic without Ontology*, by Ernest Nagel. *The Journal of Symbolic Logic* 10.1 (March): 16–18.

Cohen, Morris Raphael. 1914. "Qualities, Relations, and Things." *Journal of Philosophy, Psychology, and Scientific Methods* 11.23: 617–27.

———. 1917. "The Distinction between the Mental and the Physical." *Journal of Philosophy, Psychology, and Scientific Methods* 14.10: 261–67.

———. 1918. "The Subject Matter of Formal Logic." *Journal of Philosophy, Psychology, and Scientific Methods* 15.25 (December): 673–88.

———. 1923. "Preface" to *Chance, Love, and Logic: Philosophical Essays by the Late Charles S. Peirce, the Founder of Pragmatism*. New York: Barnes and Noble. iii–xxxiii.

———. 1931. "The Metaphysics of Reason and Scientific Method." Chapter 4 of *Reason and Nature: An Essay on the Meaning of Scientific Method*. New York: Dover Publications.

———. 1944. *A Preface to Logic*. New York: Dover Publications.

———. 1949. *Studies in Philosophy and Science*. New York: Henry Holt and Co.

Cohen, Morris R., and Ernest Nagel. 1934. *An Introduction to Logic and Scientific Method*. New York: Harcourt, Brace and Co.

Colapietro, Vincent. 1997. "Susanne Langer on Artistic Creativity and Creations." *Semiotics: Yearbook of the Semiotic Society of America*. 3–12.

Damasio, Antonio. 2000. *The Feeling of What Happens: Body and Emotion in the Making of Consciousness*. San Diego, CA: Harcourt Inc.

———. 2003. *Looking for Spinoza: Joy, Sorrow, and the Feeling Brain*. Boston: Mariner Books.

———. 2012. *Self Comes to Mind: Constructing the Conscious Brain*. New York: Vintage.

Danto, Arthur. 1964. "The Artworld." *American Philosophical Association Eastern Division Sixty-First Annual Meeting*, October 15. 571–84.

———. 1981. *Transfiguration of the Commonplace: A Philosophy of Art*. Cambridge, MA: Harvard University Press.

———. 1985. "The Philosophical Disenfranchisement of Art." *Grand Street* 4.3 (Spring 1985): 171–89.

———. 1986. *The Philosophical Disenfranchisement of Art*. New York: Columbia University Press.

———. 1998. "The Artworld Revisited: Comedies of Similarity," in *Beyond the Brillo Box: The Visual Arts in Post-Historical Perspective*. Berkeley: University of California Press.

———. 1999. "Indiscernibility and Perception: A Reply to Joseph Margolis. *British Journal of Aesthetics* 39.4 (October).

———. 2007. "Embodied Meanings, Isotopes, and Aesthetical Ideas." *Journal of Aesthetics and Art Criticism* 65.1 (Winter): 121–29.
———. 2013a. *What Art Is*. New Haven, CT: Yale University Press.
———. 2013b. "My Life as a Philosopher," in *The Philosophy of Arthur Danto*, ed. Randall Auxier and Lewis Hahn. Chicago: Open Court.
Darwin, Charles. 1860–1861. *Darwin Correspondence Project*. Jim Secord, director, November 26, 1860 and December 11. 1861 Letters to Asa Gray. www.darwinproject.ac.uk/entry-3342.
———. 1871. *The Descent of Man and Selection in Relation to Sex*. Vol. 1. New York: Appleton.
Darwin, Francis. 1887. *The Life and Letters of Charles Darwin*. Vol. 2. London: John Murray.
Davidson, Donald. 1963. "Actions, Reasons, and Causes." *Journal of Philosophy* 60.23: 685–700.
———. 1978. "What Metaphors Mean." *Critical Inquiry* 5.1 (Autumn): 31–47.
———. 1986. "A Coherence Theory of Truth and Knowledge," in *Truth and Intepretation: Perspectives on the Philosophy of Donald Davidson*, ed. Ernest Lepore. Oxford: Blackwell. 307–19.
Davies, Stephen. 1994. *Musical Meaning and Expression*. Ithaca, NY: Cornell University Press.
De Caro, Mario. 2016. *Naturalism, Realism, and Normativity*. Cambridge, MA: Harvard University Press.
Dennett, Daniel. 1997. *Kinds of Minds: Toward an Understanding of Consciousness*. New York: Basic Books.
———. 2004. *Freedom Evolves*. New York: Penguin.
———. 2018. "Comment to Clatterbuck." *Teorema: Revista Internacional de Filosofía*. 37.3: 145–50.
De Waal, Frans. 2009. *Good Natured: The Origins of Right and Wrong in Humans and Other Animals*. Cambridge, MA: Harvard University.
Dewey, John. 1896. "The Reflex Arc Concept in Psychology." *Psychological Review* 3: 357–70.
———. 1938. *Logic: The Theory of Inquiry*. New York: Holt.
———. 1992. *Theory of the Moral Life*. New York: Irvington.
———. 1989. *Art as Experience. Later Works of John Dewey*, Vol. 10. Edited by Jo Ann Boydston. Carbondale: Southern Illinois University Press.
———. 2000. *Experience and Nature*. Mineola, NY: Dover.
Dewey, John, and Arthur F. Bentley. 1964. *John Dewey and Arthur F. Bentley: A Philosophical Correspondence, 1932–1951*. Edited by Sidney Ratner and Jules Altman. New Brunswick, NJ: Rutgers University Press.
Dickie, George. 1969. "Defining Art." *American Philosophical Quarterly* 6.3 (July): 253–56.
Diffey, T. J. 1969. "The Republic of Art." *The British Journal of Aesthetics* 9.2 (April): 145–56.

Dolev, Yuval. 2007. *Time and Realism: Metaphysical and Antimetaphysical Perspectives.* Cambridge, MA: MIT Press.
Douglas, Mary. 2002. *Purity and Danger: An Analysis of the Concepts of Pollution and Taboo.* New York: Routledge.
Drake, Durant. 1920. *Essays in Critical Realism: A Co-operative Study of the Problem of Knowledge.* London: Macmillan and Co.
Dretske, Fred. 1988. *Explaining Behavior: Reasons in a World of Causes.* Cambridge, MA: MIT Press.
Dryden, Donald. 1997. "Susanne K. Langer and American Philosophic Naturalism in the Twentieth Century." *Transactions of the Charles S. Peirce Society* 33.1 (Winter): 161–82.
Du Bois, W. E. B. 1994. *The Souls of Black Folk.* New York: Dover Thrift Editions.
Durkheim, Emile. 1933. *The Division of Labor in Society.* Trans. George Simpson. Glencoe, IL: Free Press.
Dummett, Michael. 1978. *Truth and Other Enigmas.* London: Duckworth.
Dworkin, Ronald. 1986. Law's Empire. Cambridge, MA: Belknap.
Edmunds, Bruce. 1999. *Syntactic Measures of Complexity*, PhD Thesis, University of Manchester, UK.
Einstein, Albert, and David Infeld. 1966. *The Evolution of Physics.* New York: Simon & Schuster.
Ellis, Willis D. 1938. *A Sourcebook for Gestalt Psychology.* London: Routledge & Paul Kegan.
Feynman, Richard. 1985. *The Character of Physical Law.* Cambridge, MA: MIT Press.
Finnis, John. 2021. *Natural Law and the Nature of Law.* Cambridge: Cambridge University Press.
Foot, Philippa. 1958. "Moral Judgment." *Mind* 67.268 (October): 502–13.
Freud, Sigmund. 2010. *Civilization and its Discontents.* Trans. James Strachey. New York: Norton and Co.
Fukuyama, Francis. 2011. *The Origins of Political Order: From Prehuman Times to the French Revolution.* New York: Farrar, Straus and Giroux.
Garcia, Jorge. 1990. "The Primacy of the Virtuous." *Philosophia* 20.1–2: 69–91.
Geist, Valerius. 1978. *Life Strategies, Human Evolution, Environmental Design: Toward a Biological Theory of Health.* New York: Springer Verlag
———. 2004. "Big Game in the City: The Other Side of the Coin." ed. William Shaw et al., *Proceedings of the 4th International Urban Wildlife Symposium.* 20–25.
Gellner, Ernest. 1955. "Ethics and Logic." *Proceedings of the Aristotelian Society* 55.1: 157–78.
———. 1974. "Concepts and Society." in *Rationality*, ed. Bryan R. Wilson. Oxford, UK: Basil Blackwell. 18–49.
———. 1990. *Plough, Sword, and Book: The Structure of Human History.* Chicago: University of Chicago Press.

———. 2009. *Nations and Nationalism*. Ithaca, NY: Cornell University Press.
Gibson, Abraham. 2013. "Edward O. Wilson and the Organicist Tradition." *Journal of the History of Biology* 46.4 (Winter): 599–630.
Gibson, J. J. 1979. *The Ecological Approach to Visual Perception*. Boston: Houghton Mifflin.
Glazer, Trip. 2017. "The Semiotics of Emotional Expression." *Transactions of the Charles S. Peirce Society* 53.2 (Spring): 189–215.
Globus, Gordon, G. Maxwell, and I. Savodnik, eds. 1976. *Consciousness and the Brain: A Scientific and Philosophical Inquiry*. New York: Basic Books.
Goldstein, Kurt. 2000. *The Organism: A Holistic Approach to Biology Derived from Pathological Data in Man*. New York: Zone Books.
Goodman, Nelson. 1976. *Languages of Art: An Approach to a Theory of Symbols*. Indianapolis: Bobbs-Merrill (Hackett).
———. 1978. *Ways of Worldmaking*. Indianapolis: Bobbs-Merrill (Hackett).
———. 1979. "Metaphor as Moonlighting." *Critical Inquiry* 6.1 (Autumn): 125–30.
Gray, Asa. 1874. "Scientific Worthies." *Nature* 10.240 (June 4).
Gray, Michael. 2010. "Irremediable Complexity," *Science* 330.6006: 920–21.
Greenfeld Liah. 1992. *Nationalism: Five Roads to Modernity*. Cambridge, MA: Harvard University Press.
Grene, Marjorie. 1974. "People and Other Animals," in *The Understanding of Nature: Essays in the Philosophy of Biology*. Vol. 23. Boston Studies. Dordrecht: Reidel.
———. 1999. *A Philosophical Testament*. Chicago: Open Court.
Guyer, Paul. 1986. "Mary Mothersill's *Beauty Restored*." *Journal of Aesthetics and Art Criticism* 44.3 (Spring): 245–55.
———. 2008. "The Psychology of Kant's Aesthetics." *Studies in the History and Philosophy of Science* 39: 483–d94.
Habermas, Jürgen. 1985. *Theory of Communicative Action. Vol. 1, Reason and the Rationalization of Society*, and *Vol. II, Lifeworld and System: A Critique of Functionalist Reason*. Trans. Thomas McCarty. Boston: Beacon Press.
Haidt, Jonathan. 2013. *The Righteous Mind: Why Good People Are Divided by Politics and Religion*. New York: Vintage Press.
Haidt, Jonathan, and Joseph Craig. 2007. "The Moral Mind: How Five Sets of Innate Intuitions Guide the Development of Many Culture-Specific Virtues, and Perhaps Even Modules," in *The Innate Mind, Volume 3: Foundations and the Future*, ed. Peter Carruthers, Stephen Laurence, and Stephen Stich. Oxford University Press. 367–391.
Hamilton, W. D. 1964. "The Genetic Evolution of Social Behavior." *Journal of Theoretical Biology* 7: 1–16.
Hare, R. M. 1952. *The Language of Morals*. Oxford: Clarendon Press.
———. 1955. "Universalizability." *Proceedings of the Aristotelian Society* 55.1: 295–312.
———. 1981. *Moral Thinking: Its Levels, Method and Point*. Oxford: Clarendon Press.

———. 1997. "Could Kant Have Been a Utilitarian?," in *Sorting out Ethics*. Oxford: Clarendon. 147–65.

Hart, H. L. A. 1976. *The Concept of Law*. Oxford: Oxford University Press.

Hawthorne, Nathaniel. 1843. "The Celestial Railroad." *Democratic Review* 12 (May).

Heft, Harry. 2005. *Ecological Psychology in Context: James Gibson, Roger Barker, and the Legacy of William James*. London: Psychology Press.

Hickman, Larry. 2013. "Objective Relativism," in *International Encyclopedia of Ethics*, ed. Hugh LaFollette. Malden, MA: Wiley-Blackwell.

Hobson, Peter. 2002. *The Cradle of Thought: Exploring the Origins of Thinking*. Oxford: Oxford University Press.

Hollinger, David. 1975. *Morris Cohen and the Scientific Ideal*. Cambridge: MIT Press.

Holmes, Oliver Wendell. 1897. "The Path of Law." *Harvard Law Review* 10.8 March: 457–98.

Holt, Edwin Bissell, Walter Taylor Marvin, William Pepperrell Montague, Ralph Barton Perry, Walter Broughton Pitkin, and Edward Gleason Spaulding. 1910. "The Program and First Platform of Six Realists." *Journal of Philosophy, Psychology and Scientific Methods* 3.15 (July): 393–40.

Holt, Edwin Bissell, Walter Taylor Marvin, William Pepperrell Montague, Ralph Barton Perry, Walter Broughton Pitkin, and Edward Gleason Spaulding. 1925. *The New Realism: Cooperative Studies in Philosophy*. New York: Macmillan.

Hook, Sidney. 1976. "Morris Cohen—Fifty Years Later." *American Scholar* (June): 426–36.

Hooker, Brad. 1999. "Rule-Consequentialismi" in *The Blackwell Guide to Ethical Theory*, ed. Hugh LaFollette. Oxford: Blackwell. 183–204.

Huizinga, Johan. 1955. *Homo Ludens: A Study in the Play Element in Culture*. Boston: Beacon University Press.

Hume, David. 2000. *Treatise on Human Nature*. Edited by David Fate Norton and Mary J. Norton. Oxford: Oxford University Press.

Humphrey, Nicholas. 2006. *Seeing Red: A Study in Consciousness*. Cambridge, MA: Harvard University Press.

Huxley, Thomas H. 2009. *Evolution and Ethics*. Princeton, NJ: Princeton University Press.

Husserl, Edmund. 1970. *Logical Investigations*. Vol. 2. Trans. J. N. Findlay. London: Routledge & Kegan Paul.

Ibn Khaldun. 2015. *The Muqqadima: An Introduction to History*. Edited by N. J. Darwood et al. Princeton, NJ: Princeton University Press.

Illich, Ivan. 1990. *Gender*. Berkeley, CA: Heyday Books.

Innis, Robert. 2009. *Susanne Langer in Focus: The Symbolic Mind*. Bloomington: Indiana University Press.

James, William. 1904a. "Does Consciousness Exist?" *Journal of Philosophy, Psychology, and Scientific Methods* 1.18 (September): 477–91.

———. 1904b. "A World of Pure Experience." *Journal of Philosophy, Psychology, and Scientific Methods* 1.20 (September): 533–54, 561–70n21.
———. 2011. "The Will to Believe," in *The Essential William James*, ed. John Shook. Buffalo, NY: Prometheus.
Jaspers, Karl. 2011. *The Origin and Goal of History*. New York: Routledge.
Johnson, Mark. 2015. *Morality for Humans: Ethical Understanding from the Perspective of Cognitive Science*. Chicago: University of Chicago Press.
Jonas, Hans. 1982. *The Phenomenon of Life: Towards a Philosophical Biology*. Chicago: University of Chicago Press.
Juarrero, Alicia. 1999. *Dynamics in Action: Intentional Behavior as a Complex System*. Cambridge: MIT Press.
Kant, Immanuel. 1951. *Critique of Judgment*. Trans. J. H. Bernard. New York: Hafner Publishing.
Keller, Helen. 1954. *The Story of My Life*. Garden City, NY: Doubleday.
Kitcher, Philip. 2011. *The Ethical Project*. Cambridge, MA: Harvard University Press.
Kim, Jaegwon. 2000. *Mind in a Physical World: An Essay on the Mind–Body Problem and Mental Causation*. Cambridge, MA: MIT Press.
Kocka, Jürgen. 2017. *Capitalism: A Brief History*. Princeton, NJ: Princeton University Press.
Kohák, Erazim. 1984. *The Embers and the Stars: A Philosophical Inquiry into the Moral Sense of Nature*. Chicago: University of Chicago Press.
Kornblith, Hillary. 1985. *Naturalizing Epistemology*. Cambridge, MA: MIT Press.
———. 2002. *Knowledge and Its Place in Nature*. Oxford: Clarendon.
Krikorian, Yervant, ed. 1944. *Naturalism and the Human Spirit*. New York: Columbia University Press.
Kristeller, Paul Oskar. 1951. "The Modern System of the Arts: A Study in the History of Aesthetics. Part I." *Journal of the History of Ideas* 12.4 (October): 496–527.
———. 1952. "The Modern System of the Arts: A Study in the History of Aesthetics Part II." *Journal of the History of Ideas* 13.1 (January): 17–46.
Kruse, Felicia. 2005. "Emotion in Musical Meaning: A Peircean Solution to Langer's Dualism." *Transactions of the Charles S. Peirce Society* 41.4 (Fall): 762–78.
Kurtz, Paul. 1988. *The Ethics of Secularism*. Amherst, NY: Prometheus.
Lafferty, Theodore. 1949. "Empiricism and Objective Relativism in Value Theory." *Journal of Philosophy* 46.6 (March): 141–55.
Langer, Susanne. 1937. *An Introduction to Symbolic Logic*. Boston: Houghton and Mifflin.
———. 1942. *Philosophy in a New Key: A Study in the Symbolism of Reason, Rite, and Art*. Cambridge, MA: Harvard University Press.
———. 1953. *Feeling and Form: A Theory of Art*. New York: Charles Scribner's Sons.
———. 1957. *Problems of Art: Ten Philosophical Lectures*. New York: Charles Scribner's Sons.

Lewes, G. H. 1877. *Problems of Life and Mind*. London: Trubner & Co.
Lewis, Clarence I. 1929. *Mind and the World Order: Outline of a Theory of Knowledge*. New York: Charles Scribner's Sons.
———. 1962. *An Analysis of Knowledge and Valuation*. Chicago: Open Court.
Libet, Benjamin. 1985. "Unconscious Cerebral Initiative and the Role of Conscious Will in Voluntary Actions." *Behavioral and Brain Sciences* 8: 529–66.
———. 1999. "Do We Have Free Will?" *Journal of Consciousness Studies* 6.8–9: 47–57.
Lloyd Morgan, C. 1913. *Spencer's Philosophy of Science*. Oxford: Clarendon.
———. 1927. *Emergent Evolution*. New York: Henry Holt and Co.
Locke, John. 1975. *An Essay Concerning Human Understanding*. Oxford: Clarendon.
Lorenz, Konrad. 1975. "Kant's Doctrine of the A Priori in the Light of Contemporary Biology," in *Konrad Lorenz: The Man and His Ideas*, ed. Richard I. Evans. New York: Harcourt Brace Janovich. 129–217.
———. 1973. *Behind the Mirror: A Search for a Natural History of Human Knowledge*. New York & London: Harcourt Brace Janovich.
Lovejoy, Arthur O. 1930. *The Revolt against Dualism: An Inquiry Concerning the Existence of Ideas*. New York: W. W. Norton.
Luhmann, Niklas. 1982. *The Differentiation of Society*. Trans. Stephen Holmes and Charles Larmore. New York: Columbia University Press.
Lyotard, Jean-François. 1984. *The Postmodern Condition: A Report on Knowledge*. Trans. Geoff Bennington and Brian Massumi. Minneapolis: University of Minnesota Press.
MacCumhaill, Clare, and Rachael Wiseman. 2022. *Metaphysical Animals: How Four Women Brought Philosophy Back to Life*. New York: Doubleday.
Mach, Ernst. 1897. *Contributions to the Analysis of the Sensations*. Trans. C. M. Williams. Chicago: Open Court.
MacIntyre, Alasdair. 1974. "The Idea of a Social Science," in *Rationality*, ed. Bryan R. Wilson. Oxford, UK: Basil Blackwell. 112–30.
———. 1981. *After Virtue: A Study in Moral Theory*. South Bend, IN: University of Notre Dame Press.
MacLean, Paul. 1990. *The Triune Brain in Evolution: Role in Paleocerebral Functions*. New York: Springer.
Maddy, Penelope. 1990. *Realism in Mathematics*. Oxford: Clarendon.
———. 2007. *Second Philosophy: A Naturalistic Method*. Oxford: Oxford University.
Mangabeira Unger, Roberto. 2015. *The Critical Legal Studies Movement*. New York: Verso.
Mapel, David R. 1997. "Realism and the Ethics of War," in *The Ethics of War and Peace: Secular and Religious Perspectives*, ed. Terry Nardin. Princeton, NJ: Princeton University Press. 54–77.
Margolis, Joseph. 1958. "The Mode of Existence of a Work of Art." *Review of Metaphysics* 12.1: 26–34.

———. 1974. "Works of Art as Physically Embodied and Culturally Emergent Entities." *British Journal of Aesthetics* 14.3 (Summer): 187–96.
———. 1976. "Robust Relativism." *Journal of Aesthetics and Art Criticism* 35.1 (Autumn): 37–46.
———. 1977. "The Ontological Peculiarity of Works of Art." *Journal of Aesthetics and Art Criticism* 36.1 (Autumn): 45–50.
———. 1978. *Persons and Minds: The Prospects of a Nonreductive Materialism*. Dordrecht: Reidel.
———. 1998. "Farewell to Danto and Goodman." *British Journal of Aesthetics* 38.4 (October): 353–74.
———. 1999. "What, After All, Is a Work of Art?" In *What, After All, Is a Work of Art: Lectures in the Philosophy of Art*. State College: Penn State University Press.
———. 2001. *Selves and Other Texts: The Case for Cultural Realism*. State College: Penn State University Press.
———. 2015. "Preparations for a Theory of Interpretation." *Contemporary Pragmatism* 12: 11–37.
Mayr, Ernest. 1960. "The Emergence of Evolutionary Novelties," in *Evolution after Darwin*, vol. 3: *Issues in Evolution*. ed. Sol Tax and Charles Callendar. Chicago: University of Chicago Press.
———. 1974. "Teleological and Teleonomic: A New Analysis." *Boston Studies in the Philosophy of Science* 14: 91–117.
———. 1982. *The Growth of Biological Knowledge: Diversity, Evolution, and Inheritance*. Cambridge, MA: Belknap.
McCloskey, H. J. 1963. "A Note on Utilitarian Punishment." *Mind* 72.288: 599.
McCrea, W. H., and M. J. Rees. 1983. *The Constants of Physics*. Great Neck, NY: Scholium International.
McDowell, John. 1996. *Mind and World*. Cambridge, MA: Harvard University Press.
McGilvary, Evander Bradley. 1933. "Perceptual and Memory Perspectives." *Journal of Philosophy* 30.12 (June): 309–30.
———. 1977. *Toward a Perspective Realism*. Chicago: Open Court.
McLaughlin, Brian. 1992. "The Rise and Fall of British Emergentism," in *Emergence or Reduction? Essays on the Prospects of Nonreductive Physicalism*, ed. Ansgar Beckerman et al. New York: Walter de Gruyter Press.
McMahan, Jeffrey. 1997. "Realism, Morality, and War," in *The Ethics of War and Peace: Secular and Religious Perspectives*, ed. Terry Nardin. Princeton, NJ: Princeton University Press. 78–92.
McShea, Daniel. 1991. "Complexity and Evolution: What Everybody Knows." *Biology and Philosophy* 6: 303–24.
McTaggart, John. 1908. "The Unreality of Time." *Mind* 17.68: 457–74.
Mead, George Herbert. 1895. "Review of Introduction to Comparative Psychology by C. Lloyd Morgan," *Psychological Review* 2: 399–402.

———. 1927. "The Objective Reality of Perspectives," in *Proceedings of the Sixth International Congress of Philosophy*, ed. Edgar Brightman. New York: Longmans, Green, and Co. 75–85.

———. 1934. *Mind, Self and Society: Psychology from the Standpoint of a Social Behaviorist*. Chicago: University of Chicago Press.

———. 1938. *Philosophy of the Act*. Chicago: University of Chicago Press.

———. 2002. *Philosophy of the Present*. Amherst, NY: Prometheus.

Merleau-Ponty, Maurice. 1963. *The Structure of Behavior*. Trans. Alden Fisher. Boston: Beacon.

———. 1968. *The Visible and the Invisible*. Trans. Alphonso Lingis. Evanston, IL: Northwestern University Press.

———. 1995. *Nature: Course Notes from the Collège de France*. Edited by Dominique Séglard. Trans. Roébert Vallier, Evanston, IL: Northwestern University Press.

———. 2013. *The Phenomenology of Perception*. Trans. Donald Landes. New York: Routledge.

Midgley, Mary. 1994. *The Ethical Primate: Humans, Freedom, and Morality*. London: Routledge.

Mill, John Stuart. 1974. "Nature," in *Nature, The Utility of Religion, and Theism*. London: Longmans, Green, Reader and Dyer.

Milosz, Czeslaw. 1953. *The Captive Mind*. Trans. Jane Zielonko. New York: Knopf.

Misak, Cheryl. 2015. *The American Pragmatists*. Oxford: Oxford University Press.

Mitchell, Melanie. 2009. *Complexity: A Guided Tour*. Oxford: Oxford University Press.

Monod, Jacques. 1972. *Chance and Necessity: An Essay on the Natural Philosophy of Modern Biology*. Trans. Austryn Wainhouse. New York: Vintage Press.

Montague, William Pepperell. 1937. "The Story of American Realism." *Philosophy: Royal Institute of Philosophy* 12.46 (April): 140–61.

Moore, George Edward. 1903. "The Refutation of Idealism." *Mind* 12.48 (1903): 433–53.

———. 1993. *Principia Ethica*. Cambridge: Cambridge University Press.

Morgenthau, Hans. 1946. *Scientific Man versus Power Politics*. Chicago: University of Chicago Press.

Morris, Charles W. 1932. *Six Theories of Mind*. Chicago: University of Chicago Press.

———. 1970. *The Pragmatic Movement in American Philosophy*. New York: George Baziller.

Mothersill, Mary. 1984. *Beauty Restored*. Cambridge: Clarendon.

Muller, Jerry Z. 2003. *The Mind and the Market: Capitalism and Western Thought*. New York: Anchor.

Murphy, Arthur. 1927. "Objective Relativism in Whitehead and Dewey." *Philosophical Review* 36.2 (March): 121–44.

———. 1963. "Whatever Happened to Objective Relativism?," in *Reason and the Common Good: Selected Essays*. New York: Prentice-Hall. 67–79.

Nagel, Ernest. 1944. "Logic without Ontology," in *Naturalism and the Human Spirit*, ed. Yervant Krikorian. New York: Columbia University Press.

———.1949. "In Defense of Logic without Metaphysics," *The Philosophical Review* 58.1 (January): 26–34.

———. 1954. "Philosophy and the American Temper," in *Sovereign Reason: And Other Studies in the Philosophy of Science*. New York: Free Press. 50–57.

———. 1956. *Logic without Metaphysics and Other Studies in the Philosophy of Science*. New York: Free Press.

———. 1961. *The Structure of Science: Problems in the Logic of Scientific Explanation*. New York: Harcourt, Brace, & World.

Nagel, Thomas. 1986. *The View from Nowhere*. New York: Oxford University.

Nietzsche, Friedrich. 2002. *Beyond Good and Evil: Prelude to a Philosophy of the Future*. Trans. Judith Norman. Cambridge Cambridge University Press.

Nozick, Robert. 1974. *Anarchy, State, and Utopia*. New York: Basic Books.

Nussbaum, Martha. 1990. "Aristotelian Social Democracy," in *Liberalism and the Good*, ed. R. Bruch Douglass et al. New York: Routledge.

Oakeshott, Michael. 1991. *Rationalism in Politics and Other Essays*. New York: Liberty Fund.

Oliver, Sir Donald. 1938. "The Logic of Perspective Realism," *Journal of Philosophy* 35.8.

Ongley, John, and Rosalind Carey. 2013. *Russell: A Guide for the Perplexed*. New York: Bloomsbury Academic.

Ortega y Gasset, José. 1972. *Meditations on Hunting*. Trans. Howard Wescott. New York: Scribner.

Panksepp, Jaak. 2003. Review of *Looking for Spinoza: Joy, Sorrow, and the Feeling Brain* by A Damasio. *Consciousness & Emotion* 4.1: 111–34.

———. 2005. "Affective Consciousness: Core Emotional Feelings in Humans and Animals." *Consciousness and Cognition* 14: 30–80.

Passmore, John, 1968. *One Hundred Years of Philosophy*. New York: Penguin.

Peirce, Charles Sanders. 1932. *Collected Papers of Charles Sanders Peirce, Volumes One and Two: Principles of Philosophy and Elements of Logic*. Edited by Charles Hartshorne and Paul Weiss. Cambridge, MA: Harvard University Press.

———. 1935. *Collected Papers of Charles Sanders Peirce, Volumes Five and Six: Pragmatism and Scientific Metaphysics*, Edited by Charles Hartshorne and Paul Weiss. Cambridge, MA: Harvard University Press.

———. 1955. "Some Consequences of Four Incapacities," in *Philosophical Writings of Charles Sanders Peirce*, ed. Justus Buchler. Mineola, NY: Dover. 225–50.

Penrose, Roger. 2004. *The Road to Reality: A Complete Guide to the Laws of the Universe*. New York: Knopf.

Pittendrigh, Colin. 1958. "Adaptation, Natural Selection, and Behavior," in *Behavior and Evolution*, ed. A. Roe and G. G. Simpson. New Haven, CT: Yale University Press. 390–416.

Pocock, J. G. A. 2016. *The Machiavellian Moment: Florentine Political Thought and the Modern Republican Tradition*. Princeton, NJ: Princeton University Press.

Polanyi, Karl. 1944. *The Great Transformation: The Political and Economic Origins of our Time*. Boston: Beacon Press.

Popper, Karl. 1963. *Conjectures and Refutations: The Growth of Scientific Knowledge*. New York: Harper & Row.

———. 1972. *Objective Knowledge: An Evolutionary Approach*. Oxford: Clarendon.

———. 1987. "Natural Selection and the Emergence of Mind," in *Evolutionary Epistemology, Rationality, and the Sociology of Knowledge*, ed. G. Radnitzky and W. W. Bartley Jr. Chicago: Open Court. 139–56.

Pryba, Russell. 2010. "John Dewey and the Ontology of Art," in *Dewey's Enduring Impact: Essays on America's Philosopher*, ed. John Shook. Amherst, NY: Prometheus, pp. 219–35.

———. 2021. "Margolis Looks at the Arts: The Place of the Early Aesthetic Writings in the Philosophy of Joseph Margolis." *Metaphilosophy* 52.1 (February): 1–15.

Putnam, Hilary. 1975. "The Meaning of 'Meaning.'" *Minnesota Studies in the Philosophy of Science* 7: 131–193.

———. 1981. *Reason, Truth, and History*. Cambridge: Cambridge University Press.

———. 1982. "Why Reason Can't Be Naturalized." *Synthese* 52.1 (July): 3–23.

———. 1985. "A Comparison of Something with Something Else." *New Literary History* 17.1. *Philosophy of Science and Literary Theory* (Autumn): 61–79.

———. 1991. "Does Disquotationalism Really Solve All Philosophical Problems?" *Metaphilosophy* 22.1/2.

———. 1994a. "Sense, Nonsense, and the Senses: An Inquiry into the Powers of the Human Mind." *Journal of Philosophy* 91.9 (September): 445–517.

———. 2004. *The Collapse of the Fact/Value Dichotomy*. Cambridge, MA: Harvard University Press.

———. 2015. "Naturalism, Realism, and Normativity." *Journal of the American Philosophical Association* 1.2: 312–28.

Putnam, Hilary, and Ruth Anna Putnam. 2017. "What the Spilled Beans Can Spell," in *Pragmatism as a Way of Life: The Lasting Legacy of William James and John Dewey*, ed. David Macarthur. Cambridge, MA: Belknap. 159–66.

Quine, Willard V. O. 1951. "Two Dogmas of Empiricism." *The Philosophical Review* 60 (1951): 20–43.

———. 1968. "Epistemology Naturalized," in *Ontological Relativity and Other Essays*. New York: Columbia University. 69–90.

Radnitzky, Gerard, and W. W. Bartley III, eds. 1993. *Evolutionary Epistemology, Rationality, and the Sociology of Knowledge*. Chicago: Open Court.

Ramsey, F. P. 1931. *The Foundations of Mathematics and Other Logical Essays*, London: Kegan Paul, Trench, Trubner, & Co.

Randall, John Herman. 1944. "Epilogue: The Nature of Naturalism," in *Naturalism and the Human Spirit*, ed. Yervant Krikorian. New York: Columbia University Press.

———. 1958. *Nature and Historical Experience: Essays in Naturalism and in the Theory of History*. New York: Columbia University Press.

Rawls, John. 1999. *A Theory of Justice*. Cambridge, MA: Belknap Press.
———. 2005. *Political Liberalism*. New York: Columbia University Press.
Robischon, Thomas. 1958. "What is Objective Relativism?" *The Journal of Philosophy* 55.26 (December): 1117–32.
Rolston, Holmes III. 1982. Are Values in Nature Subjective or Objective?," *Environmental Ethics* 4 (1982): 125–51.
———. 1987. "The Preservation of Natural Value in the Solar System," in *Beyond Spaceship Earth: Environmental Ethics and the Solar System*, ed. Eugene C. Hargrove. San Francisco: Sierra Club Books. 140–82.
———. 1987. "Duties to Ecosystems," in *Companion to A Sand County Almanac: Interpretive and Critical Essays*, ed. Madison J. Baird Callicott. Madison: University of Wisconsin Press. 246–274.
———. 1988. *Environmental Ethics: Duties to and Values in the Natural World*. Philadelphia: Temple University Press.
Rorty, Richard. 1979. *Philosophy and the Mirror of Nature*. Princeton, NJ: Princeton University Press.
———. 1986. "From Logic to Language to Play: A Plenary Address to the Inter-American Congress of Philosophy." *Proceedings and Addresses of the American Philosophical Association* 59.5: 747–53.
———. 1991. *Objectivity, Relativism, and Truth*. Cambridge: Cambridge University Press.
Ross, David. 2003. *The Right and the Good*. Oxford: Clarendon.
Rothenberg, David. 2011. *Survival of the Beautiful: Art, Science, and Evolution*. London: Bloomsbury.
Rozin, Paul. 1976. "Selection of Food by Rats, Humans, and Other Animals. *Advances in the Study of Behavior* 6: 21–76.
Ruse, Michael. 2019. "Evolution and the Naturalistic Fallacy," in *The Naturalistic Fallacy*, ed. Neil Sinclair. Cambridge: Cambridge University Press.
Russell, Bertrand. 1903. *Principles of Mathematics*. New York: W. W. Norton.
———. 1911. "The Basis of Realism." *Journal of Philosophy, Psychology and Scientific Methods* 8.6 (March): 158–61.
———. 1914. "On the Nature of Acquaintance: II. Neutral Monism." *The Monist* 24.2 (April): 161–87.
———. 1917. "The Study of Mathematics," in *Mysticism and Logic and other Essays*. London: Longmans, Green, and Co. 1918. 58–73.
———. 1917. "A Free Man's Worship," in *Mysticism and Logic, and Other Essays*. London: George Allen & Unwin. 46–57.
———. 1921. *The Analysis of Mind*. London: Allen and Unwin.
Ryder, John. 1991. "Ordinality and Materialism," in *Nature's Perspectives: Prospects for an Ordinal Metaphysics*, ed. Armen Marsoobian, Kathleen Wallace, and Robert Corrington. Albany, NY: SUNY Press. 201–19.
Salthe, Stanley. 1985. *Evolving Hierarchical Systems: Their Structure and Representation*. New York: Columbia University.

———. 1993. *Development and Evolution: Complexity and Change in Biology*, Cambridge, MA: MIT Press.
Sartre, Jean-Paul. 1964. *Nausea*. Trans. Lloyd Alexander. New York: New Directions.
Sartwell, Crispin. 2017. *Entanglements: A System of Philosophy*. Albany, NY: SUNY Press.
Scalia, Antonin. 2018. *A Matter of Interpretation: Federal Courts and the Law*. Princeton, NJ: Princeton University Press.
Schlesinger, Arthur. 1972. "National Interests and Moral Absolutes," in *Ethics and World Politics: Four Perspectives*, ed. E. W. Lefever: Baltimore: Johns Hopkins University Press.
Schiller, Friedrich. 1965. *On the Aesthetic Education of Man*: In a Series of Letters. Trans. Reginald Snell. New York: Frederick Ungar Publishing.
Searle, John. 1970. *Speech Acts: An Essay in the Philosophy of Language*. Cambridge: Cambridge University Press.
Sellars, Roy Wood. 1922. *Evolutionary Naturalism*. Chicago: Open Court.
Sellars, Wilfred. 1963. "Philosophy and the Scientific Image of Man," in *Science, Perception, and Reality*. New York: Humanities Press.
———. 1997. *Empiricism and the Philosophy of Mind*. Edited by Robert Brandom. Cambridge, MA: Harvard University Press.
Sheffer, Henry M. 1926. "Review of A.N. Whitehead and B. Russell *Principia Mathematica*." *Isis* 1.
Shepard, Paul. 1973. *The Tender Carnivore and the Sacred Game*. New York: Scribners.
Shils, Edward. 1957. "Personal, Primordial, Sacred, and Civic Ties: Some Particular Observations on the Relationship of Sociological Research and Theory." *British Journal of Sociology* 8.2 (June): 130–45.
———. 1981. *Tradition*. Chicago: University of Chicago.
———. 1975. *Center and Periphery: Essays in Macrosociology*. Chicago: University of Chicago Press.
———. 1997. *The Virtue of Civility: Selected Essays on Liberalism, Tradition, and Civil Society*. New York: Liberty Fund.
Shimony, Abner, and Debra Nails. 1987. *Natural Epistemology: A Symposium of Two Decades*. Dordrecht: Reidel.
———. 1993. "Some Proposals Concerning Parts and Wholes." *The Search for a Naturalistic Worldview, Vol. II: Natural Science and Metaphysics*. Cambridge: Cambridge University Press. 218–27.
Shusterman, Richard. 1997. "The End of Aesthetic Experience." *Journal of Aesthetics and Art Criticism* 55.1 (Winter): 29–41.
———. 2000. *Pragmatic Aesthetics: Living Beauty, Rethinking Art*. Lanham, MD. Rowman and Littlefield.
Simon, Herbert. 1969. *Sciences of the Artificial*. Cambridge, MA: MIT Press.
Singer, Beth. 1983. *Ordinal Naturalism: An Introduction to the Philosophy of Justus Buchler*. Lewisburg, PA: Bucknell Press.

Smart, J. J. C. 2004. "Defending Utilitarianism," in *Ethics: Contemporary* Readings, ed. Harry Gensler, Earl Spurgin, and James Swindal. New York: Routledge. 202–9.
Smith, M. G. 1956. "On Segmentary Lineage Systems," *Journal of the Royal Anthropological Institute of Great Britain and Ireland* 86.2: 39–80.
Smolin, Lee. 1997. *The Life of the Cosmos*. Oxford UK: Oxford University Press.
Snow, C. P. 2012. *The Two Cultures*. Cambridge, UK: Cambridge University Press.
Sperry, R. W. 1969. "A Modified Concept of Consciousness." *Psychological Review* 76.6: 532–36.
———. 1976. "Mental Phenomena as Causal Determinants in Brain Function," in *Consciousness and the Brain: A Scientific and Philosophical Inquiry*, ed. G. Globus, G. Maxwell, and I. Savodnik. New York: Basic Books. 163–77.
Stockdale, Admiral James B. *A Vietnam Experience: Ten Years of Reflection*. Stanford, CA: Hoover Institution Press.
Stolnitz, Jerome. 1960. "On Objective Relativism in Aesthetics," *Journal of Philosophy* 57.8: 261–76.
Stueber, Karsten. 2006. *Rediscovering Empathy*. Cambridge, MA: MIT Press.
———. 2019. "Empathy," in *Stanford Encyclopedia of Philosophy*. https://plato.stanford.edu/entries/empathy.
Suddendorf, Thomas. 2013. *The Gap: The Science of What Separates us from Other Animals*. New York: Basic Books.
Suppes, Patrick. 1969. "Nagel's Lectures on Dewey," in *Philosophy, Science and Method: Essays in Honor of Ernest Nagel*, ed. Sidney Morgenbesser, Patrick Suppes, and Morton White. New York: St. Martin's Press.
Tarski, Alfred. 1983. "The Concept of Truth in Formalized Languages," in *Logic, Semantics, Metamathematics*, ed. J. Corcoran. Trans. J. H. Woodger. Indianapolis: Hackett. 152–78.
Tomasello, Michael. 2014. *A Natural History of Human Thinking*. Cambridge, MA: Harvard University Press.
———. 2016. *A Natural History of Human Morality*. Cambridge, MA: Harvard University Press.
Trivers, Robert. 1971. "The Evolution of Reciprocal Altruism." *The Quarterly Review of Biology* 46.1 (March): 35–57.
Tuomela, Raimo. 2007. *The Philosophy of Sociality: The Shared Point of View*. Oxford: Oxford University Press.
Velmans, Max. 2002. "How Could Conscious Experience Affect Brains? *Journal of Consciousness Studies* 9.11: 3–29.
Voltaire. 2010. *Philosophical Dictionary*. Trans H. I. Woolf. Mineola, NY: Dover.
Von Uexküll, Jacob. 1926. *Theoretical Biology*. Trans. D. L. Mackinnon. New York: Harcourt, Brace & Co.
———. 2010. *A Foray into the Worlds of Animals and Men: with A Theory of Meaning*. Trans. Joseph O'Neil. Minneapolis: University of Minnesota Press.

Waddington, Conrad. 1960. *The Ethical Animal*. Chicago: University of Chicago Press.
Walzer, Michael. 1973. "Political Action: The Problem of Dirty Hands." *Philosophy and Public Affairs* 2.2: 160–80.
———. 1984. *Spheres of Justice: A Defense of Pluralism and Equality*. New York: Basic Books.
———. 1996. *What It Means to Be an American*. New York: Marsilio Publishers.
———. 1997. *On Toleration*. New Haven, CT: Yale University Press.
———. 2004. *Arguing about War*. New Haven, CT: Yale University Press.
———. 2015. *Just and Unjust Wars: A Moral Argument with Historical Illustrations*. New York: Basic Books.
———. 2019. *Thick and Thin: Moral Argument at Home and Abroad*. South Bend, IN: University of Notre Dame Press.
Warnock, Mary. 1978. *Imagination*. Berkeley: University of California.
Watts, Ian. 1999 "The Origin of Symbolic Culture," in *The Evolution of Culture: A Historical and Scientific Overview*, ed. Robin Dunbar, Chris Knight, and Camilla Power. New Brunswick, NJ: Rutgers University Press. 114–136.
Weber, Max. 1949a. "Objectivity in Social Science and Social Policy," in *The Methodology of the Social Sciences*, ed. Edward Shils and Henry Finch. Glencoe, IL: Free Press. 50–112.
———. 1949b. "The Meaning of Ethical Neutrality [*Wertfrei*] in Sociology and Economics," in *The Methodology of the Social Sciences*, ed. Edward Shils and Henry Finch. Glencoe, IL: Free Press. 1–49.
———. 1946a. "Science as a Vocation," in *From Max Weber: Essays in Sociology*, ed. H. H. Gerth and C. Wright Mills. New York: Oxford University.
———. 1946b. "Politics as a Vocation," in *From Max Weber: Essays in Sociology*, ed. H. H. Gerth and C. Wright Mills. New York: Oxford University Press.
———. 2004. *The Vocation Lectures*. Trans. Rodney Livingstone. Edited by David Owen and Tracy B. Strong. Indianapolis: Hackett.
Weinberg, Steven. *The First Three Minutes: A Modern View of the Origin of the Universe*. New York: Bantam, 1979.
Werner, Heinz. 1957. "The Concept of Development from a Comparative and Organismic Point of View," in *The Concept of Development: An Issue in the Study of Human Behavior*, ed. Dale Harris. Minneapolis: University of Minnesota Press. 125–48.
Werner, Heinz, and Bernard Kaplan. 1964. *Symbol Formation: An Organismic Developmental Approach to Language and the Development of Thought*. New York: Wiley and Sons.
Wertheimer, Max. 1938. "Laws of Organization in Perceptual Forms," in *A Source Book of Gestalt Psychology*, ed. W. D. Ellis. London: Routledge & Kegan Paul. 71–94.
Wheeler, William Morton. *Emergent Evolution and the Development of Societies*. New York: W. W. Norton, 1928.

White, Morton. 1956 *Toward Reunion in Philosophy*. Cambridge, MA: Harvard University Press.
Whitehead, Alfred North. 1920. *The Concept of Nature*. Cambridge: Cambridge University Press.
———. 1967. *Science and the Modern World*. New York: Free Press
———. 1985. *Process and Reality*. New York: Free Press.
Wigner, Eugene. 1960. "The Unreasonable Effectiveness of Mathematics in the Natural Sciences." *Communications on Pure and Applied Mathematics* 13: 001–014.
Williams, Bernard. 1985. *Ethics and the Limits of Philosophy*. Cambridge, MA: Harvard University Press.
Wilson, E. O. 2013. *The Social Conquest of Earth*. New York: Liveright.
Wilson, Bryan R. 1970. *Rationality*. New York: Harper.
Wimsatt, William. 1972. "Teleology and the Logical Structure of Function Statements." *Studies in the History and Philosophy of Science* 3.1: 1–80.
———. 1976. "Reductionism, Levels of Organization, and the Mind–Body Problem," in *Consciousness and the Brain: A Scientific and Philosophical Inquiry*, ed. G. Globus, G. Maxwell, and I. Savodnik. New York: Basic Books. 199–267.
———. 2007. *Re-Engineering Philosophy for Limited Beings: Piecewise Approximations to Reality*. Cambridge, MA: Harvard University Press.
Winch, Peter. 1974a. "The Idea of a Social Science," in *Rationality*, ed. Bryan R. Wilson. Oxford, UK: Basil Blackwell. 1–17.
———. 1974b. "Understanding a Primitive Society," in *Rationality*, ed. Bryan R. Wilson. Oxford, UK: Basil Blackwell. 78–111.
Wittgenstein, Ludwig. 1922. *Tractatus Logico-Philosophicus*. Trans. C. K. Ogden. London: Routledge and Kegan Paul.
Wong, David. 2009. *Natural Moralities: A Defense of Pluralistic Relativism*. Oxford: Oxford University Press.
Wrangham, Richard. 1999. *The Goodness Paradox: The Strange Relationship between Virtue and Violence in Human Evolution*. New York: Vintage.
Wright, Robert. 1994. *The Moral Animal: Why We Are the Way We Are: The New Science of Evolutionary Psychology*. New York: Pantheon.

Index

active judgment, 139–40, 144–45. *See also* judgment
aesthetic: attitude, 255, 258, 271, 273–74; experience, 252, 256–57, 271–72. *See also* art
affect, 90, 95–98 passim, 113, 116, 128
agency, 60; teleonomic (biological), 64; human, 101–20, 145; teleological, 75, 85–86, 95–97
aggregativity, 52, 55, 57. *See also* emergence
agro-literate (cultivating) lifeway, 154–60, 178, 180–83 passim, 243, 281. *See also* history; society
Ahl, Valerie, 54
Alexander, Samuel, 34–35, 50, 72, 289
Allan, George, 31
Allen, T. F. H., 54
analytic statements (vs. synthetic): 16–18, 21–22, 26, 43, 201, 212
Andrews, Kristen, 85
animal, 86–89; cognition, 88–89; and fact-value distinction, 97–99; and human cognition, 126–30, 132–35; and mind, 87–92
Anscombe, G. E. M., 10, 210, 213–14
antirealism, 34, 122, 131, 207. *See also* realism
Arendt, Hanna, 70, 144, 238

Aristotle, 2, 18, 20, 28–29, 279; on animals, 85–86; on art, 251; and judgment 138–39, 153, 159; and life, 71–73 passim; on politics, 231; on substances, 57; on truth, 199–200; and virtue ethics, 185, 209, 214, 219, 222
art, 168–69, 251–75; Columbians on, 255–71; expressive theory of, 254, 257, 259, 273; formalist theory of, 252, 259, 273; mimetic theory of, 251–52, 263–65, 273. *See also* aesthetic, attitude; aesthetic, experience
assertive judgment, 139–40, 143–51, 154, 156, 166; and art, 263, 265, 274, 285; and ethics, 213, 222–23; and logic, 191, 200–02. *See also* judgment
Austin, John, 235
Austin, John L., 131, 213; on speech acts, 140–42, 145
Australopithecus, 102
authority, 156, 159, 163; and morality, 175–76, 178, 180–81, 185–86; in politics, 232–34. *See also* moral foundations
Axial (Jasperian) Age, 159–64 passim, 181, 185, 243, 281–85. *See also* agro-literate lifeway; civilization

Baeten, Elizabeth, 185
bands, 155, 181–82. *See also* chiefdoms; tribes; states
Bartley III, W. W., 135
Beardsley, Monroe, 258
beauty, 59, 145–46, 150, 253–54, 256, 261–63, 274
behavioral modernity, 102
Benedict, Ruth, 24
Berger, Peter, 165, 278
Bergson, Henri, 9, 34–35, 66–67, 70, 118
Berlin, Isaiah, 279
Boas, Franz, 24
Boehm, Christopher, 176, 178
Borghini, Andrea, 204
Bradley, F. H., 33, 180
Brentano, Franz, 33, 90
Broad, C. D., 35, 50
Buchanan, Brett, 68
Buchler, Justus, 46, 49, 182, 207, 252, 256, 272, 274; on art, 261–63; on identity and integrity, 44; on judgment, 138–47 passim; on logical realism, 197–99; and objective relativism, 37–39; and possibility, 42
Bunge, Mario, 267
Burge, Tyler, 88–89, 128–29, 132
Butler, Joseph, 77
Butler, Judith, 5

Cahoone, Lawrence: on civil society, 234–35; on culture, 155, 183, 240–42; on mental causation, 93; on ordinal naturalism, 8, 47, 51, 56, 63
Campbell, Donald, 1, 7, 123–25
Ĉapek, Miliĉ, 67
capitalism, 24, 160, 238–39, 248. *See also* liberalism
care, 85, 96, 104, 119, 175–88, 225, 239. *See also* moral foundations

Carnap, Rudolf, 5, 9, 16–17, 35, 195–97
Cassirer, Ernst, 69, 255–56, 258, 263
causation (causality), 42, 76; downward, 56; and final causes, 73, 76–77. *See also* mental causation
Chase, Philip, 115
chiefdoms, 183, 22. *See also* bands; tribes; states
Church, Alonzo, 205
Cicero, 234, 255
civility, 241–42, 249. *See also* civil society
civil society, 234, 237–38, 242. *See also* civility
civilization, 116, 157–60, 164–69, 178, 180–81, 185, 281–82
cognitivism, ethical, 211–12, 216, 221–23
Cohen, Morris, 31, 35–39, 45–46, 192–99, 203, 206–07
Colapietro, Vincent, 259
Coleridge, Samuel Taylor, 255, 261
Columbia Naturalism. *See* naturalism, Columbia
complexes, 36–39, 41, 43; identity and integrity of, 44–46; natural, 43, 55–57, 197–98, 207, 261
conation, 97
consciousness: analysis of, 91–93; proto-, 92; core-, 92–93, 106, 118, 128–29; self-, 92, 103, 106, 112–13, 118–19, 129–30, 134, 173, 185
consequentialism, 179, 209, 236, 244; act- vs. rule-, versions of, 216–19; and The Good, 226–28; and necessity of rules, 224–25. *See also* utilitarianism
core-consciousness. *See* consciousness, core-
correspondence. *See* truth, theories of

cosmopolitanism, 4, 165, 186, 188, 211, 238–41
culture: definition of, 114–16; and history, 154–66 passim; and liberalism, 241–43, 248; and tribalism, 187–89; and art 268–78

Damasio, Antonio, 92, 96, 106, 118, 128
Danto, Arthur, 252, 256, 265–66, 268–72
Darwin, Charles, 23, 32, 49, 64, 71–74, 123, 173–74, 180
Darwin, Francis, 74
Davidson, Donald, 17, 91, 122, 145, 200; on metaphor, 264–65
Davies, Stephen, 260
De Chardin, Teihard, 74
De Waal, Frans, 186
deflation. *See* truth, theories of
democracy, 9, 164–65, 230, 238–39, 240, 244, 246, 249
Dennett, Daniel, 85, 88, 97, 118–19, 123
deontological ethics, 144, 180, 209, 216–19, 226, 239, 244, 247
descriptivism, ethical. *See* cognitivism, ethical
Dewey, John, 9, 17, 31, 35–37, 71–72, 139, 192–95, 219, 252; on aesthetic experience, 255–57, 271
Dickie, George, 266, 271
differentiation, modern, 69, 151, 156, 161–62, 285
Diffey, T. J., 297
dirty hands, problem of, 244–45
Douglas, Mary, 182
Dretske, Fred, 94
Dryden, Donald, 259
Duchamp, Michel, 259, 265, 270
Dummett, Michael, 122

Durkheim, Emile, 116, 155–56, 161. *See also* Durkheimian reason
Durkheimian reason, 156, 281, 282
duty, 144, 178–84; and Kant, 209, 219–20, 225–26, 236, 244, 246, 278; *prima facie*, 176, 180–89 passim, 218. *See also* moral foundations
Dworkin, Ronald, 235

efficiency, 162, 238
Einstein, Albert, 33, 40, 65, 67
emergence, 49–60, 291, 135, 160, 200, 223, 252, 285; and art, 267–72 passim; and British emergentists, 72; definition of, 50–55; Mayr on, 75; Mead on, 72–73; and mind, 91; and ordinal naturalism, 55–59; and values, 59–60
empathy, 104, 179, 187, 219
entities. *See* systems
equality, 162–66 passim, 175–81, 214, 219, 226, 230; legal, 248, 286
ethics, 209–28; Hare on, 213–19, 221–25; kinds of normative, 219–21; metaethics, 211–13; relation to The Good, 225–28. *See also* morality
ethology, 10, 71, 85, 121
evolution, 3, 60, 67, 72–77 passim; 127, 134, 161, 167, 173–74, 186–87, 204–05; of mind, 85–86, 95, 98; and pragmatism, 17
evolutionary epistemology, 59, 60, 121, 123–26
evolutionary psychology, 3–4, 173–74, 176, 188. *See also* moral foundations; tribalism, problem of
excellence, 182–86, 220. *See also* virtue ethics
exhibitive judgment, 139–49, 154, 156, 166, 261, 263, 272–74. *See also* judgment

existentialism, 3, 14, 214, 284
explanation, types of, 51–53
expressivism. *See* art, theory of
externalism: of meaning, 91–92; moral, 212, 223. *See also* internalism

fact-value distinction, 13–30, 83, 98, 166; collapse of, 25–28; history of, 18–25; Weber on, 23–24. *See also* normative facts
fairness, 29, 162, 175–86 passim. *See also* moral foundations
fallibilism, 39–40, 43–44, 135, 285
Feigl, Herbert, 267
Feynman, Richard, 59
Finnis, John, 235
Foot, Philippa, 213–14
foraging era. *See* hunter-gatherers
form: aesthetic, 252–56, 258–60, 273; biological, 69–73, 76–77, 125
formalism. *See* art, theory of
foundationalism, 8, 14, 59, 178, 213, 252, 29, 168–69, 207, 281–82
free will, 93, 103, 117–19
Freud, Sigmund, 182
Fukuyama, Francis, 158, 163, 232–33, 249
function: biological, 68, 75–77, 129; explanatory, 51–52; instrumental, 27, 79; of judgments, 140–48; and meanings, 106, 108–10 passim; and objective relativism, 35, 38–39, 44; statements of, 222–23; and values, 80, 82

Garcia, Jorge, 220
Geist, Valerius, 99, 251
Gellner, Ernest, 25, 116, 137, 154–59 passim, 162, 167, 213–14, 231, 238
generals (vs. universals), 214–15
Gibson, J. J., 78, 97
Glazer, Trip, 259

Goldstein, Kurt, 10, 67–68
good, as generic value, 80, 145, 211–12
Good, The, 277–86; not ethical, 225–28; existential or spiritual, 283–86
Goodman, Nelson, 17, 256, 259, 263–68, 271–72
Gray, Asa, 73, 264
Great Leap Forward, 102, 158
Grene, Marjorie, 121
Guyer, Paul, 255, 262–63

Habermas, Jürgen, 149, 161–62
Haidt, Jonathan, 174–82, 218
Hare, Richard M., 10, 16, 143, 155, 211–24 passim, 227, 263
Hart, H. L. A., 235
Hickman, Larry, 31
history: three eras of, 154–63; uniquely human, 120
Hobbes, Thomas, 236, 239
Hobson, Peter, 104
Hollinger, David, 195
Holmes, Oliver Wendell, 77, 235, 268
Holt, Edwin B., 35
Homo erectus, 102, 175
Homo neanderthalis, 102–03, 108
Homo sapiens, 58, 147, 155–56, 175–76, 268, 281, 285; evolution of, 99, 102–03, 108, 115. *See also* humans
Hook, Sidney, 35
Hooker, Brad, 224
Huizinga, Johan, 254
humans: and animal cognition, 126–35; and culture, definition of, 114–16; distinctiveness of, 101–20; historical eras of, 154–55; and joint intentionality, 103–08; and language, 108–14; and free will, 117–19. *See also Homo sapiens*
Hume, David, 17–21 passim, 98, 103, 175, 205
Humphrey, Nicholas, 91

INDEX 323

hunter-gatherer (foraging) lifeway, 154, 157, 181, 183, 227, 234, 281–82. *See also* history; society
Husserl, Edmund, 5, 9, 14, 33–35, 66–67
Huxley, Thomas, 173
hypoicons, 109, 259. *See also* Peirce, theory of signs

Ibn Khaldun, 159
icons, 92, 109, 115, 259–60
identity, 22, 38; vs. integrity, 44–45
imitation. *See mimesis*
indices, 109, 260, 272
individuals, 57. *See also* systems
industrial society. *See* modern industrial
Innis, Robert, 259
instrumental, 46, 79, 80–81, 162, 168
integrity, 38, 44–45, 59, 80, 270. *See also* identity
intentionality, 90–92, 96. *See also* joint intentionality
internalism: aesthetic, 258; of meaning, 91; moral, 212, 215

James, Williams, 17, 33–36, 39, 67, 71–72, 94, 101, 111, 131, 284
Jaspers, Karl, 159
Johnson, Mark, 174
joint intentionality, 103–10 passim, 113–14, 120, 129, 179, 186, 221, 224, 272
Jonas, Hans, 70–71
Juarrero, Alicia, 138, 145, 265
judgment, 138–39; multifunctional theory of, 139–46; active, 139–40, 144–45, 212–13, 222, 246; assertive, 139–40, 143–51; exhibitive, 139–40, 145–46; naturalized, 147–48; and omnivalence, 150–51; validity of, 142–46; and value, 148–50

just war, theory of, 245–46
justice, 169, 179, 188, 222, 228, 234–35, 242, 244, 246, 248

Kant, Immanuel, 123, 127, 202; on aesthetic judgment, 252–55, 262, 266–67; and ethics, 209–10, 214–19, 226, 239; and judgment, 138–39; and organicism, 66–72 passim
Kaplan, Bernard, 69
Keats, John, 150, 274–75
Keller, Helen, 113
Kitcher, Philip, 174
Kohák, Erazim, 173
Kornblith, Hilary, 123
Krikorian, Yervant, 193
Kristeller, Paul O., 255
Kruse, Felicia, 259–60
Kurtz, Paul, 31

Lafferty, Theodore, 258
Langer, Susanne, 110, 252, 255–56, 258–61, 263, 265–66, 272
language, 108–16, 127–31 passim, 155, 157, 187–88; formal, 196, 199, 204, 206–07; and judgment, 141, 147–49
law (political), 160–62, 164–66, 169, 233, 235–37, 242–43; and ethics, 210, 214; natural, 230, 233, 235; theories of, 235
learning, 83, 85, 88–89, 93–98
levels, emergent, 49–55
Lewes, George H., 50, 72
Lewis, Clarence Irving, 9, 32, 35, 45, 192, 195, 203, 256–58, 261
liberalism (liberal republicanism), 131–32, 163–65, 169: and culture, 241–45; defense of, 247–50; and ethics, 178, 181; and markets, 238–39; and nationalism, 240–41; norms of, 236–38

liberty, 117, 164–66, 176, 178, 248–50. See also moral foundations
Libet, Benjamin, 117–18
life, 63–83; organicism (vs. mechanism), 65–73; and teleonomy, 73–76; and values, 77–80; and The Good, 286
Lloyd Morgan, Conwy, 10, 34–35, 50, 72, 91, 289
Locke, John, 19, 28, 117, 125, 239
logic, 191–207; in Axial Age, 159; modern logic, 191–92; Columbia Naturalists on, 192–99; and realism, 34, 193–99 passim, 202–04, 206–07
logical interpretants, 110–11, 141, 201, 260. See also Peirce, theory of signs
Lorenz, Konrad, 10, 88, 123–24, 292
Lovejoy, Arthur O., 34, 36, 44, 194
loyalty, 175–76, 178, 180–82, 186–87, 214, 234. See also moral foundations
Luhmann, Niklas, 168

MacCumhaill, Clare, 214
Mach, Ernst, 33–36 passim
MacIntyre, Alasdair, 10, 25, 27, 155, 210, 213, 282, 286
Maddy, Penelope, 192, 202–04
mammals, 57, 89, 110, 135, 221
Mangabeira Unger, Roberto, 235
Margolis, Joseph, 142, 252, 256, 265, 267–72
mark (self-recognition) test, 68, 71, 106, 185
markets, 238–39. See also capitalism; liberalism
Mayr, Ernest, 75
McDowell, John, 126, 131
McTaggart, John, 42
Mead, George H., 24, 36–37, 50, 72–73, 103, 110–11, 223, 259

Mead, Margaret, 24
meanings: cultural, 115; Frege on, 110–11; and joint intentionality, 111–14; as possibilities, 43, 110–12. See also signs
mechanism, 18, 65, 74–75, 123
mental causation, 93–95
Merleau-Ponty, Maurice, 10, 69–70
metaphor, 65, 109, 259, 264–65
Midgely, Mary, 174
Mill, John Stuart, 15, 21, 33, 50, 169, 209, 214–19, 225, 239
mimesis, 251, 257, 26–24, 273–74
mind, 85–99; animal, 89–90; human, 103–06, 111, 113, 116; kinds of, 85, 123; and organicism, 66, 70, 72, 75–78 passim, 83. See also consciousness; mental causation
Misak, Cheryl, 191, 200
modern industrial (fabricating) lifeway, 9, 24, 153–54, 160–63, 166, 211, 281. See also modernity
modernism, aesthetic, 252, 263
modernity, 2, 9–10, 24–25, 30, 60, 153–70, 178, 180, 282, 285; and morality, 169–70, 178, 180, 210; and politics, 232, 236–43, 248–49. See also modern industrial
Monod, Jacques, 74–75, 290
moral foundations, theory of, 175–83. See also moral receptors/motivators
morality, 3–4, 20–21, 140, 165, 169–70, 173–90; and judgment, 138, 140, 144; and politics, 230–31, 234–35, 243, 246–47. See also ethics; moral foundations
moral receptors/motivators, 177, 179, 181, 186, 189. See also moral foundations
Morgenbesser, Sidney, 142, 256
Morgenthau, Hans, 244, 296

Morris, Charles, 36, 46, 50, 192, 200, 259
Mothersill, Mary, 252, 256, 261–63, 274
Muller, Jerry Z., 239
Murdoch, Iris, 213
Murphy, Arthur, 36–37
Myth of the Given, the, 126–30

Nagel, Ernest, 35, 37, 46, 131; on logic, 192–99, 204–07
Nagel, Thomas, 39, 188
Nails, Debra, 123
nationalism, 25, 165, 169, 181, 238, 240–42
natural law, 230, 233, 235. *See also* law
naturalism, 3–4, 23, 35, 70, 121; Columbia, 8, 10, 37, 46–47, 192–93, 252, 255–56; and Hare, 221–25; liberal, 131–32; ordinal, 49, 55–57, 59–60, 76–78, 203, 284. *See also* evolutionary psychology; evolutionary epistemology
naturalistic fallacy, 10, 22–23, 60, 80, 121–35, 197
neurons, 85, 87–89, 104, 118; study of (neurology), 8, 55, 90
neutral monism, 35, 194
Nietzsche, Friedrich, 5, 14–15, 274–75
nominalism, 34, 65–66, 194, 205, 235, 263, 268
non-aggregative, 55. *See also* aggregativity
non-contradiction, law of (LNC), 196, 198, 205
normative facts, 82
Nozick, Robert, 181, 241

Oakeshott, Michael, 235
objective morality, 174, 177
objective relativism, 8, 10, 31–48, 55–59, 135, 194, 197–200; definition of, 37–40; and metaphysics, 40–45; problems of, 46–47; and realism, 32–37; and values, 45–46
omnivalence, 150–51, 162, 166, 170, 280–84
orders (of nature), 165, 198, 203, 270, 274; emergent, 54–58, 64; in objective relativism, 38–39, 44, 46
ordinal naturalism, 49, 59, 91, 137, 148, 229; and art, 270–71, 284; and ethical realism, 222–24; and judgment, 137, 148; and knowledge, 132–33; and logical realism, 192, 200, 203, 206, 211; and meanings, 111; and values, 76–78
Ortega y Gasset, José, 85

Panksepp, Jaak, 96
Passmore, John, 32–33
Peirce, Charles S., 7, 17, 32, 35, 43, 71–72, 139; and fallibilism, 39–40; and logic, 192–94, 197, 199, 200–01, 206; and signs, theory of, 92, 109–10, 206, 259–60
perceptual realism, 34, 36, 44. *See also* representationalism
philosophy: analytic, 5, 9–10, 14, 16–18, 25–26; continental, 5–6, 9–10; ordinary language, 10, 16, 25–26, 37, 212–13, 252; specialized vs. systematic, 4–9, 253. *See also* pragmatism
physicalism, 28–29, 49, 51, 55, 194, 265
Pittendrigh, Colin, 75
play: and art, 253–55, 266
political activity, 10, 232–33, 235–36
political realism, 34, 22, 236, 245
politics, 229–50, 274–78 passim; definition of, 231–32; norms of, 232–36; and ethics, 243–47. *See also* liberalism

Popper, Karl, 49, 88, 97, 123–24, 135
positivism, 3, 10, 16–17, 25, 37, 97, 122, 131, 192; legal, 235; Nagel's pragmatic, 194–95
possibility, 28, 39–43, 60, 70, 88, 95, 106, 111–13; and logic, 193, 196, 198, 203–07 passim; and meanings, 43, 110–12
postmodern, 168–69, 252, 265, 282
pragmatism, 7–10, 17–18, 25–26; 34, 37, 97, 103, 130–34 passim, 139, 147; and art, 252, 256–57, 263; and truth, 191–95 passim, 199–200, 256–57
prescriptivism (moral), 212, 214–15, 219, 222
prima facie duties. *See* duty, *prima facie*
progress, 5, 167–68, 237, 248, 282; and specialization, 24–25, 30, 151, 161–62; as modern value, 163–66
properties, 41, 44–46, 53–57, 203. *See also* emergence
Pryba, Russell, 267
purity, 175–76, 178, 182, 184–86. *See also* moral foundations
purpose, 15, 17–18, 27; and active judgment, 139, 143, 145; in biology, 60, 65–84, 223; and highest good, 227, 282–85; and Kant, 253–54; and mind, 97, 119
Putnam, Hilary, 6, 31, 122, 126, 144, 192; and externalism, 91; on fact-value distinction, 17–18, 25–28; and pragmatism, 25, 192; and realism, 122, 126, 130–32, 200–01

Quine, W. V. O., 17, 26, 203, 263; and evolutionary epistemology, 123, 125; on positivism, 122; and pragmatism, 192–93, 195

Radnitzky, Gerard, 135
Ramsey, Frank P., 191, 199, 207
Randall, John Herman, 34, 37, 39, 46, 193
rationality: debate on, 24, 155–56, 210, 213; and judgment, multifunctional theory of, 137–46 passim, 143–46
Rawls, John, 169, 179, 188, 209, 241–42
realism, 122, 130–33; ethical, 211–12; logical 193–207 passim; new, 32–37; and objective relativism, 31, 44; political, 229–30, 243, 245, 247; types of, 34
reason: as cultural judgment, 154–55; Durkheimian, 156–57; Axial (Jasperian), 160; Weberian, 162, 166; Hume on, 20–21; Kant on, 139
reduction, 22, 50–53, 73, 76, 206, 272. *See also* explanation, types of; emergence
relations, 32–36; objective relativism on, 38–45, internal vs external, 38; and values, 45–46, 80–83
relativism, cultural, 25, 29. *See also* objective relativism
religion, 5, 32, 74, 115, 183, 283; and ethics, 210–11; and The Good, 283; and history, 153–60; and modernity, 161–70
representation, 33, 124, 128–29, 131–32, 141; and logic, 200–01; and mind 90–94; and perception, 19–20, 33–35, 59, 88. See also *mimesis*
representationalism, 19, 34, 131
republicanism, 164, 23, 239. *See also* liberalism
Rolston, Holmes, 77, 79

Romanticism, 30
Rorty, Richard, 5, 17, 25, 29, 122, 126, 130, 200, 207
Ross, David, 176, 218
Rousseau, Jean-Jacques, 117, 231, 239
Rozin, Paul, 176, 179
rule consequentialism, 224, 226–27
rule utilitarianism. *See* utilitarianism
Ruse, Michael, 23, 287
Russell, Bertrand, 5, 9, 14, 21, 32–36, 44, 192–93, 196, 199, 203

sanctity. *See* purity
Sartre, Jean-Paul, 13, 14, 283
Scalia, Antonin, 235
Schiller, Friedrich, 254
Schlesinger, Arthur, 244
Searle, John, 141–42, 162
segmentary, 155, 165, 183, 232
self-consciousness. *See* consciousness, self-
self-determination. *See* free will
Sellars, Roy Wood, 50, 122
Sellars, Wilfred, 50, 122–32 passim, 200
Sheffer, Henry, 191, 205, 258
Shils, Edward, 153, 158–59, 183, 239, 242, 249
Shimony, Abner, 63, 123
Shusterman, Richard, 257, 271
signs: animal, 68–69, 167, 196; cultural, 115; human, 110, 112–13, 141, 259; and joint intentionality, 105–09 passim; Langer on, 259; Mead on, 103; natural, 110; Peirce on 109–10, 259–60; vs. symbols, 109, 258–59
Simon, Herbert, 54
Singer, Beth, 49
Smart, J. J. C., 217
Smith, Adam, 103, 175, 183, 242
Snow, C. P., 5, 9

society: agro-literate, 157–60; animal, 78; civil, 242, 249; distinct from culture, 115; historical forms of, 154; hunter-gatherer, 155–57; modern industrial, 160–63; in modernity, 165; political, 231–32, 235–36; postmodern, 168
speech act theory, 140–45 passim, 162
Sperry, Roger W., 74, 91
spiritual, 157, 160, 228, 254, 257, 283–36
states (political), 232–33. *See also* bands; chiefdoms; tribes
Stockdale, Admiral John, 101
Stolnitz, Jerome, 32, 258
Strawson, P. F., 213
Stueber, Karsten, 104
substances. *See* systems
success (efficacy), 29, 79–80; and morality, 29, 140, 145, 150–51, 162, 169, 179–86, 210–12, 222; and politics, 230, 232, 235, 248, 277, 280
Suddendorf, Thomas, 112
supervenience, 91, 223
Suppes, Patrick, 195
symbols, 109, 114, 258–59, 264, 275. *See also* Peirce, theory of signs
synthetic statements. *See* analytic statements
systems, 41, 50–54, 57–59

Tarski, Alfred, 122, 191–97 passim, 199–201
teleology, 74–76, 83, 94, 97, 253
teleonomy, 74–78 passim, 83, 89, 94–95, 119, 129, 167, 223
Thomas Nagel, 39
time, metaphysics of, 41–43
Tomasello, Michael, 104–05, 108, 116, 129, 174–77 passim

tools, 29, 60; and animals, 79, 80, 82; human, 103, 108, 112, 124, 147–48
tribalism, problem of, 116, 165, 186–88
tribes, 155–59, 181–84, 187, 229, 232–33. *See also* bands; chiefdoms; states
Trivers, Robert, 179
truth, 127, 134–35, 140–45, 167–68; relation to logic, 191–207; theories of, 191–92
Tuomela, Raimo, 104
Two Cultures, The, 5, 9

unifunctional (vs. omnivalent), 161–62, 166–67, 279–80, 282, 284
unity of The Good, 279
universals, 23, 28, 34, 41–43; vs. generals, 214–15
utilitarianism, 15, 21, 209–10, 225, 239, 246, 272. *See also* consequentialism

validity. *See* judgment, validity of
value, definition of, 80–83; and judgments, 139–46, 148–50
Velmans, Max, 118
virtue, 212–12, 224, 234, 262; ethics, 185, 209, 219–21. *See also* excellence
Voltaire, 239
Von Uexküll, Jacob, 68–70, 110

Waddington, Conrad, 10, 173

Walzer, Michael, 23, 239–46 passim
Warhol, Andy 259, 263, 265–66
Warnock, Mary, 104
Watts, Ian, 115
Weber, Max, 13, 30, 98, 167, 244; on modernity, 161; on polytheism of values, 277–80, 284–85; on value neutrality, 23–24. *See also* Weberian reason
Weberian reason, 162, 166, 282
Weinberg, Steven, 13
Welles, Orson, 275
Werner, Heinz, 10, 69
Wertheimer, Max, 67
Wheeler, William Morton, 50, 78
White, Morton, 17, 26, 35, 41, 192
Whitehead, Alfred North, 9, 35–36, 67, 70, 192, 255, 258
Wigner, Eugene, 205
Williams, Bernard, 10, 29, 170, 209–10, 213, 227
Wilson, Edward O., 78, 174
Wimsatt, William, 40, 51–55, 75–76, 91. *See also* emergence
Winch, Peter, 24–25, 213
Winters, Jonathan, 101
Wiseman, Rachel, 214
Wittgenstein, Ludwig, 5, 9, 16, 35, 195, 203–07 passim, 212–13, 265
Wong, David, 174
Wordsworth, William, 268, 274
Wrangham, Richard, 176
Wright, Robert, 174, 187

www.ingramcontent.com/pod-product-compliance
Lightning Source LLC
Chambersburg PA
CBHW021937240426
43668CB00036B/113